INTRODUCTION

This book breaks Britain and Ireland into their top big-city, small-town, and rural destinations. It gives you all the information and opinions necessary to wring the maximum value out of your limited time and money in each of these destinations. If you plan a month or less for Britain and Ireland and have a normal appetite for information, this lean and mean little book is all you need. If you're a travel info fiend, this book sorts through all the superlatives and provides a handy rack upon which to hang your supplemental information.

Experiencing British and Irish cultures, people, and natural wonders economically and hassle free has been my goal for more than 25 years of traveling, tour guiding, and travel writing. With this new edition I pass on to you the lessons I've learned, updated for your trip in 2000.

Rick Steves' Great Britain & Ireland is a personal tour guide in your pocket. The places I cover are balanced to include a comfortable mix of exciting big cities and great-to-be-alive-in small towns. While including the predictable biggies (such as Big Ben, Stratford, bagpipes, and the *Book of Kells*), the book also mixes in a healthy dose of Back Door intimacy (nearly edible Cotswold villages, Gaelic folk pubs, angelic boys' choirs, and windswept Roman lookouts). I've been selective. On a short trip, visiting both Oxford and Cambridge is redundant; I cover just the best (Cambridge). There are plenty of great countryside palaces; again, I recommend just the best (Blenheim).

The best is, of course, only my opinion. But after more than two busy decades of travel writing, lecturing, and tour guiding, I've developed a sixth sense for what tickles the traveler's fancy. The places featured in this book will knock your spots off.

This Information Is Accurate and Up-to-Date

Most publishers of guidebooks that cover a country from top to bottom can afford an update only every two or three years, and even then it's often by letter. Since this book is selective, covering only the top month of sightseeing, I'm able to update it each year. (Don't tell my publisher, but I'm so committed to this book, I'd do it for free.) Even with an annual update, things change, but if you're traveling with the current edition of this book, I guarantee you're using the most up-to-date information available. This book will help you have an inexpensive, hassle-free trip.

Use this year's edition. I tell you, you're crazy to save a few bucks by traveling on old information. If you're packing an old book, you'll learn the seriousness of your mistake... once you start your trip. To rescue those of you who will inevitably travel with a two-year-old edition of this book (and realize your mistake too

late), I've sent the latest edition to my lead B&Bs in each town
for you to transcribe over breakfast. Your trip costs about $10
per waking hour. Your time is valuable. This guidebook saves
lots of time.

Planning Your Trip

This book is organized by destinations, each one a minivacation
on its own, filled with exciting sights and homey, affordable places
to stay. In each chapter, you'll find the following:

Planning Your Time, a suggested schedule with thoughts on
how to best use your limited time.

Orientation, including tourist information, city transportation, and an easy-to-read map designed to make the text clear and
your entry smooth.

Sights, with ratings: ▲▲▲—Don't miss; ▲▲—Try hard to
see; ▲—Worthwhile if you can make it; No rating—Worth knowing about.

Sleeping and **Eating,** with addresses and phone numbers of
my favorite budget hotels and restaurants.

Transportation Connections to nearby destinations by train
or bus and route tips for drivers.

The Appendix is a traveler's tool kit, with information on history, architecture, TV, climate, telephoning, and a British–Yankee
vocabulary list.

Browse through this book, choose your favorite destinations,
and link them up. Then have a great trip! You'll travel like a temporary local, getting the absolute most out of every mile, minute,
and dollar. You won't waste time on mediocre sights because,
unlike others, this guidebook covers only the best. Since your
major financial pitfall is lousy, expensive hotels, I've worked hard
to assemble the best accommodation values for each stop. And as
you travel the route I know and love, I'm happy you'll be meeting
some of my favorite British and Irish people.

Trip Costs

Five components make up your trip costs: airfare, surface transportation, room and board, sightseeing/entertainment, and shop-
ping/miscellany.

Airfare: Don't try to sort through the mess. Find and use a
good travel agent. A basic, round-trip, U.S.A.-to-London flight
costs $500 to $1,000, depending on where you fly from and when.
Always consider saving time and money in Europe by flying
"open-jaws" (into one city and out of another; for instance, into
London and out of Dublin).

Surface Transportation: For a three-week whirlwind trip of
all my recommended British destinations, allow $450 per person
for public transportation (train pass and key buses), or $500 per

Rick Steves'
GREAT BRITAIN & IRELAND
2000

John Muir Publications
Santa Fe, New Mexico

Other JMP travel guidebooks by Rick Steves
Europe 101: History and Art for the Traveler (with Gene Openshaw)
Rick Steves' Mona Winks: Self-Guided Tours of Europe's Top Museums
  (with Gene Openshaw)
Rick Steves' Postcards from Europe
Rick Steves' Best of Europe
Rick Steves' Europe Through the Back Door
Rick Steves' France, Belgium & the Netherlands (with Steve Smith)
Rick Steves' Germany, Austria & Switzerland
Rick Steves' Italy
Rick Steves' Scandinavia
Rick Steves' Spain & Portugal
Rick Steves' London (with Gene Openshaw)
Rick Steves' Paris (with Steve Smith and Gene Openshaw)
Rick Steves' Rome (with Gene Openshaw)
Rick Steves' Phrase Books for: German, Italian, French,
  Spanish/Portuguese, and French/German/Italian
Asia Through the Back Door (with Bob Effertz)

Thanks to my wife, Anne, for making "home" my favorite travel destination.
Thanks also to Roy and Jodi Nicholls for their research help, to our readers for
their input, and to local friends listed in this book who put the "Great" in Britain.

John Muir Publications, P.O. Box 613, Santa Fe, NM 87504
Copyright ©2000, 1999, 1998, 1997, 1996 by Rick Steves
Cover copyright ©2000, 1999, 1998 by John Muir Publications
All rights reserved.

Printed in the United States of America
First printing January 2000

For the latest on Rick's lectures, guidebooks, tours, and public television series,
contact Europe Through the Back Door, Box 2009, Edmonds, WA 98020,
tel. 425/771-8303, fax 425/771-0833, www.ricksteves.com, or e-mail:
rick@ricksteves.com.

ISSN 1090-6843
ISBN 1-56261-499-1

Europe Through the Back Door Editor Risa Laib
John Muir Publications Editors Laurel Gladden Gillespie, Krista Lyons-Gould
Research Assistance Risa Laib
Production & Typesetting Kathleen Sparkes, White Hart Design
Design Linda Braun
Cover Design Janine Lehmann
Maps David C. Hoerlein
Printer Banta Company
Cover Photo Tower Bridge, London, England; Leo de Wys Inc./Steve Vidler

Distributed to the book trade by Publishers Group West, Berkeley, California

CONTENTS

The Best Destinations in Great Britain and Ireland

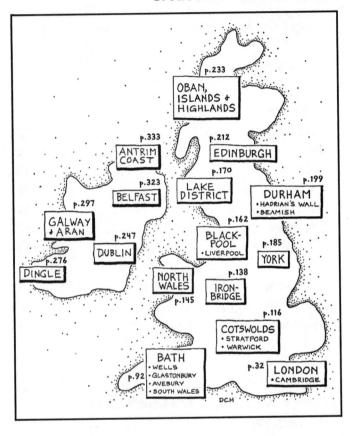

OBAN, ISLANDS & HIGHLANDS p.233

ANTRIM COAST p.333

EDINBURGH p.212

BELFAST p.323

LAKE DISTRICT p.170

DURHAM p.199
• HADRIAN'S WALL
• BEAMISH

GALWAY & ARAN p.297

DUBLIN p.247

BLACK-POOL p.162
• LIVERPOOL

YORK p.185

DINGLE p.276

NORTH WALES p.145

IRON-BRIDGE p.138

COTSWOLDS p.116
• STRATFORD
• WARWICK

BATH p.92
• WELLS
• GLASTONBURY
• AVEBURY
• SOUTH WALES

LONDON p.32
• CAMBRIDGE

DCH

person (based on two people sharing) for a three-week car rental, gas, and insurance. About $150 more covers the ferry to Ireland and train and bus connections to its major sights. Car rental is cheapest if arranged from the United States. Train passes are normally available only outside of Europe. You may save money by simply buying tickets as you go (see Transportation, below).

Room and Board: You can thrive in Britain and Ireland on $70 a day per person for room and board (allow $90 a day for London). A $70-a-day budget allows $10 for lunch, $15 for dinner, and $45 for lodging (based on two people splitting a $90 double room that includes breakfast). That's doable, particularly outside London. Students and tightwads can do it on $40 ($20 for a bed, $20 a day for meals and snacks). But budget sleeping and eating require the skills and information covered below (and in greater detail in my book *Rick Steves' Europe Through the Back Door*).

Sightseeing and Entertainment: In big cities, figure $5 to $10 per major sight (Imperial War Museum, $7.50, Edinburgh Castle, $9), $2 for minor ones (climbing church towers), $10 for guided walks, and $25 for bus tours and splurge experiences (Welsh and Scottish folk evenings). An overall average of $15 a day works for most. Don't skimp here. After all, this category directly powers most of the experiences all the other expenses are designed to make possible.

You will be tempted to buy the British Heritage Pass, which gets you into more than 500 British Heritage and National Trust properties (£30 for seven days, £42 for 15 days, £56 for 30 days; sold at airport information desks and the British Travel Centre on Regent Street in London). Of the 500 sights included (a list comes with the pass), here are the sights I describe and recommend for a three-week tour of Britain, along with their adult admission prices. A typical sightseer with three weeks will probably pay to see nearly all of these: Tower of London, £10.50 (London); Shakespeare's Birthplace and Anne Hathaway's Cottage, £7.50 (Stratford); Warwick Castle, £10.50 (near Stratford); Blenheim Palace, £8.50 (near the Cotswolds and Oxford); Roman and Medieval Baths, £6.70 (Bath); Stonehenge, £4 (near Bath); Caerphilly Castle, £2.50 and Tintern Abbey, £2.50 (South Wales); Caernarfon Castle, £4.20 (North Wales); Wordsworth's Dove Cottage, £4.80 (Lake District); Housesteads Roman Fort, £2.80 (Hadrian's Wall); Edinburgh Castle, £6.50, Georgian House, £4.30, Gladstone's Land, £3.40, and Holyrood Palace, £5.50 (Edinburgh); Culloden Battlefield, £3.20 (near Inverness); and Urquhart Castle, £4 (near Loch Ness). Your pass also saves you £1 on all Guide Friday bus tours (you'll probably take four). This totals about £95; a pass takes the pain out of all these admissions with one big pill.

Shopping and Miscellany: Figure $1 per postcard, tea, or ice cream cone and $2 per beer. Shopping can vary in cost from nearly nothing to a small fortune. Good budget travelers find that this category has little to do with assembling a trip full of lifelong and wonderful memories.

Exchange Rates
I list prices in pounds (£) throughout this book.

> 1 British pound (£1) = about $1.70
> 1 Irish pound (£1) = about $1.50

Britain: The British pound sterling (£), also called a "quid," is broken into 100 pence (p). Pence means "cents." You'll find coins ranging from 1p to £2 and bills from £5 to £50. To roughly convert pounds to dollars, multiply British prices by 2 and then subtract 10 percent: £6 is about $10.50, £3 is about $5, and 80p is about $1.40. Scotland and Northern Ireland issue their own currency in pounds, worth the same as an English pound. English, Scottish, and Northern Ireland's Ulster pounds are technically interchangeable in each region, although Scottish and Ulster pounds are "undesirable" in England. Banks in any of the three regions will convert your Scottish or Ulster pounds into English pounds at no charge.

Ireland: The Irish-English money relationship is like the Canadian-American one. The Irish call their pound a "punt." To convert punts into dollars, multiply Irish prices by 1.5: £6 is $9, £3 is $4.50, and 80p is $1.20. Use Irish, not English, money on the Emerald Isle. Ireland is a different country—treat it that way.

Prices, Times, and Discounts
The prices in this book, as well as the hours and telephone numbers, are accurate as of late 1999. The economy is flat, and inflation is low, so these prices should be pretty accurate in 2000. Britain and Ireland are always changing, and I know you'll understand that this guidebook, like any other, starts to yellow even before it's printed.

In Britain and Ireland you'll be using the 24-hour clock. After 12:00 noon, keep going—13:00, 14:00.... For anything over 12, subtract 12 and add p.m. (14:00 is 2 p.m.).

This book lists peak-season hours for sightseeing attractions (Easter–October). Off-season (roughly November–Easter) expect shorter hours, more lunchtime breaks, and fewer activities. Some places are open only on weekends or are closed entirely in the winter. Confirm your sightseeing plans locally, especially when traveling between November and April.

While discounts (called "concessions" in Britain) are not listed in this book, nearly all British and Irish sights are discounted for seniors (loosely defined as anyone retired or willing to call themselves a "senior"), youths (ages 8–18), students, groups of 10 or more, and families.

When to Go

[handwritten: rain coat + umbrella]

July and August are peak season—my favorite time—with very long days, the best weather, and the busiest schedule of tourist fun. Prices and crowds don't go up as dramatically in Britain as they do in much of Europe. Still, travel during "shoulder season" (May, early June, September, and early October) is easier and a bit less expensive. Shoulder-season travelers get minimal crowds, decent weather, the full range of sights and tourist fun spots, and the joy of being able to just grab a room almost whenever and wherever they like—often at a flexible price. Winter travelers find absolutely no crowds and soft room prices but shorter sightseeing hours. The weather can be cold and dreary, and nightfall draws the shades on sightseeing well before dinnertime. While England's rural charm falls with the leaves, city sightseeing is fine in the winter.

Plan for rain no matter when you go. Just keep going and take full advantage of "bright spells." In Ireland rainy weather is called "nice and soft." Conditions can change several times in a day, but rarely is the weather extreme. Daily averages throughout the year range between 42 and 70 degrees Fahrenheit. *[handwritten: Cool]* Temperatures below 32 or over 80 degrees are cause for headlines (see the climate chart in the Appendix). July and August are not much better than shoulder months, but May and June can be lovely. While sunshine may be rare, summer days are very long. The summer sun is up from 6:30 until 22:30. It's not uncommon to have a grey day, eat dinner, and enjoy hours of sunshine afterward.

Sightseeing Priorities

Depending on the length of your trip, here are my recommended priorities:

Britain:

[handwritten: York]

3 days:	London
5 days, add:	Bath, Cotswolds, Blenheim
7 days, add:	York
9 days, add:	Edinburgh
11 days, add:	Stratford, Warwick, Cambridge
14 days, add:	North Wales, Wells/Glastonbury/Avebury
17 days, add:	Lake District, Hadrian's Wall, Durham
21 days, add:	Ironbridge, Blackpool, Scottish Highlands
24 days, add:	South Wales

(The Whirlwind Tour map and three-week itinerary on the following pages include everything in the above 24 days. With 30 days you could slow down or add a five-day swing through Ireland.)

Best Three-Week Trip in Britain by Car

Day	Plan	Sleep in
1	Arrive in London, bus to Bath	Bath
2	Bath	Bath
3	Pick up car, Avebury, Wells, Glastonbury	Bath
4	South Wales, St. Fagans, Tintern	Stow
5	Explore the Cotswolds, Blenheim	Stow
6	Stratford, Warwick, Coventry	Ironbridge
7	Ironbridge Gorge, Ruthin banquet	Conwy
8	Highlights of North Wales	Conwy
9	Liverpool, Blackpool	Blackpool
10	Southern Lake District	Keswick area
11	Northern Lake District	Keswick area
12	Drive up west coast of Scotland	Oban
13	Highlands, Loch Ness, Scenic Drive	Highlands/ Edinburgh
14	More Highlands or Edinburgh	Edinburgh
15	Edinburgh	Edinburgh
16	Hadrian's Wall, Beamish, Durham evensong	Durham
17	York Moors, York, turn in car	York
18	York	York
19	Early train to London	London
20	London	London
21	London	London
22	Side trip to Cambridge or Greenwich, London	Whew!

While this three-week itinerary is designed to be done by car, it can be done by train and bus or, better yet, with a rail 'n' drive pass (best car days: Cotswolds, North Wales, Lake District, Scottish Highlands, Hadrian's Wall). For three weeks without a car, I'd probably cut back on the recommended sights with the most frustrating public transportation (South and North Wales, Ironbridge Gorge, the Highlands). Lacing together the cities by train is very slick. With more time, everything is workable without a car.

Whirlwind Three-Week Tour of Great Britain

Ireland:

3 days:	Not worth the trouble
5 days:	Dublin, Dingle Peninsula
7 days, add:	Galway and a day in Belfast
9 days, add:	County Clare/Burren
11 days, add:	Northern Ireland's Antrim Coast
15 days, add:	Aran Islands, Wicklow area

Itinerary Tips

Most people fly into London and remain there for a few days. Instead, consider a gentler small-town start in Bath, and visit London at the end of your trip. You'll be more rested and ready to tackle Britain's greatest city. Heathrow Airport has direct connections to Bath and other cities.

To give yourself a little rootedness, minimize one-night stands. It's worth a long drive after dinner to be settled into a town for two nights. B&Bs are also more likely to give a good price to someone staying more than one night.

Many people save a couple of days and a lot of miles by going directly from the Lake District to Edinburgh and skipping the long joyride through Scotland. I consider a trip to Wales, rather than Scotland or Ireland, the best quick look at Celtic Britain.

Ireland, because of its nature and the expense and headaches involved in getting there, is not worth a very quick visit. It requires a minimum of five days. Don't overlook the handy ferry connections from Belfast to Scotland and from southeast Ireland to France. If you ask the Irish about ferries, they'll say, "I don't believe in them. But they're there."

Red Tape and Taxes

You need a passport, but no visa or shots, to travel in Britain and Ireland.

Sales Tax: Britain's and Ireland's sales tax—the "value added tax," or VAT (17.5 percent)—is built into the price of nearly everything you buy. Tourists can get this VAT refunded on souvenirs they take out of the country. But unless you buy something worth at least $100, your refund won't be worth the trouble. Before you make a substantial purchase of merchandise, ask the store clerk if you will be able to get a VAT refund. You'll likely get a "Tax-Free Shopping Cheque" which is redeemable for cash or credit-card credit at virtually any European airport before you fly home.

Banking

Credit or debit cards are widely accepted in Britain and Ireland (and are necessary for renting a car and handy for booking rooms and theater and transportation tickets over the phone). For cash advances you'll find that Barclays, National Westminster, and places displaying an Access or Eurocard sign accept MasterCard. Visa is accepted at Barclays and Midland banks. In general, Visa is far more widely accepted than American Express.

Many travelers also carry an ATM card. They get you a better exchange rate than traveler's checks and are as commonplace in Britain and Ireland as they are in the United States. Make sure your PIN is only four numbers long.

Traveler's checks work fine in Britain and Ireland. Many people traveling exclusively in Great Britain buy traveler's checks in pounds sterling. On the road, save time and money by changing plenty of money at a time. Banks commonly charge a commission fee of £2 to £4 or even more. While policies vary, some British banks favor various traveler's checks by waiving the commission: Barclays and Visa checks at Barclays banks, American Express checks at Lloyds banks, and Thomas Cook checks at Midland banks or Cook offices. American Express exchange offices don't charge a commission on their checks or any others. This can save you around 2 percent. But don't let this cloud your assessment of their exchange rates.

On my last trip I bought all my pounds in cash from a good American foreign exchange service, stowed them safely in my money belt, and never needed a bank. Even in jolly olde England and friendly Ireland you should use a money belt. Thieves target tourists. A money belt (call 425/771-8303 for our free newsletter/ catalog) provides peace of mind. You can carry lots of cash safely in a money belt—and, given the high bank fees, you should.

Bank holidays bring most businesses to a grinding halt on Christmas, December 26, New Year's Day, Good Friday, Easter Monday, the first and last Monday in May, and the last Monday in August.

Travel Smart

Upon arrival in a new town, lay the groundwork for a smooth departure. Reread this book as you travel and visit local tourist information offices. Buy a phone card and use it for reservations and confirmations. You speak the language—use it! Enjoy the friendliness of the local people. Ask questions. Most locals are eager to point you in their idea of the right direction. Bring along a pocket-size notebook to organize your thoughts and practice the virtue of simplicity. Those who expect to travel smart do. Plan ahead for banking, laundry, post office chores, and picnics. Mix intense and relaxed periods. Every trip (and every traveler) needs at least a few slack days. Pace yourself. Assume you will return.

As you read this book, make note of festivals, colorful market days, and days when sights are closed. Sundays have pros and cons, as they do for travelers in the United States (special events, limited hours, closed shops and banks, limited public transportation, no rush hours). Saturdays are virtually weekdays. Popular places are even more popular on weekends—especially sunny weekends, which are sufficient cause for an impromptu holiday in this soggy corner of Europe.

Consider making the travel arrangements and reservations listed below before your trip or within a few days of arrival.

Before You Go

• Reserve a room for your first night.
• If you'll be traveling in late June, July, or August and want to sleep in my lead listings, book the B&Bs on your route (and the Ruthin Medieval Banquet) as soon as you're ready to commit to a date.
• Confirm car rental and pick-up plans with your rental agency (picking up a car on Saturday afternoon or Sunday may be difficult).
• If you'll be attending the Edinburgh Festival (August 13–September 2 in 2000), call the festival office at 0131/473-2000 to book a ticket by credit card (Visa, MasterCard, Amex) after April 1. And while you're at it, book your Edinburgh room.
• If you want to attend the pageantry-filled Ceremony of the Keys at the Tower of London, write for tickets (see details in the London chapter under "Sights—East London").

Within a Day or Two of Arrival

• If you'll be in London the last night of your trip, reserve a room and book tickets for a London play or concert. You can book a play from home (see details in the London chapter under "Entertainment and Theater in London"), but for simplicity, I book plays while in London.
• If the Royal Shakespeare Company will be performing at the Stratford Theater when you're in or near Stratford, consider booking a ticket (tel. 01789/295-623).

Tourist Information

Virtually every town in Britain has a helpful tourist information center (abbreviated "TI" in this book) eager to make your visit as smooth and enjoyable as possible. Take full advantage of this service. Arrive (or telephone) with a list of questions and a proposed sightseeing plan. Pick up maps, brochures, and walking-tour information. In London you can pick up everything you'll need for Britain in one stop at the National Tourist Information Centre.

The TIs in Ireland have lost their government funding and are now little more than sales outlets for the various hotels and gimmicky new attractions. They have little of value to give you except flyers printed by whoever wants your money. Avoid the room-finding service offered by TIs throughout Britain and

Ireland (bloated prices, fees, no opinions, and they take a cut
from your host).

Each country's national tourist office in the United States has a
wealth of information. Before your trip request any information you
may want (such as city maps and schedules of upcoming festivals).

British Tourist Authority (BTA): 551 Fifth Avenue, 7th
floor, New York, NY 10176, tel. 800/462-2748 or 212/986-2200,
fax 212/986-1188, www.visitbritain.com. Meaty material, responsive
to individual needs. Their free London and Britain maps are excellent (and the same maps are sold for £1.40 each at TIs in Britain).

Irish Tourist Board: 345 Park Avenue, 17th floor, New
York, NY 10154, tel. 800/223-6470 or 212/418-0800, fax
212/371-9059, www.ireland.travel.ie.

Recommended Guidebooks

You may want some supplemental travel guidebooks, especially if
you're traveling beyond my recommended destinations. I know it
hurts to spend $25 or $35 on extra books and maps, but when you
consider the money they'll save you and the improvements they'll
make in your $3,000 vacation, not buying them would be penny-
wise and pound-foolish.

While this book offers everything you'll need for the structure
of your trip, each place you will visit has plenty of great little
guidebooks to fill you in on local history. For cultural and sightseeing background in bigger chunks, Michelin and Cadogan guides
to London, England, Britain, and Ireland are good. The best budget travel guides to Britain and Ireland are the Lonely Planet and
Let's Go guidebooks. Lonely Planet's guidebook is more thorough
and informative. Let's Go is youth oriented, with good coverage of
nightlife, hosteling, and cheap transportation deals.

Rick Steves' Books and Videos

Rick Steves' Europe Through the Back Door 2000 (John Muir Publications) gives you budget-travel skills, such as minimizing jet lag,
packing light, planning your itinerary, traveling by car or train,
finding beds without reservations, changing money, avoiding rip-
offs, outsmarting thieves, hurdling the language barrier, staying
healthy, taking great photographs, and much more. The book also
includes chapters on 34 of my favorite "Back Doors," eight of
which are in Great Britain and Ireland.

Rick Steves' Country Guides (John Muir Publications,
2000) are a series of seven guidebooks—including this book—
covering my favorite continent: Best of Europe; France/Belgium/
Netherlands; Italy; Spain/Portugal; Scandinavia; and Germany/
Switzerland/Austria with Prague. All are updated annually and
come out in January.

My new **City Guides** (John Muir Publications, 2000) cover

London, Paris, and Rome. Updated annually, they offer in-depth coverage of the sights, hotels, restaurants, and nightlife in these grand cities, along with illustrated tours of their great museums.

Europe 101: History and Art for the Traveler (John Muir Publications, 1996, co-written with Gene Openshaw) gives you the story of Europe's people, history, and art. Written for smart people who were sleeping in their history and art classes before they knew they were going to Europe, *101* really helps Europe's sights come alive. However, this book is more applicable to travel on the European continent than to travel in Britain.

Rick Steves' Mona Winks (John Muir Publications, 1998, co-written with Gene Openshaw), provides fun, easy-to-follow, self-guided tours of Europe's top 20 museums. In London, *Mona* leads the way through the British Museum, the British Library, the National Gallery, the Tate Gallery, Westminster Abbey, and the historic Westminster neighborhood.

Of the 52 episodes in my television series, *Travels in Europe with Rick Steves*, eight shows feature Britain and Ireland. A new series of 13 shows, which will air in 2000, will include three shows on England. Episodes air nationally on public television and the Travel Channel. These are also available in information-packed home videos, along with my two-hour slide-show lecture on Britain (call us at 425/771-8303 for our free newsletter/catalog).

Rick Steves' Postcards from Europe (John Muir Publications, 1999), my autobiographical book, packs more than 25 years of travel anecdotes and insights into the ultimate 3,000-mile European adventure. Through my guidebooks, I share my favorite European discoveries with you. *Postcards* introduces you to my favorite European friends.

Maps

The maps in this book, designed and drawn by Dave Hoerlein, are concise and simple. Dave, who is well traveled in Britain and Ireland, has designed the maps to help you locate recommended places and get to the tourist office, where you'll find more in-depth maps of the city or region (cheap or free).

Maps to buy in England: Train travelers can do fine with a simple rail map (such as the one that comes with your train pass) and city maps from TIs. (Get a free map of London and Britain from the BTA before you go; see "Tourist Information," above.) If you're driving, get a road atlas (one inch equals three miles) covering all of Britain. Ordnance Survey, AA, and Bartholomew editions are available for about £7 in TIs, gas stations, and bookstores. Drivers, hikers, and bikers may want much more detailed maps for the Cotswolds, North Wales, and Lake District (easy to buy locally).

Tours of Britain and Ireland

Your travel agent can tell you about all the normal Britain tours.
But they won't tell you about ours. At Europe Through the Back
Door we offer 20-day tours of Britain, 14-day tours of Ireland, and
7-day winter getaways to London featuring the all-stars covered in
this book (call us at 425/771-8303). And ETBD tour guides Roy
and Jodi Nicholls lead their own garden tours and south England
tours in their spare time (call Roy and Jodi in England at
44/1749/812-873 or visit www.brittours.com).

Transportation in Britain and Ireland

By Car or Train?

Cars are best for three or more traveling together (especially families with small kids), those packing heavy, and those scouring the
countryside. Trains and buses are best for solo travelers, blitz
tourists, and city-to-city travelers.

Britain has a great train-and-bus system, and travelers who
don't want (or can't afford) to drive a rental car can enjoy an excellent tour using public transportation. Britain's 100-mph train system is one of Europe's best. Buses pick you up when the trains let
you down.

My choice is to connect big cities by train and to explore rural
areas (the Cotswolds, North Wales, Lake District, and the Highlands) footloose and fancy-free by rental car. You might consider a
BritRail Plus Car pass, which gives you various combinations of
rail days and car days to use within a month's time.

Deals on Rails, Wheels, and Wings in Britain

Regular tickets on Britain's great train system (15,000 departures
from 2,400 stations daily) are the most expensive per mile in all of
Europe. Those who go round-trip (leaving after 9:30 in the morning), buy in advance, or ride the bus save big.

Buying Train Tickets in Advance: Either go direct to any
station or call and book your ticket with a credit card. To book
ahead, call 0345/484-950 (from the States call 011/44/345-484-
950) to find out the schedule and best fare for your journey; then
you'll be referred to the appropriate number to call—depending
on the particular rail company—to book your ticket. Here are a
few of the many deals. **Bargain Return** fares offer the greatest
savings but must be booked at least seven days in advance and
usually apply to journeys of about 250 miles (i.e., London–
Edinburgh) or longer, but sometimes shorter journeys qualify—
ask. Note that a Bargain Return is a round-trip ticket, but you
can use it only one-way if you want. **Apex** fares, which must be
booked at least seven days in advance, apply to journeys of about
100 miles (i.e., London–York) or longer. (You can book Apex

Cost of Public Transportation

2000 BRITRAIL CLASSIC PASS

	Adult first class	Adult standard	Senior (60+) first class	16-25 youth standard
8 consec. days	$400	$265	$340	$215
15 consec. days	600	400	510	280
22 consec. days	760	505	645	355
1 month	900	600	765	420

"Standard" is the polite British term for "second" class. No senior discounts for standard class. For each adult pass you buy, one child (5-15) gets a free pass of the same type (ask for the "Family Pass"). Additional kids pay the normal half-adult rate. Kids under 5: free. The "Family Pass" is available with all BritRail passes, except the SouthEast pass. These rules also apply to the Flexipasses listed below.

2000 BRITRAIL FLEXIPASS

	Adult first class	Adult standard	Senior (60+) first class	16-25 youth standard
4 days in 2 months	$350	$235	$300	$185
8 days in 2 months	510	340	435	240
15 days in 2 months	770	515	655	360

1999 BRITRAIL PLUS CAR PASS (Prices may vary in 2000)

	First class	Senior (60+)	Standard class
Any 3 days by rail + 3 days by car in 1 month:	$442	$404	$358
Any 6 days by rail + 7 days by car in 1 month:	811	755	688

BritRail Plus Car gives you rail travel throughout England, Scotland and Wales and use of a Hertz car. Prices listed are per person for a manual shift 2-door economy car. An additional adult pays $250 (1st cl)/$166 (2nd cl) for a 3+3 pass, or $364/$241 for a 6+7 pass. Add about $30 per person for a compact car, and another $45 for an intermediate car. Drivers must be 25 or older. No senior discounts for standard class.

Note: For a railpass order form, or for Rick's complete Railpass Guide, visit www.ricksteves.com or call us at 425/771-8303; for Britrail Plus Car passes, call your travel agent or Rail Europe at 800/438-7245.

Britain & Ireland:
The map shows approximate point-to-point one-way 2nd-class fares in $US by rail (solid line) and bus (dashed line). Add up fares for your itinerary to see whether a railpass will save you money.

BritRail Routes

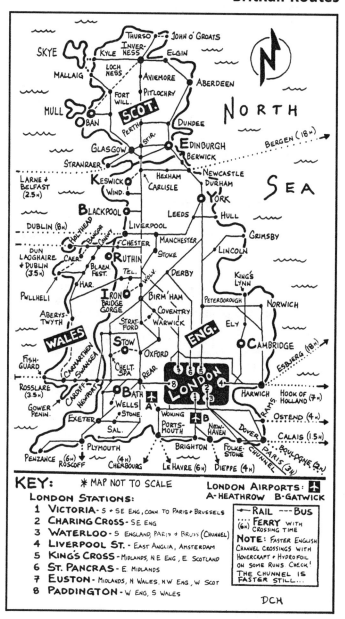

KEY: ✳ MAP NOT TO SCALE   **LONDON AIRPORTS:** ✈
A- HEATHROW   B- GATWICK

LONDON STATIONS:

1 **VICTORIA** - S + SE ENG, CONN. TO PARIS + BRUSSELS
2 **CHARING CROSS** - SE ENG
3 **WATERLOO** - S ENGLAND, PARIS + BRUSS (CHUNNEL)
4 **LIVERPOOL ST.** - EAST ANGLIA, AMSTERDAM
5 **KING'S CROSS** - MIDLANDS, N E ENG, E. SCOTLAND
6 **ST. PANCRAS** - E. MIDLANDS
7 **EUSTON** - MIDLANDS, N WALES, NW ENG, W SCOT
8 **PADDINGTON** - W ENG, S WALES

— RAIL - - - BUS
⋮⋮ FERRY WITH (6H) CROSSING TIME
NOTE: FASTER ENGLISH CHANNEL CROSSINGS WITH HOVERCRAFT + HYDROFOIL ON SOME RUNS CHECK! THE CHUNNEL IS FASTER STILL...

DCH

and Bargain Return tickets as early as six to eight weeks before your journey; be warned that cheap fares go fast in summer, tickets have refund restrictions, and you'll need to pin down dates and times—for schedules, visit http://bahn.hafas.de.) To save a few pounds, get a **Super Advance** ticket (for any journey on any day) by buying your ticket before 14:00 the day prior to your journey. If you buy a ticket the day you want to travel, leave after 9:30, and avoid traveling on Friday or summer Saturdays, you'll save a little with a **Super Saver** ticket. There can be up to 30 different prices for the same journey. A clerk at any station (or the helpful folks at tel. 0345-484-950, 24 hours daily) can figure out the cheapest fare for your trip. Savings can be significant. For a London–Edinburgh round-trip, the regular fare is £79, Super Saver is £69, Super Advance is £63, Apex is £50, and Bargain Return is £36. For a York–London round-trip, the regular fare is £63, Super Saver is £53, Super Advance is £45, Apex is £38, and Bargain Return is £31.

Railpasses: Consider getting a railpass. The BritRail pass comes in "consecutive day" and "flexi" versions, with price breaks for second class ("standard" class, available to anyone), youths, and seniors. BritRail passes cover England, Scotland, and Wales. There are now Scotland passes, England/Ireland passes, southeast Britain passes, and BritRail Plus Car passes, which allow you to take a day of rail here and a day of Hertz car rental there. Any Brit pass or Eurailpass gives a discount on the Eurostar train that zips you to continental Europe under the English Channel. These passes are sold outside of Europe only. For specifics, contact your travel agent or Europe Through the Back Door (tel. 425/771-8303).

Buses: Although trains are twice as fast as buses, they're also 50 percent more expensive. Round-trip bus tickets usually cost less than two one-way fares (e.g., London–York one way costs £17; round-trip costs £26). And buses go many places that trains don't. Budget travelers can save a wad with a bus pass. The National Express sells Tourist Trail bus passes (over the counter, tel. 0990-808-080 for a busy, or try 08705-808-080, www.nationalexpress.co.uk): a pass for three consecutive days costs £49; for eight days within 16, £119; and for 15 days within 30, £179. In Britain bus stations are normally at or near train stations (in London, the bus station is a block southwest of Victoria Station). The British distinguish between "buses" (for local runs with lots of stops) and "coaches" (long-distance express runs).

There are several **backpacker's bus circuits.** These hop-on/hop-off bus circuits take mostly youth hostelers around the country super cheap and easy with the assumption that they'll be sleeping in the hostels along the way. For instance, **Stray Travel** network does a six-day-or-more "tour," making a 1,600-kilometer circle connecting London, Bath, Stratford, the lakes, Edinburgh, York, Cambridge, and London hostels (£129 for six days, three buses weekly, commentary from driver, tel. 020/7373-7737, www.straytravel.com). **Haggis Backpacker** offers a similar deal, with hop-on/hop-off buses circling Scotland (£95, 1,000 km: Edinburgh, Inverness, Skye, Fort William, Glencoe, Oban, Edinburgh; buses run daily in summer, otherwise 4/wk; ticket good for a year, tel. 0131/557-9393, www.radicaltravel.com). The **Hairy Hog** does Wales for the same crowd, but as a tour (five-day trip for £160, including four nights in hostels, not hop-on/hop-off, tel. 020/7706-1539, www.hairyhog.co.uk).

    Flights: For reasonable flights, try **British Midland Airline.** If you've got more money than time, don't buy a ticket for a long train trip without considering a BM flight such as Heathrow–Dublin (8/day, 75 min, about £107 one way plus tax, as little as £70 round-trip with a stay over Saturday, plus tax) and Heathrow–Edinburgh (8/day, 75 min, as little as £60 round-trip with a stay over Saturday, plus tax). BM also offers good £130 one-way fares on flights to Frankfurt, Amsterdam, Brussels, and Paris (about £110 round-trip with a stay over Saturday). For reservations and information, call 0870-607-0555 or, in the United States, 800/788-0555. (The U.S. office of British Midland sells Discover Europe air passes: flights out of London that are less than 500 miles—say, to Paris or Amsterdam—cost $109 plus tax; flights over 500 miles cost $159 plus tax. For information, visit www.britishmidland.com.) More cut-rate airlines are getting into the fray: Consider Easy Jet (www.easyjet.com), Virgin Express (www.virgin-express.com), Ryanair (www.ryanair.ie), and Debonair (www.debonair.co.uk).

Transportation within Ireland

Ireland's train system matches its sparse population. Trains work like spokes, connecting Dublin with each corner of the country (Rosslare in the southeast, Cork in the south, Limerick and Tralee in the southeast, Galway in the west, and Belfast in the north). Between the bus and train systems you can get around the Emerald Isle quite handily. Departures are not as frequent as the European norm.

    Irish Explorer Passes make a public bus and train tour of Ireland inexpensive. All can be purchased easily and cheapest in Ireland at major stations (Dublin information tel. 01/836-6111, London office on Bond Street at tel. 020/7493-3201).

    Rail only: "Irish Explorer Rail Only" passes cover the Republic—any 5 days in 15 (£67). "Irish Rover Rail Only" passes cover all of Ireland—any 5 days in 15 (£83).

    Bus only: Rambler passes cover the Republic—3 days in 8 (£28), 8 days in 15 (£68), and 15 days in 30 (£98). Rover passes

Public Transportation in Ireland

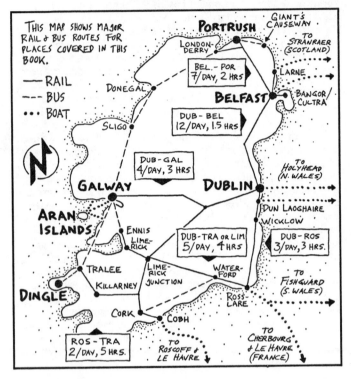

THIS MAP SHOWS MAJOR RAIL & BUS ROUTES FOR PLACES COVERED IN THIS BOOK.

— RAIL
--- BUS
••• BOAT

GIANT'S CAUSEWAY
PORTRUSH
LONDON-DERRY
TO STRANRAER (SCOTLAND)
BEL.- POR 7/DAY, 2 HRS
LARNE
DONEGAL
BANGOR/CULTRA
BELFAST
DUB - BEL 12/DAY, 1.5 HRS
SLIGO
DUB - GAL 4/DAY, 3 HRS
TO HOLYHEAD (N. WALES)
GALWAY
DUBLIN
ARAN ISLANDS
DUN LAOGHAIRE
WICKLOW
ENNIS
LIMERICK
DUB - TRA OR LIM 5/DAY, 4 HRS
DUB - ROS 3/DAY, 3 HRS.
TRALEE
LIMERICK JUNCTION
WATERFORD
TO FISHGUARD (S. WALES)
KILLARNEY
DINGLE
ROSS LARE
CORK
COBH
ROS - TRA 2/DAY, 5 HRS.
TO ROSCOFF & LE HAVRE
TO CHERBOURG & LE HAVRE (FRANCE)

cover all of Ireland—3 days in 8 (£36), 8 days in 15 (£85), and 15 days in 30 (£130).

Rail and bus: Irish Explorer passes cover the Republic—8 days in 15 (£100). Emerald Cards cover all of Ireland—8 days in 15 (£115) and 15 days in 30 (£200).

Car Rental

Car rental for this tour is cheapest if arranged in advance through your hometown travel agent. The best rates are weekly with unlimited mileage or leasing (possible for rentals of over three weeks). You can pick up and drop off just about anywhere, anytime. For a trip covering both Britain and Ireland you're better off with two separate car rentals. If you pick up the car in a smaller city, such as Bath, you'll more likely survive your first day on the British roads. If you drop it off early or keep it longer, you'll be credited or charged at a fair, prorated price.

Big companies have offices in most cities. (Ask to be picked up at your hotel.) Small local rental companies can be cheaper but aren't as flexible.

The Ford 1.3-liter Escort-category car costs about $50 per week more than the smallest cars but feels better on the motorways and safer on the small roads. Remember, minibuses are a great budget way to go for five to nine people.

For peace of mind, spring for the CDW insurance (Collision Damage Waiver, about $15 per day), which gives a zero (or low) deductible rather than the standard value-of-the-car "deductible." A few "gold" credit cards cover CDW insurance; quiz your credit-card company on the worst-case scenario.

Driving

Your U.S. license is all you need to drive in Britain and Ireland. Set your car up for a fun road trip. Establish a cardboard-box munchies pantry. Buy a rack of liter boxes of juice for the trunk. Buy some Windex and a roll of paper towels for cleaner sightseeing.

Britain: Driving in Britain is basically wonderful—once you remember to stay on the left and after you've mastered the "round-abouts." But be warned: Every year I get a few cards from traveling readers advising me that, for them, trying to drive British was a nerve-racking and regrettable mistake. If you want to get a little slack on the roads, drop by a gas station or auto shop and buy the red "L" (inexperienced driver) or green "L" (student driver, stay off motorways) sign to put in your window.

A British Automobile Association membership comes with most rentals. Understand its towing and emergency road service benefits. Gas (petrol) costs over $4 per gallon and is self-serve. Green pumps are unleaded. Seat belts are required by law. Speed limits are 30 mph in town, 70 mph on the motorways, and 50 or 60 mph elsewhere. The national sign for 60 mph is a white circle with a black slash. Note that a new system of road-surveillance cameras strictly enforces speed limits. Any driver (including foreigners renting cars) photographed speeding will get a nasty bill in the mail. (Cameras—you'll see the foreboding grey boxes—flash on your rear license plate in order not to invade the privacy of anyone sharing the front seat with someone who they shouldn't be with.) Avoid driving in big cities whenever possible. Most have modern ring roads to skirt the congestion. The shortest distance between any two points is usually the motorway. Road signs can be confusing, too little, and too late. Study your map before taking off. Know the cities you'll be lacing together since road numbers are inconsistent. Miss a motorway exit and you can lose 30 minutes. A Britain road atlas (sold at gas stations and bookstores) is $10 very well spent.

Parking is confusing. One yellow line marked on the pavement means no parking Monday through Saturday during work

Standard European Road Signs

hours. Double yellow lines mean no parking at any time. Broken yellow lines mean short stops are OK, but you should always look for explicit signs or ask a passerby. White lines are good news.

Even in small towns, rather than fight it, I just pull into the most central and handy "pay and display" car park I can find. Rates are reasonable by U.S. standards. Locals love to share "pay and display" stickers. If you stand by the machine, invariably someone on their way out with time left on their sticker will give it to you. I keep a bag of 10p and 20p coins in the ashtray for parking meters.

Ireland: In Ireland you'll be dealing with the same left-hand drives and roundabouts. Traffic and parking are rarely a problem. Ireland's roads, while getting much better with the financial help of the European Union, are still among the worst in Europe. There simply aren't enough people to justify big, slick roads. Except for rush hour in the big cities, traffic is wonderfully sparse. But roads are so narrow that every passing car or truck comes with a slight adrenaline rush. Take things slowly. If you rush, you'll wear yourself out, hit a pothole, and blow a tire—or worse. In Ireland, a single yellow line means parking is regulated (look for a street sign explaining the hours or limits on that street). A double yellow line means parking is not permitted at any time. Some towns require a disk, which you can buy at the TI or newsstands. Parking lots are cheap and central. While theft is rare in Ireland, tourists' cars are likely targets. Don't tempt thieves needlessly.

Telephones, Mail, and E-mail

Use the telephone routinely. You can make long-distance calls directly, cheaply, and easily, and there's no language barrier. Call ahead to reserve or reconfirm rooms, check opening hours, confirm tour times, and reserve theater tickets.

To call long distance you'll need the correct area code. Britain and Ireland have about as many area codes as we have prefixes. For long distance you'll find area codes listed by city on phone booth walls and throughout this book, or you can get them from directory assistance (free and happy to help, dial 192 in Britain). Phone numbers and area codes rarely have a standard number of digits. For information on telephoning throughout Europe, see the Appendix.

The British telephone system is great. Easy-to-find public phone booths are either coin- or card-operated. Phones take any coin from 10p to £1, and a display shows how your money supply's doing. Only completely unused coins will be returned, so put in biggies with caution. (If money's left over, rather than hang up, push the "make another call" button.) The more convenient phone-card booths are common only in cities. Some "credit-card phones" have a slot that will take—but not accept—a British Telecom phone card.

The British Telecom (BT) phone cards (available for £3, £10, or £20 at newsstands, hotels, tourist offices, and post offices) are facing competition from new, cheaper-per-minute PIN cards (which allow you to call home at the rate of about five minutes per dollar). The main difference is that a BT phone card, which must be inserted into a phone, can only be used at a phone card booth. The new PIN cards, which are not inserted into a phone, allow you to dial from any type of phone, even from your hotel room. To use a PIN card, dial the access number and Personal Identification Number listed on the card. There are many different brands of PIN cards; simply ask for an international calling card (sold for £3, etc., at most newsstands, exchange bureaus, and minimarts). If you're making numerous calls with a PIN card, you can avoid re-dialing the long access number by pressing whatever key (usually the pound sign) allows you to launch directly into your next call. Phone cards are your key to easy telephoning in Ireland as well.

The only tricky British phones you'll use are the expensive Mickey Mouse coin-op ones in bars and B&Bs. Some require money before you dial, while others wait until after you've connected. Many have a button you must push before you begin talking. But all have clear instructions. Long distance in Britain is most expensive from 8:00 to 13:00 and cheapest from 17:00 to 8:00. A short call across the country is quite inexpensive. Don't hesitate to call long distance.

Direct Dialing: When calling long distance within either Britain or Ireland, first dial the area code (which starts with zero), then the local number. When dialing internationally, dial the international access code (00 for Britain and Ireland), the country code (of the country you're calling to), the area code (without its initial zero), and the local number. For example, London's area code is 020. To call one of my listed London B&Bs from New York, I dial 011 (the U.S. international access code), 44 (Britain's country code), 20 (London's area code without its initial zero), then 7730-8191 (the B&B's number). To call it from Britain's old York, dial 020/7730-8191.

To call my office from Britain, I dial 00 (Britain's international access code), 1 (the U.S. country code), 425 (Edmonds' area code), then 771-8303. For a listing of international access codes and country codes, see the Appendix.

USA Direct Services (with an AT&T, MCI, or Sprint calling card) are popular for calling the United States from any kind of phone. While these used to be a fine deal, direct-dial rates were recently cut in half, and now you can more cheaply call home using coins or British or Irish phone cards. For a list of calling-card operators, see the Appendix. It's ridiculously expensive to use USA Direct for making calls between European countries—instead, call direct.

Mail: To arrange for mail delivery, reserve a few hotels along your route in advance and give their addresses to friends or use American Express mail services (available to anyone who has at least one Amex traveler's check). Allow 10 days for a letter to arrive. Phoning is so easy that I've dispensed with mail stops altogether.

E-mail: E-mail is gradually getting more common among hoteliers. I've listed e-mail addresses where possible. Cyber cafés are becoming popular in the bigger cities, giving you reasonably inexpensive and easy Internet access.

Sleeping

In the interest of smart use of your time, I favor accommodations (and restaurants) handy to your sightseeing activities. Rather than list hotels scattered throughout a city, I choose two or three favorite neighborhoods and recommend the best accommodations values in each, from $15 bunk beds to fancy-for-my-book $200 doubles. Outside of London you can expect to find good doubles for $60 to $100, including full-cooked breakfasts and tax.

I've described my recommended hotels and B&Bs with a standard code. Prices listed are for one-night stays in peak season, include a hearty breakfast, and assume you're going direct and not through a TI. Prices may be soft for off-season and longer stays. While many places have larger rooms and offer families special deals, Britain is peculiar in its insistence on charging per person rather than per room. Because of this, small groups often pay the same for a single and a double as they would for a triple. (Note: In this book, room prices are listed per room, not per person.)

Almost every place has three floors of rooms, steep stairs, and no elevator. Offhand, I can't think of a single elevator among my recommended places. If you're concerned about stairs, call and ask about ground-floor rooms.

All rooms have sinks. Any room without a bathroom has access to a free bath or shower on the corridor. In Britain and Ireland, rooms with private plumbing are called "en suite"; rooms that lack private plumbing are "standard." As more rooms go en suite, the hallway bathroom is shared with fewer standard rooms. If money's tight, ask for standard rooms.

Sleep Code

To give maximum information with a minimum of space, I use this code to describe accommodations listed in this book. *Prices in this book are listed per room, not per person.* Breakfast is included.

S = Single room, or price for one person in a double.

D = Double or twin room. (I specify double- and twin-bed rooms only if they are priced differently, or if a place has only one or the other. When reserving, you should specify.)

T = Three-person room (often a double bed with a single).

Q = Four-person room (adding an extra child's bed to a T is usually cheaper).

b = Private bathroom with toilet and shower or tub.

t = Private toilet only. (The shower is down the hall.)

s = Private shower or tub only. (The toilet is down the hall.)

CC = Accepts credit cards (**V** = Visa, **M** = MasterCard, **A** = American Express). If CC isn't mentioned, assume you'll need to pay cash.

No smoking—With this edition, about 80 percent of my recommended B&Bs are smoke free. While some places allow smoking in the sleeping rooms, breakfast rooms are nearly always smoke free.

Family deal—Indicates that parents with young children can easily get a room with an extra child's bed or a discount for larger rooms. Call to negotiate the price. Teenage kids are generally charged as adults. Little kids sleep almost free.

According to this code, a couple staying at a "Db-£55, CC:VM" hotel would pay a total of £55 (about $88) per night for a room with a private toilet and shower (or tub). The hotel accepts Visa, MasterCard, or cash.

British showers confuse (and scald) many tourists. A place built as a hotel has simple showers. But most B&Bs are retrofitted with showers, and water is heated individually for each shower rather than by one central heating system. While the switch is generally left on, in many rooms you'll have a hot-water switch to consider. Any cord hanging from the ceiling is for lights (not emergencies). Once in the shower you'll find a multitude of overly clever mechanisms designed to somehow get the right amount and temperature of water. Good luck.

Bed-and-Breakfasts (B&Bs)

Thank God Britain and Ireland have such lousy hotels, because the bed-and-breakfast alternative gives you double the cultural intimacy for half the price.

I'm assuming you have a reasonable but limited budget. Skip hotels. Go the B&B way. If you can use a telephone and speak English, you'll enjoy homey, friendly, clean rooms at a great price by sticking to my listings. Always call first.

If you're traveling beyond my recommended destinations, you'll find B&Bs where you need them. Any town with tourists has a TI that books rooms or can give you a list and point you in the right direction. In the absence of a TI, ask people on the street for help.

B&Bs range from large guest houses with 15 to 20 rooms to small homes renting out a spare bedroom. The philosophy of the management determines the character of a place more than its size and facilities offered. Avoid places run as a business by absentee owners. My top listings are run by couples who enjoy welcoming the world to their breakfast table.

The B&Bs I've recommended are nearly all stocking-feet comfortable and very "homely," as they say in England. I look for a place that is friendly (i.e., enjoys Americans); located in a central, safe, quiet neighborhood; clean, with good beds, a sink in the room, and shower down the hall; a good value; not mentioned in other guidebooks (and therefore filled mostly by English or Irish travelers); and willing to hold a room until 16:00 or so without a deposit (though more and more places are requiring a deposit or credit-card number). In certain cases my recommendations don't meet all of these prerequisites. I'm more impressed by a handy location and a fun-loving philosophy than hair driers and shoe-shine machines.

A few tips: B&B proprietors are selective as to whom they invite in for the night. Risky-looking people (two or more single men are often assumed to be troublemakers) find many places suddenly full. If you'll be staying for more than one night you are a "desirable." Sometimes staying several nights earns you a better price—ask about it. If you book through a TI, it takes a 10 percent commission. If you book direct, the B&B gets it all (and you'll have a better chance of getting a discount). I have negotiated special prices with this book (often for cash). You should find prices quoted here good through 2000 (except for major holidays and festivals). In popular weekend getaway spots you're unlikely to find a place to take you for Saturday night only. If my listings are full, ask for guidance. (Mentioning this book can help.) Owners usually work together and can call up an ally to land you a bed.

B&Bs are not hotels. If you want to ruin your relationship with your hostess, treat her like a hotel clerk. Americans often assume they'll get new towels each day. The British and Irish don't, and neither will you. Hang them up to dry and reuse. You'll climb plenty of stairs. Expect good exercise and be happy you packed light.

In Britain and Ireland you'll pay £15 to £32 ($27–50) per person for a B&B in 2000. Small places, with a gross income of under £46,000, can offer cheaper prices. They don't have to pay a 17 percent tax, don't have hired help, and can skimp on safety regulations. Prices include a big cooked breakfast. How much coziness, teddies, tea, and biscuits are tossed in varies tremendously.

"Twin" means two single beds, and "double" means one double bed. If you'll take either one, let them know or you might be needlessly turned away. "Standard" rooms come with just a sink. More and more are going en suite, meaning with a private shower/tub and a loo. Many better places have a basic room (with a shower down the hall) that they don't even advertise.

Both Britain and Ireland have rating systems for hotels and B&Bs. These diamonds, stars, and shamrocks are supposed to imply quality, but I find that they mean only that the place sporting symbols is paying dues to the tourist board. Rating systems often have little to do with value.

Making Reservations

It's possible to travel at any time of year without reservations, but given the high stakes, erratic accommodations values, number of people traveling with this book, and the quality of the gems I've listed, I highly recommend calling ahead for rooms at least a day or two in advance as you travel. When tourist crowds are down, you might make a habit of calling your hotel between 9:00 and 10:00 on the day you plan to arrive, when the hotel knows who'll be checking out and just which rooms will be available. I've taken great pains to list telephone numbers with long-distance instructions (see "Telephones, Mail, and E-mail" above; also see Appendix). Get a British or Irish phone card and use it to confirm and reconfirm as you travel. A hotel receptionist will trust you and hold a room until 16:00 without a deposit, though some will ask for a credit-card number.

Honor your reservations or cancel by phone: Trusting travelers to show up is a huge, stressful issue and a financial risk for small B&B owners. I promised the owners of the places I list that you will be reliable when you make a telephone reservation; please don't let them (or me) down. If you'll be delayed or won't make it, simply call in. Americans are notorious for "standing up" B&Bs. Being late is no problem if you are in telephone contact. Long distance is cheap and easy from public phone booths. While it's generally easy to find a room, a few national holidays jam things up (especially "bank holiday" Mondays) and merit reservations long in advance. Mark these dates in red on your travel calendar:

Christmas, December 26, New Year's Day, Good Friday, Easter plus Easter Monday, the first and last Monday in May, and the last Monday in August. Monday holidays are preceded by busy weekends; book the entire weekend in advance.

If you know exactly which dates you need and really want a particular place, reserve a room before you leave home. To reserve from home, call, fax, e-mail, or write the hotel. To fax, use the form in the Appendix (online at www.ricksteves.com/reservation). If you're writing, add the postal code and confirm the need and method for a deposit. A two-night stay in August would be "two nights, 16/8/00 to 18/8/00"—Europeans write the date day/month/year, and hotel jargon uses your day of departure. You'll often receive a letter back requesting one night's deposit. Your credit-card number and expiration date will usually be accepted as a deposit, though you may need to send a signed traveler's check or a bank draft in the local currency. If your credit card is the deposit, you can pay with your card or cash when you arrive; if you don't show up you'll be billed for one night. Reconfirm your reservations a day in advance for safety (or you may be bumped—really). Also, don't just assume you can extend. Take the time to consider in advance how long you'll stay.

Hostels

Britain and Ireland have more than 400 hostels of all shapes and sizes. They can be historic castles or depressing huts, serene and comfy or overrun by noisy children. Unfortunately, many of the international youth hostels have become overpriced, and, in general, I no longer recommend them. The only time I do is if you're on a very tight budget, want to cook your own meals, or are traveling with a group that likes to sleep on bunk beds in big rooms. The informal private hostels are often more fun, easygoing, and cheaper. These alternatives to the International Youth Hostel Federation (IYHF) hostels are more common than ever. If you're traveling alone, hosteling is the best way to conquer hotel loneliness. Hostels are also a tremendous source of local and budget travel information. If you hostel selectively, you'll enjoy historical and interesting buildings.

You'll pay an average of £9 for a bed, £1 for sheets, and £2 for breakfast. Anyone of any age can hostel in Britain and Ireland. While there are no membership concerns for private hostels, IYHF hostels require membership. Those without cards simply buy one-night guest memberships for £1.50.

Forte Travelodge in Britain

The Forte Travelodge chain has 120 freeway-friendly motels throughout Britain. These are superconvenient, offering simple, clean, and comfortable rooms for up to four people (two adults/

two children or three adults/one child) for £40 to £70, depending on location. Each room has a double bed, a single bed, a five-foot trundle bed, a private shower, a WC, and a TV. Each hotel has an attached restaurant, good security, and a 24-hour staffed reception desk. Of course they are as cozy as a Motel 6, but they're great for families, and many travelers love them. (If you call particular hotels direct, you can sometimes get discounts.) You can reserve by credit card (CC:VMA, tel. 01384/78884 or toll-free tel. 0800-850-950 in Britain, www.travelodge.co.uk/index.html) and pay when you check in (any time after 15:00, as late as you like). When you're ready to go (before noon), you just drop off the key, Lee. The Travel Inn chain is also opening up huge hotels with similarly tight and modern little rooms, ranging in price from £45 to £65 for up to two adults and two kids (tel. 01582/414-341).

Eating

I don't mind English food. But then, I liked dorm food. True, England isn't famous for its cuisine and probably never will be, but we tourists have to eat. If there's any good place to cut corners to stretch your budget in Britain and Ireland, it's in eating. Here are a few tips on budget eating.

The traditional "fry" is famous as a hearty way to start the day. Also known as a "heart attack on a plate," the breakfast is especially feasty if you've just come from the land of the skimpy continental breakfast across the Channel. Your standard fry gets off to a healthy start with juice and cereal or porridge. (Try Weet-abix, a soggy English cousin of shredded wheat. Scotland serves great porridge.) Next, with tea or coffee, you get a heated plate with a fried egg, lean Canadian-style bacon, a bad sausage, a grilled tomato, and often a slice of delightfully greasy pan toast and sautéed mushrooms. Toast comes on a rack (to cool quickly and crisply) with butter and marmalade. Order kippers (herring filets smoked in an oak fire). This meal tides many travelers over until dinner. Order only what you'll eat. A B&B hostess, your temporary local mother, doesn't like to see food wasted. And there's nothing un-British about skipping the "fry"—few locals actually start their day with this heavy traditional breakfast.

These days, the best coffee is served in a *cafetiére* (also called a French press). When your coffee has steeped as long as you like, plunge down the filter and pour. To revitalize your brew, pump the plunger again.

Many B&Bs don't serve breakfast until 8:00. If you need an early start, ask politely if it's possible. While they may not make you a cooked breakfast, they can usually put out cereal, toast, juice, and coffee.

Picnicking saves time and money. Try boxes of orange juice (pure, by the liter), fresh bread (especially Irish soda bread), tasty

English cheese, meat, a tube of Colman's English mustard, local eatin' apples, bananas, small tomatoes, a small tub of yogurt (they're drinkable), rice crackers, gorp or nuts, plain "Digestive Biscuits" (the chocolate-covered ones melt), and any local specialties. At open-air markets and supermarkets you can get food in small quantities. (Three tomatoes and two bananas cost me 50p.) Decent sandwiches (£2) are sold everywhere. I often munch a relaxed "meal on wheels" in a car, train, or bus to save 30 precious minutes.

British restaurants are fairly expensive, but cheap alternatives abound: fish-and-chips joints, Chinese and Indian take-outs, cafeterias, pubs (see below), B&Bs that serve evening meals, and your typical good old greasy-spoon cafés. At a sit-down place with table service, tip no more than 10 percent.

For fresh, fast, and cheap lunches, bakeries have meat pies (and microwaves), pastries, yogurt, and cartons of "semiskimmed" milk. Pasties (PASTE-eez) are "savory" (not sweet) meat pies that originated in the mining country. They had big crust handles so miners with filthy hands could eat them and toss the crust. Today you'll find them in bakeries and cafés. They make a quick, hot meal.

People of leisure punctuate their day with a "cream tea" at a tea room. You'll get a pot of tea, two homemade scones, jam, and thick, creamy-as-honey clotted cream. For maximum pinkie-waving taste per calorie, slice your scone thin like a miniature loaf of bread. Tea rooms, which often serve appealing light meals, are usually open for lunch and close around 17:00, just before dinner.

Pub Grub and Beer

Pubs are a basic part of the British and Irish social scene, and whether you're a teetotaler or a beer guzzler they should be a part of your travel here. Pub is short for "public house." It's an extended living room where, if you don't mind the stickiness, you can feel the pulse of Britain and Ireland. Most traditional atmospheric pubs are in the countryside and smaller towns. Unfortunately, many city pubs have been afflicted with an excess of brass, ferns, and video games. In any case, smart travelers use the pubs to eat, drink, get out of the rain, watch the latest sporting event, and make new friends.

Pub grub gets better each year. It's Britain's and Ireland's best eating value. For £5 you'll get a basic budget hot lunch or dinner in friendly surroundings. The *Good Pub Guide*, published annually by the British Consumers Union, is excellent. Pubs attached to restaurants often have fresher food and a chef who knows how to cook.

I recommend certain pubs, but food can spoil, and your B&B host is usually up-to-date on the best neighborhood pub grub. Ask for advice (but adjust for nepotism and cronyism, which run rampant). Locals will rarely recommend a rough pub that's a local hangout. If you want this experience (the food will be cheaper but not very good), ask for a "spit-and-sawdust" place. Big-city spit-and-sawdust places may not welcome tourists. Rural and village ones will. They are the most interesting.

Pubs generally serve assorted meat pies, such as steak and kidney pie or shepherd's pie, curried dishes, fish, quiche, vegetables, and (invariably) chips and peas. Better pubs let you substitute a "jacket potato" (baked potato) for your fries. Meals are usually served from 12:00 to 14:00 and 18:00 to 20:00, not throughout the day. Servings are hearty, service is quick, and you'll rarely spend more than £4 to £6 ($6–9). Your beer or cider adds another pound or two. Free tap water is always available. In Britain a "ploughman's lunch" is a modern "traditional English meal" that nearly every tourist tries... once. Pubs that advertise their food and are crowded with locals are less likely to be the kind that serve only lousy microwaved snacks.

In a pub you order your beer at the bar. Part of the experience is standing before a line of "hand pulls" and wondering which on-tap beer you want. The British and Irish take great pride in their beer. They think that drinking beer cold and carbonated, as Americans do, ruins the taste. At pubs, long hand pulls are used to pull the traditional rich-flavored "real ales" up from the cellar. These are the connoisseur's favorites: They're fermented naturally, vary from sweet to bitter, and often include a hoppy or nutty flavor. Notice the fun names. Experiment with the obscure local microbrews. Short "hand pulls" at the bar mean colder, fizzier, mass-produced, and less interesting keg beers. Mild beers are sweeter, with a creamy malt flavor. Stout is dark and more bitter, like Guinness. For a cold, refreshing, basic American-style beer, ask for a "lager." Try the draft cider (sweet or dry)... carefully. Proper English ladies like a half-beer and half-lemonade "shandy." Teetotalers can order a soft drink. Drinks are served by the pint or the half-pint. (It's almost feminine for a man to order just a half; I order mine with quiche.) There's no table service. Order drinks and meals at the bar. Pay as you order and don't tip.

Pub hours vary. The strictly limited wartime hours (designed to keep the wartime working force sober and productive) finally ended a few years ago, and now pubs can serve beer from 11:00 to 23:00, and Sunday from noon to 22:30. Children are served food and soft drinks in pubs, and you must be 18 to order a beer. A cup of darts is free for the asking. People go to a "public house" to be social. They want to talk. Get vocal with a local. Pubs are the next best thing to relatives in every town.

Stranger in a Strange Land

We travel all the way to Europe to enjoy differences—to become temporary locals. You'll experience frustrations. There are certain truths that we find God-given and self-evident, such as cold beer, ice in drinks, bottomless cups of coffee, easy shower faucets, and driving on the right side of the road. One of the benefits of travel is the eye-opening realization that there are logical, civil, and even better alternatives. A willingness to go local ensures that you'll enjoy a full dose of European hospitality.

Send Me a Postcard, Drop Me a Line

If you enjoy a successful trip with the help of this book and would like to share your discoveries, please fill out and send the survey at the end of this book to me at Europe Through the Back Door, Box 2009, Edmonds, WA 98020. I personally read and value all feedback. Thanks in advance—it helps a lot.

For our latest travel information, tap into our Web site: www.ricksteves.com. To check on any updates for this book, visit www.ricksteves.com/update. My e-mail address is rick@ricksteves .com. Anyone can request a free issue of our newsletter.

Judging from the happy postcards I receive from travelers, it's safe to assume you'll enjoy a great, affordable vacation—with the finesse of an independent, experienced traveler. Thanks, and happy travels!

BACK DOOR TRAVEL PHILOSOPHY
As Taught in *Rick Steves' Europe Through the Back Door*

Travel is intensified living—maximum thrills per minute and one of the last great sources of legal adventure. Travel is freedom. It's recess, and we need it.

Experiencing the real Europe requires catching it by surprise, going casual... "Through the Back Door."

Affording travel is a matter of priorities. (Make do with the old car.) You can travel—simply, safely, and comfortably—anywhere in Europe for $70 a day plus transportation costs. In many ways, spending more money only builds a thicker wall between you and what you came to see. Europe is a cultural carnival and, time after time, you'll find that its best acts are free and the best seats are the cheap ones.

A tight budget forces you to travel close to the ground, meeting and communicating with the people, not relying on service with a purchased smile. Never sacrifice sleep, nutrition, safety, or cleanliness in the name of budget. Simply enjoy the local-style alternatives to expensive hotels and restaurants.

Extroverts have more fun. If your trip is low on magic moments, kick yourself and make things happen. If you don't enjoy a place, maybe you don't know enough about it. Seek the truth. Recognize tourist traps. Give a culture the benefit of your open mind. See things as different but not better or worse. Any culture has much to share.

Of course, travel, like the world, is a series of hills and valleys. Be fanatically positive and militantly optimistic. If something's not to your liking, change your liking. Travel is addictive. It can make you a happier American as well as a citizen of the world. Our Earth is home to nearly 6 billion equally important people. It's humbling to travel and find that people don't envy Americans. They like us, but with all due respect, they wouldn't trade passports.

Globetrotting destroys ethnocentricity. It helps you understand and appreciate different cultures. Travel changes people. It broadens perspectives and teaches new ways to measure quality of life. Many travelers toss aside their hometown blinders. Their prized souvenirs are the strands of different cultures they decide to knit into their own character. The world is a cultural yarn shop. And Back Door Travelers are weaving the ultimate tapestry. Come on, join in!

LONDON

London is more than 600 square miles of urban jungle. With 9 million struggling people—many of whom speak English—it's a world in itself and a barrage on all the senses. On my first visit I felt very, very small. London is much more than its museums and famous landmarks. It's a living, breathing, thriving organism.

London has changed dramatically in recent years, and many visitors are surprised to find how "un-English" it is. Whites are now a minority in major parts of the city that once symbolized white imperialism. Arabs have nearly bought out the area north of Hyde Park. Chinese take-outs outnumber fish-and-chips shops. Many hotels are run by people with foreign accents (who hire English chambermaids), while outlying suburbs are home to huge communities of Indians and Pakistanis. London is learning— sometimes fitfully—to live as a microcosm of its formerly vast empire. With the English Channel Tunnel complete, many see more foreign threats to the Britishness of Britain.

With just a few days here, you'll get no more than a quick splash in this teeming human tidal pool. But, with a quick orientation, you'll get a good taste of its top sights, history, and cultural entertainment, as well as its ever-changing human face.

Have fun in London. Blow through the city on the open deck of a double-decker orientation tour bus, and take a pinch-me-I'm-in-Britain walk through downtown. Ogle the crown jewels at the Tower of London, hear the chimes of Big Ben, and see the Houses of Parliament in action. Hobnob with the tombstones in Westminster Abbey, duck WWII bombs in Churchill's underground Cabinet War Rooms, and brave the earthshaking Imperial War Museum. Overfeed the pigeons at Trafalgar Square. Visit with Leonardo, Botticelli, and Rembrandt in the National Gallery. Whisper across the dome of St. Paul's Cathedral and rummage through our civilization's attic at the British Museum. Cruise down the Thames River. You'll enjoy some of Europe's best people watching at Covent Garden and snap to at Buckingham Palace's Changing of the Guard. Just sit in Victoria Station, at a major tube station, at Piccadilly Circus, or in Trafalgar Square, and observe. Spend one evening at a theater and the others catching your breath.

Planning Your Time

The sights of London alone could easily fill a trip to Britain. It's a great one-week getaway. On a three-week tour of Britain I'd give it three busy days. If you're flying in, consider starting your trip in Bath and make London your British finale. Especially if you hope to enjoy a play or concert, a night or two of jet lag is bad news.

Here's a suggested schedule:

Day 1: 9:00–Tower of London (Beefeater tour, crown jewels), 12:00–Munch a sandwich on the Thames while cruising from the Tower to Westminster Bridge, 13:00–Follow the self-guided "Hello London" walk (see below) with a quick visit to the Cabinet War Rooms, 15:30–Trafalgar Square and National Gallery, 17:30–Visit the National Tourist Information Centre near Piccadilly, planning ahead for your trip, 18:30–Dinner in Soho. Take in a play or 19:30 concert at St. Martin-in-the-Fields.

Day 2: 9:00–If traveling around Britain, spend 30 minutes in a phone booth getting all essential elements of your trip nailed down. If you know where you'll be and when, call those B&Bs now. 9:30–Take the Round London bus tour (consider hopping off for the 11:30 Changing of the Guard at Buckingham Palace), 12:30–Covent Gardens for lunch and people watching, 14:00–Tour the British Museum. Have a pub dinner before a play, concert, or evening walking tour.

Days 3 and 4: Choose among these remaining London highlights: Tour Westminster Abbey, the British Library, the Imperial War Museum, the two Tate Galleries (British art on the north bank and modern art on the south bank), St. Paul's Cathedral, or the Museum of London; cruise to Kew or Greenwich (Millennium Dome); do some serious shopping at one of London's elegant department stores or open-air markets; or consider another historic walking tour.

After considering nearly all of London's tourist sights, I have pruned them down to just the most important (or fun) for a first visit of up to seven days. You won't be able to see all of these, so don't try. You'll keep coming back to London. After 25 visits myself, I still enjoy a healthy list of excuses to return.

Orientation
(tel. code: 020)

To grasp London comfortably, see it as the old town without the

Millennium London

London seems hell-bent on hosting the world's grandest millennium celebrations. The year 2000 brings London revamped museums, a huge Ferris wheel, and a giant dome at Greenwich.

Greenwich, site of the world's prime meridian and "the place from where time is measured," kicked off the millennium with gusto, playing host to Her Majesty and Prince Charles' big New Year's Eve 2000 bash in the Millennium Dome. This exhibition hall, fifty meters high and a kilometer around, is the biggest millennium project anywhere. Fourteen theme zones (such as Mind, Body, Spirit, Work, National Identity, Play, and a display of Princess Diana's dresses) surround a vast central stage. Expect lots of live entertainment, huge video screens, virtual reality gimmicks, and enthusiastic interactivity. After 2000, the dome will be redeveloped as a theme park or exhibition center. In the town of Greenwich, the Queen's House hosts the new "The Story of Time" exhibit (until Sept 24) and the Old Royal Naval College opens its Painted Hall and Chapel to the public. (For details, see "Greenwich," below.)

On London's South Bank, a grand Ferris wheel spins opposite Big Ben—at 450 feet high, it's the highest public viewpoint in London. The new Tate Gallery of Modern Art, opening this May, will be linked to St. Paul's Cathedral by the new pedestrian Millennium Bridge, London's first bridge in a hundred years. And the Globe Theater has expanded its exhibit on the history of the Globe to cover Shakespeare, his contemporaries, and the beginnings of theater. (For details, see "Sights—South London," below.)

The British Museum opens its Great Court and elegant, round Reading Room (that Karl Marx liked so much) to the public this fall. The museum hosts a thought-provoking exhibit exploring the legacy of the book of Revelations—*The Apocalypse and the Shape of Things to Come*—tracing the devil and ideas about the apocalypse from the 11th century to World War II (through April 24, 2000).

The "Arts 2000" movement plans to free art from its normal places all over Britain and hang it in unusual, everyday places, from train stations to shopping malls.

Like nowhere else in Europe, London and Greenwich know how to throw a party. They make it easy to turn 2000.

modern, congested sprawl. Most of the visitor's London lies between the Tower of London and Hyde Park—about a three-mile walk. Mentally—maybe even physically—scissor down your map to include only the area between the Tower, King's Cross Station, Paddington Station, the Victoria and Albert Museum, and Victoria Station. With this focus and a good orientation, you'll find London manageable and even fun.

Tourist Information

The **British Visitors Centre** is the best information service in town (Mon–Fri 9:00–18:30, Sat–Sun 10:00–16:00, just off Piccadilly Circus at 1 Lower Regent Street, tel. 020/8846-9000, www.visitbritain .com). It's great for London information. If you're traveling beyond London, take advantage of its well-equipped London/England desk, Wales desk (tel. 020/7803-3838), Ireland desk (tel. 020/7493-3201), and Scotland desk. At the center's extensive bookshop, gather whatever guidebooks, youth hostel directories, maps, and information you'll need. If venturing beyond London, consider the *Michelin Green Guide* to London or Britain (£9), the Britain road atlas (£10), and Ordnance Survey maps for areas you'll be exploring by car. There's also a travel agency upstairs.

The **Scottish Tourist Centre** (19 Cockspur Street, tel. 020/7930-8661) and the slick new **French National Tourist Office** (Mon–Sat 9:00–17:30, closed Sun, 179 Piccadilly Street, tel. 0990-848-848) are nearby.

Unfortunately **London's Tourist Information Centres** (TIs) are now owned by the big hotels and are simply businesses selling advertising space to companies with fliers to distribute. They are not very helpful. Avoid their 50p-per-minute telephone information service (instead try the **British Visitors Centre** at 020/8846-9000). Locations include Heathrow Airport's Terminal 3 (daily 6:00–23:00, most convenient and least crowded); Heathrow Airport's Terminal 1 and 2 tube station (daily 8:00–18:00); Victoria Station (daily 8:00–18:00, shorter hours in winter, crowded and commercial); and Waterloo International Terminal Arrivals Hall (serving trains from Paris, daily 8:30–22:30).

At any of the TIs, bring your itinerary and a checklist of questions. Pick up these publications: *London Planner* (a great free monthly that lists all the sights, events, and hours), walking-tour schedule fliers, and a theater guide. Consider buying their fine £1.40 London map, which rivals the £4 maps sold in newsstands (free from the British Tourist Authority in the U.S.A.: tel. 800/462-2748 or 212/986-2200, 551 Fifth Avenue, 7th floor, New York, NY 10176, www.visitbritain.com). The TIs sell BT phone cards, long-distance bus tickets and passes, British Heritage Passes, and tickets to plays (steep booking fee). They also book rooms (avoid their £5 booking fee by calling hotels direct).

Helpful Hints

Theft Alert: The Artful Dodger is alive and well in London. Be on guard, particularly on public transportation and in places crowded with tourists. Tourists, considered naive and rich, are targeted. Over 7,500 handbags are stolen annually at Covent Garden alone. Thieves paw you so you don't feel the pickpocketing.

Changing Money: ATMs are really the way to go. Standard transaction fees at banks are £2–4. American Express Offices offer a fair rate and change any brand of traveler's checks for no fee. There are several offices (Heathrow Terminal 4 tube station and at 6 Haymarket near Piccadilly, daily 9:00–18:00, tel. 020/7930-4411). Avoid changing money at exchange bureaus. Their latest scam: they advertise very good rates with a same-as-the-banks fee of 2 percent. But the fine print explains that the fee of 2 percent is for *buying* pounds. The fee for *selling* pounds is 9.5 percent. Ouch!

What's Up: For the best listing of what's happening (plays, movies, restaurants, concerts, exhibitions, protests, walking tours, shopping, and children's activities) and a look at the trendy London scene, pick up a current copy of *Time Out* (£1.80, www.timeout .co.uk) or *What's On* at any newsstand. The TI's free monthly *London Planner* lists sights, plays, and events at least as well. For a fun Web site on London's entertainment, theater, restaurants, and news, go to www.thisislondon.com.

Free Sights: The British Museum, British Library, National Gallery, National Portrait Gallery, and both Tate Galleries are always free. These museums are free from 16:30 to closing (17:30 or 18:00), saving you £5 or so: The Imperial War Museum, Museum of London, Natural History Museum, and Victoria and Albert Museum. More museums will be free in the next few years.

Travel Bookstores: Stanfords Travel Bookstore—near Victoria Station (52 Grosvenor Gardens), at Covent Garden (12 Long Acre, tel. 020/7836-1321), and at 156 Regent Street—is good and stocks current editions of my books. Waterstones Bookstore, on the corner of Trafalgar Square, is also handy, with a fine travel selection next to the Coffee Republic café (WC upstairs, tel. 020/7839-4411). The best London map I've seen is the Bensons Mapguide of London (£2, May 1999 edition has the Greenwich Dome).

Travel Agency: The student travel agency USIT, across from Victoria Station, has great deals on flights for people of all ages (Mon–Fri 9:00–18:00, Sat–Sun 10:00–17:00, Buckingham Palace Road, tel. 0870-240-1010, www.usitcampus.co.uk). Also, look in the Sunday *Times* travel section for great deals on flights.

Arrival in London

By Train: London has eight train stations, all connected by the tube (subway), all with exchange offices and luggage storage. From any station, ride the tube or taxi to your hotel.

By Bus: The bus station is one block southwest of Victoria Station, which has a TI and tube entrance.

By Plane: For detailed information on getting from London's airports to downtown London, see "Transportation Connections" at the end of this chapter.

Getting around London

London's taxis, buses, and subway system make a private car unnecessary. To travel smart in a city this size, you must get comfortable with public transportation.

By Taxi: London is the best taxi town in Europe. Big, black, carefully regulated cabs are everywhere. I never met a crabby cabbie in London. They love to talk and know every nook and cranny in town. I ride in one a day just to get my London questions answered. Rides start at £1.40 and cost about £1.50 per tube stop. Connecting downtown sights is quick and easy and will cost you about £4 (e.g., St. Paul's to the Tower of London). For a short ride, three people in a cab travel at tube prices. Groups of four or five should taxi everywhere. If a cab's top light is on, just wave it down. (Drivers flash lights when they see you.) They have a tiny turning radius, so you can wave at cabs going both directions. If waving doesn't work, ask someone where you can find a taxi stand. Stick with metered cabs. While telephoning a cab gets one in minutes, it's generally not necessary and adds to the cost. London is such a great wave-'em-down taxi town that most cabs don't even have a radio phone.

By Bus: London's extensive bus system is easy to follow. Just pick up a free map from a TI or tube station. Signs at stops list routes clearly. Conductors are terse but helpful. Ask to be reminded when it's your stop. Just hop on, tell the driver where you're going, pay what he says, grab a ticket, take a seat, and relax. (The best views are upstairs.) Rides start at 90p. If the driver is not taking money, hop in and grab a seat. The conductor will eventually sell you a ticket. If you have a transit pass, get in the habit of hopping buses for quick little straight shots (even just to get to a metro stop). During bump-and-grind rush hours (8:00–10:00 and 16:00–19:00), you'll go faster by tube.

By Tube: London's subway is one of this planet's great people movers and the fastest (and cheapest) long-distance transport in town. Any ride in the Central Zone (on or within the Circle Line, including virtually all my recommended sights and hotels) costs £1.40. You can avoid ticket window lines in tube stations by buying tickets from coin-op machines; practice on the punchboard to see how the system works (hit "adult single" and your destination). Again, nearly every ride will be £1.40. (These tickets are valid only on the day of purchase.) Beware: Overshooting your zone will get you a £10 fine.

London

Most city maps include a tube map with color-coded lines and names (free at any station window). Each line has a name (such as Circle, Northern, or Bakerloo) and two directions (indicated by end stop). In stations you'll have a choice of two platforms per line. Navigate by signs leading to the platforms (usually labeled north, south, east, or west) and clearly listing the stops served by each line, or ask a local or an orange-vested staff person for help. All city maps have north on top. Know which general direction you're heading, and tube navigation suddenly becomes easier. Some tracks are shared by several lines, and electronic signboards announce which train is next and the minutes remaining until various arrivals. Each train has its final destination or line name above its windshield. Read the system notices clearly posted at the platform; they explain the tube's latest flood, construction, or bomb scare. Bring something to do to pass the waits productively. And always... mind the gap.

You can't leave the system without feeding your ticket to the turnstile. Save time by choosing the best street exit (look at the maps on the walls). "Subway" means pedestrian underpass in "English." For tube and bus information, call 020/7222-1234.

London Tube and Bus Passes: Consider using these passes, valid on both the tube and buses. The "Travel Card," covering Zones 1 and 2, gives you unlimited travel for a day, starting after 9:30 and anytime on weekends, for £3.80. The all-zone version of this card costs £4.50 (and includes Heathrow airport). The "LT Card," a one-day, two-zone pass with no time restriction, costs £4.80. Families save with the one-day "Family Travel Card." The "Weekend Travel Card," covering Zones 1 and 2 for £5.70, costs 25 percent less than two one-day cards. The "7-Day Travel Card" costs £18, covers Zone 1, and requires a passport-type photo (cut one out of any snapshot and bring it from home). All passes are available for more zones and are purchased as easily as a normal ticket at any station. If you figure you'll take three rides in a day, get a day pass.

If you want to travel a little each day or if you're part of a group, a £10 "carnet" is a great deal: you get 10 separate tickets for tube travel in Zone 1 (£1 each rather than £1.40). Wait for the machine to lay all 10 tickets.

Tours of London

▲▲▲**Hop-on Hop-off Double-Decker Bus Tours**—Two very competitive companies ("Original" and "Big Bus") offer essentially the same tours, with live (English-only) guides on board. This two-hour, once-over-lightly bus tour drives by all the most famous sights, providing a stressless way to get your bearings and at least see the biggies. You can sit back and enjoy the entire two-hour orientation tour (a good idea if you like the guide and the weather) or "hop on and hop off" at any of the 20 plus stops and catch a later bus. Buses run about every 10 minutes in summer, every 20 minutes in winter. It's an inexpensive form of transport as well as an informative tour. Grab one of the maps and study it. Buses run daily, except on Christmas (from about 9:00 in summer—9:30 in winter—until early evening), from Victoria Street (one block north of Victoria Station), Marble Arch, Piccadilly Circus, Trafalgar Square, and so on. Each company offers a core two-hour overview tour and two other routes (buy ticket from driver, ticket good for 24 hours; bring a sweater and extra film). Note: if you start at Victoria at 9:30, you can hop off near the end of the two-hour loop at the Buckingham Palace stop (Bressenden Place), a five-minute walk from the palace and the Changing of the Guard at 11:30. Sunday morning, with light traffic and many museums closed, is a fine time for the tour.

Original London Sightseeing Bus Tour: Live guided buses have a Union Jack flag and a yellow triangle on the front of the bus. If the front has many flags or a green triangle, it's a tape-recorded multilingual tour—avoid it, unless you have kids who'd enjoy the more entertaining recorded kids' tour (£12.50, £3.50 off with this book—limit two discounts per book, they'll rip off the corner of this page, ticket good for 24 hours, tel. 020/8877-1722).

Big Bus Hop-on Hop-off London Tours: These are also good. For £15 you get the same basic tour plus coupons for four different one-hour London walks and the scenic and entertainingly guided Thames boat ride (normally £4.60) between Westminster Pier and the Tower of London. The pass and extras are valid for 24 hours. While the price is steeper, Big Bus guides seem more dynamic than the Original guides, and the Big Bus system is probably better organized (tel. 020/8944-7810, www.bigbus.co.uk).

▲▲**Walking Tours**—Many times a day top-notch local guides lead small groups through specific slices of London's past. Schedule fliers litter the desks of TIs, hotels, and pubs. (The beefy, plain black-and-white *Original London Walks* newsletter lists their extensive daily schedule.) *Time Out* lists many but not all scheduled walks. Simply show up at the announced location, pay £5, and enjoy two chatty hours of Dickens, the Plague, Shakespeare, Legal London, the Beatles, Jack the Ripper, or whatever is on the agenda. Original London Walks is the dominant company (for schedule, tel. 020/7624-3978, www.walks.com). They do private tours for £80.

Robina Brown, who winters in Seattle (a bizarre concept), leads tours on foot or with small groups in her Toyota Previa. Standard rates for London's registered guides: £83/4 hrs, £125/9 hrs. For car and guiding she charges £145 for 3 hours and about £300 per day per group (tel. & fax 020/7228-2238, e-mail: robina.brown@which.net). Brit Lonsdale, an energetic mother of twins, is another registered London guide (tel. 020/7386-9907,

fax 020/7386-9807). Chris Salaman, while semiretired, tailors specialty walks (his favorite: industrial tours). He does daylong private
walks, including lunch, a tube travel card, and museum admissions,
for £120 for up to six people (tel. 020/8871-9048). For other
guides call 020/7403-2062, www.touristguides.org.uk.

▲▲**Cruise the Thames**—Boat tours with an entertaining
commentary sail regularly from Westminster Pier (at the base of
Westminster Bridge under Big Ben). You can cruise to the Tower
of London (£4.60, round-trip £5.80, included with Big Bus
London tour, 3/hrly, 10:20–21:00 in peak season, until 18:00 in
winter, 30 min, tel. 020/7930-9033), Greenwich (£6, round-trip
£7.30, 2/hrly, 10:00–17:00, 50 min, tel. 020/7930-4097), and Kew
Gardens (£6, round-trip £10, 5/day, 90 min, 30 min narrated,
tel. 020/7930-2062). For pleasure and efficiency, consider com-
bining a one-way cruise with a tube ride back.

Sights—From Westminster Abbey to Trafalgar Square

▲▲**"Hello London" Walk**—Just about every visitor to London
strolls the historic Whitehall boulevard from Big Ben to Trafalgar
Square. Beneath London's modern traffic and big-city bustle lies
2,000 fascinating years of history. This three-quarter-mile, self-
guided orientation walk gives you a whirlwind tour and connects
the sights listed in this section.

Start halfway across **Westminster Bridge** for the great view.
For that "Wow, I'm really in London!" feeling, get a close-up
view of the **Houses of Parliament** and **Big Ben** (floodlit at
night). Downstream you'll see the new **Millennium Ferris wheel**.
Downstairs are boats to the Tower of London and Greenwich.

To thrill your loved ones (or bug the envious), call home
from a pay phone near Big Ben at about three minutes before the
hour. You'll find a phone on Great George Street, across from
Parliament Square. As Big Ben chimes, stick the receiver outside
the booth and prove you're in London: Ding dong ding dong…
dong ding ding dong.

Wave hello to Churchill in the park. To his right is **Westminster Abbey** with its two stubby, elegant towers.

Walk north up Parliament Street (which turns into Whitehall) toward Trafalgar Square. As you stroll along this center-
of-government boulevard, you'll see the thought-provoking **Cenotaph** in the middle of the street, reminding passersby of Britain's
many war dead. To visit the Cabinet War Rooms (see "Sights,"
below) take a left before the Cenotaph, on King Charles Street.

Continuing on Whitehall, stop at the barricaded and guarded
little **Downing Street** to see the British "White House" at **#10,**
home of the prime minister. Break the bobby's boredom and ask
him a question.

Central London

Nearing Trafalgar Square, look for the **Horse Guards** behind the gated fence (11:00 inspection Mon–Sat, 10:00 on Sun; dismounting ceremony daily at 16:00) and the 17th-century **Banqueting House** across the street (see "Sights," below).

The column topped by Lord Nelson marks **Trafalgar Square**. The stately domed building on the far side of the square is the **National Gallery** (free) which has a classy café (upstairs in the Sainsbury wing). To the right of the National Gallery is **St. Martin-in-the-Fields Church** and its Café in the Crypt (see "Eating," below).

To get to Piccadilly from Trafalgar Square, walk up Cockspur Street to Haymarket and then take a short left on Coventry Street to colorful **Piccadilly Circus.**

Near Piccadilly you'll find the **British Tourist Information Centre** and piles of theaters. **Leicester Square** (with its half-price ticket booth for plays) thrives just a few blocks away. Walk through seedy **Soho** (north of Shaftesbury Avenue) for its fun pubs (see "Eating," below, for "Food is Fun" Dinner Crawl). From Piccadilly or Oxford Circus, you can taxi, bus, or tube home.

▲▲▲**Westminster Abbey**—England's historic coronation church is a crowded collection of famous tombs. Like a stony refugee camp huddled outside St. Peter's gates, this is an English hall of fame. Choose among tours (Walkman-£2 or live-£3). Consider attending an evensong (weekdays except Wed at 17:00, Sat and Sun at 15:00) or the Sunday 17:45 organ recital (£5 for abbey entry, tours extra; Mon–Fri 9:15–16:45, Sat 9:00–14:45, technically no visitors on Sun, also open for half price on Wed 18:00–19:45—the only time photography is allowed; last admission one hour before closing, lattés in the cloister, tube: Westminster, tel. 020/7222-7110). For a free peek at the nave with no line, enter via Deans Yard (arch near west end of church) and go through the group entrance as if you're going to the museum. At the cloister, turn left and enter the nave. Since the church is often closed to the public for special services, it's wise to call first. Praying is free; use separate marked entrance.

▲▲**Houses of Parliament (Palace of Westminster)**—This neo-Gothic icon of London, the royal residence from 1042 to 1547, is now the meeting place of the legislative branch of government. While Parliament is too tempting to terrorists to be opened wide to tourists, you can view debates in either the bickering House of Commons or the genteel House of Lords if they're in session—indicated by a flag flying atop the Victoria Tower (Mon, Tue, and Thu 14:30–22:00, Wed 9:30–22:00, Fri 9:30–15:00, generally less action and no lines after 18:00, use St. Stephen's entrance, tube: Westminster, tel. 020/7219-4272 for schedule).

While it's not worth a long wait and the actual action is generally extremely dull, it is a thrill to be inside and see the British government inaction. The House of Lords has more pageantry, shorter lines, and less-interesting debates (tel. 020/7219-3107 for schedule). If confronted with a too-long House of Commons line, see the House of Lords first. Once you've seen the Lords (hide your HOL flier), you can often slip directly to the Commons—joining the gang waiting in the lobby. If there's only one line outside, it's for the House of Commons. Go to the gate and tell the guard you want the Lords. You may pop right in. While other guidebooks tout the U.S. Embassy "entry cards," which get you directly in, they only give out four per day, and landing one is most likely hopeless.

After passing security, slip to the left and study the big dark **Westminster Hall**, which survived the 1834 fire. The hall is 11th century, and its famous self-supporting hammer-beam roof was added in 1397. The Houses of Parliament are located in what was once the Palace of Westminster, long the palace of England's medieval kings, until it was largely destroyed by fire in 1834. The palace was rebuilt in Victorian Gothic style (a move away from Neoclassicism back to England's Christian and medieval heritage, true to the Romantic age). It was completed in 1860; only a few of its 1,000 rooms are open to the public.

The **Jewel Tower** is (along with Westminster Hall) about the only surviving part of the old Palace of Westminster. It contains a fine little exhibit on Parliament: first floor—history, second floor—Parliament today, with a 30-minute video and lonely picnic-friendly benches (£1.50, daily 10:00–18:00, closing at 16:00 or 17:00 off-season, across the street from St. Stephens Gate, tel. 020/7222-2219).

The clock tower (315 feet high) is named for its 13-ton bell, Ben. The light above the clock is lit when the House of Commons is sitting. For a hip HOP view, walk halfway over Westminster Bridge.

▲▲**Cabinet War Rooms**—This is a fascinating walk through the underground headquarters of the British government's fight against the Nazis in the darkest days of the Battle for Britain. The 21-room nerve center of the British war effort was used from 1939 to 1945. Churchill's room, the map room, and so on, are just as they were in 1945. For all the blood, sweat, toil, and tears details, pick up the headsets at the entry and follow the included and excellent 45-minute audio guide (£4.80, daily 9:30–18:00, last admission 17:15, on King Charles Street 200 yards off Whitehall, follow the signs, tube: Westminster, tel. 020/7930-6961).

Horse Guards—The Horse Guards change daily at 11:00 (10:00 on Sunday), and there's a colorful dismounting ceremony daily at 16:00. The rest of the day they just stand there—terrible for camcorders (on Whitehall, between Trafalgar Square and #10 Downing Street, tube: Westminster). While Buckingham Palace pageantry is canceled when it rains, the horse guards change regardless of the weather.

▲**Banqueting House**—England's first Renaissance building was designed by Inigo Jones around 1620. It's one of the few London landmarks spared by the 1666 fire and the only surviving part of the original Palace of Whitehall. Don't miss its Rubens ceiling, which, at Charles I's request, drove home the doctrine of the legitimacy of the divine right of kings. In 1649, divine right ignored, Charles I was beheaded on the balcony of this building by a Cromwellian parliament. Admission includes a restful 15-minute audiovisual history, which shows the place in banqueting action, a 30-minute tape-recorded tour that is interesting only to history buffs, and a look at a fancy banqueting hall (£3.80, Mon–Sat 10:00–17:00, last entry at 16:15, subject to closure for government functions, aristocratic WC, immediately across Whitehall from the Horse Guards, tube: Westminster, tel. 020/7930-4179). Just up the street is...

Sights—Trafalgar Square

▲▲**Trafalgar Square**—London's central square is a thrilling place to just hang out. Lord Nelson stands atop his 185-foot-tall fluted granite column, gazing out to Trafalgar, where he lost his life but defeated the French fleet. Part of this 1842 memorial is made from the melted-down cannons of his victims at Trafalgar. He's surrounded by giant lions, hordes of people, and even more pigeons. Buy a 25p cup of bird-pleasing seed. To make the birds explode into flight, simply toss a sweater into the air. (When bombed, resist the impulse to wipe immediately—it'll smear. Wait for it to dry and flake off gently.) This high-profile square is the climax of most marches and demonstrations (tube: Charing Cross).

▲▲▲**National Gallery**—Wonderfully renovated, displaying Britain's top collection of European paintings from 1250 to 1900 (works by Leonardo, Botticelli, Velázquez, Rembrandt, Turner, van Gogh, and the Impressionists), this is one of Europe's great galleries. While the collection is huge, following the 30-stop route suggested on the map on pages 46 and 47 will give you my best quick tour. Don't miss the "Micro Gallery," a computer room even your dad could have fun in (closes 30 minutes earlier than museum). You can study any artist, style, or topic in the museum and even print out a tailor-made tour map (free, daily 10:00–18:00, Wed until 21:00, free one-hour tours weekdays at 11:30 and 14:30, on Trafalgar Square, tube: Charing Cross or Leicester Square, tel. 020/7747-2885). The CD Walkman tours are the best I've used in Europe (£3 donation requested).

▲**National Portrait Gallery**—Put off by halls of 19th-century characters who meant nothing to me, I used to call this "as interesting as someone else's yearbook." But a select walk through this five-centuries-long Who's Who of British history is quick and free and puts faces on the story of England. A bonus is the chance to admire some great art by painters such as Holbein, Van Dyck, Hogarth, Reynolds, and Gainsborough. The collection is well described, not huge, and in historical sequence, from the 16th century on the top floor to today's royal family on the bottom.

Some highlights: Henry VIII and wives; several fascinating portraits of the "Virgin Queen" Elizabeth I, Sir Francis Drake, and Sir Walter Raleigh; the only real-life portrait of Shakespeare; Oliver Cromwell and Charles I with his head on; self-portraits and other portraits by Gainsborough and Reynolds; the Romantics (Blake, Byron, Wordsworth, and company); Queen Victoria and her era; and the present royal family, including the late Princess Diana. For more information, follow the fine CD Walkman tours (£3 donation requested, tells more about history than art, hear actual interviews with 20th-century subjects) or get the 60p quick overview guidebooklet (free, Mon–Sat 10:00–18:00, Sun 12:00–18:00, entry 100 yards off Trafalgar Square, around the corner from the National Gallery, opposite Church of St. Martin-in-the-Fields, tel. 020/7306-0055).

▲**St. Martin-in-the-Fields**—This church, built in the 1720s, with a Gothic spire placed upon a Greek-type temple, is an oasis of peace on wild and noisy Trafalgar Square. St. Martin cared for the poor.

National Gallery Highlights

Medieval and Early Renaissance

1. Wilton Diptych
2. UCCELLO—Battle of San Romano
3. VAN EYCK—Arnolfini Marriage
4. CRIVELLI—Annunciation With St. Emidius
5. BOTTICELLI—Venus and Mars

"In the fields" was where the first church stood on this spot (in the 13th century), between Westminster and the City. Stepping inside, you still feel a compassion for the needs of the people in this community. The church is famous for its concerts. Consider a free lunchtime concert (most weekdays at 13:05) or an evening concert (Thu, Fri, and Sat at 19:30, £6–15, tel. 020/7930-0089). Downstairs you'll find a ticket office for concerts, a good shop, a brass-rubbing centre, and a fine budget support-the-church cafeteria (see "Eating").

More Top Squares: Piccadilly, Soho, and Covent Garden

▲▲Piccadilly Circus—London's touristy "Town Square" is surrounded by fascinating streets and swimming with youth on the rampage. The Rock Circus offers a commercial but serious history of rock music with Madame Tussaud wax stars. While overpriced,

High Renaissance
6. LEONARDO DA VINCI—Virgin and Child (painting and cartoon)
7. MICHELANGELO—Entombment
8. RAPHAEL—Pope Julius II

Venetian Renaissance
9. TINTORETTO—Origin of the Milky Way
10. TITIAN—Bacchus and Ariadne

Northern Protestant Art
11. VERMEER—Young Woman Standing at a Virginal
12. REMBRANDT—Self Portrait
13. REMBRANDT—Belshazzar's Feast

Baroque and Rococo
14. RUBENS—The Judgment of Paris
15. VAN DYCK—Charles I on Horseback
16. VELÁZQUEZ—The Rokeby Venus

17. CARAVAGGIO—Supper at Emmaus
18. BOUCHER—Pan and Syrinx

British
19. CONSTABLE—The Hay Wain
20. TURNER—The Fighting Téméraire
21. TURNER—Rain, Steam, Speed

Impressionism and Beyond
22. DELAROCHE—The Execution of Lady Jane Grey
23. MONET—Gare St. Lazare
24. MANET—The Waitress (La Servante de Bocks)
25. DEGAS— Miss La La at the Cirque Fernando
26. RENOIR—The Umbrellas
27. SEURAT—Bathers at Asnieres
28. VAN GOGH—Sunflowers
29. CÉZANNE—Bathers
30. MONET—Water Lilies

it's an entertaining hour under radio earphones for rock 'n' roll romantics—many enter with a beer buzz and sing happily off-key under their headphones—nearly as entertaining as the exhibit itself (£8, daily 10:00–20:00, plenty of photo ops, tube: Piccadilly Circus). For overstimulation, drop by the extremely trashy Pepsi Trocadero Center's "theme park of the future" for its Segaworld virtual reality games, nine-screen cinema, and thundering IMAX theater (admission to Trocadero is free; individual attractions cost £2–8; find a discount ticket at brochure racks at TI or hotels before paying full price for IMAX; between Coventry and Shaftesbury, just off Piccadilly). Chinatown, to the east, has swollen since Hong Kong lost its independence. Nearby Shaftesbury Avenue and Leicester Square teem with fun seekers, theaters, Chinese restaurants, and street singers.

Soho—North of Piccadilly, seedy Soho is becoming trendy and is well worth a gawk. Soho is London's red-light district, where "friendly models" wait in tiny rooms up dreary stairways and scantily clad con artists sell strip shows. While venturing up a stairway to check out a model is interesting, anyone who goes into any one of the shows will be ripped off. Every time. Even a £3 show comes with a £100 cover or minimum (as it's printed on the drink menu) and a "security man." You may accidently buy a £200 bottle of bubbly. And suddenly, the door has no handle. By the way, telephone sex is hard to avoid these days in London. Phone booths are littered with racy fliers of busty ladies "new in town." Some travelers gather six or eight phone booths' worth of fliers and take them home for kinky wallpaper.

▲▲**Covent Garden**—This boutique-ish shopping district is a people watcher's delight with cigarette eaters, Punch-and-Judy acts, food that's good for you (but not your wallet), trendy crafts, sweet whiffs of pot, two-tone hair (neither natural), and faces that could set off a metal detector (tube: Covent Garden). For better Covent Garden lunch deals, walk a block or two away from the eye of this touristic hurricane (check out the places a block or two north of the tube station along Endell Street and Neal Street—try Food for Thought at #31), and for a "Food is Fun" dinner crawl from Covent Garden to Soho, see "Eating," below.

Sights—North London

▲▲▲**British Museum**—This is the greatest chronicle of our civilization anywhere. Visiting this immense museum is like hiking through Encyclopedia Britannica National Park. After an overview ramble, cover just two or three sections of your choice more thoroughly. The Egyptian, Mesopotamian (Assyrian), and Greek (Parthenon) sections are highlights.

The huge winged lions (which guarded Assyrian palaces 800 years before Christ) guard the museum's three great ancient galleries. For a brief tour, connect these ancient dots:

Start with the **Egyptian.** Wander from the Rosetta Stone past the many statues. At the end of the hall, climb the stairs to mummy land.

Back at the winged lions, wander through the dark, violent, and mysterious **Assyrian** rooms. The Nimrud Gallery is lined with royal propaganda reliefs and wounded lions.

The most modern of the ancient art fills the **Greek** section. Find room 1 behind the winged lions and start your walk through Greek art history with the simple and primitive Cycladic fertility figures. Later, painted vases show a culture really into partying. The finale is the Elgin Marbles. The much-wrangled-over bits of the Athenian Parthenon (from 450 B.C.) are even more impressive than they look. To best appreciate these ancient carvings, read through the orientation material in the tiny area between rooms

7 and 8 (free, £2 donation requested, Mon–Sat 10:00–17:00, Sun 12:00–18:00, least crowded weekday late afternoons, guided 90-minute £7 tours offered daily—4/day—call museum for times, free "eye-opener" 50-minute talks on particular subjects nearly hourly—schedule at entry, Great Russell Street, tube: Tottenham Court Road, tel. 020/7636-1555, www.british-museum.ac.uk).

The British Museum is undergoing a major transformation for the millennium and for its 250th birthday in 2003. With more than 6 million visitors a year, Britain's most popular museum was due for an upgrade. In the fall, the Great Court, previously unused, will become a two-acre, glass-domed hub of a new cultural complex. From here you enter a reorganized (better-flowing) British museum, a restored and once-again-public Round Reading Room (Marx's hangout), new Ethnographic Galleries (collections on life in Africa, Asia, and the Americas), and a bustling people zone of shops and restaurants. For the latest, see www.british-museum.ac.uk.

▲▲▲**British Library**—In the new and impressive British Library, wander through the manuscripts that have enlightened and brightened our lives for centuries. While the library contains 180 miles of bookshelves in London's deepest basement, one beautiful room filled with state-of-the-art glass display cases shows you the treasures: ancient maps, early Gospels on papyrus, illuminated manuscripts from the early Middle Ages, the Gutenberg Bible, the Magna Carta, pages from Leonardo's notebooks, and original writing by the titans of English literature, from Chaucer and Shakespeare to Dickens and Wordsworth. There's also a wall dedicated to music, with manuscripts from Beethoven to the Beatles. To virtually flip through the pages of a few precious books, drop by the "Turning the Pages" room (free, Mon–Fri 9:30–18:00, Tue 9:30–20:00, Sat 9:30–17:00, Sun 11:00–17:00, tube: King's Cross/St. Pancras, leaving station, turn right and walk a block to 96 Euston Road, tel. 020/7412-7332, www.bl.uk).

▲**Madame Tussaud's Waxworks**—This is expensive but dang good. The original Madame Tussaud did wax casts of heads lopped off during the French Revolution (e.g., Marie Antoinette). She took her show on the road and ended up in London. And now it's much easier to be featured. The gallery is one big Who's Who photo op—a huge hit with the kind of travelers who skip the British Museum. Don't miss the "make a model" exhibit (showing Jerry Hall getting waxed) or the gallery of has-been heads that no longer merit a body (such as Sammy Davis Jr. and Nikita Khrushchev). After looking a hundred famous people in the glassy eyes and surviving a silly hall of horror, you'll board a Disney-type ride and cruise through a kid-pleasing "Spirit of London" time trip (£11, children £7, under five free, daily 9:00–18:00, last admission 17:30, closes at 17:00 in winter, Marylebone Road, tube: Baker Street, tel. 020/7935-6861; combined ticket for Tussaud's and Planetarium is £13 adults, £8.50 kids). Avoid a wait by arriving late in the day—90 minutes is plenty of time for the exhibit.

Sir John Soane's Museum—Architects and fans of eclectic knick-knacks love this quirky place (free, Tue–Sat 10:00–17:00, closed Sun and Mon, 13 Lincoln's Inn Fields, five blocks east of British Museum, tube: Holborn, tel. 020/7405-2107).

Sights—Buckingham Palace

▲**Buckingham Palace**—This has been the royal residence since 1837. When the queen's at home, the royal standard flies; otherwise the Union Jack flaps in the wind. To pay for the restoration of fire-damaged Windsor Castle, the royal family is opening its lavish home to the public through 2000 (£10 to see the state apartments and throne room, open Aug and Sept only, daily 9:30–16:30, only 8,000 visitors a day—come early to get an appointed visit time or call 020/7321-2233 and reserve a ticket with your credit card, tube: Victoria). *overrated*

▲▲**Changing of the Guard at Buckingham Palace**—The guards change with much fanfare at 11:30 daily through May and June and generally every even-numbered day July through April (no band when wet; worth a phone call any day to confirm that they'll change; tel. 020/7930-4832). Join the mob at the back side of the palace (the front faces a huge and extremely private park). You'll need to be early or tall to see much of the actual changing of the guard, but for the pageantry in the street you can pop by at 11:30. Stake out the high ground on the circular Victoria Monument for the best general views. The marching troops and bands are colorful and even stirring, but the actual changing of the guard is a nonevent. It is interesting, however, to see nearly every tourist in London gathered in one place at the same time. Hop into a big black taxi and say, "Buck House, please." The show lasts about 30 minutes: three troops parade by, the guard changes with much shouting, the band plays a happy little concert, and then they march out. On a balmy day, it's a fun happening.

For all the color with none of the crowds, see the **Inspection of the Guard Ceremony** at 11:00 in front of the **Wellington Barracks**, 500 yards east of the palace on Birdcage Walk. Afterwards, stroll through nearby St. James' Park. (tube: Victoria, St. James' Park, or Green Park).

Sights—West London

▲**Hyde Park and Speakers' Corner**—London's "Central Park"—originally Henry VIII's hunting ground—has more than 600 acres of lush greenery, a huge man-made lake, the royal Kensington Palace (not worth touring), and the ornate neo-Gothic Albert Memorial across from the Royal Albert Hall. Early afternoons on Sunday, Speaker's Corner offers soapbox oratory at its best (tube: Marble Arch). "The grass roots of democracy" is actually a holdover from when the gallows stood here and the criminal was allowed to say just about anything he wanted to before he swung. I dare you to raise your voice and gather a crowd—it's easy to do.

▲**Apsley House (Wellington Museum)**—Having beat Napoleon at Waterloo, the Duke of Wellington was the most famous man in Europe. He was given London's ultimate address, #1 London. His newly refurbished mansion offers one of London's best palace experiences. An 11-foot-tall marble statue (by Canova) of Napoleon clad only in a fig leaf greets you. Downstairs is a small gallery of Wellington memorabilia (including a 30-minute video and a pair of Wellington boots). The lavish upstairs shows off the duke's fine collection of paintings, including works by Velázquez and Steen (well described by included CD tour wand, £4.50, Tue–Sun 11:00–17:00, closed Mon, 20 yards from Hyde Park Corner tube station, tel. 020/7499-5676). Hyde Park's pleasant and picnic-wonderful rose garden is nearby.

▲▲**Victoria and Albert Museum**—The world's top collection of decorative arts is a gangly (150 rooms over 12 miles of corridors) but surprisingly interesting assortment of artistic stuff from the West as well as Asian and Islamic cultures. The V&A, which grew out of the Great Exhibition of 1851—that ultimate festival celebrating the Industrial Revolution and the greatness of Britain—was originally for manufactured art. But after much support from Queen Victoria and Prince Albert, it was renamed after the royal couple, and its present building was opened in 1909. The idealistic Victorian notion that anyone can be continually improved by education and example remains the driving force behind this museum.

While just wandering works well here, consider catching one of the regular 60-minute orientation tours, buying the fine £5 Hundred Highlights guidebook, or walking through these ground-floor highlights: Medieval Treasury (room 43, well-described treasury of Middle Age European art), the finest collection of Indian decorative art outside India (room 41), the Dress Gallery (room 40, 400 years of English fashion corseted into 40 display cases), the Raphael Gallery (room 48a, seven huge watercolor "cartoons" painted as designs for tapestries to hang in the Sistine Chapel, among the greatest art treasures in Britain and the best works of the High Renaissance), reliefs by the Renaissance sculptor Donatello (room 16), a close-up look at medieval stained glass (room 28, much more upstairs), the fascinating Cast Courts (rooms 46a and 46b, filled with plaster copies of the greatest art of our civilization—such as Trajan's Column and Michelangelo's David—made for the benefit of 19th-century art students who couldn't afford a railpass), and the hall of "great" fakes and forgeries (room 46). Upstairs you can walk through the British Galleries for centuries of aristocratic living rooms (£5, daily 10:00–18:00, and usually Wed evenings until 21:30 in summer, free after 16:30; the museum café is in the delightfully ornate Gamble Room from 1868, just off room 14, tube: South Kensington, a long tunnel leads directly from the tube station to the museum, tel. 020/7938-8500).

▲**Natural History Museum**—Across the street from the Victoria and Albert Museum, this mammoth museum is housed in a giant and wonderful Victorian neo-Romanesque building. Built in the 1870s specifically to house the huge collection (50 million specimens), it presents itself in two halves: the Life Galleries (creepy-crawlies, human biology, the origin of the species, "our place in evolution," and awesome dinosaurs) and the Earth Galleries (meteors, volcanoes, earthquakes, and so on). Exhibits are wonderfully explained with lots of creative interactive displays (£6.50, children under 16 free, free to anyone after 16:30 on weekdays and after 17:00 on weekends—pop in if only for the wild collection of dinosaurs, Mon–Sat 10:00–18:00, Sun 11:00–18:00, a long tunnel leads directly from the South Kensington tube station to the museum, tel. 020/7938-9123, www.nhm.ac.uk).

Sights—East London: "The City"

▲▲**The City of London**—When Londoners say "The City," they mean the one-square-mile business, banking, and journalism center that 2,000 years ago was Roman Londinium. The outline of the Roman city walls can still be seen in the arc of roads from Blackfriars Bridge to Tower Bridge. Within the City are 24 churches designed by Christopher Wren. Today, while home to only 5,000 residents, the City thrives with over 500,000 office workers coming and going daily. It's a fascinating district to wander, but since almost nobody actually lives there, it's dull on Saturday and Sunday.

▲**Old Bailey**—An hour sitting in the public galleries of the City's Central Criminal Courts, known as "Old Bailey," is always interesting (free, Mon–Fri 10:30–13:00, 14:00–16:30, quiet in August, ask at door which trials are where, no cameras, no bags, no cloakroom, no kids under 14, at Old Bailey and Newgate Streets, tube: St. Paul's, tel. 020/7248-3277).

▲▲▲**St. Paul's Cathedral**—Wren's most famous church is the great St. Paul's, its elaborate interior capped by a 365-foot dome. During World War II, when Nazi bombs failed to blow it up, St. Paul's became Britain's symbol of resistance. The crypt (free with admission) is a world of historic bones and memorials, including Admiral Nelson's tomb and interesting cathedral models. This was the wedding church of Prince Charles and the late Princess Diana (1981). Sit under the second-largest dome in the world and eavesdrop on guided tours. Climb the dome for some fun in the whispering gallery (where the precisely designed barrel of the dome lets sweet nothings circle audibly around to the

The City

opposite side) and a great city view (£4 entry, free on Sun but restricted viewing due to services, £3.50 extra to climb dome—allow an hour to climb up and down; open daily 9:00–16:30, last entry 16:00, £3.50 for guided 90-minute cathedral and crypt tours offered at 11:00, 11:30, 13:30, and 14:00 or £3 for a Walkman tour anytime, Sunday services at 8:00, 10:15, 11:30, and 15:15, evensong weekdays at 17:00, good restaurant and cheap and cheery café in the crypt, tube: St. Paul's, tel. 020/7236-8348).

▲**Museum of London**—Stroll through London history from pre-Roman times through the Blitz up to today. This regular stop for the local schoolkids gives the best overview of London history in town (£5, free after 16:30, Mon–Sat 10:00–18:00, Sun 12:00–18:00, tube: Barbican or St. Paul's, tel. 020/7600-3699).

Geffrye Decorative Arts Museum—Walk through British front rooms from 1600 to 1990 (free, Tue–Sat 10:00–17:00, Sun 12:00–17:00, closed Mon, tube: Liverpool Street, then bus 149 or 242 north, tel. 020/7739-9893).

▲▲▲**Tower of London**—The Tower has served as a castle in wartime, a king's residence in peace, and, most notorious, as the prison and execution site of rebels. This historic fortress is host to more than 3 million visitors a year. Enjoy the free, and riotously entertaining, 50-minute Beefeater tour (leaves regularly from inside the gate, last one is usually at 15:25). The crown jewels, dating from the Restoration, are the best on earth—and come with hour-long lines for most of the day. To avoid the crowds, arrive at

9:00 and go straight for the jewels, doing the tour and tower later—or do the jewels after 16:30 (£10.50, Mon–Sat 9:00–18:00, Sun 10:00–18:00, the long but fast-moving ticket line is worst on Sundays, last entry at 17:00, tube: Tower Hill, tel. 020/7709-0765, recorded info: 020/7680-9004).

Ceremony of the Keys: Every night at 21:30, with pageantry-filled ceremony, the Tower of London is locked up (as it has been for the last 700 years). To attend this free 30-minute event, you need to request an invitation at least five weeks before your visit. Write to: Ceremony of the Keys, H.M. Tower of London, London EC3N 4AB. Include your name; the addresses, names, and ages of all people attending (up to seven, nontransferable); requested date; alternative dates; and an international reply coupon (buy at a U.S. post office).

Sights next to the Tower—The best remaining bit of London's **Roman Wall** is just north of the tower (at the Tower Hill tube station). Freshly painted and restored, **Tower Bridge**—the neo-Gothic maritime gateway to London—has an 1894 to 1994 history exhibit (£6.20, daily 10:00–18:30, last entry at 17:15, good view, poor value, tel. 020/7403-3761). **St. Katherine Yacht Harbor**, chic and newly renovated, just east of the Tower Bridge, has mod shops and the classic old Dickens Inn, fun for a drink or pub lunch. Across the bridge is the South Bank, with the upscale Butlers Wharf area, museums, and promenade.

Sights—South London, on the South Bank

The South Bank is rapidly becoming a thriving arts and cultural center tied together by a riverside path. This trendy, pub-crawling walk—called the Jubilee Promenade—stretches from the Tower of London bridge past Westminster Bridge, with grand views of the Houses of Parliament. (The promenade hugs the river except just east of London Bridge, where it cuts inland for a couple of blocks.)

▲▲**Globe Theater**—The original Globe Theater has been rebuilt—half-timbered and thatched—exactly as it was in Shakespeare's time. It's open as a museum and hosts authentic old-time performances of Shakespeare's plays. The theater is open to tour when there are no plays (£6, daily 9:00–12:00, Oct–Apr 10:00–17:00, includes guided 30-minute tour offered on the half hour). In 2000 the Globe expands its exhibition on the history of the Globe Theater to include the beginnings of theater plus more on Shakespeare, his workplace, and his contemporaries. Expect interactive displays and possibly film presentations, a sound lab, a script factory, and a costume exhibit (included in £6 theater admission, daily 10:00–17:00, Oct–Apr 9:00–16:00, on the South Bank directly across the Thames over Southwark Bridge from St. Paul's, tube: Mansion House, tel. 020/7902-1500, for details on seeing a play, see "Entertainment," below).

▲▲**Tate Gallery of Modern Art**—Open in May of 2000, this new museum across the river from St. Paul's opens the new century with art from the old one (remember the 20th century?) This powerhouse collection of Monet, Matisse, Dalí, Picasso, Warhol, and much more is displayed in a converted power house (free, special exhibitions cost extra, probably daily 10:00–18:00, Walkman tours, free guided tours, call for schedule, walk the new Millennium Bridge from St. Paul's or tube: Southwark plus a 7-minute walk, tel. 020/7887-8000).

▲▲**Millennium Bridge**—Linking St. Paul's Cathedral and the new Tate Gallery of Modern Art, this new bridge opens in April 2000. Its sleek minimalist design—370 meters long, 4 meters wide, stainless steel with teak planks—has clever aerodynamic handrails to deflect wind over the heads of pedestrians. London's only pedestrian bridge is the first new bridge in a century (free, always open).

▲▲▲**Millennium Ferris Wheel (a.k.a. The British Airways London Eye)**—Towering above London opposite Big Ben on the South Bank of the Thames, this is the world's highest observational wheel—and a chance to fly British Air without leaving London. At 450 feet high, it offers the highest public viewpoint in London. Built like a giant bicycle wheel, it's a pan-European undertaking: British steel and Dutch engineering, with Czech, German, French, and Italian mechanical parts. It's also very "green," running extremely efficiently and virtually silently. Twenty-five people will ride in each of its 32 capsules for the 30-minute rotation. In 2005 it will be dismantled and moved to a lower-profile location (probably £5, tel. 020/7738-8080).

▲▲**Imperial War Museum**—This impressive museum covers the wars of this century, from heavy weaponry to love notes and Varga Girls, from Monty's Africa campaign tank to Schwartzkopf's Desert Storm uniform. You can trace the development of the machine gun, watch footage of the first tank battles, hold your breath through the gruesome WWI trench experience, and buy WWII-era toys in the fun museum shop. Rather than glorify war, the museum does its best to shine a light on the powerful human side of one of mankind's most persistent traits (£5.20, free for kids under 16, daily 10:00–18:00, free for anyone after 16:30, 90 minutes is enough time for most visitors, tube: Lambeth North, tel. 020/7416-5000).

Bramah Tea and Coffee Museum—Aficionados of tea or coffee will find this small museum fascinating. It tells the story of each drink almost passionately. The owner, Mr. Bramah, comes from a big tea family and wants the world to know how the advent of commercial television, with breaks not long enough to brew a proper pot of tea, required a faster hot drink. In came the horrible English instant coffee. Tea countered with finely chopped leaves in tea bags, and it's gone downhill ever since.

(£4, daily 10:00–18:00, in the Butlers Wharf complex just across the bridge from the Tower, behind the Design Museum, tel. 020/7378-0222). Its café, which serves more kinds of coffees and teas than cakes, is open to the public, not just museum goers (same hours as museum).

Sights—South London, on the North Bank

▲▲**Tate Gallery of British Art**—One of Europe's great art houses, the Tate specializes in British painting: 16th century through the 20th, including Pre-Raphaelites. Commune with the mystical Blake and romantic Turner (free, daily 10:00–18:00, fine £3 CD Walkman tours, free tours weekdays, call for schedule, tube: Pimlico, tel. 020/7887-8000). In May 2000 the Tate's modern collection opens at the new Tate Gallery of Modern Art (on the South Bank; see above).

Sights—Greater London

▲**Kew Gardens**—For a fine riverside park and a palatial green-house jungle to swing through, take the tube or the boat to every botanist's favorite escape, Kew Gardens. While to most visitors the Royal Botanic Gardens of Kew is simply a delightful opportunity to wander among 33,000 different types of plants, it's run by a hardworking organization committed to understanding and preserving the botanical diversity of our planet. The Kew tube station drops you in an herbal little business community a two-block walk from Victoria Gate (the main garden entry). Watch the five-minute orientation video and pick up a map brochure with a monthly listing of best blooms.

Garden lovers could spend days exploring Kew's 300 acres. For a quick visit, spend a fragrant hour wandering through three buildings: the Palm House—a humid Victorian world of iron, glass, and tropical plants—built in 1844; a Waterlily House—hottest in the gardens—that Monet would swim for; and the Princess of Wales Conservatory—a modern greenhouse with many different climate zones growing countless cacti, bug-munching carnivorous plants, and more (£5, Mon–Sat 9:30–18:00, Sun 9:30–19:30, until 16:30 off-season, galleries and conservatories close a half hour earlier, entry discounted to £3.50 90 minutes before closing, consider the £2 narrated floral joyride on the little train departing from Victoria Gate, tube: Kew Gardens, tel. 020/8332-5000). For a sun-dappled lunch, hike 10 minutes from the Palm House to the Orangery (£6 hot meals, daily 10:00–17:30). For tea, consider the Maids of Honor (280 Kew Road, near garden entrance, tel. 020/8940-2752).

▲**Hampton Court Palace**—Fifteen miles up the Thames from downtown (£16 taxi ride from Kew Gardens) is the 500-year-old palace of Henry VIII. Actually, it was the palace of his minister,

Greater London

Cardinal Wolsey. When Wolsey, a clever man, realized Henry VIII was experiencing a little palace envy, he gave it to his king. The Tudor palace was also home to Elizabeth I and Charles I. And parts were updated by Christopher Wren for William and Mary. The palace stands stately overlooking the Thames and includes some impressive Tudor rooms, including a Great Hall, with its magnificent hammer-beam ceiling. The industrial-strength Tudor kitchen was capable of keeping 600 schmoozing courtesans thoroughly—if not well—fed. The sculpted garden features a rare Tudor tennis court and a popular maze. The palace, fully restored since its 1986 fire, tries hard to please, but it doesn't quite sparkle. From the information center in the main courtyard, visitors book times for tours with tired costumed guides or grab CD-ROM wands for self-guided tours of various wings of the palace (all free). The Tudor Kitchens, Henry VIII's Apartments, and the King's Apartments are most interesting. The Georgian Rooms are pretty dull. The maze in the nearby garden is a curiosity some find fun. The train (2/hrly, 30 min) from London's Waterloo station drops you just across the river from the palace (£10, Tue–Sun 9:30–18:00, 10:15–18:00 on Mondays, Nov–Mar until 16:30, tel. 020/8781-9500).

▲▲▲**Greenwich and New Millennium Dome**—See "Near London" at the end of this chapter.

Disappointments of London

The venerable BBC broadcasts from Broadcasting House. Of all
its productions, its "BBC Experience" tour for visitors is among
the worst. On the South Bank, the London Dungeon, a much-
visited but amateurish attraction, is just a highly advertised, overpriced haunted house—certainly not worth the £10 admission,
much less your valuable London time. It comes with long and
rude lines. Wait for Halloween and see one in your hometown
to support a better cause. The Design Museum (next to Bramah
Tea and Coffee Museum) and "Winston Churchill's Britain at
War Experience" (next to London Dungeon) waste your time.
The Kensington Palace State Apartments are lifeless and not
worth a visit.

Shopping in London

Harrods—Filled with wonderful displays, Harrods is London's
most famous and touristy department store. Big yet classy,
Harrods has everything from elephants to toothbrushes. The
food halls are sights to savor, with cafeterias (Mon, Tue, and Sat
10:00–18:00, Wed–Fri 10:00–19:00, closed Sun, on Brompton
Road, tube: Knightsbridge, tel. 020/7730-1234). Many readers
report that Harrods is now overpriced (its £1 toilets are the most
expensive in Europe), snooty, and teeming with American and
Japanese tourists. Still, it's the palace of department stores—an
experience for even nonshoppers. The nearby Beauchamp Place
is lined with classy and fascinating shops.

Harvey Nichols—Princess Diana's favorite, this is the department
store du jour. Its fifth floor is a food fest with a fancy restaurant
and a Yo! Sushi bar. Consider a take-away tray of sushi to eat on
a bench in the Hyde Park rose garden two blocks away (Mon–Tue
and Sat 10:00–19:00, Wed–Fri 10:00–20:00, Sun 12:00–18:00,
near Harrods, 109 Knightsbridge, tube: Knightsbridge).

Street Markets—Antique buffs, people watchers, and folks who
brake for garage sales love London's street markets. There's good
early morning market activity somewhere any day of the week.
The best are Portobello Road (Fri–Wed 9:00–18:00, Thu
9:00–13:00, go Saturday for antiques until 16:00—plus the regular
junk, clothes, and produce; tube: Notting Hill Gate) and Camden
Market (Sat–Sun 10:00–18:00, trendy arts and crafts, tube: Camden Town). The tourist office has a complete, up-to-date list. If
you like to haggle, there are no holds barred in London's street
markets. Warning: Markets attract two kinds of people—tourists
and pickpockets.

Famous Auctions—London's famous auctioneers welcome the
curious public for viewing and bidding. For schedules, call Sothe-
by's (Mon–Fri 9:00–16:30, 34 New Bond Street, tube: Oxford
Circus, tel. 020/7293-5000) or Christie's (during sales season:

Mon and Wed–Fri 9:00–16:30, Tue 9:00–20:00, 8 King Street, tube: Green Park, tel. 020/7839-9060).

Entertainment and Theater in London

London bubbles with top-notch entertainment seven days a week. Everything's listed in the weekly entertainment magazines, available at newsstands. Choose from classical, jazz, rock, and far-out music, Gilbert and Sullivan, dance, comedy, Baha'i meetings, poetry readings, spectator sports, film, and theater.

London's theater rivals Broadway's in quality and beats it in price. Choose from the Royal Shakespeare Company, top musicals, comedy, thrillers, sex farces, and more. Performances are nightly except Sunday, usually with one matinee a week. Matinees (Wed, Thu, or Sat) are cheaper and rarely sold out. Tickets range from about £8 to £35.

Most theaters, marked on tourist maps, are in the Piccadilly–Trafalgar area. Box offices, hotels, and TIs have a handy "Theater Guide" brochure listing what's playing.

To book a seat, simply call the theater box office directly, ask about seats and dates available, and buy one with your credit card. You can call from the U.S.A. as easily as from England (photocopy your hometown library's London newspaper theater section or check out www.officiallondontheatre.co.uk). Pick up your ticket 15 minutes before the show.

Ticket agencies are scalpers with an address. Booking through an agency (at most TIs or scattered throughout London) is quick and easy, but prices are inflated by a standard 25 percent fee. If buying from an agency, look at the ticket carefully (your price should be no more than 30 percent over the printed face value; the 17 percent VAT tax is already included in the face value) and understand where you're sitting according to the floor plan (if your view is restricted it will state this on ticket). Agencies are worthwhile only if a show you've got to see is sold out at the box office. They scarf up hot tickets, planning to make a killing after the show is sold out. U.S.A. booking agencies get their tickets from another agency, adding even more to your expense by involving yet another middleman. Many tickets sold on the streets are forgeries. With cheap international phone calls and credit cards, there's no reason not to book direct.

Theater lingo: stalls (ground floor), dress circle (first balcony), upper circle (second balcony), balcony (sky-high third balcony).

Cheap theater tricks: Most theaters offer cheap returned tickets, standing room, matinee, and senior or student standby deals. These "concessions" are indicated with a *conc* or *s* in the listings. Picking up a late return can get you a great seat at a cheap-seat price. Standing room can be very cheap. If a show is "sold out," there's usually a way to get a seat. Call the theater box office and ask how. I buy the second-cheapest tickets directly from the theater box office. The famous "half-price booth" in Leicester (pronounced "Lester") Square sells discounted tickets for good seats to shows on the push list the day of the show only (Mon–Sat 12:00–18:30). Note: The real half-price booth is a free-standing kiosk at the edge of the garden actually in Leicester Square. Several dishonest outfits advertise "official half-price tickets" at agencies closer to the tube station. Avoid these. Many theaters are so small that there's hardly a bad seat. After the lights go down, "scooting up" is less than a capital offense. Shakespeare did it.

Royal Shakespeare Company—If you'll ever enjoy Shakespeare, it'll be in Britain. The RSC splits its season between the Royal Shakespeare Theatre in Stratford (Jun–Sept, tel. 01789/403-403) and the Barbican Centre in London (Oct–May, daily 9:00–20:00, credit-card booking, tel. 020/7638-8891, or for recorded information, tel. 020/7628-9760). To get a schedule, either request it by phone (tel. 020/7638-8891), write to the Royal Shakespeare Theatre, Stratford-upon-Avon, CV37 6BB Warwickshire, or visit www.rsc.org.uk. Tickets range in price from £10 to £30. The best way to book is direct, by telephone and credit card. You can pick up your ticket at the door (Barbican Centre, Silk Street, tube: Barbican). Students, seniors, and those under 16 can get tickets for half price.

Shakespeare at the Globe Theater—To see Shakespeare in an exact replica of the theater for which he wrote his plays, attend a play at the Globe. This thatch-roofed, open-air round theater does the plays as Shakespeare intended (with no amplification). There are performances from May through September (usually Tue–Sat 14:00 and 19:30, Sun at either 13:00 and 18:30 or at 16:00 only, and no plays on Monday). You'll pay £5 to stand and £10 to £25 to sit (usually on a backless bench; only a few rows and the pricier Gentlemen's Rooms have seats with backs). The £5 "yard" (or "groundling") tickets—while the only ones open to rain—are most fun. You're a crude peasant. You can walk around, munch a picnic dinner, lean your elbows on the stage, and even interact with the actors. I've never enjoyed Shakespeare as much as here, performed as it was meant to be in the "wooden O." The theater is on the South Bank directly across the Thames over Southwark Bridge from St. Paul's (tube: Mansion House, tel. 020/7902-1500, box office 020/7401-9919 to book a ticket with your credit card). Plays are long. Many groundlings leave before the end. If you like, hang out an hour before the finish and beg or buy a ticket off someone leaving early (groundlings are allowed to come and go). The Globe is far from public transport, but the courtesy phone in the lobby gets a minicab in minutes. Confirm the cost, but they seem to be much cheaper than the official black cabs (£5 or £6 to Victoria Station).

London Day Trips

Music—For easy, cheap, or free concerts in historic churches, check the TI's listings for lunch concerts (especially Wren's St. Bride's Church, tel. 020/7353-1301, St. James at Piccadilly, and St. Martin-in-the-Fields, Mon–Tue and Fri at 13:00, tel. 020/7930-1862). St. Martin-in-the-Fields also hosts fine evening concerts by candlelight (Thu–Sat at 19:30, £6–16, tel. 020/7839-8362). For a fun classical event (Jun–Sept only), attend a "Prom Concert." This is an annual music festival with almost nightly concerts in the Royal Albert Hall at give-a-peasant-some-culture prices (£3 standing-room spots sold at the door, tel. 020/7589-8212).

Day Trips from London

You could fill a book with the many easy and exciting day trips from London (Earl Steinbicker did: *Daytrips London: Fifty One-Day Adventures by Rail or Car, in and around London and Southern England*). Several tour companies take London-based travelers out and back every day. Original London Walks offers a variety of day trips using the train for about £10 plus transportation costs (see their walking-tour brochure). Some big bus tours can be used by those without a car as a "free" way to get to Bath or Stow-on-the-Wold (saving you, for instance, the £32.50 London–Bath train ticket). Evan Evans' tours leave from behind Victoria Station daily at 9:00 (with your bag stowed under the bus), include a day of sightseeing, and leave you in Bath before returning to London (£25 for Stonehenge and Bath covers transportation only, or £46 to include tours and admissions; tel. 020/8332-2222). Travelline does a tour of Bath and Stonehenge for £25 (tel. 020/8668-7261, office in Fountain Square directly south of Victoria Station).

The British rail system uses London as a hub and normally offers round-trip fares (after 9:30) that cost virtually the same as one-way fares. "Day return" tickets are best (and cheapest) for day trips. You can save a little money if you purchase Super Advance tickets before 14:00 on the day before your trip. But given the high cost of big-city living and the charm of small-town England, rather than side-tripping I'd see London and get out.

Sleeping in London
(£1 = about $1.70, tel. code: 020)
Sleep Code: **S** = Single, **D** = Double/Twin, **T** = Triple, **Q** = Quad, **b** = bathroom, **t** = toilet only, **s** = shower only, **CC** = Credit Card (**V**isa, **M**asterCard, **A**mex). Unless otherwise noted, prices include a generous breakfast and all taxes.

London is expensive. For £50 ($80), you'll get a sleepable double with breakfast in a safe, cramped, and dreary place with minimal service. For £60 ($95) you'll get a basic, clean, reasonably cheery double in a usually cramped, cracked-plaster building or a soulless but comfortable room without breakfast in a huge Motel 6-type place. My London splurges, at £100 to £140 ($170–240), are spacious, thoughtfully appointed places you'd be happy to entertain or make love in. Hearty English or generous buffet breakfasts are included unless otherwise noted, and TVs are nearly standard in rooms.

Reserve your London room with a phone call or e-mail as soon as you can commit to a date. A few places will hold a room with no deposit if you promise to arrive by midday. Most take your credit-card number as security. Most have expensive cancellation policies. Some fancy £120 rooms rent for half price if you arrive late on a slow day and ask for a deal.

Sleeping in Victoria Station Neighborhood, Belgravia
The streets behind Victoria Station teem with budget B&Bs. It's a safe, surprisingly tidy, and decent area without a hint of the trashy touristy glitz of the streets in front of the station. Here in Belgravia, your neighbors include Andrew Lloyd Webber and Margaret Thatcher (her policeman stands outside 73 Chester Square). Decent eateries abound (see "Eating"). The cheaper listings are dumpy. Don't expect £90 cheeriness in a £50 room. Off-season save money by arriving late without a reservation and checking around. Fierce competition softens prices, especially for multinight stays. Particularly for Warwick Way hotels (and on hot summer nights), request a quiet back room. All are within a five-minute walk of the Victoria tube, bus, and train stations. There's

London, Victoria Station Neighborhood

1. TUBE, TOURIST INFO, TAXIS, & CITY BUSES
2. CITY BUS TOURS
3. WOODVILLE HOUSE B&B
4. LIME TREE HOTEL
5. CHERRY COURT HOTEL
6. LIMEGROVE HOTEL
7. WINCHESTER HOTEL
8. ELIZABETH HOTEL
9. QUALITY HOTEL ECCLESTON
10. STARLIGHT EXPRESS

an £8-per-day garage and a nearby launderette (daily 8:00–20:30, self-serve or full-serve, past Warwick Square at 3 Westmoreland Terrace, tel. 020/7821-8692).

Winchester Hotel is family run and perhaps the best value, with 18 fine rooms, no claustrophobia, and a wise and caring management (Db-£75, Tb-£100, Qb-£115, no CC, no groups, no small children, 17 Belgrave Road, London SW1V 1RB, tel. 020/7828-2972, fax 020/7828-5191, Jimmy #1 cooks, Jimmy #2 greets).

In **Woodville House,** the quarters are dollhouse tight, showers are down the hall, and several rooms are on the noisy street (doubles on quiet backside, twins and singles on street), but this well-run, well-worn place is a good value, with lots of travel tips and friendly chat—especially about the local rich and famous—from Rachel

* Westminster 82-86 Belgrave Rd or further

Joplin (S-£42, D-£62, bunky family deals-£80–110 for up to 5, CC:VM, 107 Ebury Street, SW1W 9QU, tel. 020/7730-1048, fax 020/7730-2574, e-mail: woodville.house@cwcom.net).

Lime Tree Hotel, enthusiastically run by David and Marilyn Davies, comes with spacious and thoughtfully decorated rooms and a fun-loving breakfast room. While priced a bit steep, the place has character plus (Sb-£75, Db-£95–105, Tb-£130, family room-£145, David deals in slow times and is creative at helping travelers in a bind, CC:VMA, 135 Ebury Street, SW1W 9RA, tel. 020/7730-8191, fax 020/7730-7865).

Elizabeth House feels institutional and a bit bland—as you might expect from a former YMCA—but the rooms are clean and bright, and the price is right (S-£30, D-£50, Db-£60, T-£75, Q-£85, CC:VM, 118 Warwick Way, SW1 4JB, tel. 020/7630-0741, fax 020/7630-0740).

Quality Hotel Eccleston is big, modern, well located, and a fine value for no-nonsense comfort (Db-£96, on slow days drop-ins can ask for "saver prices"—33 percent off on first night, breakfast extra, CC:VMA, nonsmoking floor, elevator, 82 Eccleston Square, SW1V 1PS, tel. 020/7834-8042, fax 020/7630-8942, e-mail: admin@gb614.u-net.com).

These three places come with cramped rooms and claustrophobic halls. While they generate a lot of reader complaints, I list them because they offer cheap beds at youth hostel prices and are beautifully located a few minutes' walk from Victoria Station:

Cherry Court Hotel is run by the friendly and industrious Patel family (S-£30, Sb-£40, Db-£45, T-£50, Tb-£65, price promised with this book, CC:VMA, fruit basket breakfast in room, no twins—only double beds, 23 Hugh Street, SW1V 1QJ, tel. 020/7828-2840, fax 020/7828-0393, e-mail: info@cherrycourthotel .co.uk). **Cedar Guest House,** run by a Polish organization to help Poles afford London, welcomes all (D-£38, Db-£45, T-£54, 30 Hugh Street, SW1V 1RP, tel. 020/7828-2625). **Limegrove Hotel,** run by harried Joyce, more musty and run-down, serves a humble breakfast in the room (S-£28, D-£38, Db-£50, T-£48, Tb-£60, cheaper off-season, lots of stairs, 101 Warwick Way, SW1V 1QL, tel. 020/7828-0458). Back rooms are quieter.

Big, Cheap, Modern Hotels

These places—popular with budget tour groups—are well run and offer elevators and all the modern comforts in a no-frills practical package. Their £60 doubles are a great value for London.

London County Hall Travel Inn, literally down the hall from a $400-a-night Marriott Hotel, fills one end of London's massive former City Hall. This place is wonderfully located across the Thames from Big Ben. Its 300 slick and no-frills rooms come with all the necessary comforts (Db-£60 for two adults and up to two kids under age 17, couples can request a bigger family room—same price, breakfast extra, book in advance, no-show rooms are released at 16:00, elevator, some smoke-free and easy-access rooms, CC:VMA, 500 yards from Westminster tube stop and Waterloo Station where the Chunnel train leaves for Paris, Belvedere Road, SE1 7PB, tel. 020/7902-1600, fax 020/7902-1619, www.travelinn.co.uk).

Other London Travel Inns charging £60 per room include **London Euston** (141 Euston Road, NW1 2AU, tube: Euston), **Tower Bridge** (tube: London Bridge), and **London Putney Bridge** (farther out, tube: Putney Bridge). For any of these, call 01582/414-341.

Hotel Ibis London Euston, which feels classier than a Travel Inn, is located on a quiet street a block behind Euston Station (Sb-£60, Db-£63, breakfast extra, CC:VMA, nonsmoking floor, 3 Cardington St, NW1 2LW, tel. 020/7388-7777, fax 020/7388-0001, e-mail: ho921@accor-hotels.com).

Jurys Inn rents 200 mod, compact, and comfy rooms near King's Cross station (Db/Tb-£75, 2 adults and 2 kids in one room is O.K., breakfast extra, CC:VMA, nonsmoking floors, 60 Pentonville Road, Islington, N1 9LA, tube: Angel, tel. 020/7282-5500, fax 020/7282-5511).

"South Kensington," She Said, Loosening His Cummerbund

To live on a quiet street so classy it doesn't allow hotel signs, surrounded by trendy shops and colorful restaurants, call "South Ken" your London home. Shoppers like being a short walk from Harrods and the designer shops of King's Road and Chelsea. When I splurge, I splurge here. Sumner Place is just off Old Brompton Road, 200 yards from the handy South Kensington tube station (on Circle Line, two stops from Victoria Station, direct Heathrow connection). There's a taxi rank in the meridian at the end of Harrington Road. The handy "Wash & Dry" Laundromat is on the corner of Queensberry Place and Harrington Road (daily 8:00–21:00, bring 20p and £1 coins).

Aster House Hotel—run by friendly and accommodating Simon and Leona Tan—has a sumptuous lobby, lounge, and break-fast room. Its well-worn rooms are comfy and quiet, with TV, phone, and fridge but ramshackle bathrooms. Enjoy breakfast or just lounging in the whisper-elegant Orangery, a Victorian green-house (Sb-£65–85, Db-£125, deluxe four-poster Db-£145, CC:VM, entirely nonsmoking, 3 Sumner Place, SW7 3EE, tel. 020/7581-5888, fax 020/7584-4925, www.welcome2london.com).

Five Sumner Place Hotel was recently voted "the best small hotel in London." In this 150-year-old building, rooms are tastefully decorated and the breakfast room is a Victorian-style conservatory/

greenhouse (13 rooms, Sb-£88, Db-£141, third bed-£24; Oct–Mar 10 percent discount with this book—this makes it the best Sumner Place value off-season; CC:VMA, TV, phones, and fridge in rooms, nonsmoking rooms, elevator, 5 Sumner Place, South Kensington, SW7 3EE, tel. 020/7584–7586, fax 020/7823-9962, www .sumnerplace.com, reservations@sumnerplace.com, run by Tom).

Sixteen Sumner Place—a lesser value for classier travelers—has over-the-top formality and class packed into its 37 unnumbered but pretentiously named rooms, plush lounges, and quiet garden (Db-£160 with showers, £185 with baths, CC:VMA, breakfast in your room, elevator, 16 Sumner Place, SW7 3EG, tel. 020/7589-5232, fax 020/7584-8615, U.S. tel. 800/592-5387, e-mail: reservations@numbersixteenhotel.co.uk).

Kensington Jurys Hotel is big and stately (Sb/Db/Tb-£100–170 depending upon "availability," ask for a deal, breakfast extra, CC:VMA, piano lounge, nonsmoking floor, elevator, Queen's Gate, South Kensington, SW7 5LR, tel. 020/7589-6300, fax 020/7581-1492).

The Claverley, two blocks from Harrods, is on a quiet street similar to Sumner Place. The warmly furnished rooms come with all the comforts (S-£70, Sb-£75–115, Db-£110–145, sofabed Tb-£160–215, flexible during slow times, CC:VMA, plush lounge, nonsmoking rooms, elevator, 13–14 Beaufort Gardens, SW3 1PS, tube: Knightsbridge, tel. 020/7589-8541, fax 020/7584-3410, U.S. tel. 800/747-0398).

Sleeping in Notting Hill Gate Neighborhood

Residential Notting Hill Gate has quick bus and tube access to downtown, is on the A2 Airbus line from Heathrow, and, for London, is very "homely." It has a self-serve launderette, an artsy theater, a late-hours supermarket, and lots of fun budget eateries (see "Eating").

Westland Hotel is comfortable, convenient, and hotelesque, with a fine lounge and spacious 1970s-style rooms (Sb-£80, Db-£95, cavernous deluxe Db-£110, sprawling Tb-£120, gargantuan Qb-£135, 10 percent discount with this book through 2000, CC:VMA, elevator, free garage, between Notting Hill Gate and Queensway tube stations, 154 Bayswater Road, W2 4HP, tel. 020/7229-9191, fax 020/7727-1054, e-mail: 106411.3060 @compuserve.com).

Vicarage Private Hotel, understandably popular, is family run and elegantly British in a quiet, classy neighborhood. It has 19 rooms furnished with taste and quality, a TV lounge, and facilities on each floor. Mandy, Richard, and Tere maintain a homey and caring atmosphere. Reserve long in advance. There's no better room for the price (S-£43, D-£68, T-£87, Q-£92, a 6-minute walk from the Notting Hill Gate and High Street Kensington

London, Notting Hill Gate Neighborhood

1/4 MILE

❶ WESTLAND HOTEL	❺ KENSINGTON GARDENS HOTEL	❿ CHURCHILL ARMS PUB
❷ VICARAGE & ABBEY HOUSE HOTELS	❻ VANCOUVER STUDIOS	⓫ GEALE'S FISH & CHIPS
❸ NORWEGIAN YWCA	❼ PHOENIX HOUSE	⓬ MODHUBON INDIAN REST.
❹ GARDEN COURT HOTEL	❽ LONDON HOUSE BUDGET	⓭ MAGGIE JONES REST.
	❾ LADBROKE ARMS PUB	⓮ MR. WU'S CHINESE REST.

tube stations, near Kensington Palace at 10 Vicarage Gate, Kensington, W8 4AG, tel. 020/7229-4030, fax 020/7792-5989, www.londonvicaragehotel.com).

Abbey House Hotel, next door, is similar, but—while also a fine value—it has no lounge and is less cozy (16 rooms, S-£43, D-£68, T-£85, Q-£95, Quint-£105, 11 Vicarage Gate, Kensington, W8 4AG, tel. 020/7727-2594, Rodrigo).

Norwegian YWCA (Norsk K.F.U.K.) is for women under 30 only (and men with Norwegian passports). Located on a quiet, stately street, it offers nonsmoking rooms, a study, TV room, piano lounge, and an open-face Norwegian ambience. They have mostly quads, so those willing to share with strangers are most likely to get a place (Jul–Aug: Ss-£27, bed in shared double-£25, shared triple-£21 apiece, shared quad-£18 apiece, with breakfast; Sept–Jun: same prices include dinner; CC:VM, 52 Holland Park, W11 3RS, tel. & fax 020/7727-9897). With each visit I wonder which is easier to get—a sex change or a Norwegian passport?

Sleeping on Kensington Gardens

Several big old hotels line the quiet Victorian Kensington Gardens, a block off the bustling Queensway shopping street near the Bayswater tube station. Popular with young travelers from around the world, Queensway is a multicultural festival of commerce and lively eateries (such as Mr Wu's Chinese buffet, stuffing locals for £4.50, on Queensway, see "Eating," below). These hotels come with the least traffic noise of all my downtown recommendations. Brookford Wash & Dry is at Queensway and Bishop's Bridge Road (daily 7:00–19:30, service from 9:00–17:30, computerized pay point takes all coins).

Garden Court rents 34 large, comfortable rooms, offering one of London's best accommodations values. The breakfast room is sticky, and the public bathrooms are a bit unkempt, but it's friendly, with a great lounge and super prices (S-£34, Sb-£48, D-£52, Db-£76, T-£72, Tb-£86, Q-£78, Qb-£92, CC:VM, 30 Kensington Gardens Square, W2 4BG, tel. 020/7229-2553, fax 020/7727-2749, e-mail: gardencourthotel@londonw24bg.freeserve.co.uk).

Kensington Gardens Hotel laces 17 fine, fresh rooms together in a tall, skinny place with lots of stairs (S-£50, Sb-£55, Db-£75, 9 Kensington Gardens Square, W2 4BH, tel. 020/7221-7790, fax 020/7792-8612, www.kensingtongardenshotel.co.uk).

Vancouver Studios is a different concept, giving you a fully equipped kitchenette (plates, stove, microwave, and fridge) rather than breakfast (Sb-£55–72, Db-£85–100, Tb-£123, CC:VMA, homey lounge and private garden, rooms with all the modern comforts, 30 Prince's Square, W2 4NJ, tel. 020/7243-1270, fax 020/7221-8678, e-mail: hotels@vienna-group.co.uk).

Phoenix Hotel, a Best Western modernization of a 130-room hotel, offers American business-class comforts; spacious, plush public spaces; and big, fresh, modern-feeling rooms (Sb-£72, Db-£92, Tb-£120, CC:VMA, nonsmoking rooms, elevator, 8 Kensington Gardens Square, W2 4BH, tel. 020/7229-2494, fax 020/7727-1419, U.S. tel. 800/528-1234, www.phoenixhotel.co.uk).

London House Budget Hotel is a threadbare, nose-ringed slumbermill renting 220 beds in 76 stark but sleepable rooms (S-£40, twin-£54, dorm bed-£20, includes continental breakfast, CC:VMA, lots of school groups, 81 Kensington Gardens Square, W2 4DJ, tel. 020/7727-0696, fax 020/7243-8626, e-mail: hotels@vienna-group.co.uk).

Sleeping in Other Neighborhoods

Euston Station: The **Methodist International Centre** (new in 1998) is a youthful Christian residence, its lower floors filled with international students and its top floor open to travelers. Rooms are modern and simple yet comfortable, with fine bathrooms, phones, and desks. The atmosphere is friendly, safe, clean, and controlled, with a spacious lounge and game room (Sb-£38, Db-£58, Tb-£70, includes breakfast, three-course buffet dinner-£11, CC:VM, nonsmoking rooms, elevator, on a quiet street a block southwest of Euston Square, 81–103 Euston Street, not Euston Road, W1 2EZ, tube: Euston Station, tel. 020/7380-0001, fax 020/7387-5300, e-mail: sales@micentre.com).

Cottage Hotel is tucked away a block off the west exit of Euston Station. Established in 1950—a bit tired, cramped, and smoky—it feels like 1950. But it's cheap, quiet, and has a fine breakfast room (40 rooms, S-£35, Sb-£45, D-£45, Db-£55, 67 Euston Street, tel. 020/7387-6785, fax 020/7383-0859).

Bloomsbury, near the British Museum: The **Cambria House,** a fine value, is run by the Salvation Army (a plus when it comes to cheap big-city hotels). This smoke-free old building with a narrow maze of halls is all newly painted and superclean, if institutional. The rooms are large and perfectly good. You'll find ample showers and toilets on each floor, a TV lounge, and a warm welcome (S-£29, D-£46, Db-£57, T-£70, CC:VM, north of Russell Square, 37 Hunter Street, WC1N 1BJ, tel. 020/7837-1654, fax 020/7837-1229).

Downtown near Baker Street: For a less hotelesque alternative in the center, consider renting one of 18 stark, hardwood, comfortable rooms in **22 York Street B&B** (Db-£94, Tb-£141, CC:VMA, strictly smoke-free, inviting lounge, social breakfast, from Baker Street tube station walk two blocks down Baker Street and take a right, 22 York Street, tel. 020/7224-3990, fax 020/7224-1990, e-mail: mc@22yorkstreet.prestel.co.uk, energetically run by Liz and Michael).

Near St. Paul's: The **City of London Youth Hostel** is clean, modern, friendly, and well run. You'll pay about £24 for a bed in three- to five-bed rooms, £26 in a single (youth hostel membership required, 200 beds, CC:VM, cheap meals, 36 Carter Lane, EC4V 5AD, tube: St. Paul's, tel. 020/7236-4965, fax 020/7236-7681).

South of London: Caroline Cunningham's humble guest house is on a quiet street in a well-worn neighborhood south of Victoria near Clapham Common (3 rooms, S-£15, D-£30 with English breakfast, 98 Hambalt Road, Clapham Common, London SW4 9EJ, tel. 020/8673-1077). It's 15 minutes by tube to Clapham Common, then a bus ride or a 12-minute walk—exit left down Clapham South Road, left on Elms, right on Abbeville

Road, left on Hambalt. Rooms in Caroline's brother's house are an equally good value. A good, cheap Thai restaurant (the Pepper Tree) is near the tube station.

Near Gatwick Airport: These two B&Bs are both in the peaceful countryside and have tennis courts, small swimming pools, and a good pub within walking distance. **Barn Cottage,** a converted 17th-century barn, has two wood-beamed rooms, antique furniture, and a large garden that makes you forget Gatwick is 10 minutes away (S-£35, D-£50, can drive you to airport or train station for £5–6—a taxi costs £10—Leigh, Reigate, Surrey, RH2 8RF, tel. 01306/611-347, warmly run by Pat and Mike Comer). The idyllic **Crutchfield Farm B&B** offers three comfortable rooms, a great sitting room, and an elegant dining room in a 600-year-old renovated farmhouse surrounded by lots of greenery and a pond. Gillian Blok includes a ride to the airport and its train station, whether you're leaving Britain or day-tripping to London (Sb-£45, Db-£75, Tb-£85, Qb-£95, two miles from Gatwick Airport—£5 by taxi, 30 minutes by train from London, at Hookwood, Surrey, RH6 OHT, tel. 01293/863-110, fax 01293/863-233, e-mail: TonyBlok@compuserve.com).

Near Heathrow Airport: It's so easy to get to Heathrow from central London, I see no reason to sleep there. But for budget beds near the airport, consider the **Heathrow Ibis** (Db-£60, breakfast extra, CC:VMA, shuttle bus to terminals, 112 Bath Road, tel. 020/8759-4888, fax 020/8564-7894).

Sleeping and Eating in Hampstead, the Small-Town Alternative

If you must "do" London but wish it was a small town, make Hampstead your home-base-on-the-hill. Just 15 to 25 minutes north of the center by tube (to Hampstead on the sometimes tardy Northern Line) and you're in the former resort of wealthy Londoners—drawn by spas in the 1700s and the brilliant views of London from the popular Hampstead Heath, an 800-acre park.

Hampstead today glows with Georgian village elegance— narrow cobblestone lanes, gas lamps (now electrified), blue plaques noting where Keats, Freud, and other famous locals lived. Even McDonald's has a mock-Tudor facade.

The tube station marks the center of the town (note that in tube terms, Hampstead is in Zone 2, covered by day passes but not carnet tickets). From the station, busy High Street cuts downhill though the center. Following it downhill takes you into a cheery business district with side streets flickering with gaslit charm. The hotel is a three-minute walk uphill. The B&B is a brisk 10-minute walk downhill. The **Freemason's Arms** pub (best for dinner) is a couple of blocks beyond the B&B. And all other pubs and restaurants are within five minutes of the tube station. Everything's near the park.

Make a point to explore the back lanes, where you can pop into churches and peek into windows—drapes are left open so their elegant interiors can be envied.

Hampstead Village Guesthouse is run in a laissez-faire style by Anne Marie van der Meer, who rents eight rooms and raised her family in this Victorian house. The homey rooms, most named after her children, don't have locks, but the house is secure. All rooms come with a phone, miniature fridge, TV, and even a hot-water bottle (small S-£40, S-£45, Sb-£55, D-£60, Db-£70, price varies for studio/kitchenette for 1–5 people; £100 for 2, breakfast-£6, CC:VMA for reservation deposit only, payment in cash, nonsmoking, extremely quiet, book well in advance, walk 10 minutes from tube downhill on High Street, left at Lloyds Bank on Pilgrims Lane to 2 Kemplay Road, Hampstead, NW3 1SY, tel. 020/7435-8679, fax 020/7794-0254, e-mail: hvguesthouse @dial.pipex.com).

La Gaffe Hotel is a sweet Italian-run hotel and restaurant right on Heath Street. Its 14 rooms are small and worn but floral, comfy, and quiet (Sb-£60–75, Db-£85–120, 4-poster room priciest, includes breakfast, CC:VM, TV, phones, nonsmoking, walk uphill from tube station three minutes to 107 Heath Street, Hampstead, London, NW3 6SS, tel. 020/7435-8965, fax 020/7794-7592, e-mail: la-gaffe@msn.com).

Eating in Hampstead: Freemason's Arms is the place for classy pub grub. If the lighting doesn't make your partner look delicious, the Czech lager will. Set on the edge of the heath, with a spacious interior and sprawling beer garden for summer outdoor seating, the Freemason's Arms serves great English food (£9 meals, Mon–Sat 11:00–23:00, Sun 12:00–23:00, CC:VM, skittles downstairs on Thursday and Saturday night—private but peeking permitted; down High Street, left on Downshire Hill Road to #32, tel. 020/7433-6811).

Down High Street from the tube stop you'll find Hampstead swinging at **The House on Rosslyn Hill**. Serving international cuisine, this trendy, modern brasserie attracts a young crowd wearing black, grey, and white (meals start at £10, daily 11:00–24:00, CC:VM, 34 Rosslyn Hill, tel. 020/7435-8037).

French Hampstead cooks a block below the tube station. For a quick bite, **Maison Blanc** on Hampstead High Street not only has the best croissants in town but also makes great savories, like Roquefort and walnut *fougasse* (focaccia pockets) or tarte Provençal (tomato, zucchini, and Gruyère miniquiche)—all this for £3 to £4, including lovely strong French coffee. **Cafe des Arts** serves French food in a rustic, candlelit English setting (daily 12:00–23:30, CC:VMA, 82 Hampstead High Street), but just around the corner, a little crêpe cart in search of Paris is more popular (on Perrins Lane, a few steps off High Street).

For village atmosphere, shop at the **Hampstead Foodhall** on Fitzjohn Avenue (within a block of the tube, cross High Street to the only level street). There's no place better for a dinner picnic with a view than Hampstead Heath (a 10-minute hike away, up Heath Street).

For a laid-back crowd, visit the **Holly Bush** pub (daily 12:00–23:30, serves sandwiches 12:00–15:00 except Sunday, hidden on a quiet lane uphill from the tube, from Heath Street turn left on Holly Bush Steps). For a livelier, spit-and-sawdust pub, toss your darts with the locals at **The Flask** (on Flask Walk, two blocks below the tube station).

Eating in London

If you want to dine (as opposed to eat), check out the extensive listings in the weekly entertainment guides sold at London newsstands (or catch a train for Paris). The thought of a £30 meal in Britain generally ruins my appetite, so my London dining is limited mostly to easygoing, fun, but inexpensive alternatives. I've listed places by neighborhood—handy to your sightseeing or hotel.

Your £6 budget choices are pub grub, a café, fish and chips, pizza, ethnic, or picnic. Pub grub is the most atmospheric budget option. Many of London's 7,000 pubs serve fresh, tasty buffets under ancient timbers, with hearty lunches and dinners priced from £6 to £8. Ethnic restaurants from all over the world add spice to England's lackluster cuisine scene. Eating Indian or Chinese is "going local" in London. It's also going cheap (cheaper if you take out). Most large museums (and many churches) have inexpensive, cheery cafeterias. Sandwich shops are a hit with local workers eating on the run. Of course, picnicking is the fastest and cheapest way to go. Good grocery stores and sandwich shops, fine park benches, and polite pigeons abound in Britain's most expensive city.

Eating near Trafalgar Square

For a tasty meal on a monk's budget sitting on somebody's tomb in an ancient crypt, descend into the **St. Martin-in-the-Fields Café in the Crypt** (Mon–Sat 10:00–20:00, Sun 12:00–20:30, £5–7 cafeteria plates, cheaper sandwich bar, profits go to the church; underneath St. Martin-in-the-Fields on Trafalgar Square, tel. 020/7839-4342).

Chandos Bar's Opera Room floats amazingly apart from the tacky crush of tourism around Trafalgar Square. Look for the pub opposite the National Portrait Gallery (corner of William Street and St. Martin's Lane) and climb the stairs to the Opera Room. They serve £6 pub lunches and dinners (last orders at 19:00, 18:00 on weekends, tel. 020/7836-1401). This is a fine Tragalfar rendezvous point—smoky, but wonderfully local.

Gordon's Wine Bar is ripe with atmosphere. A simple steep staircase leads into a 14th-century cellar filled with candlelight, dusty old wine bottles, faded British memorabilia, and local nine-to-fivers (hot meals only for lunch, fine cheese-and-salad buffet all day until 21:00—one plate of each feeds two for £7). While it's crowded, you can normally corral two chairs and grab the corner of a table (Mon–Sat 11:00–23:00, closed Sun, two blocks from Trafalgar Square, bottom of Villiars Street at #47, near Embankment tube station, tel. 020/7930-1408).

Down Whitehall (toward Big Ben), a block from Trafalgar Square, you'll find the touristy but atmospheric **Clarence Pub** (decent grub) and several cheaper cafeterias and pizza joints.

For a classy lunch in the National Gallery, treat your palate to the pricier **Brasserie** (hot meals £8–10, open daily, first floor of Sainsbury Wing).

Simpson's in the Strand serves a stuffy, aristocratic, old-time carvery dinner—where the chef slices your favorite red meat from a fancy trolley at your table—in their elegant smoky old dining room (£20, Mon–Sat 12:15–14:30, 17:30–23:00, tel. 020/7836-9112).

Eating near Piccadilly

Hungry and broke in the theater district? Head for Panton Street (off Haymarket, two blocks southeast of Piccadilly Circus) for a line of decent eateries. **Stockpot** is a mushy-peas kind of place, famous and rightly popular for its edible, cheap meals (Mon–Sat 8:00–23:00, Sun 8:00–22:00, 40 Panton Street). The **West End Kitchen** (across the street at #5, same hours and menu) is a direct competitor that's just as good. The original **Stockpot**, a few blocks away, has better atmosphere (daily 12:00–23:00, a block north of Shaftesbury near Cambridge Circus at 18 Old Compton Street).

The palatial **Criterion Brasserie** serves a £15 two-course "Anglo-French" menu under gilded tiles and chandeliers in a dreamy Byzantine church setting from 1880. It's right on Piccadilly Circus but a world away from the punk junk (12:00–14:30, 18:00–18:30 only, pricier later, tel. 020/7930-0488).

Just off Leicester Square, **Luigi Malone's**, a chain restaurant, serves inexpensive salads and pasta (12 Irving Street, tel. 020/7925-0457).

Near Covent Garden, the area around Neal's Yard is busy with fun eateries. One of the best is **Food for Thought** (serving until 20:15, closed Sun, very good £4 vegetarian meals, nonsmoking, two blocks north of tube: Covent Garden, 31 Neal Street, tel. 020/7836-0239). Neal's Yard itself is a food circus of trendy, healthy eateries.

Eating near St. Paul's
Ye Olde Cheshire Cheese Pub, rebuilt a year after the great fire of 1666, is a creaky half-timbered tangle of eateries (explained on a chart outside the door). Characteristic restaurants are upstairs, while fast, cheap pub meals are served in the rustic cellar bar (Mon–Fri 11:30–23:00, 145 Fleet Street, tel. 020/7353-6170). There's also a good restaurant and cafe in St. Paul's crypt.

The "Food Is Fun" Dinner Crawl: From Covent Garden to Soho
London has a trendy, generation X scene that most Beefeater seekers miss entirely. For a multicultural movable feast and a chance to sample some of London's most popular eateries, consider sampling these. Start around 18:00 to avoid lines, get in on early specials, and find waiters willing to let you split a meal. Prices, while reasonable by London standards, add up. Servings are large enough to share. All are open nightly.

Suggested nibbler's dinner crawl for two: Arrive before 18:00 at **Belgo** and split the early-bird dinner special: a kilo of mussels, fries, and dark Belgian beer; at **Yo! Sushi**, have beer or sake and a few dishes; slurp your last course at **Wagamama**; for dessert, people watch at Leicester Square, where the serf's always up.

Belgo Centraal is a space-station world overrun with Trappist monks serving hearty Belgian specialties. The classy restaurant section requires reservations, but just grabbing a bench in the boisterous beer hall is more fun. Belgians claim they eat as well as the French and as hearty as the Germans. Specialties include mussels, great fries, and a stunning array of dark, blond, and fruity Belgian beers. Belgo actually makes things Belgian trendy—a formidable feat (£12 meals; open daily till very late; Mon–Fri 17:00–18:30 "beat the clock" meal specials cost only the time... £5 to £6.30, and you get mussels, fries, and beer; no meal-splitting after 18:30; £5 lunch special daily, 12:00–17:00; one block north of Covent Garden tube station at the intersection of Neal and Shelton Streets, 50 Earlham Street, tel. 020/7813-2233).

Soho Spice Indian is where modern Britain meets Indian tradition—fine Indian cuisine in a trendy jewel-tone ambience. The £15 "Tandoori selections" meal is the best "variety" dish and big enough for two (daily 12:00–24:00, nonsmoking section, five blocks due north of Piccadilly Circus at 124 Wardour Street, tel. 020/7434-0808).

Yo! Sushi is a futuristic Japanese food extravaganza experience. With thumping rock, Japanese cable TV, a 60-meter-long conveyor-belt sushi bar (the world's longest), automated sushi machines, and a robotic drink trolley, just sipping a sake on a bar stool here is a trip. For £1 you get unlimited tea (on request), water (from spigot at bar, with or without gas), or miso soup.

From Covent Garden to Soho, "Food is Fun"

❶ CHANDO'S BAR	❺ BELGO CENTRAAL	❾ SOHO SOHO BISTRO
❷ GORDON'S WINE BAR	❻ SOHO SPICE INDIAN	❿ ANDREW EDMUNDS REST.
❸ CRITERION BRASSERIE	❼ YOI SUSHI	
❹ NEAL'S YARD	❽ WAGAMAMA NOODLE BAR	

Grab dishes as they rattle by (priced by color of dish; see their chart) and a drink off the trash-talking robot (daily 12:00–24:00, two blocks south of Oxford Street, where Lexington Street becomes Poland Street, 52 Poland Street, tel. 020/7287-0443). For more serious drinking on tatami mats, go downstairs into "Yo Below."

Wagamama Noodle Bar is a noisy, pan-Asian slurp-athon. As you enter, check out the kitchen and listen to the roar of the basement, where benches rock with happy eaters. Everything's organic—stand against the wall to feel the energy of all this "positive eating" (daily 12:00–23:00, crowded after 20:00, just past the porno and prostitution core of Soho but entirely smoke free, 10A Lexington Street, tel. 020/7292-0990).

Soho Soho French Bistro-Rotisserie is a chance to go French in a Matisse-esque setting. The ground floor is a trendy wine bar. Upstairs is an oasis of peace serving £17 three-course

French "pretheater specials"—order from 18:00 to 19:30 (near Cambridge Circus, two blocks east of Charing Cross Road at 11 Frith Street, tel. 020/7494-3491).

Andrew Edmunds Restaurant is a tiny candlelit place where you'll want to hide your camera and guidebook and act as local as possible. The modern-European cooking is worth the splurge (three courses for £20, 12:30–15:00, 18:00–23:00, 46 Lexington Street in Soho, reservations are smart, tel. 020/7437-5708).

Eating near Recommended Victoria Station Accommodations

Here are places a couple of blocks southwest of Victoria Station where I've enjoyed eating:

Jenny Lo's Tea House is a simple, for-the-joy-of-good-food kind of place serving up £5 Chinese-style meals to locals in the know (Mon–Sat 12:00–15:00, 18:00–22:00, 14 Eccleston Street, tel. 020/7259-0399).

For pub grub with good local atmosphere, consider the **Plumbers Arms** (filling £5 hot meals and cheaper sandwiches Mon–Fri only, indoor/outdoor seating, 14 Lower Belgrave Street, tel. 020/7730-4067—ask about the murdered nanny).

Next door, the small but classy **La Campagnola** is Belgravia's favorite budget Italian restaurant (£12–15, closed Sun, 10 Lower Belgrave Street, tel. 020/7730-2057).

Across the street, the **Maestro Bar** is the closest thing to an English tapas bar I've seen, with salads, sandwiches, and 10 bar stools (very cheap, closed Sat).

The **Ebury Wine Bar** offers a French candlelit ambience and pricey but delicious meals (£15, daily 12:00–15:00, 18:00–22:30, 139 Ebury Street, at the intersection with Elizabeth Street, near the bus station, tel. 020/7730-5447). Several cheap places are around the corner on Elizabeth Street (#23 for take-out or eat-in fish and chips).

The **Duke of Wellington** pub is good, if smoky, for dinner (£5 meals, Mon–Sat 12:00–15:00, 18:00–21:30, Sun 12:00–15:00, 63 Eaton Terrace). **Peter's Restaurant** is the cabbie's hangout for cheap food, smoke, and chatter (closed Sun, end of Ebury, at the intersection with Pimlico).

The **Country Pub in London** lives up to its name and serves good £6 to £12 meals (12:00–15:00, 19:00–21:30, corner of Warwick and Cambridge Streets, tel. 020/7834-5281).

The late-hours **Whistle Stop** grocery at the station has decent sandwiches and a fine salad bar. The **Marche** is an easy cafeteria a couple of blocks north of Victoria Station at Bressenden Place. If you miss America, there's a mall-type food circus at Victoria Place, upstairs in Victoria Station. **Cafe Rouge** is probably the best food there.

Eating near Recommended Notting Hill Gate B&Bs and Bayswater Hotels

The exuberantly rustic and very English **Maggie Jones** serves my favorite £20 London dinner. You'll get solid English cuisine, with huge plates of crunchy vegetables, by candlelight (daily 18:30–23:00, CC:VMA, 6 Old Court Place, just east of Kensington Church Street, near High Street Kensington tube stop, reservations recommended, tel. 020/7937-6462). If you eat well once in London, eat here (and do it quick, before it burns down).

The **Churchill Arms** pub is a local hangout, with good beer and old English ambience in front and hearty £5 Thai plates in an enclosed patio in the back (you can bring the Thai food into the more atmospheric pub section, Mon–Sat 12:00–15:00, 18:00–21:30, closed Sun, 119 Kensington Church Street, tel. 020/7792-1246).

The friendly **Ladbroke Arms Pub** serves country-style meals that are one step above pub grub in quality and price (£8 meals, daily 12:00–14:30, 19:00–22:00, great indoor/outdoor ambience, 54 Ladbroke Road, behind Holland Park tube station, tel. 020/7727-6648).

For fish and chips, the almost-too-popular **Geale's** has long been considered one of London's best (£8, Mon–Sat 12:00–15:00, 18:00–23:00, closed Sun, 2 Farmer Street, just off Notting Hill Gate behind Gate Cinema, tel. 020/7727-7528). Get there early for a place to sit (they take no reservations) and the best selection of fish.

The **Modhubon** Indian restaurant is not too spicy, "vedy, vedy nice," and has cheap lunch specials (Sun–Fri 12:00–15:00, 18:00–24:00, Sat 12:00–24:00, 29 Pembridge Road, tel. 020/7727-3399). Next door is a cheap Chinese take-out (daily 17:30–24:00, 19 Pembridge Road) and the tiny **Organic Restaurant** at #35, which busily keeps yuppie vegetarians as well as carnivores happy (£10, 100 percent organic, Mon–Fri 17:30–23:00, Sat–Sun 10:30–23:00, 35 Pembridge Road, tel. 020/7727-9620).

Cafe Diana is a healthy little sandwich shop decorated with photos of Princess Diana (daily 8:00–22:30, 5 Wellington Terrace, on Bayswater Road, opposite Kensington Palace Garden Gates, tel. 020/7792-9606).

Mr Wu's Chinese Restaurant serves a tasty 10-course buffet in a bright and cheery little place. Just grab a plate and help yourself (£4.50, daily 12:00–23:00, across from Bayswater tube station, 54 Queensway, tel. 020/7243-1017). Queensway is lined with lively and inexpensive eateries.

Eating near Recommended Accommodations in South Kensington

Popular eateries line Old Brompton Road and Thurloe Street (tube: South Kensington).

Luigi Malone's is an Italian-food chain restaurant serving good £6 salads and pasta (73 Old Brompton Road, tel. 020/7584-4323). Its twin brother is just off Leicester Square at 12 Irving Street.

Daquise, an authentic-feeling Polish place, is ideal if you're in the mood for kielbasa and kraut. It's fast, cheap, faded, family run, and a part of the neighborhood (£8 meals, daily until 23:00, nonsmoking, 20 Thurloe Street, tel. 020/7589-6117).

For Indian food, the **Khyber Pass Tandoori Restaurant** is a nondescript but handy place serving good £8 dinners nightly (12:00–15:00, 18:00–24:00, 21 Bute Street, tel. 020/7589-7311).

La Bouchee Bistro Café is a classy hole-in-the-wall touch of France serving early bird three-course £11 meals before 19:30 and plats du jour for £8 all *jour* (daily 12:00–23:00, CC:VM, 56 Old Brompton Road, tel. 020/7589-1929).

La Brasserie fills a big plain room with a Parisian ambience and good French-style food at reasonable prices (two-course £14 "regional menu," £12 bottle of house wine, CC:VMA, nightly until midnight, 272 Brompton Road, tel. 020/7581-3089).

PJ's Bar and Grill is popular with the yuppie Chelsea crowd for a good reason. Traditional "New York Brasserie"-style yet trendy, it serves modern Mediterranean cuisine (£15 meals, nightly until 23:30, 52 Fulham Road, tel. 020/7581-0025).

Transportation Connections—London

Flying into London's Heathrow Airport

Heathrow Airport is the world's busiest. Think about it: 60 million passengers a year on 425,000 flights from 200 destinations riding 90 airlines... some kind of global Maypole dance. While many complain about it, I like it. It's user-friendly. Read signs, ask questions. For Heathrow's airport, flight, and transfers information, call 020/8759-4321. It has four terminals: T-1 (mostly domestic flights), T-2 (mostly European flights), T-3 (mostly flights from the U.S.), T-4 (British Air trans-Atlantic flights).

Each terminal has an airport information desk, car-rental agencies, exchange bureaus and ATMs, a pharmacy, a VAT refund desk (VAT info tel. 020/8745-4216; you must present the VAT claim form from the retailer here to get your 17.5 percent tax rebate on items purchased in Britain), and a £3.50/day baggage check desk (open 5:30–23:00). There's a post office in T-2 and T-4. The best value eating at T-3 and T-4 is the cheap and cheery **Granary** self-service cafeteria. The American Express desk (with rates no better than the exchange bureaus) is in the tube station at Terminal 4.

Heathrow's TI gives you all the help that London's Victoria Station does, with none of the crowds (daily 8:30–18:00, a 5-minute walk from Terminal 3 in the tube station, follow signs to "underground"). If you're riding the Airbus into London, have your partner stay with the bags at the terminal. At the TI, get a free simple map and brochures, and if you're taking the tube (subway) into London, buy a Travel Card day pass to cover the ride (see below).

Transportation to London from Heathrow Airport

By Tube (Subway): For £3.40, the tube takes you 14 miles to Victoria Station in 45 minutes (6/hrly, one change). Even better, buy a £4.50 Travel Card that covers your trip into London and all your tube travel for the day (starting at 9:30).

By Airbus: The A2 Airbus serves the Notting Hill Gate and Kensington Gardens/Queensway neighborhoods—see recommended hotels, above (departs from each terminal, £6, 4/hrly, 5:15–22:00, buy ticket from the driver, tel. 020/8400-6655 or 020/7222-1234). The tube works fine, but with baggage I prefer the Airbus—there are no connections underground and a lovely view from the top of the double-decker bus. Ask the driver to remind you when to get off. If you're going to the airport, exact pick-up times are clearly posted at each bus stop.

By Taxi: Taxis from the airport cost about £35. Especially for four people traveling together this can be a deal. Hotels can often line up a cab back to the airport for £30. For the cheapest taxi to the airport don't order one from your hotel. Simply flag down a few and ask them for their best "off-meter" rate (I managed a ride for £25).

By Heathrow Express Train: This new train service zips air travelers between Heathrow Airport and London's Paddington Station; at Paddington, you're in the thick of the tube system, with easy access to any of my recommended neighborhoods—Notting Hill Gate is just two stops away (£10 but ask about discount promos at Heathrow ticket desk, children under 16 ride free if you buy tickets before boarding, 4/hrly, 5:10–23:00, 15 min to downtown from Terminals 1, 2, 3; 20 min from T-4; works as a free transfer between terminals, tel. 0845/600-1515). For one person going to the airport, the tube or a taxi to Paddington and the Express to Heathrow is as fast and half the cost of a cab to the airport.

Buses from Heathrow to Destinations beyond London

The **National Express Central Bus Station** offers direct bus connections to **Cambridge** (hrly, 3.5 hrs, £17), **Cheltenham** (6/day, 2 hrs, £19), **Gatwick Airport** (2/hrly, 1 hr, £12), and **Bath** (10/day, at 8:40, 10:10, 11:40, 13:10, 14:40, 16:40, 18:10, 19:10, 20:10, 21:40, 2.5 hrs, £19.50, direct, tel. 0990-808-080). Or try the slick 2.5-hour Heathrow–Bath bus/train connection via Reading. Either use your BritRail pass or buy the £26 ticket at the desk in the terminal (credit cards accepted), then catch the twice-hourly RailAir Link shuttle bus to Reading (RED-ding) to hop on the hourly express train to Bath. Most Heathrow buses depart from the common area serving terminals 1, 2, and 3, although some depart from T-4 (bus info tel. 0990-747-777).

Flying into London's Gatwick Airport

More and more flights, especially charters, land at Gatwick Airport, halfway between London and the southern coast. Trains—clearly the best way into London from here—shuttle conveniently between Gatwick and London's Victoria Station (4/hrly, 30 min, £9).

Trains and Buses

London, Britain's major transportation hub, has a different train station for each region. Waterloo handles the Eurostar to Paris. King's Cross covers northeast England and Scotland (tel. 08457/ 225-225). Paddington covers west and southwest England (Bath) and South Wales (tel. 08457/000-125). For the others, call 0345-484-950. Also see the BritRail map in the introduction.

National Express's excellent bus service is considerably cheaper than trains. (For a busy signal, call 0990-808-080, or visit www.nationalexpress.co.uk or the bus station a block southwest of Victoria Station.)

To Bath: Trains leave London's Paddington Station every hour (at a quarter after) for the £32.50, 75-minute ride to Bath. As an alternative, consider taking a guided bus tour from London to Stonehenge and Bath and abandoning the tour in Bath. Both Evan Evans (tel. 020/7950-1777) and Travelline (tel. 020/8668-7261) offer Stonehenge/Bath day trips from London. Evan Evans' tours come fully guided, with admissions for £46 or just the bus trans-portation (free time at Stonehenge and then in Bath) for £25.

To points north: Trains run hourly from London's King's Cross Station, stopping in York (2 hrs), Durham (3 hrs), and Edinburgh (5 hrs).

To Dublin, Ireland: The boat/rail journey takes 10 hours, all day or all night (£40–60). Consider a cheap 70-minute Ryanair or British Midland flight instead (see below).

Discounted Flights from London

British Midland, the local discount airline, can often get you somewhere cheaper than the train. You can fly cheaply domesti-cally (as little as £60 for a round-trip London–Edinburgh ticket if you stay over Saturday), to Ireland (as little as £70 return to Dublin if you stay over a Saturday), and to Paris, Amsterdam, or Frankfurt (round-trip over a Saturday for around £110). For the latest, call 0870-607-0555 or in the U.S., 800/788-0555.

Virgin Air is a Belgian company with incredible rates (no advance purchase deals, one way is half the round-trip, book by phone with credit card and pick up at the airport an hour before your flight, tel. 020/7744-0004, www.virgin-express.com). Virgin Air flies from Stansted and Gatwick in London to Shannon, Ireland (£47) and Brussels (£30 from Stansted, £40 from Gatwick). From its hub in Brussels you can connect cheaply to Barcelona, Madrid, Nice, Copenhagen, Rome, or Milan (e.g., London–Milan, £50).

Ryanair is a creative Irish airline with more complicated but potentially even cheaper fares. They fly mostly from London's Stansted airport to Dublin, Glasgow, Frankfurt, Lyons, Stockholm, Oslo, Venice, and Turin. Sample fares: London–Dublin—£80 round-trip or £30 one way if purchased a week in advance; London–Frankfurt—£70 round-trip or £30 with three-day advance purchase. They tend to book up a couple of weeks in advance (tel. 0541/569-569, www.ryanair.ie).

Crossing the English Channel

By Eurostar Train: The fastest and most convenient way to get from Big Ben to the Eiffel Tower is by rail. In London, advertisements claim "more businessmen travel from London to Paris on the Eurostar than on all airlines combined." Eurostar is the speedy passenger train which zips you (and up to 800 others in 18 sleek cars) from downtown London to downtown Paris (12/day, 3 hrs) or Brussels (6/day, 3 hrs) faster and easier than flying. The train goes 80 mph in England and 190 mph on the Continent. (When the English segment gets up to speed the journey time will shrink to two hours.) The actual Tunnel crossing is a 20-minute black, silent, 100 mph nonevent. Your ears won't even pop. You can change at Lille to catch a TGV directly to Paris' Charles de Gaulle airport or Disneyland Paris. Yes!

Channel fares (essentially the same to Paris or Brussels) are reasonable but complicated. For the latest, call 800/EURO-STAR in the U.S. (or go to www.eurostar.com). These are prices for 2000: The "Leisure Ticket" is cheap ($119 second class, $199 first class, 50 percent refundable up to three days before departure). "Full Fare" first class costs $239 and includes a meal (a dinner departure nets you more grub than breakfast); second class (or "standard") costs $159 (fully refundable even after departure date).

Discounts for first- or second-class travel are available to rail-pass holders ($84 off "Full Fare"), youths under 26 ($80 off "Full Fare"), and children under 12 (about half the fare of your ticket). Cheaper seats can sell out. Book from home if you're ready to commit to a date and time. Call your travel agent or call direct (800/EUROSTAR). Prices do not include Fed Ex delivery. Note: Britain's time zone is one hour earlier than the Continent's. Times listed on tickets are local times.

Buying your Eurostar ticket in London is also easy. Here are some sample London–Paris standard—that's second-class—fares (London–Brussels fares are up to £20 less). Avoid the basic standard fare: one way—£145, round-trip—£249. Those with a railpass pay £50 one way, any day. Without a railpass, a same-day round-trip on a Saturday or Sunday costs £99. Those staying at least three nights pay £130 round-trip. Excursion fares (round-trip over a Saturday) are cheaper: £100. "Saturday Night Away" tickets (round-trip, purchased a week in advance, and staying over a Saturday) are the best deal: £90 standard, £160 first class. One-way tickets for departures after 14:00 Friday or anytime Saturday or Sunday cost £90. Youth tickets (for those under 26) are £80 to Paris, £65 to Brussels (round-trip any time and changeable). First-class and business-class fares are substantially higher. The only seven-day advance deal is the Saturday Night Away. Remember, round-trip tickets over a Saturday are much cheaper than the basic one-way fare...you know the trick.

In Europe, get your Eurostar ticket at any major train station (in any country) or at any travel agency that handles train tickets (expect a booking fee). In Britain, you can book and pay for tickets over the phone with a credit card by calling 0990-186-186; pick up your tickets at London's Waterloo station an hour before the Eurostar departure.

By Bus and Boat or Train and Boat: The old-fashioned way of crossing the Channel is competitive and cheaper than Eurostar; it's also twice as romantic, complicated, and time-consuming. You'll get better prices arranging your trip in London than you would in the U.S. Taking the bus is cheapest, and round-trips are a bargain. By bus to Paris or Amsterdam from Victoria Coach Station: £40 one way, £50 round-trip, 10 hours, day or overnight, on Eurolines (tel. 0990-143-219) or Hoverspeed (tel. 0990-240-241). By train and ship: £42 one way overnight, £59 by day, seven hours.

By Plane: Typical fares are £110 regular, less for student standby. Call in London for the latest fares. Consider British Midland (see "Discounted Flights," above) for its cheap round-trip fares.

NEAR LONDON: GREENWICH AND CAMBRIDGE

GREENWICH
The palace at Greenwich was favored by the Tudor kings. Henry VIII was born here. Later kings commissioned Inigo Jones and Christopher Wren to beautify the town and palace. In spite of Greenwich's architectural and royal treats, this is England's maritime capital, and visitors go for things salty. Greenwich hosts

historic ships, nautical shops, and hordes of tourists. Now, in 2000, the home of the Zero Meridian will host more visitors than ever, drawn by the huge Millennium Dome.

If you plan to tour the Millennium Dome and Greenwich, do the Dome first (to get your money's worth out of the hefty ticket price—£25), and go straight to the Dome, rather than Greenwich, from London via tube (on the Jubilee Line, tube: North Greenwich) or boat (from Westminster Pier). If you decide to roam the Dome all day, it's easy to return to Greenwich another day to see the sights.

When you tour Greenwich, visit the two great ships upon arrival. Then walk the shoreline promenade with a possible lunch or drink in the venerable Trafalgar Tavern before heading up to the National Maritime Museum and Old Royal Observatory. Or, if you're rushed or tired, consider taking the handy shuttle bus that runs from Greenwich Pier (near the *Cutty Sark*) to the Old Royal Observatory, saving a 15-minute gradual uphill walk; then walk down, sightseeing as you go (£1.50, 4/hrly 10:45–17:00, Apr–Sept, Meridian Line Shuttle).

Getting to the town of Greenwich is a joy by boat or a snap by tube. You have good choices: Cruise down the Thames from central London's piers at Westminster, Charing Cross, or Tower of London; tube to Cutty Sark in Zone 2 (free with tube pass); or catch the train from Charing Cross station (2/hrly, £2). I'd take the tube to Greenwich, see the sights, and cruise back.

The TI is on 46 Greenwich Church Street (daily 10:00–17:00, tel. 020/8858-6376). Most of Greenwich's sights are covered by combo tickets, a pricier one for nearly everything and sometimes a cheaper one for a couple of sights; each year the combination of sights is shuffled slightly and the prices go up. Greenwich throbs with day-trippers on weekends, particularly on Sunday because of its arts and craft market; to avoid crowds, visit on a weekday.

Sights—Greenwich

▲▲*Cutty Sark*—The Scottish-built *Cutty Sark* was the last of the great China tea clippers. Handsomely restored, she was the queen of the seas when first launched in 1869. With 32,000 square feet of sail, she could blow with the wind 300 miles in a day. Below deck you'll see the best collection of merchant-ship figureheads in Britain and exhibits giving a vivid peek into the lives of Victorian sailors back when Britain ruled the waves. Stand at the big wheel and look up at the still-rigged main mast towering 150 feet above. During summer afternoons costumed storytellers tell tales of the high seas (£3.50, £12 combo ticket covers most Greenwich town sights, Mon–Sat 10:00–18:00, Sun 12:00–18:00; Oct–Apr Mon–Sat 10:00–17:00, Sun 12:00–17:00, tel. 020/8858-3445, www.cuttysark.org.uk).

Greenwich

▲**Gipsy Moth IV**—Tiny next to the *Cutty Sark*, the 53-foot *Gipsy Moth IV* is the boat Sir Francis Chichester used for the first solo circumnavigation of the world in 1966 and 1967. Upon Chichester's return, Queen Elizabeth II knighted him in Greenwich, using the same sword Elizabeth I had used to knight Francis Drake in 1582 (free, viewable anytime, but interior not open to public).

Stroll the Thames to Trafalgar Tavern—From the *Cutty Sark* and *Gipsy Moth*, pass the pier and wander east along the Thames on Five Foot Walk (the width of the path) for grand views in front of the Old Royal Naval College (listed below). Founded by William III as a naval hospital and designed by Wren, the college was split in two because Queen Mary didn't want the view from Queen's House blocked. The riverside view's good, too, with the twin-domed towers of the college (one giving the time; the other the direction of the wind) framing Queen's House and the Old Royal Observatory crowning the hill beyond.

Continuing downstream, just past the college, you'll see the Trafalgar Tavern. Dickens knew the pub well and even used it as the setting for the wedding breakfast in *Our Mutual Friend*. Built in 1837 in the Regency style to attract Londoners downriver, the tavern is still popular with Londoners for its fine lunches. And the upstairs Nelson Room is still used for weddings. Its formal moldings and elegant windows with balconies over the Thames are a step back in time (Mon–Sat 11:30–23:00, Sun 12:00–23:00, lunch 12:00–15:00, dinner 17:00–21:00, CC:VM, Park Row, tel. 020/ 8858-2437).

From the Trafalgar Tavern, you can walk the two long blocks up Park Row and turn right onto the park leading up to the Royal Observatory.

Old Royal Naval College—Now that the Royal Navy has moved out, the public is invited in to see the elaborate Painted Hall and Chapel, grandly designed by Wren and completed by other architects in the 1700s (fee not yet set, Mon–Sat 10:00–17:00, Sun 12:00–17:00, in the two college buildings farthest from river, choral service Sunday at 11:00 in chapel—all are welcome).

▲**Queen's House**—In 2000, this royal house—the architectural centerpiece of Greenwich—will host an exhibit, *The Story of Time* (until Sept 24). The building, the first Palladian-style villa in Britain, was designed in 1616 by Inigo Jones for James I's wife, Anne of Denmark. Exploring its Great Hall and Royal Apartments offers a sumptuous look at royal life in the 17th century—or lots of stairs if you're suffering from manor-house fatigue (£12 combo ticket covers most Greenwich town sights, daily 10:00–17:00).

▲▲▲**National Maritime Museum**—At the largest and most important maritime museum in the world visitors can taste both the romance and harshness of life at sea. Experience 20th-century naval warfare on a WWII frigate or get to know Britain's greatest naval hero, Nelson, whose display covers both his public career and his scandalous private life (don't miss the uniform coat in which he was fatally shot). The museum's newly opened Neptune Court greatly increases the number of galleries and better profiles the sweep of the Empire and the role of the sea in British history (£12 combo ticket covers most Greenwich town sights, daily 10:00–17:00, look for the events board at entrance: singing, treasure hunts, storytelling, particularly on weekends, tel. 020/8312-6565, www.nmm.ac.uk).

▲▲**Old Royal Observatory**—Whether you think the millennium starts in 2000 or 2001, it happened/happens here first. All time is measured from longitude zero degrees, the prime meridian line—the point from which the millennium began/begins. However, the observatory's early work had nothing to do with coordinating the world's clocks to GMT, Greenwich mean time. The observatory was founded in 1675 by Charles II to find a way to determine longitude at sea. Today the Greenwich time signal is linked with the BBC (which broadcasts the "pips" worldwide at the top of the hour). In the courtyard, set your wristwatch to the digital clock showing GMT to a 10th of a second and straddle the prime meridian (called the Times meridian at the observatory, in deference to the *London Times*, which paid for the courtyard sculpture and the inset meridian line that runs banner headlines of today's *Times*—I wish I were kidding). It's less commercial—and cheaper—to straddle the meridian marked on the path outside the museum's courtyard. Nearby (also outside the courtyard), see how your foot measures up to the foot where the public standards of length are cast in bronze. Look up to see the orange Time Ball, also visible from the Thames, which drops daily at 13:00. Inside, check out the historic astronomical instruments and camera obscura. Finally, enjoy the view: the symmetrical royal buildings; the Thames; the square-mile "City" of London, with its skyscrapers and the dome of St. Paul's; the Docklands, with its busy cranes; and the Millennium Dome itself (£12 combo ticket covers most Greenwich town sights, daily 10:00–17:00). Planetarium shows twinkle on weekdays at 14:30, sometimes on weekends—ask (£2, buy tickets at the observatory, a two-minute walk from the planetarium).

Greenwich Town—Save time to browse the town. Sunday is best for markets: The arts-and-crafts market is an entertaining mini–Covent Garden between College Approach and Nelson Road (Fri–Sun, best on Sun), and the antique market sells old ends and odds at high prices on Greenwich High Road near the post office. Wander beyond the touristy Church Street and Greenwich High Road to where flower stands spill into the side streets and antique shops sell brass nautical knickknacks. King William Walk, College Approach, Nelson Road, and Turnpin Lane are all worth a look. Covered markets and outdoor stalls make weekends colorful and lively.

Sights—Near Greenwich

▲▲▲**Millennium Dome**—Housed under a vast dome a mile from Greenwich, the show's theme is "who we are, how we live, what we do." The dome—at 20 acres the largest ever built—is separated into 14 zones, each with a focus: body, mind, spirit, work, rest, and so on. In the body zone, listen to the magnified sounds of human organs as you walk through the giant 90-foot-tall sculptures of a reclined man and woman (exit through leg). The town zone daily features a different British town telling its story. At center stage, an acrobatic drama troupe performs five times daily. Your admission includes a filmed 30-minute joke history of Britain by Mr. Bean (Rowan Atkinson) shown at the Skyscape "baby dome," a 5,000-seat theatre boasting the two biggest screens in Britain (in the Millennium Plaza in front of the dome).

The organizers plan (or pray) for 12 million visitors this year; a limit of 35,000 tickets will be sold daily. Even from the outside the dome will be a spectacle, especially on the nights it becomes an outdoor light show, with bright lights flickering over its white surface.

Skeptical media, an upset church, and problems getting transportation connections together in time have tempered this Y2K blowout. Still, it's an awesome construction and promises to be a happening worth the steep admission—£25 (daily from Jan 1– Dec 31, 10:00–18:00, until 23:00 in peak times). Tickets are sold at the door, in advance at National Lottery Ticket outlets in Britain, or over the phone at tel. 0870-606-2000, www.dome2000 .co.uk and www.greenwich2000.com. At the end of 2000, the contents of the Dome will be dismantled, and the Dome will be sold.

From London, it's easiest to reach the Dome by tube. The new Jubilee Line Extension, with the largest tube station in Europe, will zip up to 22,000 people an hour from central London directly to the Millennium Dome in 12 minutes (tube: North Greenwich). Boats shuttle people more scenically in about 45 minutes (6/hrly from Westminster Pier). To get to the Dome from the town of Greenwich, take a boat, bus, or the mile-long path. **Thames Barrier**—East of Greenwich, the world's largest movable flood barrier welcomes visitors. You'll get a good video and exhibition on the river they claim is the cleanest urban waterway in the world, its floods, and how it was tamed (£3.40, Mon–Fri 10:00– 17:00, Sat–Sun 10:30–17:30; catch the 70-minute boat from Westminster Pier or take the 30-minute boat from Greenwich Pier— first boats from either location leave about 11:00; or a 20-minute train ride from London's Charing Cross station to Charlton, then a 15-minute walk, tel. 020/8305-4188).

CAMBRIDGE

Cambridge, 60 miles north of London, is world famous for its prestigious university. Wordsworth, Isaac Newton, Tennyson, Darwin, and Prince Charles are a few of its illustrious alumni. This historic town of 100,000 people is more pleasant than its rival, Oxford. Cambridge is the epitome of a university town, with busy bikers, stately residence halls, plenty of bookshops, and proud locals who can point out where electrons and DNA were discovered and where the first atom was split.

In medieval Europe, higher education was the domain of the Church and was limited to ecclesiastical schools. Scholars lived in "halls" on campus. This scholarly community of residential halls, chapels, and lecture halls connected by peaceful garden courtyards survives today in the colleges that make the universities at Cambridge and Oxford. By 1350 Cambridge had eight colleges (Oxford is roughly 100 years older), each with a monastic-type courtyard and lodgings. Today Cambridge has 31 colleges. While a student's life revolves around his or her independent college, the university organizes lectures, presents degrees, and promotes research.

The university dominates—and owns—most of Cambridge. The approximate term schedule is late January to late March (called Lent term), mid-April to mid-June (Easter term), and early October to early December (Michaelmas term). The colleges are closed to visitors during exams, from mid-April until late June, but King's College Chapel and the Trinity Library stay open, and the town is never sleepy.

Planning Your Time

Cambridge is worth most of a day but not an overnight. Accommodations are frustrating in Cambridge. While Cambridge can be visited on your way from London to York, the cheap day-return train plan makes Cambridge easiest and economical as a side trip from London (from London's King's Cross Station, £13.50, 2/hrly, one hour, fast trains depart at :15 and :45 past each hour each way; the budget ticket requires a departure after 9:30 except on Sat and Sun). You can arrive in time for the 11:30 walking tour—an essential part of any visit—and spend the afternoon touring King's College and Fitzwilliam Museum (closed Mon) and simply enjoying the ambience of this stately old college town.

Orientation
(tel. code: 01223)

Cambridge is small but congested. There are two main streets separated from the river by the most interesting colleges. The town center, brimming with tearooms, has a TI and a colorful open-air market (daily 9:00–16:00 on Market Hill Square; on Sunday arts and crafts, otherwise clothes and produce). Also on the main square is a Marks & Spencer grocery (Mon–Sat 8:30–19:00, Sun 11:00–17:00). A J. Sainsbury supermarket, with longer hours and a better deli, is three blocks away on Sidney Street, just north of Green Street. A good picnic spot is Laundress Green, a grassy park on the river, at the end of Mill Lane near the Silver Street punts. Everything is within a pleasant walk.

Tourist Information: At the station, a Guide Friday TI dispenses free Guide Friday maps of Cambridge and sells more detailed ones. The official TI, well signed and just off Market Hill

Square, is more harried than helpful (40p maps, Mon–Fri 10:00–18:00, Sat 10:00–17:00, Sun 11:00–16:00; Nov–Easter Mon–Sat 10:00–17:00, closed Sun, tel. 01223/322-640).

Arrival in Cambridge: To get to downtown Cambridge from the train station, take a 20-minute walk (the Guide Friday map is fine for this); a £3 taxi ride; or bus #3 (90p, every 10 minutes). Drivers can follow signs to any of the handy, central Short Stay Parking Lots.

Tours of Cambridge

▲▲**Walking Tour of the Colleges**—A walking tour is the best way to understand Cambridge's mix of "town and gown." Walks give a good rundown on the historic and scenic highlights of the university as well as some fun local gossip. Walks are run by and leave from the tourist office. From mid-June through August, tours start at 10:30, 11:30, 13:30, and 14:30; September 10:30, 11:30, 13:30; the rest of the year often at 11:30 and always at 13:30. Tours cost £6.50 and include admission to King's College Chapel. Drop by the TI 30 minutes early to snare a spot; off-season you can call ahead and book with your credit card (TI tel. 01223/322-640 or 01223/463-290). Particularly if you're coming from London, try calling at least to confirm that a tour is scheduled and not full. Private guides are also available.

Bus Tours—Guide Friday hop-on hop-off bus tours are informative and cover the outskirts (£8, departing every 15 minutes, can use CC if you buy tickets in train station office), but walking tours go where the buses can't—right into the center.

Sights—Cambridge

▲▲**King's College Chapel**—Built from 1446 to 1515 by Henrys VI through VIII, England's best example of Perpendicular Gothic is the single most impressive building in town. Stand inside, look up, and marvel, as Christopher Wren did, at what was the largest single span of vaulted roof anywhere—2,000 tons of incredible fan vaulting. Wander through the Old Testament via the 25 16th-century stained-glass windows (the most Renaissance stained glass anywhere in one spot; it was taken out for safety during World War II then painstakingly replaced). Walk to the altar and admire Rubens' masterful *Adoration of the Magi* (£3.50, erratic hours depending on school and events, but usually daily 9:30–15:30 in term, till 16:30 otherwise). During term you're welcome to enjoy an evensong service (Mon–Sat at 17:30, Sun at 15:30).

▲▲**Trinity College**—Half of Cambridge's 63 Nobel Prize winners came from this richest and biggest of the town's colleges, founded in 1546 by Henry VIII. Don't miss the Wren-designed library, with its wonderful carving and fascinating original manuscripts (free, 10p leaflet, Mon–Fri 12:00–14:00,

Cambridge

also Sat 10:30–12:30 during term). Just outside the library entrance, Sir Isaac Newton, who spent 30 years at Trinity, clapped his hands and timed the echo to measure the speed of sound as it raced down the side of the cloister and back. In the library's display cases (covered with brown cloth that you flip back), you'll see handwritten works by Newton, Milton, Byron, Tennyson, and Housman, alongside Milne's original *Winnie the Pooh* (the real Christopher Robin attended Trinity College).

▲▲**Fitzwilliam Museum**—Britain's best museum of antiquities and art outside of London is the Fitzwilliam. Enjoy its wonderful paintings (Old Masters and a fine English section featuring Gainsborough, Reynolds, Hogarth, and others, plus works by all the famous Impressionists), old manuscripts, and Greek, Egyptian, and Mesopotamian collections (free, £2 guided tour at 14:30 on Sun only, Tue–Sat 10:00–17:00, Sun 14:15–17:00, closed Mon, tel. 01223/332-900).

Museum of Classical Archeology—While this museum contains no originals, it offers a unique chance to see accurate copies (19th-century casts of the originals) of virtually every famous ancient Greek and Roman statue. More than 450 statues are on display (free, Mon–Fri 10:00–17:00; sometimes also Sat 10:00–13:00 during term; Sidgwick Avenue, tel. 01223/335-153). The museum is a five-minute walk west of Silver Street Bridge; after crossing the bridge, continue straight till you reach the sign "Sidgwick Site" (museum is on your right, its entrance away from street).

▲**Punting on the Cam**—For a little levity and probably more exercise than you really want, try hiring one of the traditional (and inexpensive) flat-bottom punts at the river and pole yourself up and down (around and around, more likely) the lazy Cam. Once you get the hang of it, it's a fine way to enjoy the scenic side of Cambridge. After 17:00 it's less crowded and less embarrassing. Three places, one at each bridge, rent punts (£25–50 deposit required, CC okay) and also offer chauffeured rides (minimum £25 for 40-minute ride). Trinity Punt, at Garrett Hostel Bridge near Trinity College, has the best prices (£6/hour rental, ask for short lesson, free). Scudamore runs the other two locations: the central Silver Street (£10/hr rentals) and the less convenient Quayside at Great Bridge, at the north end of town (£8/hr). Depending on the weather, punting season runs daily Easter through October, with Silver Street open weekends year-round.

Transportation Connections—Cambridge

By train to: London's King's Cross or Liverpool Station (departures at :15 and :45 past each hour, 1 hr, one way £13.40, cheap day-return for £13.50), **York** (hrly, 2.5 hrs, transfer in Petersborough), Birmingham (6/day, 3 hrs), **Liverpool** (5/day, 5 hrs), **Heathrow** (hrly buses, 3.5 hrs). Train info tel. 0345-484-950.

BATH

Any tour of Britain that skips Bath stinks. Two hundred years ago this city of 80,000 was the trendsetting Hollywood of Britain. If ever a city enjoyed looking in the mirror, Bath's the one. It has more "government-listed" or protected historic buildings per capita than any other town in England. The entire city, built of the creamy warm-tone limestone called "Bath stone," beams in its cover-girl complexion. An architectural chorus line, it's a triumph of the Georgian style. Proud locals remind visitors that the town is routinely banned from the "Britain in Bloom" contest to give other towns a chance to win. Bath's narcissism is justified. Even with its mobs of tourists, it's a joy to visit.

Long before the Romans arrived in the first century, Bath was known for its hot springs. What became the Roman spa town of Aquae Sulis has always been fueled by the healing allure of its 116-degree mineral hot springs. The town's importance carried through Saxon times, when it had a huge church on the site of the present-day Abbey and was considered the religious capital of Britain. Its influence peaked in 973, when England's first king, Edgar, was crowned in the Abbey. Bath prospered as a wool town.

Bath then declined until the mid-1600s, when it was just a huddle of huts around the Abbey and some hot springs, with 3,000 residents oblivious to the Roman ruins 18 feet below their dirt floors. Then, in 1687, Queen Mary, fighting infertility, bathed here. Within 10 months she gave birth to a son . . . and a new age of popularity for Bath.

The town boomed as a spa resort. Ninety percent of the buildings you'll see today are from the 18th century. Local architect John Wood was inspired by the Italian architect Palladio to build a "new Rome." The town bloomed in the neoclassical style, and streets were lined not with scrawny sidewalks but with wide "parades," upon which the women in their stylishly wide dresses could spread their fashionable tails.

Beau Nash (1673–1762) was Bath's "master of ceremonies." He organized both the daily regimen of the aristocratic visitors and the city, lighting and improving street security, banning swords, and opening the Pump Room. Under his fashionable baton, Bath became a city of balls, gaming, and concerts and the place to see and be seen in England. This most civilized place became even more so with the great neoclassical building spree that followed.

Planning Your Time

Bath needs two nights even on a quick trip. There's plenty to do, and it's a joy to do it. On a three-week British trip, spend three nights in Bath, with one day for the city and one for a side trip to Wells, Glastonbury, and Avebury. Bath could easily fill another day. Ideally, use Bath as your jet-lag recovery pillow and do London at the end of your trip.

Consider starting a three-week British vacation this way:
Day 1: Land at Heathrow. Catch the National Express bus to Bath (10/day, 2.5-hr trip). While you don't need or want a car in Bath, and most rental companies have an office there, those who pick up their cars at the airport can visit Stonehenge on their way to Bath on this day.
Day 2: 9:00–Tour the Roman Baths, 10:30–Catch the free city walking tour, 12:30–Picnic on the open deck of a Guide Friday bus tour, 14:30–Free time in the shopping center of old Bath, 16:00–Tour the Costume Museum.
Day 3: Pick up your rental car and tour Avebury, Glastonbury (Abbey and Tower), and Wells (17:15 evensong weekdays at the cathedral, 15:00 on Sunday). Without a car, consider a one-day Avebury/Stonehenge/cute towns minibus tour from Bath ("Mad Max" tours are best; see "Near Bath," below).
Day 4: 9:00–Leave Bath for South Wales, 10:30–Tour Welsh Folk Museum, 15:00–Stop at Tintern Abbey, then drive to the Cotswolds, 18:00–Set up in your Cotswold home base.

Orientation (tel. code: 01225)

Bath's town square, three blocks in front of the bus and train station, is a bouquet of tourist landmarks, including the Abbey, Roman and medieval baths, and the royal Pump Room.

Tourist Information: The TI is in the Abbey churchyard (Mon–Sat 9:30–18:00, Sun 10:00–16:00; Oct–Apr closes at 17:00 Mon–Sat, tel. 01225/477-101). Pick up the 25p Bath map/guide; the free "Museums in Bath" brochure; and the free, info-packed *This Month in Bath*. Browse through scads of fliers, books, and maps (including the Cotswolds) in their bookshop. Skip their

room-finding service (£3 fee for walk-ins, £5 for callers) and go
direct. An American Express office is tucked into the TI (decent
rates, no commission on any checks, open same hours as TI).

Arrival in Bath: The Bath train station is a pleasure (small-
town charm, an international tickets desk, and a Guide Friday
office masquerading as a tourist information service). The bus
station is immediately in front of the train station. To get to the
TI, walk two blocks up Manvers Street from either station and turn
left, following TI signs. My recommended B&Bs are all within a
10- or 15-minute walk or a £3.50 taxi ride from the station.

Driving within Bath is a nightmare of one-way streets. Nearly
everyone gets lost. Ask for advice from your hotelier and minimize
driving in town.

Helpful Hints

Festivals: The International Music Festival bursts into song from
mid-May to early June (classical, folk, jazz, contemporary, tel.
01225/462-231) overlapped by the eclectic Fringe Festival from
late May to mid-June (theatre, walks, talks, bus trips, tel.
01225/480-079, www.bathfringe.co.uk). The Mozart festival
strikes a universal chord every November. Bath's box office sells
tickets for most every event (2 Church Street, tel. 01225/463-362).

Internet Access: Try the Itchy Feet Café & Travel Store
(Bartlett Street), the click-cafe.com (Broad Street, near the
YMCA), or the Bath Backpackers Hostel (13 Pierrepont Street,
near train station, you pass hostel on your way to TI).

Farmers' Market: First and third Saturday of the month at
Green Park Station (9:00–15:00).

Car Rental: Avis (behind the station and over the river at
Unit 4B Riverside Business Park, Lower Bristol Road, tel.
01225/446-680), Enterprise (Lower Bristol Road, tel. 01225/443-
311), and Hertz (just outside the train station, tel. 01225/442-911)
are all trying harder. Most offices are a 10-minute walk from most
recommended accommodations. Consider hotel delivery (usually
£5, free with Enterprise). Most offices close Saturday afternoon
and all day Sunday, complicating weekend pickups. Ideally, pick
up your car only on the way out and into the countryside. Take
the train or bus from London to Bath and rent a car as you leave
Bath rather than in London.

Tours of Bath

▲▲**City Bus Tours**—The Guide Friday green-and-cream open-
top tour bus makes a 70-minute figure-eight circuit of Bath's main
sights with an exhaustingly informative running commentary. For
one £8.50 ticket (buy from the driver), tourists can stop and go at
will for a whole day. The buses cover the city center and the surrounding hills (17 signposted pick-up points, 5/hrly in summer,

[handwritten: T Print your Bathes] *[handwritten: walle 10:30 – 12:30]*

[handwritten: high tea 2:30 →]

hrly in winter, about 9:30–18:00, until 16:00 in winter, tel. 01225/ 464-446). This is great in sunny weather and a feast for photographers. You can munch a sandwich, work on a tan, and sightsee at the same time. Several competing hop-on hop-off tour bus companies offer basically the same tour, but in 45 minutes and without the swing through the countryside, for a couple pounds less. (Ask a local what he or she thinks about all of these city-tour buses.) Generally, the Guide Friday guides are better. Save your ticket to get a £1 discount on a Guide Friday tour in another town.

▲▲▲**Walking Tours**—These two-hour tours, offered free by trained local volunteers who want to share their love of Bath with its many visitors, are a chatty, historical, gossip-filled joy, essential for your understanding of this town's amazing Georgian social scene. How else will you learn that the old "chair ho" call for your sedan chair evolved into today's "cheerio" greeting? Tours leave from in front of the Pump Room (year-round daily at 10:30, plus May–Oct 14:00 weekdays, 14:30 Sunday, and several evenings a week at 19:00; confirm at TI). For Ghost Walks and Bizarre Bath Comedy Walks, see "Nightlife," below. For a private walking tour from a local gentleman who's an excellent guide, contact Patrick Driscoll (2 hours for £41, tel. 01225/462-010).

Sights—Bath

▲▲▲**Roman and Medieval Baths**—In ancient Roman times, high society enjoyed the mineral springs at Bath. From Londinium, Romans traveled so often to Aquae Sulis, as the city was called, to "take a bath" that finally it became known simply as Bath. Today a fine museum surrounds the ancient bath and is, with its well-documented displays, a one-way system leading you past Roman artifacts, mosaics, a temple pediment, and the actual mouth of the spring, piled high with Roman pennies. Enjoy some quality time looking into the eyes of Minerva, goddess of the hot springs. The included self-guided tour audio-wand makes the visit easy and plenty informative. For those with a big appetite for Roman history, in-depth 40-minute tours leave from the end of the museum at the edge of the actual bath (included, on the hour, a pool-side clock is set for the next departure time). You can revisit the museum after the tour (£6.70, £8.70 combo ticket includes Costume Museum at a good savings, a family combo costs £22.60, combo tickets good for one week; daily 9:00–18:00, in August also 20:00–22:00, Oct–Apr closes at 17:00, tel. 01225/477-000).

▲**Pump Room**—After a centuries-long cold spell, Bath was reheated when the previously barren Queen Mary bathed here and in due course bore a male heir to the throne (1687). Once Bath was back on the aristocratic map, high society soon turned the place into one big pleasure palace. The Pump Room, an elegant Georgian hall just above the Roman baths, offers the visitor's best chance to raise a

Bath

① MEET TOURS HERE
② HARINGTON'S HOTEL
③ PARADE PARK HOTEL
④ HENRY GUEST HOUSE
⑤ PRATT'S HOTEL
⑥ BACKPACKER'S HOSTEL

pinky in this Chippendale elegance. Drop by to sip coffee or tea to the rhythm of a string trio or pianist (live music all year 10:00–12:00, summers until 17:00, tea/coffee and pastry available for £4 anytime except during lunch, traditional high tea served after 14:30). Above the newspaper table and sedan chairs a statue of Beau Nash himself sniffles down at you. Now's your chance to have a famous (but forgettable) "Bath bun" and split (and spit) a 45p drink of the awfully curative water. Public WCs are in the entry hallway that connects the Pump Room with the Baths. A new spa facility will open here in 2001.

▲**Abbey**—Bath town wasn't much in the Middle Ages. But an important church has stood on this spot since Anglo-Saxon times. In 973, Edgar, the first king of England, was crowned here. Dominating the town center, the present church—the last great medieval church of England—is 500 years old and a fine example of Late Perpendicular Gothic, with breezy fan vaulting and enough stained glass to earn it the nickname "Lantern of the West" (Mon–Sat 9:00–18:00, Sun 13:00–17:30 with 15:15 evensong service; closes at 16:30 in winter; concert and evensong schedule posted on door, worth the £2 donation, handy flier narrates an

18-stop tour). The *Abbey's Heritage Vaults*, a small but interesting exhibit, tells the story of Christianity in Bath since Roman times (£2, Mon–Sat 10:00–16:00, closed Sun). Take a moment to really appreciate the Abbey's architecture from the Abbey Green square.

▲**Pulteney Bridge and Cruises**—Bath is inclined to compare its shop-lined Pulteney Bridge to Florence's Ponte Vecchio. That's pushing it. To best enjoy a sunny day, pay £1 to enter the Parade Gardens below the bridge (daily 10:00–20:00, free after 20:00).

Across the bridge at Pulteney Weir, tour boats run cruises from under the bridge (£4, up to 7/day if the weather's good, 50 minutes to Bathampton and back, WCs on board). Just take whatever boat is running. Avon Cruisers stop in Bathampton if you'd like to walk back; Pulteney Cruisers come with a sundeck ideal for picnics.

▲▲**Royal Crescent and the Circus**—If Bath is an architectural cancan, these are the kickers. These first elegant Georgian "condos" by John Wood (the Elder and the Younger) are well explained in the city walking tours. "Georgian" is British for "neoclassical," or dating from the 1770s. Pretend you're rich. Pretend you're poor. Notice the "ha ha fence," a drop in the front yard offering a barrier, invisible from the windows, to sheep and peasants.

▲▲**Georgian House at #1 Royal Crescent**—This museum (on the corner of Brock Street and the Royal Crescent) offers your best look into a period house. It's worth the £4 admission to get behind one of those classy exteriors. The volunteers in each room are determined to fill you in on all the fascinating details of Georgian life ... like how high-class women shaved their eyebrows and pasted on carefully trimmed strips of furry mouse skin in their place (Tue–Sun 10:30–17:00, closed Mon, closes at 16:00 in Nov, closed Dec–Jan, "no stiletto heels, please," tel. 01225/428-126).

▲▲▲**Costume Museum**—One of Europe's great museums, displaying 400 years of fashion—one frilly decade at a time— is housed within Bath's elegant Assembly Rooms. Follow the included and excellent CD-wand self-guided tour. Learn why Yankee Doodle "stuck a feather in his cap and called it macaroni" and much more (£4, an £8.70 combo ticket includes Roman Baths, family combo costs £22.60, daily 10:00–17:00, tel. 01225/477-789).

▲▲**Industrial Heritage Centre**—This is the grand title for Mr. Bowler's Business, a turn-of-the-century engineer's shop, brass foundry, and fizzy-drink factory with a Dickensian office. It's just a pile of meaningless old gadgets until a volunteer guide lovingly resurrects Mr. Bowler's creative genius. Fascinating hour-long tours go regularly; just join the one in session upon arrival. (£3.50, plus a few pence for a glass of genuine Victorian lemonade, daily 10:00–17:00, weekends only in winter, two blocks up Russell Street from the Assembly Rooms, call to be sure a volunteer is available to give a tour, café upstairs tel. 01225/318-348.)

The Building of Bath Museum—This offers a fascinating look behind the scenes at how the Georgian city was actually built. It's just one large room of exhibits, but those interested in construction find it worth the £3.50 (Tue–Sun 10:30–17:00, closed Mon, near the Circus on a street called "the Paragon," tel. 01225/333-895).

Royal Photographic Society—A hit with shutterbugs, this focuses on the earliest cameras, photos, and their development (£3, daily 9:30–17:30, on Milsom Street, tel. 01225/462-841).

More Museums—Consider the new **Jane Austen Centre** (£4, daily 9:30–17:00, 40 Gay Street, just south of the Circus), the **Museum of East Asian Art** (daily, 12 Bennett Street, near the Circus), or the **Bath Postal Museum** (daily, 8 Broad Street). For the rundown, get the TI's brochure "Museums in Bath."

▲**American Museum**—This museum offers a fascinating look at colonial and early-American lifestyles. Guides fill you in on the details that make domestic Yankee history surprisingly interesting (£5, Tue–Sun 14:00–17:00, closed Mon and early Nov–late Mar, at Claverton Manor, tel. 01225/460-503).

Activities in Bath

Walking, Biking, and Swimming—Get brochures at the TI. Consider the idyllic walk up the canal path to Bathampton: from downtown, walk over Pulteney Bridge, through Sydney Gardens, turn left on canal, and in 30 minutes you'll hit Bathampton, with its much-loved Old George Pub. The Bath Skyline Walk is a six-mile wander around the hills surrounding Bath (95p leaflet at TI). Consider *Country Walks around Bath*, by Tim Mowls (£5 at TI). Sailors enjoy the river cruise up to Bathampton; hikers like walking back (see "Pulteney Bridge and Cruises," above). From Bathampton it's two hours along the canal to the fine old town of Bradford-on-Avon, from which you can train back to Bath. You can bike this route (rent bikes at Avon Valley Cyclery behind train station, £9/half day, £14/all day, tel. 01225/442-442). The scenic 12-mile path along the old Bath–Bristol train tracks is also popular. Cyclists like *Short Cycles around Bath*, by John Plaxton (£4.50, available at TI).

The Bath Sports and Leisure Centre has a swimming pool and more (£2.50, daily 8:00–22:00, just across North Parade Bridge, call for free swim times, tel. 01225/462-563).

Shopping—There's great browsing between the Abbey and the Assembly Rooms (Costume Museum). Shops close at 17:30, later on Thursday. Explore the antique center on Bartlett Street just below the Assembly Rooms. You'll find the most stalls open on Wednesday. Pick up the local paper (usually out on Friday) and shop with the dealers at estate sales and auctions listed in "What's On."

Nightlife in Bath

This Month in Bath (available at TI) lists events.

Plays—The Theatre Royal, newly restored and one of England's loveliest, offers a busy schedule of London West End–type plays, including many "pre-London" dress rehearsal runs (£10–25, cheap standby tickets and late returns, tel. 01225/448-844).

Bizarre Bath Walks—For a walking comedy act "with absolutely no history or culture," follow J. J. or Noel Britten on their creative and entertaining Bizarre Bath walk. This 90-minute "tour," which plays off local passersby as well as tour members, is a kick (£3.50, 20:00 nightly Apr–Sept; heavy on magic, careful to insult all minorities and sensitivities, just racy enough but still good family fun; leave from Huntsman pub near the Abbey, confirm at TI or call 01225/335-124). **Ghost Walks** are another way to pass the after-dark hours (£4, 20:00, 2 hrs, unreliably Mon–Sat Apr–Oct; in winter Fridays only; leave from Garrick's Head pub near Theatre Royal, tel. 01225/463-618). Scholarly types can try the free historical walking tours offered several times a week (19:00, 2 hrs, May–Oct, ask at TI).

Drinks—Drink real ale at the Star Pub (top of Paragon Street).

Sleeping in Bath
(£1 = about $1.70, tel. code: 01225)

Sleep Code: **S** = Single, **D** = Double/Twin, **T** = Triple, **Q** = Quad, **b** = bathroom, **t** = toilet only, **s** = shower only, **CC** = Credit Card (Visa, MasterCard, Amex).

Bath is a busy tourist town. To get a good B&B, make a telephone reservation in advance. Competition is stiff, and it's worth asking any of these places for a nonweekend, three-nights-in-a-row, or off-season deal. Friday and Saturday nights are tightest, especially if you're staying only one night, since B&Bs favor those staying longer. If staying only Saturday night, you're very bad news. Expect lots of stairs and no lifts. A launderette is around the corner from Brock's Guest House on the pedestrian lane called Margaret's Buildings (Sun–Fri 8:00–21:00, Sat 8:00–20:00), and another scruffier launderette, closer to the Marlborough Lane listings, is on Upper Bristol Road (daily 9:00–20:00, tel. 01225/429-378).

Sleeping in B&Bs near the Royal Crescent

From the train station, these listings are all a 10- to 15-minute uphill walk or an easy £3.50 taxi ride.

Brock's Guest House will put bubbles in your Bath experience. Marion and Geoffrey Dodd have redone their Georgian townhouse (built by John Wood in 1765) in a way that would make the famous architect proud. It's located between the prestigious Royal Crescent and the elegant Circus (Db-£60–67, 1 deluxe Db-£72, Tb-£83–85, Qb-£95–99, reserve with a credit-card number far in advance, CC:VM, strictly nonsmoking, little library on top floor, 32 Brock Street, BA1 2LN, tel. 01225/338-374, fax 01225/334-245, e-mail: marion@brocks.force9.net). Marion can occasionally arrange a reasonable private car hire.

Woodville House is run by Anne and Tom Toalster. This grandmotherly little house has three charming rooms, one shared shower/WC, an extra WC, and a TV lounge. Breakfast is served at a big, family-style table (D-£40, minimum two nights, strictly nonsmoking, below the Royal Crescent at 4 Marlborough Lane, BA1 2NQ, tel. & fax 01225/319-335, e-mail: toalster@compuserve.com).

Other recommended B&Bs on Marlborough Lane: **Elgin Villa** is also a fine value, with five comfy, well-maintained rooms (Ds-£45, Db-£50, discounts for 3-night stays, kids £15 extra, continental breakfast served in room, parking, nonsmoking, 6 Marlborough Lane, BA1 2NQ Bath, tel. & fax 01225/424-557, www.elginvilla.co.uk, Alwyn and Carol Landman).

Athelney Guest House, which also serves a continental breakfast in your room, has three spacious rooms with two shared bathrooms (D-£38, T-£57, nonsmoking, parking, 5 Marlborough Lane, BA1 2NQ, tel. & fax 01225/312-031, Sue and Colin Davies).

Parkside Guest House is more upscale, renting four classy Edwardian rooms (Db-£60, nonsmoking, access to pleasant backyard, 11 Marlborough Lane, BA1 2NQ, tel. & fax 01225/429-444, e-mail: parkside@lynall.freeserve.co.uk, Erica and Inge Lynall).

Marlborough House is both Victorian and vegetarian, with five comfortable rooms and optional £12 veggie dinners (Sb-£45–55, Db-£70–85, CC:VM, room service, 1 Marlborough Lane, BA1 2NQ, tel. 01225/318-175, fax 01225/466-127, www.s-h-systems.co.uk/hotels/marlbor1.html, Americans Laura and Charles).

Prior House B&B, with four rooms, is run by helpful, friendly Lynn and Keith Shearns (D-£35, Db-£40, nonsmoking, 3 Marlborough Lane, tel. 01225/313-587, fax 01225/443-543, e-mail: keith@shearns.freeserve.co.uk).

Armstrong House B&B is basic, well-run, and closer to town on a busier road, with five rooms behind double-paned windows (Db-£50–55, continental breakfast in room, nonsmoking, 41 Crescent Gardens, Upper Bristol Road, BA1 2NB, tel. 01225/442-211, fax 01225/460-665, Tony Conradi).

Sleeping in B&Bs East of the River
These listings are about a 10-minute walk from the city center.

Near North Parade Road: Holly Villa Guest House, with a cheery garden and a cozy TV lounge, is enthusiastically and thoughtfully run by Jill and Keith McGarrigle (Ds-£42, Db-£48, deluxe Db-£50, Tb-£65, 6 rooms, strictly nonsmoking, easy parking, 8-minute walk from station and city center, 14 Pulteney Gardens, BA2 4HG, tel. 01225/310-331, fax 01225/339-334, e-mail: hollyvilla.bb@ukgateway.net). From the city center, walk over North Parade Bridge, take the first right, then the second left.

Near Pulteney Road: Muriel Guy's B&B is another good value, mixing Georgian elegance with homey warmth and fine city views (Db-£48, 4 rooms, nonsmoking, 10-minute walk from city center, go over bridge on North Parade Road, left on Pulteney Road, cross to church, Raby Place is first row of houses on hill, 14 Raby Place, BA2 4EH, tel. 01225/465-120, fax01225/465-283).

Siena Hotel, next door to a lawn bowling green, has comfy, attractive rooms that hint of a more genteel time. Though this well-maintained hotel fronts a busy street, it feels tranquil inside, with double-paned windows. Rooms in the back have pleasant views of sports greens and Bath beyond (Db-£70–90, 4-poster Db-£100, CC:VMA, access to garden in back, easy parking, 10-minute walk from center, 24/25 Pulteney Road, BA2 4EZ, tel. 01225/425-495, fax 01225/469-029).

In Sydney Gardens: Sydney Gardens Hotel is a classy Casablanca-type place with six tastefully decorated rooms, garden views, and an entrance to Sydney Gardens park. The elegant breakfast room overlooking the park is a magnet (Db-£69/week-days, £75/weekends, Tb-£95, CC:VM, 2 nights preferred, request garden view, located between park and canal, easy parking, 10-minute walk from center, Sydney Road, BA2 6NT, tel. 01225/464-818, fax 01225/484-347, Geraldine and Peter Beaven).

Sleeping in Hotels near Pulteney Bridge

These listings are just a few minutes' walk from the center.

Kennard Hotel is comfortable, with 14 charming Georgian rooms. Richard Ambler runs this place warmly, with careful attention to detail (S-£48, Db-£88–98 depending upon size, CC:VMA, nonsmoking, just over Pulteney Bridge, turn left at Henrietta, 11 Henrietta Street, BA2 6LL, tel. 01225/310-472, fax 01225/460-054, www.kennard.co.uk).

Laura Place Hotel is another elegant Georgian place (8 rooms, 2 on the ground floor, Db-£80–90 from small and high up to huge and palatial, 2-night minimum stay, 10 percent discount with cash and this book, CC:VMA, family suite, nonsmoking, easy parking, 3 Laura Place, Great Pulteney Street, BA2 4BH, just over Pulteney Bridge, tel. 01225/463-815, fax 01225/310-222, Patricia Bull).

Henrietta Hotel is a very plain place with nearly no character in the same elegant neighborhood (10 rooms, Db-£45–65, cash discount when quiet, CC:VM, 32 Henrietta Street, tel. 01225/447-779, fax 01225/444-150).

Sleeping in Hotels in the Town Center

Harington's of Bath Hotel, with 13 newly renovated rooms on a quiet street in the town center, is run by Susan Pow (Db-£78–95, Tb-£95–120, prices decrease midweek and increase on weekends, CC:VMA, nonsmoking, lots of stairs, attached restaurant/bar serves simple meals throughout day, extremely central at 10

Queen Street, BA1 1HE, tel. 01225/461-728, fax 01225/444-804, www.haringtonshotel.co.uk).

Parade Park Hotel, in a Georgian building, has comfortable rooms, helpful owners, and a central location (35 rooms, Db-£60–65, special 4-poster Db-£75, Tb-£90, Qb-£105, CC:VM, nonsmoking, beaucoup stairs, attached restaurant/bar, 10 North Parade, BA2 4AL, tel. 01225/463-384, fax 01225/442-322, www.paradepark.co.uk, Nita and David Derrick).

Henry Guest House is a plain, vertical little eight-room, family-run place two blocks in front of the train station on a quiet side street (S-£20, D-£40, T-£57, TVs in rooms, lots of narrow stairs, 1 shower and 1 bath for all, 6 Henry Street, BA1 1JT, tel. 01225/424-052). This kind of decency at this budget price, centrally located, is found nowhere else in Bath.

Pratt's Hotel is as proper and old English as you'll find in Bath. Its creaks and frays are aristocratic. Its public places make you want to sip a brandy, and its 46 rooms are bright, spacious, and come with all the comforts (Sb-£75, Db-£105, prices promised with this book in 2000, dogs £2.95 but children free, CC:VMA, attached restaurant/bar, elevator, two blocks immediately in front of the station on South Parade, BA2 4AB, tel. 01225/460-441, fax 01225/448-807, e-mail: admin@prattshotel.demon.co.uk).

The Abbey Hotel, a Best Western hotel, overprices its 60 slightly worn rooms, but has a great location and offers a rare elevator as well as some ground floor rooms (standard Db-£115, deluxe Db-£125, CC:VMA, attached restaurant, nonsmoking rooms available, North Parade, BA1 1LF, tel. 01225/461-603, fax 01225/447-758, e-mail: ahres@compasshotels.co.uk).

Sleeping in Dorms

The **YMCA,** institutional but friendly, and wonderfully central on a leafy square down a tiny alley off Broad Street, has industrial-strength rooms and scuff-proof halls (S-£15, D-£28, T-£42, Q-£55, beds in big dorms-£11, cheaper for 2-night stays, includes breakfast, families offered a day nursery for kids under 5, cheap dinners, CC:VM, Broad Street Place, BA1 5LH, tel. 01225/460-471, fax 01225/462-065, e-mail: info@ymcabath.u-net.com).

Bath Backpackers Hostel bills itself as a totally fun-packed, mad place to stay. This Aussie-run dive/hostel rents bunk beds in 6- to 10-bed coed rooms (£12 per bed, no lockers, Internet access for nonguests as well, a couple of blocks toward the city center from the station, 13 Pierrepont Street, tel. 01225/446-787, fax 01225/446-305, www.backpackers-uk.demon.co.uk, e-mail: backpackers_uk@hotmail.com).

The Youth Hostel is in a grand old building on Bathwick Hill outside of town (£11 per bed without breakfast in 2- to 12-bed rooms, bus #18 from station, tel. 01225/465-674).

Eating in Bath

While not a great pub grub town, Bath is bursting with quaint eateries. There's something for every appetite and budget—just stroll around the center of town. A picnic dinner of take-out fish and chips in the Royal Crescent Park is ideal for aristocratic hoboes.

Eating between the Abbey and the Station

Three fine and popular places share North Parade Passage, a block south of the Abbey: **Tilley's Bistro** serves healthy French, English, and vegetarian meals with ambience (£15 3-course lunches, £20 dinners, daily 12:00–14:30, 18:30–23:00, CC:VM, nonsmoking, North Parade Passage, tel. 01225/484-200). **Sally Lunn's House** is a cutesy, quasi-historic place for expensive doily meals, tea, pink pillows, and lots of lace (£12 meals, nightly, CC:VM, 4 North Parade Passage, tel. 01225/461-634). It's fine for tea and buns, and customers get a free peek at the basement museum (otherwise 30p). Next door, **Demuth's Vegetarian Restaurant** serves good three-course £15 meals (daily 10:00–22:00, CC:VM, vegan options available, tel. 01225/446-059).

Crystal Palace Pub, with hearty meals under rustic timbers or in the sunny courtyard, is a handy standby (£6 meals, Mon–Fri 11:00–20:30, Sat 11:00–15:30, Sun 12:00–14:30, children welcome on patio, not indoors; 11 Abbey Green, tel. 01225/423-944).

Seafoods offers the best eat-in or take-out fish-and-chips deal in town (daily from noon until near midnight, 27 Kingsmeads Street, just off Kingsmead Square). For more cheap meals, try **Spike's Fish and Chips** (open very late) and the neighboring café just behind the bus station.

Eating between the Abbey and the Circus

George Street is lined with cheery eateries: Thai, Italian, wine bars, and so on. **Caffé Martini** is purely Italian with class (£9 entrees, £7 pizzas, daily 12:00–14:30, 18:00–22:00, CC:VM, 9 George Street, tel. 01225/460-818), while the **Mediterraneo,** also Italian, is homier (12 George Street, tel. 01225/429-008).

Eastern Eye serves Indian food under the domes of a Georgian auction hall (£15 meals, £9 minimum, daily 12:00–14:30, 18:00–23:00, CC:VMA, 8a Quiet Street, tel. 01225/422-323).

The **Old Green Tree Pub** on Green Street is a rare pub with good grub, microbrews, and a nonsmoking room (lunch only, served 12:00–14:15, no children).

Browns, a popular chain, offers affordable English food throughout the day without the customary afternoon closure (£5 lunch special, Mon–Sat 11:00–23:30, Sun 12:00–23:30, CC:VMA, live music sometimes Sun–Thur eve, half block east of the Abbey, Orange Grove, tel. 01225/461-199).

Locals prize **The Moon and Sixpence** for its quality

(£7 lunch, 3-course dinner menu for £18–22, daily 12:00–14:30, 17:30–22:30, CC:VM, indoor/outdoor seating, 6a Broad Street, tel. 01225/460-962).

Pasta Galore serves decent Italian food and homemade pasta outside on a patio or inside; the ground floor is brighter than the basement (daily 12:00–14:30, 18:00–22:30, CC:VM, 1 Barton Street, tel. 01225/463-861).

Devon Savouries serves greasy, delicious take-out pasties, sausage rolls, and vegetable pies (Mon–Sat 9:00–17:30, hours vary on Sun; on Burton Street, the main walkway between New Bond Street and Upper Borough Walls).

The **Waitrose supermarket,** at the Podium shopping center, is great for groceries (Mon–Fri 8:30–20:00, Sat 8:30–19:00, Sun 11:00–17:00, just west of Pulteney Bridge and across from post office on High Street).

Guildhall Market, across from Pulteney Bridge, is fun for browsing and picnic shopping, with an inexpensive Market Café if you'd like to sip tea surrounded by stacks of used books, overripe bananas, and honest-to-goodness old-time locals (Mon–Sat 7:30–17:00, closed Sun).

Eating East of Pulteney Bridge

For a classy, intimate setting and "new English" cuisine worth the splurge, dine at **No. 5 Bistro** (main courses with vegetables £12–15, Mon and Tue are "bring your own bottle of wine" nights—no corkage charge, Mon–Sat 18:30–22:00, closed Sun, just over Pulteney Bridge at 5 Argyle Street, smart to reserve, tel. 01225/444-499).

Eating near the Circus and Brock's Guest House

Circus Restaurant is intimate and a good value, with Mozartian ambience and candlelight prices: £16.50 for a three-course dinner special including great vegetables and a selection of fine desserts (daily 12:00–14:00, 18:30–23:00, 34 Brock Street, tel. 01225/318-918, Felix Rosenow).

Woods Restaurant serves modern English cuisine to well-dressed locals in a sprawling candlelit brasserie (£7 lunches, £13–25 three-course dinners, daily 12:00–15:00, 18:00–23:00 except closed Sun eve, CC:VM, 9–13 Alfred Street, near Assembly Rooms, tel. 01225/314-812).

Transportation Connections—Bath

To London's Paddington Station: By train (hrly, 75 min, £32.50 one way), or cheaper by National Express bus (nearly hrly, 3 hrs, £11.25 one way, £19.50 round-trip, ask about £11.50 day returns). To get from London to Bath, consider an all-day Stonehenge-and-Bath organized bus tour from London. For about the same cost as the train ticket, you can see Stonehenge, tour Bath, and leave the tour before it returns to London (they'll let you stow your bag underneath). Evan Evans (£25 for transportation only, £46 includes admissions and tour, tel. 020/8332-2222) and Travelline (tel. 020/8668-7261) offer Stonehenge/Bath day trips from London. Train info tel. 0345/484-950.

To London's airports: By National Express bus to **Heathrow** Airport—and continuing on to London (10/day, leaving Bath at 5:00, 6:30, 7:30, 8:45, 10:00, 12:00, 13:30, 15:00, 16:30, and 18:30, 2.5 hrs, £11.50, tel. 0990-808-080), and to **Gatwick** (2/hrly, 4.5 hrs, £19.50, change at Heathrow). Trains are faster but more expensive (hrly, 2.5 hrs, £28.20, see "London Connections" section for details). Coming from Heathrow you can also take the tube from the airport to London's Paddington station and then catch the Exeter train to Bath.

To the Cotswolds: A new Cotswold Link bus service runs twice daily in both directions between Bath and **Stratford,** stopping at 13 towns en route, including the Cotswold towns of **Chipping Camden, Stow-on-the-Wold,** and **Moreton-in-Marsh** (Bath–Stratford ticket costs £7 one way; buy ticket on bus). You're allowed to break the journey within the same day and continue on the next bus; this allows you to easily day trip to one Cotswold town from Bath or see one Cotswold town en route to another (e.g., see Stow, stay in Chipping Camden).

Other (lesser) Bath–Cotswolds options: By train to **Moreton-in-Marsh** (2.5 hrs, with either one transfer in Reading or two transfers in Didcot Parkway and Oxford). By National Express bus to **Cheltenham** (1 direct bus a day, 2 hrs, more trips if you transfer), **Stratford** (1/day, 3 hrs, more with transfer), and **Oxford** (1/day, 2 hrs, more with transfer); bus info tel. 0990-808-080.

To Birmingham, points north: By train to **Birmingham** (hrly, 2.5 hrs, transfer in Bristol). From Birmingham, a major transportation hub, trains depart for **Blackpool, York, Durham, Scotland,** and **North Wales.** Use a train/bus combination to reach **Ironbridge Gorge** and the **Lake District.**

NEAR BATH: GLASTONBURY, WELLS, AVEBURY, STONEHENGE, AND SOUTH WALES

Oooo, mystery, history. Glastonbury is the ancient home of Avalon, King Arthur, and the Holy Grail. Nearby, medieval Wells gathers around its grand cathedral, where you can enjoy an evensong service. Then get neolithic at every Druid's favorite stone circles, Avebury and Stonehenge.

An hour east of Bath, at the Museum of Welsh Life, you'll find South Wales' story vividly told in a park full of restored houses. Relish the romantic ruins and poetic wax of Tintern Abbey, the lush Wye River Valley, and the quirky Forest of Dean.

Sights near Bath

Planning Your Time

Avebury, Glastonbury, and Wells make a wonderful day out from Bath. Splicing in Stonehenge is possible but stretching it. Everybody needs to see Stonehenge. But I'll tell you now, it looks just like it looks. You'll know what I mean when you pay to get in and rub up against the rope fence that keeps tourists at a distance. Avebury is the connoisseur's circle: more subtle and welcoming. Wells is simply a cute town, much smaller and more medieval than Bath, with a uniquely beautiful cathedral that's best experienced at the 17:15 evensong service. Glastonbury is normally done surgically, in two hours: See the abbey, climb the tower, ponder your hippie past (and where you are now), then scram.

Think of the South Wales sights as a different grouping. Ideally, they fill the day you leave Bath for the Cotswolds. Anyone interested in Welsh culture can spend four hours in the Museum of Welsh Life. Castle lovers and romantics will want to consider the Caerphilly Castle, Tintern Abbey, and Forest of Dean. See the beginning of this chapter for a day-by-day schedule.

Getting around near Bath

Wells and Glastonbury are easily accessible by bus from Bath; **Badgerline** offers several day tours from Bath as well as a "Day Rambler" ticket (£5.50, £11 per family, tel. 01225/464-446). You can get to South Wales by train via Bristol, connecting by bus from the Welsh train station to the various sights.

Avebury and Stonehenge are trickier. The most convenient and quickest way to see Avebury and Stonehenge if you don't have a car is to take an all-day bus tour. Of those tours leaving from Bath, "Mad Max" offers the cheapest and liveliest.

"Mad Max" minibus tours (£14, 6–14 people) are thoughtfully organized, informative, and inexpensive. They last from 8:45 to 16:40 and cover 110 miles with stops in Avebury, Stonehenge, and two cute villages—Lacock and Castle Combe. Castle Combe, the southernmost Cotswold village, is as cute as they come. The Mad Max bus picks up passengers at 8:45 at the statue on Cheap Street (behind Bath Abbey). To reserve a seat, call the Bath youth hostel (tel. 01225/465-674, please honor or cancel your seat reservation, e-mail: maddy@madmax.abel.co.uk). The same outfit also does a half-day "Stone Circles" tour visiting Stonehenge and Avebury (£12, 3/wkly, departing 13:00, returning 18:00).

If Mad Max is booked up, don't fret. Plenty of companies in Bath offer tours of varying lengths, prices, and destinations. Guide Friday, in partnership with Badgerline Buses, runs a reasonable Stonehenge/Avebury tour in the afternoon (£15, 12:30–18:15, usually daily Apr–Sept, leave from Bath bus station, book at Guide Friday office at train station, tel. 01225/444-102, or Badgerline at bus station, tel. 01225/481-318). Danwood Tours offers a daily daylong City Safari tour of the Cotswolds, Avebury, Stonehenge, Salisbury, and Longleat for £16 (departs outside Abbey Hotel at 10:15, returns at 17:30, book at TI or call 01373/465-965). Danwood also rents out guides and minibuses for people who want to design their own tour. The cost of admission to sites is usually not included with any tour.

Drivers can do a loop from Bath to Avebury (25 miles) to Glastonbury (56 miles) to Wells (6 miles) and back to Bath (20 miles). A loop from Bath to South Wales is 100 miles, mostly on the 80-mph motorway. Each of the Welsh sights is just off the motorway.

GLASTONBURY

Marked by its hill, or "tor," and located on England's most powerful line of prehistoric sights (called a "ley" line), the town of Glastonbury gurgles with history and mystery.

In A.D. 37, Joseph of Arimathea carried vessels containing the blood and sweat of Jesus to Glastonbury; and with them, Christianity came to England. While this is "proven" by fourth-century writings and accepted by the Church, the Holy Grail legend that sprang from this in the Middle Ages isn't. Many think the Grail trail ends at the bottom of the Chalice Well (described below), a natural spring at the base of the Glastonbury Tor.

In the 12th century, England needed a morale-boosting folk hero for inspiration during a war with France. The fifth-century

Celtic fort at Glastonbury was considered proof enough of the greatness of the fifth-century warlord Arthur. His supposed remains (along with those of Queen Guinevere) were dug up from the abbey floor, and Glastonbury became woven into the Arthurian legends. Reburied in the abbey choir, their grave site is a shrine today.

The Glastonbury Abbey was England's most powerful in the 10th century. By the year 1500, English monasteries owned one-sixth of all English land and had four times the income of the crown. Henry VIII dissolved the abbeys in 1536. He was particularly harsh on Glastonbury. He not only destroyed the abbey but also hung and quartered the abbot, sending the parts of his body on four different national tours ... at the same time.

But Glastonbury rebounded. In an 18th-century tourism campaign, thousands signed affidavits stating that water from the Chalice Well healed them, and once again Glastonbury was on the tourist map. Today Glastonbury and its tor are a center for searchers, too creepy for the mainstream church but just right for those looking for a place to recharge their crystals.

Orientation (tel. code: 01458)

The tourist information office (daily 10:00–17:00, until 16:00 in winter, tel. 01458/832-954) is on High Street—as are many of the dreadlocked folks who walk it. The Lake Village Museum in the TI is nothing special (£1.50). Tuesday is market day—a combo crafts, flea, and produce gathering behind the TI (9:00–15:00).

Glastonbury, quickly becoming "the windy city," has no short-age of healthy eateries. The vegetarian **Rainbow's End** (next to TI, 17 High Street, tel. 01458/833-896) is one of several fine cafés for beans, salads, and New Age people watching. If you're looking for a midwife or a male-bonding tribal meeting, check their notice board. If this all causes you to wonder if you need spiritual guidance or just an odd rune read, wander through the **Glastonbury Experience,** a New Age mall at the bottom of High Street.

The **Tor Bus** shuttles visitors from the town center and abbey to the base of the tor, stopping at the Rural Life Museum and the Chalice Well (50p, 2/hrly, 9:30–17:00 throughout the summer). Their brochure outlines a good tor-to-town walk (a brisk, 10-minute walk).

Sights—Glastonbury

▲▲**Glastonbury Abbey**—The evocative ruins of the first Christian sanctuary in the British Isles stand mysteriously alive in a lush, 36-acre park. Start your visit in the museum, where a model shows the abbey in its pre–Henry VIII splendor and exhibits tell the story of a place "grandly constructed to entice even the dullest minds to prayer." Today the abbey attracts people who find God within. Tie-dyed starry-eyed pilgrims seem to float through the grounds naturally high. Others lie on the grave of King Arthur, whose burial site is marked off in the center of the abbey ruins. The only surviving building is the Abbot's conical kitchen, which often comes with a cheery singing monk demonstrating life in the abbey kitchen (£2.50, Jun–Aug daily 9:00–18:00, off-season 9:30 to dusk, tel. 01458/832-267).

Somerset Rural Life Museum—Exhibits include peat digging, cider making, and cheese making. The Abbey Farmhouse is now a collection of domestic and work mementos that illustrate the life of farmer John Hodges "from the cradle to the grave." The fine 14th-century barn, with its beautifully preserved wooden ceiling, is filled with Victorian farm tools (£2.50, Easter–Oct Tue–Fri 10:00–17:00, Sat–Sun 14:00–18:00, closed Mon and off-season, free car park, tel. 01458/831-197).

Chalice Well—The well is surrounded by a peaceful garden. According to tradition, Joseph of Arimathea brought the chalice of the Lord's Supper to Glastonbury in A.D. 37. Even if the chalice is not in the bottom of the well and the water is red from rust and not Jesus' blood, the tranquil setting is one where nature's harmony is a joy to ponder. Have a drink (£1.50, daily 10:00–18:00, in winter 13:00–16:00, tel. 01458/831-154).

Glastonbury Tor—Seen by many as a Mother Goddess symbol, the tor, a natural plug of sandstone on clay, has an undeniable geological charisma. The tower is the remnant of a 14th-century church of St. Michael. A fine Somerset view rewards those who hike to its 520-foot summit.

Transportation Connections—Glastonbury

By bus to: Wells (2/hrly, 30 min, tel. 0117/955-3231) and **Bath** (hrly, 75 min). The nearest train station is in Bath.

WELLS

This wonderfully preserved little town has a cathedral, so it can be called a city. It's England's smallest cathedral city, with one of its most interesting cathedrals and more medieval buildings still doing what they were originally built to do than in any town you'll visit. Market day fills the town square on Wednesday and Saturday.

Tourist Information: The TI, on the main square, offers occasional £2 town walks in the summer at 14:30 (daily 9:30–17:30, in winter 10:00–16:00, tel. 01749/672-552, e-mail: wells.tic @ukonline.co.uk).

Sights—Wells

▲▲**Wells Cathedral**—England's first completely Gothic cathedral (dating from about 1200) is the highlight of the city. The newly restored west front displays nearly 300 original 13th-century carvings (the Last Judgment, lots of kings, bottom row of niches empty—all too easily reached by Cromwell's men, who were hell-bent on destroying "graven images"). Stand back and imagine it as a grand Palm Sunday welcome with a cast of hundreds—all gaily painted back then, choristers singing boldly from holes above the doors and trumpets tooting through the holes up by the 12 Apostles.

Inside you're immediately struck by the general lightness and the unique "scissors" or hourglass-shaped double arch (added in 1338 to transfer weight from the west, where the foundations were sinking under the tower's weight, to the east, where they were firm). You'll be warmly greeted, reminded how expensive it is to maintain the cathedral, and given a map of its highlights.

Don't miss the fine 14th-century stained glass (the "Golden Window" on the east wall). The medieval clock does a silly but much-loved joust on the quarter hour (north transept, its face dates from 1390). The embroidery work in the choir (the central zone where the daily services are sung) is worth a close look. Walk the well-worn steps up to the grand fan-vaulted chapter house—an intimate place for the theological equivalent of a huddle among church officials. The cathedral library (14:00–16:00 only, 50p), with a few old manuscripts, offers a peek into a real 15th-century library. The requested £4 donation for the cathedral is not intended to keep you out (daily 7:30–19:00 or dusk, 45-minute-long tours at 10:15, 11:15, 12:15, 14:15, and 15:15, good shop and a handy restaurant, tel. 01749/674-483). See "Evensong," below.

Lined with perfectly pickled 14th-century houses, the oldest complete street in Europe is **Vicar's Close** (just a block north of the cathedral). It was built to house the vicar's choir, and it still houses church officials. The mediocre city museum is next door to the cathedral. For a fine cathedral-and-town view from your own leafy hilltop bench, hike 10 minutes up Tor Hill.

▲▲**Cathedral Evensong Service**—Weekdays at 17:15 and Sunday at 15:00, the cathedral choir takes full advantage of heavenly acoustics with a 45-minute entirely sung evensong service (boys' and men's voices, great pipe organ, you'll sit right in the old "quire." Note: generally not sung when school is out in July and August unless a visiting choir is performing, tel. 01749/674-483 to check). At 17:05 the verger ushers visitors to their seats. There's generally plenty of room. Unfortunately, the last bus to Bath is at 17:43 (and you can't leave the service early), so on weekdays those without a car or a bed in Wells can't enjoy this experience.

Bishop's Palace—Next to the cathedral stands the moated Bishop's Palace. On the grounds (past the old-timers playing a proper game of croquet) is a fine garden with the idyllic springs that gave the city its name. The interior offers a look at elegant furniture and clothing (£3, Aug daily 10:30–18:00; Apr–Oct Tue–Fri 10:30–18:00, Sun 14:00–18:00, closed Mon; closed in winter, tel. 01749/678-691).

Cheddar Cheese—If you're in the mood for a picnic, drop by an aromatic cheese shop for a great selection of tasty Somerset cheeses. Real farmhouse cheddar puts "American" cheddar to Velveeta shame. The Laurelbank Dairy Company is a traditional cheese shop with all the local edibles (Mon–Sat 9:00–17:30, closed Sun, 14 Queen St., tel. 01749/679-803). Ask for a pound's worth of the most interesting mix. The Cheddar Gorge (and the Cheddar Gorge Cheese Company, which welcomes and educates guests) is six miles down the road.

Sleeping and Eating in Wells
(£1 = about $1.70, tel. code: 01749)
Wells is a pleasant overnight stop. The first two guest houses and the Fountain Inn are all within a block of each other behind (east of) the cathedral. Coming in on B3139 from Bath, they're just before the cathedral. The last B&B is idyllic and in the next village.

Tor Guest House, with eight rooms in a 17th-century building facing the east end of the cathedral, is a good value (D-£42–48, Db-£45–55, family deals, 3-night discount, CC:VM, cozy lounge stocked with great regional coffee-table books, breakfast room, quiet, nonsmoking, car park, 20 Tor Street, BA5 2US, tel. & fax 01749/672-322, e-mail: letitia@torhouse.demon.co.uk, warmly and expertly run by Letitia Corray).

Furlong House B&B, a grand old house with a huge and peaceful garden, is more homey and laid-back (Db-£40, £44 on Friday and Saturday nights, nonsmoking, easy parking, a block from Fountain Inn, behind the gate at the end of Lorne Place, a tiny and quiet lane off St. Thomas Street just east of cathedral, Wells, BA5 2XF, tel. 01749/674-064, e-mail: howardwells @compuserve.com, by Lyn and John Howard).

Swan Hotel, an elegant old place facing the cathedral, is now run as a big, normal hotel by Best Western (Sb-£74, Db-£93, often cheaper if you just turn up, CC:VMA, Sadler Street, BA5 2RX, tel. 01749/678-877, fax 01749/677-647, e-mail: swan@heritagehotels.co.uk).

Manor Farm B&B in the village of Dulcote, a mile or so outside Wells, rents four fine rooms in a cozy 17th-century farmhouse (D-£40, Db-£45, huge ground floor easy-access Db suite-£55, nonsmoking, BA5 3PZ, tel. 01749/672-125). The place comes complete with friendly farm animals and the good care and cooking of Rosalind Bufton. It's a peaceful 20-minute walk through wispy farmland to the Wells Cathedral.

Fountain Inn is great for pub grub (£6–10 meals nightly, creative vegetarian meals, real ales, and draft cider, CC:VMA, behind the cathedral on St. Thomas Street, tel. 01749/672-317). Their award-winning cheese plate lets you sample cheddar and its local cousins. For a good, traditional local dish, try their founders beef pie. In town, consider **Anton's Bistro** in the Crown Hotel. For a healthy lunch, consider the **Cathedral Cloister Restaurant** (in the cathedral) or the vegetarian **Good Earth** (Mon–Sat 9:30–17:30, closed Sun, Priory Road at bottom of Broad Street, tel. 01749/678-600).

Transportation Connections—Wells
By bus to: Bath (hrly, 75 min, Badgerline Buses, tel. 01749/673-084), **Glastonbury** (2/hrly, 30 min), **London** (£16, London Flyer departs daily except Sun from Glastonbury at 6:50 and Wells at 7:00 and from London at 18:00, 3 hrs, tel. 01934/616-000).

Sights—Near Wells
▲**Wookey Hole**—This lowbrow commercial venture, possibly worthwhile as family entertainment, is a real hodgepodge. It starts with a wookey-guided tour of some big but mediocre caves complete with history, geology lessons, and witch stories. Then you're free to wander through a traditional paper-making mill, with a demonstration, and into a 19th-century amusements room—a riot of color, funny mirrors, and old penny-arcade machines that visitors can actually play for as long as their pennies (on sale there) last. They even have old girlie shows. (£7, May–Sept daily 9:30–19:00, Oct–Apr daily 10:30–18:00, tickets sold until 2 hours before closing, two miles east of Wells, tel. 01749/672-243.)

Scrumpy Farms—Scrumpy is the wonderfully dangerous hard cider brewed in this part of England. You don't find it served in many pubs because of the unruly crowd it attracts. (The Beehive pub in Bath still serves its Scrumpy and seems to enjoy the consequences.) Scrumpy, 8 percent alcohol, will rot your socks. "Scrumpy Jack," carbonated mass-produced cider, is not real Scrumpy. The real stuff is "rough farmhouse cider." This is potent stuff. It's said some farmers throw a side of beef into the vat, and when fermentation is done only the teeth remain. TIs list local cider farms open to the public, such as Mr. Wilkins Land's End Cider Farm—a great "back door" travel experience (Mon–Sat 10:00–20:00, Sun 10:00–13:00, near Wells in Mudgeley a quarter mile off the B3151 2 miles south of Wedmore—tough to find, get close and ask locals, tel. 01934/712-385). Glastonbury's Somerset Rural Life Museum has a cider exhibit. Apples are pressed from September through December. Hard cider, while not quite Scrumpy, is still West-country typical but more fashionable, decent, and accessible. You can have a pint drawn for you at nearly any pub.

AVEBURY
The stone circle at Avebury is bigger (16 times the size), less touristy, and, for many, more interesting than Stonehenge. You're free to wander among 100 stones, ditches, mounds, and curious

patterns from the past, as well as the village of Avebury, which grew up in the middle of this fascinating, 1,400-foot-wide neolithic circle.

In the 14th century, in a kind of frenzy of religious paranoia, Avebury villagers buried many of these mysterious pagan stones. Their 18th-century descendants broke up the remaining stones and used them for building material. Today the buried stones have been resurrected, and concrete markers show where the broken-down stones once stood.

Take the mile walk around the circle. Visit the archaeology museum (£1.60, daily 10:00–18:00). Notice the pyramid-shaped Silbury Hill, a 130-foot-high, yet-to-be-explained mound of chalk just outside of Avebury. Nearly 5,000 years old, this mound is the largest man-made object in prehistoric Europe (with the surface area of London's Trafalgar Square and the height of the Nelson Memorial). It's a reminder that you've just scratched the surface of Britain's mysterious ancient and religious landscape.

The pleasant **Stones Café** serves nice and healthy vegetarian meals and unhealthy cream teas (daily in summer, weekends only in winter, check out their mouthwatering £18 cookbook, next to the National Trust store, tel. 01672/539-514). The **Red Lion Pub** has inexpensive pub grub, a creaky, well-worn, dart-throwing ambience, and a medieval well in its dining room (cooking daily, overpriced rooms upstairs, CC:VM, tel. 01672/539-266).

Sleeping in Avebury makes lots of sense since the stones are lonely and wide open all night. **Mrs. Dixon's B&B**, directly across from Silbury Hill on the main road just beyond the tourist parking lot, rents three small but tidy rooms for a fine price (S-£25, D-£34, T-£40, 6 Beckhampton Road, Avebury, Wiltshire, SN8 1QT, tel. 01672/539-588).

For transportation connections, see "Getting around near Bath," above.

STONEHENGE

England's most famous stone circle, with parts older than the oldest pyramid, was built between 3100 and 1100 B.C. Many of these huge stones were rafted and then rolled on logs all the way from Wales to form a remarkably accurate celestial calendar. Even today, every summer solstice (around June 21) the sun sets in just the right slot, and Druids boogie. The monument is roped off, so even if you pay the £4 entry fee (which includes a worthwhile one-hour audio tour), you're kept at a distance. Cheapskates see it free from the road (Jun–Aug daily 9:00–19:00, less off-season, tel. 01980/625-368).

For transportation connections, see "Getting around near Bath," above.

SOUTH WALES

▲**Cardiff**—The Welsh capital (pop. 300,000) has a pleasant modern center across from its castle. A castle visit is interesting only if you catch one of the entertaining tours (every 30 minutes). The interior is a Victorian fantasy.

▲▲**St. Fagans' Welsh Folk Museum**—This best look at traditional Welsh folk life displays more than 30 carefully reconstructed old houses from all corners of this little country in a 100-acre park under a castle. Each is fully furnished and comes equipped with a local expert warming herself by a toasty fire and happy to tell you anything you want to know about life in this old cottage. Ask questions!

A highlight is the Rhyd-y-Car 1805 row house, which displays ironworker cottages as they might have looked in 1805, 1855, 1895, 1925, 1955, and 1985, offering a fascinating zip through Welsh domestic life. You'll see traditional crafts in action and a great gallery displaying crude washing machines, the earliest matches, elaborately carved "love spoons," an impressive costume exhibit, and even a case of memorabilia from the local man who pioneered cremation. While everything is well explained, the £2 museum guidebook is a good investment.

The museum has three sections: houses, museum, and castle/garden. If the sky's dry, see the scattering of houses first. Spend an hour in the large building's fascinating museum. The castle interior is royal enough and surrounded by a fine garden, but if you're tired, it's not worth the hike. While the cafeteria near the entrance (Vale Restaurant) is handy, you'll eat light lunches better, cheaper, and with more atmosphere in the park at the **Gwalia Tea Room**. The **Plymouth Arms** pub just outside the museum serves the best food (£6, daily 10:00–18:00, until 17:00 off-season, tel. 01222/573-500). City bus #56 runs hourly between Cardiff Castle and the Welsh Folk Museum (which is in the village of St. Fagans). Drivers leave the M4 at Junction 33 and follow the signs. Leaving the museum, jog left on the freeway, take the first exit, and circle back, following signs to the M4.

▲**Caerphilly Castle**—This impressive but gutted old castle is the second largest in Europe (after Windsor). With two concentric walls, it was considered to be a brilliant arrangement of defensive walls and moats (£2.50, daily 9:30–18:00, shorter hours in winter, nine miles north of Cardiff, 30 minutes from the Welsh Folk Museum, take train from Cardiff to Caerphilly—2/hrly, 20 minutes—and walk 5 minutes, tel. 01222/883-143).

▲▲**Tintern Abbey**—Inspiring monks to prayer, Wordsworth to poetry, Turner to a famous painting, and rushed tourists to a thoughtful moment, this poem-worthy ruined-castle-of-an-abbey is worth a five-mile detour off the motorway. Founded in 1131 on a site chosen by Norman monks for its tranquility, it functioned as an austere Cistercian abbey until its dissolution in 1536 (£2.50, daily 9:30–18:00, until 16:00 in winter, tel. 01291/689-251, several buses/ day from Chepstow, easy 15-minute walk up to St. Mary's Church for a view of England just over the River Wye). Visit late to miss crowds. The abbey's shop sells fine Celtic jewelry and other gifts.

If seduced into spending the night, you'll find plenty of **B&Bs** near the abbey or in the charming castle-crowned town of Chepstow just down the road. Tintern TI: tel. 01291/689-566.

▲**Wye River Valley and Forest of Dean**—This land is lush, mellow, and historic. Local tourist brochures explain the Forest of Dean's special dialect, its strange political autonomy, and its oaken ties to Trafalgar and Admiral Nelson.

For a medieval night, check into the **St. Briavels' Castle Youth Hostel** (£9 beds in 8- to 12-bed dorms, members only, tel. 01594/530-272). An 800-year-old Norman castle used by King John in 1215—the year he signed the Magna Carta, it's comfortable (as castles go), friendly, and in the center of the quiet village of St. Briavels just north of Tintern Abbey. For dinner, eat at the hostel or walk "just down the path and up the snyket" to the **Crown Pub** (decent food and local pub atmosphere).

Transportation Connections—Cardiff

By train to: Caerphilly (2/hrly, 20 min), **Bath** (hrly, 90 min, transfer in Bristol), **Birmingham** (8/day, 2 hrs), **London** (hrly, 2 hrs), **Chepstow** (hrly, 30 min, 6 miles to Tintern by bus). Train info: tel. 0345-484-950.

Route Tips for Drivers

Bath to South Wales: Leave Bath following signs for A4, then M4, then Stroud. It's 10 miles north (on A46 past a village called Pennsylvania) to the M4 superfreeway. Zip westward, crossing a huge suspension bridge into Wales (£4.20 toll westbound only). Stay on the M4 (not M48) past Cardiff, take exit 33, and follow the brown signs south to the Welsh Folk Museum. To get to Tintern Abbey, take the M4 to Exit 21 and get on M48. The abbey is six miles (up A466, signs to Chepstow then Tintern) off M48 at Exit 2, right where the northern bridge across the Severn hits Wales.

Cardiff to the Cotswolds via Forest of Dean: On the Welsh side of the big suspension bridge, take the Chepstow exit and follow signs up A466 to Tintern Abbey and the Wye River Valley. Carry on to Monmouth and, if you're running late, follow the A40 and the M50 to the Tewksebury exit, where small roads will take you into the Cotswolds.

THE COTSWOLDS

The Cotswold Hills, a 25-by-50-mile chunk of Gloucestershire, are dotted with villages and graced with England's greatest countryside palace, Blenheim.

As with many fairy-tale regions of Europe, the present-day beauty of the Cotswolds was the result of an economic disaster. Wool was a huge industry in medieval England, and Cotswold sheep grew the best wool. The region prospered. Wool money built fine towns and houses. Local "wool" churches are called "cathedrals" for their scale and wealth. Stained-glass slogans say things like "I thank my God and ever shall, it is the sheep hath paid for all."

With the rise of cotton and the Industrial Revolution, the woolen industry collapsed. Ba-a-a-ad news. The wealthy Cotswold towns fell into a depressed time warp, so poor that nobody even bothered to knock them down. Today visitors enjoy a harmonious blend of man and nature—the most pristine of English countrysides decorated with time-passed villages, rich wool churches, tell-me-a-story stone fences, kissing gates you wouldn't want to experience alone, and the gracefully dilapidated homes of an impoverished nobility. Appreciated lately by hordes of 20th-century romantics, the Cotswolds are enjoying new prosperity.

Planning Your Time

The Cotswolds are an absolute delight by car and, with the new Cotswold Link bus, enjoyable even without a car. On a three-week British trip, I'd spend two nights and a day in the Cotswolds (sleeping in Chipping Campden or Stow-in-the-Wold). The Cotswolds' charm has a softening effect on many tight itineraries. You could spend days of enjoyable walking from a home base here.

One-day driver's 100-mile Cotswold blitz (includes Blenheim; use a good map; reshuffle to fit your home base): 9:00–Browse through Chipping Camden; 10:00–Joyride through Snowshill, Stanway, Stanton, Guiting Power, the Slaughters, and Bourton; 13:00–Lunch and explore Stow-on-the-Wold; 15:00– Drive 30 miles to Blenheim Palace, take the hour-long tour (last tour departs at 16:45); 18:00–Drive home for a pub dinner in home village.

Orientation

The north Cotswolds are best. Two of the region's coziest towns, Chipping Camden and Stow-on-the-Wold, are eight and four miles, respectively, from workaday Moreton, the only Cotswold town with a train station. Any of these three towns, now connected by the new Cotswold Link bus (running twice daily between Bath and Stratford), would make a fine home base for your exploration of the thatch-happiest of Cotswold villages and walks.

Cotswold Appreciation 101

Much history can be read into the names of the area. *Cotswold* could come from the Saxon phrase meaning "hills of sheeps' coats." Or it could mean shelter ("cot" like *cottage*) on the open upland ("wold").

In the Cotswolds, a town's main street (called High Street) needed to be wide to accommodate the sheep and cattle being marched to market (and today, to park tour buses). Some of the most picturesque cottages were once humble row houses of weavers' cottages, usually along a stream for their water wheels (Bibury, Castle Combe). The towns run on slow clocks and yellowed calendars. An entire village might not have a phone booth that accepts a telephone card.

Fields of yellow (rapeseed) and pale blue (linseed) separate pastures dotted with black and white sheep. In just about any B&B, when you open your window in the morning you'll hear sheep baa-ing. The decorative "toadstool" stones that litter front yards throughout the region are medieval staddle stones. Buildings were set upon these to keep the rodents out.

Cotswold walls and roofs are made of limestone. The limestone roof tiles hang by pegs. To make the weight more bearable, smaller, lighter tiles are higher up. An extremely strict building code keeps towns looking what many locals call "overly quaint."

The area is provincial and gossipy. People are ever so polite but commonly catch themselves saying, "It's all very... ummm... yyya." Rich people open their gardens to support their favorite charities, while—until recently—the less couth enjoyed "badger baiting" (a gambling cousin of cockfighting in which a badger, with his teeth and claws taken out, is mangled by right-wing dogs).

The Cotswolds

This is walking country. The English love their walks and vigorously defend their age-old right to free passage. Once a year the Rambling Society organizes a "Mass Trespass," when each of the country's 50,000 miles of public footpaths is walked. By assuring each path is used at least once a year, they stop landlords from putting up fences. Any paths found blocked are unceremoniously unblocked.

Questions to ask locals: Does badger-baiting survive? Do you approve of foxhunting with hounds? How has mad cow disease hurt the Cotswolds? Who are the Morris men? What's a kissing gate?

Getting around the Cotswolds

By Bus: A new Cotswold Link bus service runs twice daily in both directions between Bath and Stratford, making up to 13 stops en route and hitting the highlights of the Cotswolds, including Chipping Camden, Stow-on-the-Wold, and Moreton-in-Marsh. You

Cotswold Link X55 Bus Schedule*

From Bath to Stratford

Bath	10:00	14:30
Cirencester	11:24	15:54
Stow-on-the-Wold	12:15	16:45
Moreton-in-Marsh	12:30	17:00
Chipping Camden	13:05	17:35
Hidcote Manor	13:15	17:45
Stratford	13:40	18:10

From Stratford to Bath

Stratford	10:00	14:30
Hidcote Manor	10:22	14:52
Chipping Camden	10:33	15:00
Moreton-in-Marsh	11:09	15:40
Stow-on-the-Wold	11:22	15:52
Cirencester	12:07	16:37
Bath	13:40	18:10

Schedule from 1999, and not all stops are included.

can use this service to day trip from Bath to visit one Cotswold town, as transportation through the Cotswolds (stopping where you like for an overnight), or to day trip from a Cotswold town to see Stratford. A Bath–Stratford ticket costs £7 one way (buy on bus; you can break journey within the same day; arrive early at bus stop and keep alert, stops are quick; Badgerline tel. 01225/ 464-446). Several other bus companies make different runs to different towns; if the Cotswold Link bus doesn't suit your plans, ask for other bus schedules at any local TI.

By Bike: In Moreton-in-Marsh, Country Lanes Cycle Centre rents 21-speed bikes for £14 a day and offers bike tours (Easter– Oct Tue–Sun 9:00–17:00, helmets included, at train station, reserve ahead, tel. 01608/650-065, www.countrylanes.co.uk). In Chipping Camden, try Cotswolds Cycles (£10/day, daily 9:00–dusk, helmets included, delivery for a fee, Longlands Farm Cottage, tel. 01386/438-706, cell phone 0850-354-353).

By Foot: Walking guidebooks abound, giving you a world of choices for each of my recommended stops. Villages are generally no more than three miles apart, and most have pubs that would love to feed and water you. For guided walks, ask at any TI for the free quarterly booklet *Guided Walks & Events in the Cotswolds* or call 01285/643-643 for information.

By Car: Several car-rental companies offer one-day rentals from £25 including everything but gas; figure £5 for a taxi or delivery to just about anywhere in the Cotswolds (Robinson's, near Moreton, tel. 01608/661-681; or Paxford Garage near Chipping Camden, tel. 01386/700-814). Offices are closed Saturday afternoon and Sunday.

Car hiking is great. Distances are minuscule. In this chapter, I cover the postcard-perfect (but discovered) villages. With a car and the local Ordnance Survey map you can easily ramble about and find your own gems. The problem with having a car is that you are less likely to hike. Try to taxi or bus somewhere so you can hike back to your car and enjoy the scenery.

By Taxi: Two or three taxi trips can make more sense than renting a car. While taking a cab cross-country seems extravagant at £1.20 per mile, the distances are short (Stow–Moreton is 4 miles, Stow–Chipping Campden is 10), and one-way walks are lovely.

By Tour: From Bath, take a Mad Max tour to Castle Combe, the charming southernmost Cotswold town (book by calling 01225/465-674) or try Danwood Tour's City Safari tours (personalized tours available, tel. 01373/465-965). From Stratford, catch the Guide Friday tour (£17, Apr–Oct daily 13:45–17:15, drive through 15 villages and stop briefly in Stanton, Chipping Campden, and Stow, depart from Civic Hall near Market Square, buy tickets at Guide Friday office in Civic Hall, tel. 01789/294-466).

John Hopkins, who offers Secret Cotswolds tours, will take you on a six-hour tour tailored to your interests: churches, silver work, thatching, castles, and so on, with a pub stop at lunch (£70 for two people, can take up to seven, persons 3–7 each pay £10 extra, lunch and admissions not included, half-day tours possible, tel. 01451/810-212, e-mail: lcarter123@aol.com).

Sights—North Cotswolds

▲▲**Chipping Campden**—Ten miles north of Stow-on-the-Wold and less touristy, Chipping Campden is a working market town, home of some incredibly beautiful thatched roofs and the richest Cotswold wool merchants. Both the great British historian Trevelyan and I call Chipping Campden's High Street the finest in England.

Walk the full length of High Street (its width is characteristic of market towns) and around the block on both ends. On one end you'll find impressively thatched homes (out Sheep Street, past the public WC and ugly gas station, and right on Westington Street). Walking north on High Street you'll pass the Market Hall (built in 1627), the wavy roof of the first great wool mansion (the house of William Grevel, from 1380, on left), a fine and free memorial garden (on right), and, finally, the town's famous 15th-century Perpendicular "wool" church, down Church Street.

Chipping Campden's TI is opposite the town hall on High Street (daily 10:00–17:30, 10p town maps, tel. 01386/841-206). Stop by the Guild of Handicrafts Museum on Sheep Street for an endearing look at Cotswold crafts from the late 1800s (downstairs) to today (upstairs; watch silversmithing in action weekdays but not weekends). For accommodations, see "Sleeping," below.

Stanton, Snowshill, and Guiting Power—Located between Chipping Camden and Stow, these are my nominations for the cutest Cotswold villages. Like marshmallows in hot chocolate, they nestle side by side, awaiting your arrival.

▲▲**Stanway House**—Stanway is notable for its manor house. Lord Neidpath, whose family tree charts relatives back to 1270, occasionally opens his melancholy home to visitors (£3, Aug–Sept Tue and Thu 14:00–17:00, tel. 01386/584-469). The 14th-century Tithe Barn predates the manor and was originally where monks—in the days before money—would accept one-tenth of whatever the peasants produced. Peek inside—this is a great hall for village hoedowns.

While the Tithe Barn is no longer used to greet motley peasants with their feudal "rents," the lord still collects rents from his vast landholdings. But the place feels musty and poor, even though the lord has recently remarried.

Ask the ticket taker (inside) to demonstrate the spinning rent-collection table. In the great hall marvel at the one-piece oak shuffleboard table and the 1780 Chippendale exercise chair (half an hour of bouncing on this was considered good for the liver).

The manor dogs have their own cutely painted "family tree," but Lord Neidpath admits that his current dog, CJ, is "all character and no breeding." The place has a story to tell. And so do the docents stationed in each room—modern-day peasants who, even without family trees, probably have relatives going back just as far in this village. Really. Talk to these people. Probe. Learn what you can about this side of England.

To get to Stanway, leave the B4077 at a statue of (Christian) George slaying the dragon (of pagan superstition); you'll round the corner and see the manor's fine 17th-century Jacobean gatehouse.

Stanway and Stanton are separated by a great oak forest and grazing land, with parallel waves echoing the furrows plowed by medieval farmers. Centuries ago, farmers were allotted long strips of land (called a "furlong"—an attempt to dole out good and bad land equitably). Over centuries of plowing these furrows were formed. Let someone else drive so you can sit on the roof under a canopy of oaks as you pass stone walls and sheep. The first building outside Stanway (on the left) is a thatched cricket pavilion overlooking the village cricket green. Dating only from 1930, it's raised up on rodent-resistant staddle stones, like in the Middle Ages. Stanton's just ahead.

▲▲**Stanton**—Pristine Cotswold charm cheers visitors down this village's main street. Stanton's Church of St. Michael betrays a pagan past. It's safe to assume any church dedicated to St. Michael (the archangel who fought the devil) sits upon a sacred pagan site. Stanton is actually at the intersection of two ley lines (lines of prehistoric sights). You'll see St. Michael's well-worn figure (with a sundial) above the door as you enter. Inside, above the capitals in the nave, find the pagan symbols for the sun and the moon. While the church probably dates back to the ninth century, today's building is mostly 15th century with 13th-century transepts. On the north transept, medieval frescoes weakly show through the 17th-century whitewash. (Once upon a time, medieval frescos were considered too "papist.") Imagine the church interior colorfully decorated throughout. There's original medieval glass behind the altar. The list of rectors (left side wall) goes back to 1269. Finger the grooves in the back pews, worn away by sheepdog leashes. A man's sheepdog accompanied him everywhere.

▲**Snowshill Manor**—Another nearly edible little bundle of cuteness, Snowshill has a photogenic triangular square with a fine pub at its base. The Snowshill Manor is a dark and mysterious old palace filled with the lifetime collection of Charles Paget Wade. It's one big, musty celebration of craftsmanship, from finely carved spinning wheels to frightening samurai armor to tiny elaborate figurines carved by prisoners from the bones of meat served at dinner. Taking seriously his family motto, "Let Nothing Perish," Wade dedicated his life and fortune to preserving things finely crafted. The house (whose management made me promise not to promote it as an eccentric collector's pile of curiosities) really shows off Mr. Wade's ability to recognize and acquire fine examples of craftsmanship. It's all very...ummm...yyya. The manor overlooks the town square, but, ridiculously—to stoke business for the overpriced manor shop 300 yards away—there's no direct access from the town square (£6, Apr–Oct Wed–Mon 13:00–17:00, closed Tue and off-season, car park and shop are a pleasant 500-yard walk from the house, tel. 01386/852-410).

Broadway—This very crowded town is worth a drive-through but not a stop. There won't be a parking place anyway (a couple of miles west of Chipping Camden).

▲**Hidcote Manor**—If you like gardens, the grounds around this manor house are worth a look. Garden designers here pioneered the notion of creating a series of outdoor "rooms," each with a unique theme and separated by a yew-tree hedge. Follow your nose through a clever series of small gardens that lead delightfully from one to the next. Among the best in England, Hidcote gardens are at their fragrant peak in May, June, and July (£5.60, Apr–Oct 11:00–19:00, always closed Fri, also closed Tue except in June and July, last entrance 18:00, four miles northeast of Chipping Campden, tel. 01386/438-333).

Sights—Central Cotswolds

▲▲**Stow-on-the-Wold** (which means "meeting place on the uplands") has become a crowded tourist town. Most of these tourists, however, are day-trippers, so even summer nights are peaceful. Stow has no real sights other than itself, some good pubs, cutesy shops, and art galleries draped seductively around a big town square. A visit to Stow is not complete until you've locked your partner in the stocks on the green. At the TI on the main square, get the handy little 25p walking-tour brochure called *Town Trail* (Mon–Sat 9:30–17:30, Sun 10:30–16:00; off-season Mon–Sat 9:30–16:30, closed Sun). The TI also books tickets for events (Stratford plays) and rooms for a £1.50 fee (save money and book direct). For accommodations, see "Sleeping," below. You can generally find a parking spot on the main square (free for two hours).

▲**Moreton-in-Marsh**—This workaday town is like Stow or Chipping Campden without the touristic sugar. Rather than gift and antique shops you'll find streets lined with real shops: ironmongers selling cottage nameplates and carpet shops strewn with the remarkable patterns that decorate B&B floors. A traditional market with 260 stalls filling High Street gets the town shin-kicking each Tuesday as it has for the last 400 years (8:00–16:00). There is an economy outside of tourism in the Cotswolds, and you'll feel it here. Moreton has a tiny, sleepy train station two blocks from High Street (office open Mon–Sat 6:15–13:00), lots of bus connections, and an unusually proficient—for the Cotswolds—tourist information office (Mon–Fri 9:00–17:00, Thu 9:00–19:30, offers £1 luggage check, ticket booking, rail and bus schedules, racks of flyers, possible Internet access in 2000, tel. 01608/650-881). For accommodations, see "Sleeping," below.

Bourton-on-the-Water—I can't figure out if they call this "the Venice of the Cotswolds" because of its quaint canals or its miserable crowds. If you can avoid the midday and weekend crowds, it's worth a drive-through, a few cynical comments, and maybe a short stop. It's easiest to enjoy after dark. The Motor Museum shows off a lifetime's accumulation of vintage cars, old lacquered signs, a village life exhibit, threadbare toys, and prewar memorabilia (£2.25, daily 10:00–18:00, in the Old Mill facing the town center, tel. 01451/821-255). Bourton is four miles south of Stow and a mile from the Slaughters.

Upper and Lower Slaughter—Lower Slaughter is a classic village, with ducks, a working watermill, and usually an artist busy at her easel somewhere. Just behind the skippable Old Mill Museum, two kissing gates lead to the path that goes to nearby Upper Slaughter. In Upper Slaughter walk between the yew trees (sacred in pagan days) down a lane between the raised graveyard (a buildup of centuries of graves) to the peaceful church. In the back of the fine graveyard, a wistful woman looks over the tomb of an

18th-century rector (sculpted by his son). By the way, "Slaughter" has nothing to do with lamb chops. It comes from the sloe tree (the one used to make sloe gin). From June through August, Guide Friday buses do a handy 35-minute loop from Bourton to Upper and Lower Slaughter (£4, hrly in summer, handy for hikers who'd like to hop off here and on there). These towns are an easy one-hour round-trip walk from Bourton. You could also walk from Bourton through the Slaughters to Stow. The small roads from Upper Slaughter to Ford and Kineton are some of England's most scenic.

Sights—South Cotswolds

▲**Cirencester**—Nearly 2,000 years ago, Cirencester (pron. SIGH-ren-sester) was the ancient Roman city of Corinium. It's 20 miles from Stow down A429, which was called Foss Way in Roman times. In Cirencester (towns ending in "cester" were Roman camps), stop by the Corinium Museum to find out why they say, "If you scratch Gloucestershire, you'll find Rome" (£2.50, Apr–Oct Mon–Sat 10:00–17:00, Sun 14:00–17:00, closed Mon off-season). Cirencester's church is the largest of the Cotswolds "wool" churches. The cutesy Brewery Art crafts center and workshops entertain visitors with traditional weaving and potting in action, an interesting gallery, and a good coffee shop. Monday and Friday are general market days, Tuesday is cattle market day, and Saturday is a craft market unless it's the fifth Saturday in a month (TI tel. 01285/654-180).

▲**Bibury**—Six miles northeast of Cirencester, this is an entertaining but money-grubbing and not-very-friendly village with a trout farm, a Cotswolds museum, a stream teeming with fat trout and proud ducks, a row of very old weavers' cottages, and a church surrounded by rosebushes, each tended by a volunteer of the parish. Don't miss the scenic Coln Valley drive from A429 to Bibury through the enigmatic villages of Coln St. Dennis, Coln Rogers, Coln Powell, and Winson.

▲▲▲**Blenheim Palace**—Too many palaces can send you into a furniture-wax coma. Visiting one is enough … as long as it's Blenheim. The Duke of Marlborough's home, the largest in England, is still lived in. And that's wonderfully obvious as you prowl through it. (Note: Americans who pronounce the place "blen-HEIM" are the butt of jokes. It's "BLEN-em.")

John Churchill, first duke of Marlborough, beat the French at the Battle of Blenheim in 1704. So the king built him this nice home, perhaps the finest Baroque building in England. Ten dukes of Marlborough later, it's as impressive as ever. The 2,000-acre yard, well designed by "Capability" Brown, is as impressive to some as the palace itself. The view just past the outer gate as you enter is a classic. (The current 11th Duke considers the 12th more of an error than an heir, and what to do about him is quite an issue.)

The well-organized palace tour begins with a fine Churchill exhibit centered around the bed in which Sir Winston was born in 1874 (prematurely... while his mother was at a Blenheim Palace party). Take your time in the Churchill exhibit. Then catch the guided tours (5/hrly, 1 hr, included with ticket, £8.50, family rates, CC:VM, mid-Mar–Oct 10:30–17:30, last tour at 16:45, gardens open year-round, tel. 01993/811-325).

For a more extensive visit, follow up the general tour with a 30-minute guided walk through the actual private apartments of the duke. Tours leave on the top and bottom of each hour (£4, 12:00–16:30, tickets are limited, buy from table in library— last room of main tour, enter in corner of courtyard to left of grand palace entry).

Kids enjoy the pleasure garden (a tiny train takes you from the palace parking lot to the garden, but if you're driving it's more efficient simply to drive there). A lush and humid greenhouse flutters with butterflies. A kid zone (£1) includes a few second-rate games and the "world's largest symbolic hedge maze." The maze is worth a look if you haven't seen one and could use some exercise. Another £1 buys you a rowboat for a half hour.

Churchill fans can visit his tomb, a short walk away, in the Bladon town churchyard. The train station nearest Blenheim Palace (Hanborough, 1.5 miles away) has no taxi or bus service. Your easiest train connection is to Oxford; then take a bus to Blenheim (from the Oxford train station it's a 5-minute walk to Gloucester Green bus station, then catch bus #20a, #20b, or #20c to the palace gate, 2/hrly, 30–40 min; Oxford TI: tel. 01865/726-871).

Blenheim Palace sits at the edge of the cute cobbled town of Woodstock. The grandmotherly Wishaw House B&B rents two big and comfortable rooms in a humble old house a five-minute walk from the palace (Db-£40, 2 Browns Lane, 0X20 1ST, tel. 01993/811-343).

Sleeping and Eating in the Cotswolds
(£1 = about $1.70)
Sleep Code: **S** = Single, **D** = Double/Twin, **T** = Triple, **Q** = Quad, **b** = bathroom, **t** = toilet only, **s** = shower only, **CC** = Credit Card (Visa, MasterCard, Amex).

Sleeping in Chipping Campden
Sandalwood House B&B is a big, comfy, modern home with a royal lounge and a sprawling back garden. Just a five-minute walk from the center of town, it's in a quiet, woodsy, pastoral setting. Its two cheery pastel rooms are bright and spacious (D-£43–47, family deals, nonsmoking, GL55 6AU, tel. & fax 01386/840-091, well run by Diana Bendall). Head south on High Street; at the

011-44

church and Volunteer Inn turn right and right again; look for the sign in the hedge on your left, then head up the long driveway.

Kettle House B&B has four comfortable rooms (named by colors) above a furniture store in a 17th-century building. The sitting room and small deck have a lovely view. The hosts will pack picnic lunches for £6.50, make £12.50 dinners, and offer historical talks on the Cotswolds for £6 per person (Db-£50–55, CC:VM, nonsmoking, near old church, High Street, Leysbourne, GL55 6HN, tel. 01386/840-328, fax 01386/841-740, www.kettlehouse .co.uk, run by gracious Charles and Susie Holdsworth Hunt).

Dragon House B&B has two tight and tidy rooms right on the center of High Street, with parking and a fine garden (Db-£47, near market hall, tel. & fax 01386/840-734, Valerie).

Taplins' B&B, a fine 100-year-old house a five-minute walk from the town center, rents a tastefully decorated double and twin, each with antique furniture and a fireplace (D-£42 with this book, nonsmoking, farm views, garden access, easy parking, 5 Aston Road, GL55 6HR, tel. 01386/840-927, Rachel Hall).

Sparlings B&B, grandfather-clock tidy (perhaps similarly musty) and run by the very proper Mr. Douglass, is a not-quite-cramped 17th-century townhouse with a newly added conservatory (D-£50, Db-£53, nonsmoking, High Street, GL55 6HL, tel. 01386/840-505, fax 01386/841-676).

Badgers Hall Tea Room and B&B has three cozy medieval attic rooms (Db-£45–50, nonsmoking, center of High Street, tel. 01386/840-839, Karen Pinfold).

Noel Arms Hotel is the characteristic old hotel on the main square that has been welcoming guests for 600 years. Its lobby is decorated with armor, guns, and heraldry; its medieval air is infused with complex, but not unpleasant, odors; and its 26 rooms have top-quality furnishings (Sb-£80, Db-£110, CC:VM, some ground-floor doubles, attached restaurant/bar, High Street, GL55 6AT, tel. 01386/840-317, fax 01386/841-136).

Holly House, a mile out of town, has three spacious rooms in a newish-style house, plus laundry service (Sb-£26, Db-£39–43, parking, Ebrington 6L55 6NL, tel. 01386/593-213, fax 01386/ 593-181, Mrs. Hutsby).

Lygon Arms Hotel in town is borderline dumpy but likely to have space when all else fails (D-£45, Db-£55, CC:VMA, High Street, tel. 01386/840-318).

Eating in Chipping Campden

Huxley's (in town center on High Street) and **Eight Bells** (near church, just off High Street) are popular with locals. **Volunteer Inn** serves decent and smoky pub grub (Park Road). In the Cotswolds House Hotel, the **Forbes Brasserie** (skip the formal restaurant) has good food, quick service, and vintage Cotswolds

photos on its walls (12:00–20:00). **Lygon Pub** serves old English…
"cuisine" (not quite the right word). **Alexio's,** a reputable Greek
restaurant on High Street, breaks dishes at closing every Saturday
night (closed Sunday to clean up, tel. 01386/840-826). In Broad
Campden, a mile out of Chipping Camden, vegetarians and carnivores alike flock to the **Baker's Arms** for dinner (daily 12:00–
14:00, 18:00–21:00, can be smoky and crowded, slow service,
indoor/outdoor seating, live folk music every third Tuesday,
tel. 01386/840-515). Since things change constantly, it's important
to take your B&B host's pub-grub advice seriously.

Sleeping near Chipping Campden
A tiny village locally famous for its Baker's Arms pub, Broad
Campden has several very well-run B&Bs (one mile from Chipping Campden—addresses unnecessary, you'll see the signs, zip
code: GL55 6UR). Janet Rawling's **Marnic House B&B** is in a
delightful 150-year-old stone cottage with a cozy living room,
three well-appointed rooms, and a prize-winning garden (Db-£42,
more for one-nighters, nonsmoking, easy parking, tel. 01386/840-
014, fax 01386/840-441). June Wadey's **Wyldlands** is a comfortable modern house with a breezy, relaxing mini-Hidcote of a
garden (Db-£42, Db-£40 for 3 nights, nonsmoking, can loan
maps, tel. 01386/840-478, fax 01386/849-031).

    Pond House, three miles from Chipping Camden, has four
tidy, large rooms and a conservatory with countryside views
(Db-£48, nonsmoking, Bretforton, WR11 5QA, near Evesham,
tel. 01386/831-687, fax 01386/831-558, www.smoothhound.co.uk
/hotels/pondhous.html, Anne and Ray Payne).

    Didbrook Fields Farm, near Broadway, offers four oak-
beamed suites in a restored 19th-century barn surrounded by a
40-acre environmental farm complete with a wildflower meadow,
a riding stable (horses available) and an indoor saltwater pool—available unless swimming lessons are in session (Db-from £65, cheaper
for 3-night stays, 7 miles west of Chipping Camden, Toddington,
GL54 5PE, tel. 01242/620-950, Frank and Jane Kennedy).

Sleeping in Stow-on-the-Wold (tel. code: 01451)
The **Old Stocks Hotel** is the best hotel value in town, with 18
big, comfy rooms in a classy historic building facing the town
square. It's family run but professional as can be (Db-£75
promised through 2000 with this book, CC:VM, The Square,
Stow-on-the-Wold, GL54 1AF, tel. 01451/830-666, fax
01451/870-014, Alan and Julie Rose).

    Stow Lodge Hotel, on the town square in its own sprawling
and peaceful garden, offers 21 large, thoughtfully appointed rooms
and stately public spaces (Sb-£70–85, Db-£85–100, higher on
Saturday and holidays, CC:VM, closed January, The Square,

GL54 1AB, tel. 01451/830-485, fax 01451/831-671, www
.stowlodge.com, Chris Hartley).

West Deyne B&B, with two homey rooms, a peaceful garden,
a fountain, and a small conservatory overlooking the countryside,
has a comforting grandmotherly charm. This is a super place
(D-£35, evening tea and biscuits, Lower Swell Road, GL54 1LD,
tel. 01451/831-011, run by thoughtful Joan Cave).

The Pound is the quaint, restored 500-year-old heavy-
beamed home of Patricia Whitehead. She offers two bright,
inviting twin-bedded rooms and a classic old fireplace lounge
(S-£25, D-£36, nonsmoking, downtown on Sheep Street, GL54
1AU, tel. 01451/830-229).

Rosemary Quinn's B&B, on a peaceful cul-de-sac two
blocks off the main square in a tidy modern building, rents two
no-nonsense, comfy rooms (S-£18, D-£36, nonsmoking, 22 Glebe
Close, GL54 1DJ, tel. 01451/830-042).

Top of the Wold B&B rents three spacious and well-
appointed rooms that overlook Stow's market square from
the third floor of a furniture shop (Db-£48, nonsmoking,
CC:VM, across from Queen's Head pub, tel. 01451/870-364,
fax 01451/870717, e-mail: topofthewold@btinternet.com, warmly
run by Bob Whittock).

Tall Trees B&B, on the Oddington Road at the edge of Stow,
rents three modern rooms in an old-style building overlooking a
farm (Db-£50, tel. 01451/831-296, fax 01451/870-049, Jennifer).

The **Limes B&B** has four pleasant rooms in a Victorian
home two blocks out of town on the Evesham Road (D-£36,
Db-£41, tel. & fax 01451/830-034, friendly Helen and Graham).

Cross Keys Cottage, offering three thoughtfully decorated
rooms in a lovingly maintained 350-year-old beamed cottage, is a
cover-girl B&B (D with private bath in hall-£42–45, Db-£48–52,
Park Street, GL54 1AQ, tel. 01451/831-128, Margaret and Roger
Welton).

The **Beeches** has two fine rooms and congenial hosts (D-£40,
nonsmoking, near town center, Fosse Lane, GL54 1EH, tel.
01451/870-836, Ken and Marian Wilson).

The **Stow-on-the-Wold Youth Hostel,** on Stow's main
square, has been completely renovated. It has a friendly atmosphere, good hot meals, and a do-it-yourself members' kitchen
(£10.50 per bed with sheets, nonmembers £1.80 extra, 50 beds
in 9 rooms, some family 4-bed rooms, closed 10:00–17:00, no
lockers, CC:VM, reserve long in advance in summer, tel. 01451/
830-497, fax 01451/870-102).

Eating in Stow-on-the-Wold

The formal but friendly bar in the **Stow Lodge** serves fine £6
lunches and £8 dinners (daily 12:00–14:00, 19:00–21:00; their

Stow-on-the-Wold

TO EVESHAM, BROADWAY + CHIPPING CAMPDEN

TO MORETON IN MARSH, STRATFORD + WARWICK

TO UPPER SWELL

A.424
B-4077

10

N

HIGH ST

BUS STOP

PARSON'S CORNER

FOSSEWAY

WC

6 STOCKS

1

THE SQUARE

9

2

5

8

ELL LANE

CHURCH

INFO

DIGBETH

12

POST

4 B-4068

TO LOWER SWELL + GUITING POWER

SHEEP ST.

3

PARK ST.

13

11

7

WC

BACK WALLS

A-429

↓ TO BOURTON ON WATER + THE SLAUGHTERS

DCH

1 OLD STOCKS HOTEL
2 STOW LODGE HOTEL
3 THE POUND B&B
4 WEST DEYNE B&B
5 ROSEMARY QUINN'S B&B
6 TOP OF THE WOLD B&B
7 TALL TREES B&B
8 STOW YOUTH HOSTEL
9 QUEEN'S HEAD PUB
10 LIMES B&B
11 CROSS KEYS COTTAGE
12 FOX INN PUB
13 PRINCE OF INDIA

pricier restaurant serves £17 dinners). Next door, the more pub-esque **Queen's Head** serves an inexpensive decent meal and the local Cotswold brew, Donnington Ale (daily 11:00–14:30, 18:00–23:00). Locals like the **Talbot Inn** for lunch (at south end of square, tel. 01451/830-631). Consider **The Prince of India** for Indian food (nightly 18:00–23:30, CC:VM, Park Street) or the nearby **Fox Inn** for English food (daily 11:00–15:00, 17:30–21:30, Digbeth Street, tel. 01451/831-609).

Those with a car are likely to eat well at any of these pubs (all near Stow): **Plough Pub** in Ford, **King's Head** in Bledington (moderately priced, closed Sun), **Churchill Arms** at Paxford, **The Plough** in Cold Aston (a 10-minute drive from Stow), or **The Fox** in Oddington (two miles from Stow).

Sleeping near Stow-on-the-Wold
Holmleigh B&B, in a farmhouse in the nearby hamlet of Donnington, rents two rooms, the cheapest around (D-£28, tel. 01451/830-792, Mrs. Garbett).

Fairview Farmhouse B&B feels more like a countryside mansion than a farmhouse. It's regally situated a mile outside Stow, and its six rooms come with all the thoughtful touches (Db-£45, deluxe Db-£50, nonsmoking, just down Bledington Road, GL54 1JH, tel. & fax 01451/830-279, Susan and Andrew Davis).

Guiting Guest House, six miles west of Stow in the tiny village of Guiting Power, is my favorite sleepy-village alternative. Kindly Mrs. Yvonne Sylvester rents five modern, delightful doily rooms in her 400-year-old house. It's a winner (Sb-£30, Db-£53, CC:VM, Post Office Lane, Guiting Power, Cheltenham, GL54 5TZ, tel. 01451/850-470, fax 01451/850-034, www.information -britain.co.uk/bandbs/guiting/). If you're tired of pub grub, Yvonne serves a fine home-cooked dinner with the works for £17. Guiting Power is a great base for walking excursions.

The **Vine B&B,** eight miles west of Stow in the postcard-pretty village of Stanton, is another idyllic hideaway. This classic Cotswolds home, run by Jill Gabb, is a block from the Stanton church. Jill's passion is horse riding. She rents horses by the hour (4 rooms, Db-£45, CC:VM, most rooms with 4-poster beds, WR12 7NE, tel. 01386/584-250, fax 01386/584-385).

Sleeping in Moreton-in-Marsh (tel. code: 01608)

A handy self-serve laundrette is a block in front of the train station on New Road (Laundercentre, Mon–Fri 7:30–20:00).

Townend Cottage and Coach House is a fun 17th-century English-style hacienda enthusiastically run by Chris and Jenny Gant. Two large rooms are in the main building, and two smaller rooms, including the upstairs treehouse, are across the courtyard (Sb-£32–35, D/Db-£38–45, less off-season, nonsmoking, big garden, good breakfast, attached tearoom; near police station, supermarket, and park; end of High Street, GL56 0AD, tel. 01608/650-846, e-mail: chris.gant@talk21.com). The Gants will meet you at the train station.

The Cottage dates back to 1620 and has low ceilings, an inglenooky lounge, and lots of character (S-£30, D-£40; charming, pastel, open-beamed "annex cottage" in the garden: Db-£50; nonsmoking, two blocks from the station on Oxford Street, GL56 0LA, tel. & fax 01608/651-740, e-mail:lcarter123 @aol.com, Lorraine Carter). The twin is quieter and more spacious than the front double. I'd pay extra to sleep with Peter Rabbit in the garden. If the manager's off, the place can get a bit dingy with unvacuumed carpets.

Treetops B&B is plush, with six spacious, attractive rooms, a sun lounge, and a three-quarter-acre backyard (Db-£42–45, CC:VM, easy parking, set far back from the busy road, London Road, GL56 0HE, tel. & fax 01608/651-036, Liz and Brian Dean). It's a five-minute walk from town and an eight-minute walk from the railway station (exit station, keep left, go left over bridge over train tracks, look for sign, then long driveway).

Acacia B&B, with four tight but clean and cheery rooms on the third floor, is friendly and handy (S-£20, D-£36, Db-£40, less for longer stays and off-season, bunky family deals, nonsmoking, on a quiet lane between the train station and High Street, at New Road, GL56 0AS, tel. 01608/650-130, Dot and Mick Ellwood).

Blue Cedar House has four comfortable rooms, though the breakfast room is oddly plain. It's on a busy road but has double-paned windows and a pleasing setting, surrounded by a bright green half-acre garden (S-£21, D-£39, Db-£41, easy parking, five-minute walk from center, Stow Road, GL56 0DW, tel. 01608/650-299, Sandra and Graham Billinger).

Manor House Hotel is Moreton's most elegant hotel, dating from 1545 but sporting such modern amenities as an indoor pool (open year-round). Its 39 classy rooms and garden invite relaxation (Sb-£85, Db-£100, 4-poster bed Db-£135, family suite-£145, CC:VMA, elevator, car park, log fire in winter, attached Mulberry Restaurant, High Street, GL56 0LJ, tel. 01608/650-501, fax 01608/651-481).

Moreton House Guest House offers 11 basic rooms above an Old World lounge on the Stow end of High Street (S-£22, D-£42, Db-£48–52, CC:VM, High Street, GL56 0LQ, tel. 01608/650-747, fax 01608/652-747, run by the Dempster family).

Eating in Moreton-in-Marsh

A stroll up and down High Street lets you survey your small-town options. Consider the upscale but affordable **Marshmallow** (£8 entrees, 15 different teas, daily 10:00–17:00, Wed–Sun until 21:30, CC:VM, tel. 01608/651-536) or the **Black Bear Inn,** offering English food with a French accent (daily 12:00–14:00, 18:30–21:00, head to dining room on the left, not the smoky pub on the right, CC:VM, tel. 01608/650-705). The friendly **Hassan Balti,** with tasty Bangladeshi food, is a fine value for sit-down or takeout (daily 12:00–14:00, 18:00–23:30, tel. 01608/650-798). **Mermaid Fish** is popular for its take-out fish; **Ice 'n' Slice** on Oxford Street makes good sandwiches to go (Oxford Street); and the **Budgens** supermarket is indeed super (Mon–Fri 8:30–22:00, Sun 10:00–16:00, far end of High Street, near Townend Cottage). Across the busy street from the supermarket is pleasant Victoria Park with picnic tables.

Transportation Connections—Cotswolds

Your best bus option, sans car, is the Cotswold Link bus, which runs daily, including Sunday, between Stratford and Bath, stopping at Moreton, Chipping Camden, and Stow (see "Getting around the Cotswolds," above). Here are other bus possibilities (service gets sparse on Sunday):

Moreton by bus to: Chipping Camden and **Stratford** (6/day, same bus connects all three towns, Moreton–Chipping

Camden 20 min, Moreton–Stratford 1.25 hrs, Stratford Blue bus company, tel. 01789/292-630), **Circencester** via **Stow** and **Burton** (13/day, Moreton–Cirencester 1 hr, Moreton–Stow 10 min, on Stagecoach buses), **Cheltenham** (8/day, Moreton–Cheltenham 1 hr, with stops at a few untouristy towns, Pulham buses). Ask for specific schedules at a local TI; Moreton's TI has the most comprehensive.

　　Moreton by train to: London's Paddington Station (£19 one way, £18 round-trip after 8:00, 10/day, 1.75 hrs), **Heathrow** (2/hrly, 2.5 hrs, train to Reading, then RailAir Link shuttle bus to airport), **Bath** (10/day, 2.5 hrs, transfers at Oxford and Didcot Parkway; Cotswold Link bus is better), **Oxford** (10/day, 1.25 hrs), **Ironbridge Gorge** (3.5 hrs total, with train transfers at Worcester Forgate and Birmingham New Street, arrive Telford, take £7.50 cab or £1 bus seven miles to Ironbridge Gorge). Train info: tel. 0345-484-950.

　　Drivers' Tips: Distances are wonderfully short (but only if you invest in the Ordnance Survey map of the Cotswolds—sold locally everywhere): Moreton to Broadway (10 miles), Chipping Campden (8 miles), Stratford (17 miles), Warwick (23 miles), Stow (4 miles).

NEAR THE COTSWOLDS: STRATFORD, WARWICK, AND COVENTRY

Shakespeare's hometown, Stratford...to see or not to see? A walking tour with a play's the thing to bring the Bard to life in this touristy town. Explore Warwick, England's finest medieval castle, and stop by Coventry, a workaday town with a spirit that Nazi bombs couldn't destroy.

Planning Your Time

Stratford, Warwick, and Coventry are a made-to-order day for drivers connecting the Cotswolds with Ironbridge Gorge (IBG) or North Wales. While connections from the Cotswolds to IBG are tough, Stratford, Warwick, and Coventry are well served by public transportation.

　　Stratford is a classic tourist trap. But since you're passing through, it's worth a morning. (Don't spend the night.) Warwick is England's single most spectacular castle. It's very touristy but historic and fun for three hours. Lunch in Warwick town. Coventry, the least important stop on a quick trip, is most interesting as a chance to see a real, struggling, north-English industrial city (with some decent sightseeing).

　　The area is worth only a one-day drive-through. If you're speedy, hit all three sights. If you're more relaxed, do Stratford and Warwick and get to your Ironbridge Gorge B&B in time to enjoy the evening ambience of that more interesting stop.

Cotswolds to North Wales

STRATFORD-UPON-AVON

Stratford is the most overrated tourist magnet in England, but nobody back home would understand if you skipped Shakespeare's house. The old town is compact, with the TI and theater along the riverbank and Shakespeare's birthplace a few blocks off the river; you can walk easily to everything except Anne Hathaway's and Mary Arden's places. The river has an idyllic yet playful feel, with a park along the opposite bank, paddleboats, and an old, one-man, crank-powered ferry just beyond the theater.

Tourist Information: The TI has an American Express office and a town map that welcomes you in seven languages (Mon–Sat 9:00–18:00, Sun 11:00–17:00; Nov–Mar 9:00–17:00 and closed Sun, tel. 01789/293-127).

Sights—Stratford-upon-Avon

▲**Shakespeare's Birthplace**—This half-timbered Elizabethan building—entirely rebuilt in the 1900s—is furnished as it was when young William was growing up and is filled with bits about his life and work. This is most worthwhile if you get the attendants in each room talking. Ask questions. The attached Shakespeare exhibition gives a fine historical background.

While William Shakespeare (1564–1616) was born in this house, he spent most of his career in London, where he taught his play-going public about human nature with plots that entertained the highest and the lowest minds at the same time. His tool was an unrivaled mastery of the English language. He retired—rich and famous—back in Stratford, spending his last five years at "New Place."

Little is known about Shakespeare the man. The scope of his brilliant work, his humble beginnings, and the fact that no original Shakespeare manuscripts survive raise a few scholarly eyebrows. But while some wonder who penned all these plays, most scholars accept his authorship (£5, Mon–Sat 9:00–17:00, Sun 9:30–17:00, last admission an hour before closing; mid-Oct–mid-Mar Mon–Sat 9:30–16:00, Sun 10:00–16:00, in the town center, tel. 01789/204-016).

▲**Four Other Shakespeare Properties**—Shakespeare's hometown is blanketed with opportunities for "Bardolatry." There are four other "Shakespearian properties," all run by the Shakespeare Birthplace Trust, in and near Stratford. Each has a garden and helpful docents who love to tell a story. **Anne Hathaway's Cottage,** a mile out of town in Shottery, is a picturesque thatched 12-room farmhouse where the bard's wife grew up. It has little to do with Shakespeare but offers an intimate peek at lifestyles in Shakespeare's day. Guides in each room do their best to lecture to the stampeding hordes. **Mary Arden's House,** the girlhood home of William's mom, is in Wilmcote, about three miles from town. This 16th-century farmhouse sees far fewer tourists, so the guides in each room have a chance to do a little better guiding. A 19th-century farming exhibit and a falconry demonstration are on the grounds. **Hall's Croft,** the home of Shakespeare's daughter, who married a doctor, is in the town. This fine old Tudor house, the richest house of the group, is interesting only if you're into 16th-century medicine. **Nash's House,** where the Bard lived in retirement, is the least impressive of the properties. (Nash was the first husband of Shakespeare's granddaughter.) While Shakespeare's retirement home (New Place) is long gone, Nash's house has survived. It has the town's only general history exhibit—fascinating if you like chips of Roman pottery. All properties charge £3.50 to £4.50 each. Pilgrims save money buying combo tickets: £7.50 for three sights or £11 for all. (Anne Hathaway's Cottage has the same opening hours as Shakespeare's Birthplace; the other sights are open daily Mon–Sat 9:30–17:00, Sun 10:00–17:00; mid-Oct–mid-Mar Mon–Sat 10:00–16:00, Sun 10:30–16:00.) **Shakespeare's grave** is in the riverside Holy Trinity Church (a 10-minute walk past the theater).

Avon Riverfront—The River Avon is a playground with swans and canal boats. These canal boats, which saw their workhorse days during a short window of time between the start of the Industrial Revolution and the establishment of the railways, are now mostly pleasure boats. They are long and narrow, so two can pass in the narrow canals. There are 2,000 miles of canals here in the Midlands. These were built to connect centers of industry with seaports and provided vital transport during the early days of the Industrial Revolution.

▲▲**Guide Friday Bus Tours**—These open-top buses constantly make the rounds, allowing visitors to hop on and hop off at every sight in town. The full circuit takes about an hour and comes with a steady and informative live commentary (£8.50, buses leave from the TI every 15 minutes 9:30–17:30, every half-hour off-season, runs year-round, buy tickets on bus, tel. 01789/294-466).

Guide Friday offers longer tours of the Cotswolds (£17, 13:45–17:15, drive through 15 villages with brief stops in Stanton—15 min, Chipping Campden—20 min, and Stow—30 min, depart from Civic Hall near Market Square, buy tickets at Guide Friday office in Civic Hall, tel. 01789/294-466).

▲▲**Walking Tour**—A guided walk makes this historic but oversold town endearing. Mrs. Pat Bouverat gives a great 90-minute walk (from £20, tel. 01789/269-890).

▲▲**Royal Shakespeare Company**—The RSC, undoubtedly the best Shakespeare company on earth, splits its season between London (winter) and Stratford (summer). If you're a Shakespeare fan, see if the RSC schedule fits into your itinerary either here or in London. Tickets range from £5 to £49 (Mon–Sat at 19:30, Thu and Sat matinees at 13:30). You'll probably need to buy your tickets in advance, although 50 restricted-view and standing-room places are saved to be sold each morning (from 9:30, £5–10) and returned tickets can sometimes be picked up the evening of an otherwise-sold-out show (box office tel. 01789/295-623, Mon–Sat 9:00–20:00, closed Sun). If you have a car, Stow and Chipping Campden are only 30 minutes from Stratford and an evening of classy entertainment.

Theater tours are given most days (£4, 13:30 and 17:30, not on matinee days, tours also given after performances but booked in advance; Mon–Sat 9:15–18:00, Sun 11:30–16:00, tel. 01789/412-602). The theater sponsors Shakespeare's Life in Stratford walks on Thursdays and Saturdays at 10:30 (£5, 2 hrs).

Transportation Connections— Stratford-upon-Avon

To: London (£15, £18 round-trip, 4 trains/day, 2.5 hrs, direct from Paddington Station, maybe 9:18–11:30 or 11:18–13:25), **Chipping Camden** (6 buses/day, 60 min, on Stratford Blue bus, tel. 01789/292-630; plus 2 buses/day, 35 min, on Cotswold Link bus—

continues to Moreton, Stow, and Bath), **Warwick** (hrly, 15 min, by bus or train), **Coventry** (hrly buses, 1 hr, tel. 01788/535-555). There is a Stratford–Warwick–Cambridge bus service (£12, 3/day, 2.5 hrs, tel. 01223/423-900). Train info: tel. 0345-484-950.

Driving is easy: Stow to Stratford (20 miles), Warwick (8 miles), Coventry (10 miles).

WARWICK AND COVENTRY

▲▲Warwick Castle—England's finest medieval castle is almost too groomed and organized, giving its hordes of visitors a decent value for the steep £10.50 entry fee. This cash-poor but enterprising lord hired the folks at Madame Tussaud's to wring maximum tourist dollars out of the castle. The latest marketing strategy is to build up the "kingmaker" reputation of the Earl of Warwick (WAR-ick).

With a lush, green, grassy moat and fairy-tale fornifications, Warwick will entertain you from dungeon to lookout. Standing inside the castle gate, you can see the mound where the original Norman castle of 1068 stood. Under this "motte," the wooden stockade, or "bailey," defined the courtyard as the castle walls do today. The castle is a 14th- and 15th-century fortified shell holding an 18th- and 19th-century royal residence surrounded by another dandy "Capability" Brown landscape job.

There's something for every taste—a fine and educational armory, a terrible torture chamber, a knight in shining armor on a horse that rotates with a merry band of musical jesters, a Madame Tussaud re-creation of a royal weekend party with an 1898 game of statue-maker, a grand garden, and a peacock-patrolled, picnic-perfect park. The Great Hall and Staterooms are the sumptuous highlights. The "King Maker" exhibit (It's 1471 and the town's folk are getting ready for battle....) is highly promoted but not quite as good as a Disney ride. Be warned: The tower is a one-way, no-return, 250-step climb offering a view not worth a heart attack. The £2 CD-ROM audio tour provides 60 easy-listening minutes of number-coded descriptions of the individual rooms (rent from kiosk on the lane after the turnstile). The £3.25 guide-book gives you nearly the same script in souvenir booklet form. Either are worthwhile if you want to understand the various rooms. If you tour without its help, pick the brains of the earnest and talkative docents (£10.50, daily 10:00–18:00, Nov–Mar until 17:00, tel. 01926/406-600, 24-hour recorded message).

The Stables self-serve restaurant upstairs is much nicer than the cafeteria near the turnstiles. From the castle a lane leads into the old town center, a block away, where you'll find the TI (daily 9:30-16:30, tel. 01926/492-212), doll museum, county museum, and several pubs serving fine lunches.

▲Coventry's Cathedral—The Germans bombed Coventry to smithereens in 1940. From that point on, the German phrase for "to really blast the heck out of a place" was "to coventrate" it. But Coventry rose from its ashes, and its message to our world is one of forgiveness and reconciliation. The symbol of Coventry is the bombed-out hulk of its old cathedral with the huge new one adjoining it. The inspirational complex welcomes visitors. Climb the tower (180 steps). If you're touring the church, first go downstairs to see the 18-minute "Audiovisual Spectacle" on the cathedral's history (£1.25 for the movie, plus a requested £2 donation at the church door, Mon–Sat 10:00–16:00, closed Sun, tel. 02476/227-597).

Coventry's most famous hometown girl, Lady Godiva, rode bareback through the town in the 11th century to help lower taxes. You'll see her bronze statue a block from the cathedral (near Broadgate). Just beyond that is the Museum of British Road Transport—the first, fastest, and most famous cars and motorcycles came from this British "Detroit" (free, daily 10:00–17:00). Other sights include the Herbert Art Gallery and Museum, which cover the city's history (free, Mon–Sat 10:00–17:30, Sun 12:00–17:00), and St. Mary's Guildhall, with 14th-century tapestries, stained glass, and an ornate ceiling (free, Sun–Thu 10:00–16:00, closed if event scheduled). Browse through Coventry, the closest thing to normal workaday urban England you'll see. (TI tel. 02476/832-303.)

Route Tips for Drivers
Stratford to Ironbridge Gorge via Warwick and Coventry: Entering Stratford from the Cotswolds, you cross a bridge. Veer right (following "through traffic," "P," and "Wark" signs), go around the block, turning right and right and right over the speed humps, then enter the multistory garage (50p/hr, you'll find no place easier or cheaper). The TI and Guide Friday bus stop are a block away. Leaving the garage, circle to the right around the same block but stay on the "Wark" (Warwick, A439) road. Warwick is eight miles away. The castle is just south of town on the right. If the free castle lot is full, you'll be directed to a city lot. You might lurk across the street until someone leaves. After touring the castle, carry on through the center of Warwick, following signs to Coventry (still A439, then A46). If stopping in Coventry, follow signs painted on the road into the "city centre" and then to cathedral parking. Grab a place in the high-rise car park. Leaving Coventry, follow signs to Nuneaton and M6 North through lots of sprawl and you're on your way. If skirting Coventry, M69 (Leicester) leads to M6. M6 threads through giant Birmingham. Try to avoid the 14:00-to-20:00 rush hour (see Ironbridge Gorge chapter for tips). From M6 (northwest), take M54 to the Telford/Ironbridge exit. Following the Ironbridge signs, you do-si-do through a long series of roundabouts until you're there.

IRONBRIDGE GORGE

The Industrial Revolution was born in the Severn River Valley. In its glory days, this valley (blessed with abundant deposits of iron ore and coal and a river for transport) gave the world its first iron wheels, steam-powered locomotive, and cast-iron bridge. The museums in Ironbridge Gorge (IBG) take you back into the days when Britain was racing into the modern age and pulling the rest of the West with her.

Planning Your Time

Without a car, IBG isn't worth the headache. Drivers can slip it in between the Cotswolds/Stratford/Warwick and North Wales. For a short, reasonable visit, arrive in the early evening to browse the town and spend the morning and early afternoon touring the sights before driving on to North Wales (10:00–Museum of the Gorge, 11:00–Blists Hill Victorian Town for lunch and sightseeing, 15:30–Drive to Wales).

Speed demons zip in for a midday tour of Blists Hill, look at the bridge, and speed out. With a month in Britain I'd spend two nights and a leisurely day: 9:30–Iron Bridge and the town, 10:30–Museum of the Gorge, 11:30–Coalbrookdale Museum of Iron, 14:30–Blists Hill, dinner at Coalbrookdale Inn.

Orientation (tel. code: 01952)

The town is just a few blocks gathered around the Iron Bridge, which spans the peaceful, tree-lined Severn River. While the smoke-belching bustle is long gone, knowing that this wooded, sleepy river valley was the Silicon Valley of the 19th century makes wandering its brick streets almost a pilgrimage. The actual museum sites are scattered over three miles. The modern cooling towers (for coal, not nuclear energy) that loom ominously over these red-brick remnants seem strangely appropriate.

Tourist Information: The TI is a block downhill from the Iron Bridge (Mon–Fri 9:00–17:00, Sat–Sun 10:00–17:00, room-finding service, tel. 01952/432-166). The TI has lots of booklets for sale; hikers like the home-grown *Walks in the Severn Gorge* (8 walks, £1) or the farther-ranging *Ten Walks That Changed the World* (£6).

Bike Rental: The nearest is Wenlock Bike Hire in Much Wenlock (£12/day, free delivery to IBG, helmets available, tours, 3 Sheinton Street, tel. 01952/727-089, Geoff and Mandy).

Sights—Ironbridge Gorge

▲▲**Iron Bridge**—This first iron bridge was built in 1779, while England was at war with her American colonies, to show off a wonderful new building material. Lacking experience with iron, the builders erred on the side of sturdiness and constructed it as if it was made out of wood. The valley's centerpiece is free, open all the time, and thought provoking. Walk across the bridge to the toll booth/gift shop/free museum. Read the fee schedule and notice the subtle slam against royalty (England was not immune to the revolutionary sentiment brewing in the colonies at this time). Pedestrians paid half a penny to cross (poor people crossed cheaper by coracle—a crude tublike wood-and-canvas shuttle ferry). Cross back to the town and walk downstream along the towpath; near the bridge, peek through the dirty cracked windows of a riverside shack to glimpse a couple of these coracles.

▲▲▲**Ironbridge Gorge Industrial Revolution Museums**— This group of widely scattered sites has varied admission charges (usually £2–4.50; Blists Hill is £6.80). The £9.50 Passport ticket (£29 for families) gets you into all the sights, which all have the same hours (Apr–Oct daily 10:00–17:00; from Nov–Mar, a few Coalbrookdale sights close, Blists Hill's hours are Sat–Wed 10:00–16:00, closed Thu–Fri, tel. 01952/433-522 or 01952/432-166, www.vtel.co.uk/igmt). Even though several of the sights may not be worth your time, seeing Blists Hill Victorian Town, the Museum of the Gorge, and the Coalbrookdale Museum of Iron costs £13.50 without the Passport ticket.

Museum of the Gorge: Orient yourself to the valley here in the Severn Warehouse (£2, daily 10:00–17:00, 500 yards upstream from the bridge, pay £1 to park). See the eight-minute introductory movie, check out the exhibit and the model of the gorge in its heyday, and buy a Blists Hill guidebook and Passport ticket. From the parking lot, a tiny tour boat sometimes does a 45-minute round-trip Severn River tour (£3.50, look for sign near WC, slow-moving taped commentary, peaceful photo opportunity for

Ironbridge Gorge

bridge and lazy fishermen along riverbanks, tel. 01952/418-844).
Farther upstream is the fine riverside Dale End Park, with picnic
areas and a playground.

Blists Hill Victorian Town: Save most of your time and
energy for this wonderful town. You'll wander through 50 acres
of Victorian industry, factories, and a re-created community from
the 1890s, complete with carriage rides, chemists, a candy shop,
an ancient dentist's chair, candlemakers, a working pub, a green-
grocer's shop, a fascinating squatter's cottage, and a snorty, slip-
pery pigsty. Don't miss the explanation of the winding machine at
the Blists Hill Mine (first demonstration usually at 11:15, confirm
at entry). Walk along the canal to the "inclined plane." Grab lunch
in the Victorian Pub or the cafeteria near the squatter's cottage
and old-time children's rides. The board by the entry lists which
exhibits are staffed and lively (with docents in Victorian dress).
The £2 Blists Hill guidebook gives a good step-by-step rundown
(£7, tel. 01952/583-003).

Coalbrookdale Museum of Iron: This does a fine job of
explaining the original iron-smelting process (£4.50, opposite
Darby's furnace—see below).

The Coalbrookdale neighborhood is the birthplace of the Industrial Revolution. Abraham Darby's blast furnace sits like a shrine inside a big glass pyramid (free), surrounded by the evocative Industrial Age ruins. This is where, in 1709, Darby first smelted iron using coke as fuel. If you're like me, "coke" is a drink, and "smelt" is the past tense of smell.... Nevertheless, this event kicked off the modern Industrial Age.

All the ingredients of the recipe for big industry were here in abundance—iron ore, top-grade coal, and water for power and shipping. Wander around Abraham Darby's furnace. Before this furnace was built, iron ore was laboriously melted by charcoal. With a huge waterwheel-powered billows, Darby burned top-grade coal super hot (burning off the impurities to make "coke"). Local iron ore was dumped into the furnace and melted. Impurities floated to the top, while the pure iron sank to the bottom of a clay tub in the bottom of the furnace. Twice a day the plugs were knocked off, allowing the "slag" to drain away on the top and the molten iron to drain out on the bottom. The low-grade slag was used locally on walls and paths. The high-grade iron trickled into molds formed in the sand below the furnace. It cooled into pig iron (named because the molds look like piglets suckling their mother). The pig iron "planks" were broken off by sledgehammers and shipped away. The Severn River became one of Europe's busiest, shipping pig iron to distant foundries, where it was remelted and made into cast iron (for projects such as the Iron Bridge), or to forges, where it was worked like toffee into wrought iron.

Rosehill House, just up the hill, is the 18th-century Darby mansion furnished as a Quaker ironmaster's home would have been in 1850 (daily 10:00–17:00). The adjacent Dale House from the 1780s is less interesting.

Coalport China Museum, Jackfield Tile Museum, and Broseley Pipeworks: Housed in their original factories, these showcase the region's porcelain, decorated tiles, and clay pipes. These industries were developed to pick up the slack when the iron industry shifted away from Severn Valley. Each museum features finely decorated pieces, and the china and tile museums offer low-energy workshops.

Skiing, Swimming, Fishing, and More—There's a small, brush-covered ski slope with two poma lifts at Telford Ski Centre in Madeley, which is two miles from Ironbridge Gorge; you'll see the signs for it as you drive into IBG (£8.20/hr including gear, less for kids, CC:V, daily 10:00–20:00, tel. 01952/586-862). There's a public swimming pool next door. The Woodlands Farm, on Beech Road, runs a private fishing business where only barbless hooks are used and locals toss their catch back to hook again (kind of a fish hell).

Sleeping in Ironbridge Gorge
(£1 = about $1.70, tel. code: 01952)
Sleep Code: **S** = Single, **D** = Double/Twin, **T** = Triple, **Q** = Quad,
b = bathroom, **t** = toilet only, **s** = shower only, **CC** = Credit Card
(Visa, MasterCard, **Amex**).

Sleeping in Farmhouses
Hill View Farm is a peaceful, thrifty, brave, clean, and reverent
B&B run by Rosemarie Hawkins while her husband John raises
a "beef suckler herd." If you're looking for calm and country—
Auntie Em–style—this is it, in a great rural setting overlooking the
ruins of a 12th-century abbey (D-£36 for 1 night, less for longer
stays, nonsmoking, Buildwas, Ironbridge, Shropshire, TF8 7BP,
tel. 01952/432-228). It's just outside of Ironbridge on the Much
Wenlock road (A4169); pass the huge power plants, take a left
over the bridge, and go about a quarter mile (sign on right).
    If you like the country and Hill View Farm is full, try **Grove
Farm House B&B** (D-£36, Db-£40, less for 2 nights, nonsmoking, 3 miles from IBG on the road to Shrewsbury in Buildwas,
tel. 01952/433-572, fax 01952/433-650, e-mail: clive@g-f-h.demon
.co.uk, Pat and Clive Pygott).
    Bridge House, two miles north of town, dates from 1620,
with four warmly decorated rooms (S-from £30, Db-from £52,
big garden, parking, on fairly busy road B4380, river views, near
Buildwas Abbey, TF8 7BN, tel. 01952/432-105, fax 01952/
432-105, Janet Hedges).

Sleeping in the Town Center
Library House is "better-homes-and-gardens" elegant. In the
town center, a half block downhill from the bridge, it's classy,
friendly, and a fine value. It's hard to stay just one night. Helpful
Chris and George Maddocks run this smoke-free place, and their
breakfast won a "healthy heartbeat" award. The complimentary
drink upon arrival is a welcome touch (Sb-£45, Db-£55, Tb-£70,
family room-£70, video library, free parking, 11 Severn Bank,
Ironbridge Gorge, TF8 7AN, tel. 01952/432-299, fax 01952/
433-967, www.libhouse.enta.net). George will pick you up from
the Telford train station if you request it in advance.
    Three places right in the town center overlook the bridge:
Eley's Bridge View B&B rents five bright and comfy rooms
(Db-£40 with this book through 2000, CC:VM, tel. 01952/432-
541, fax 01952/433-405, Jo or Rich). The **Post Office House
B&B** is literally above the post office. The postmaster's wife, Janet
Hunter, rents three spacious rooms (D-£38, Ds-£40, Db with tiny
kitchenette-£42, 6 The Square, Ironbridge, Shropshire TF8 7AQ,
tel. 01952/433-201). The **Tontine Hotel** is the town's big, musty,

Industrial Age hotel (12 rooms, S-£22, D-£40, Db-£56, 10 percent discount promised with this book, CC:VM, attached restaurant with set menu, tel. 01952/432-127, fax 01952/432-094). Check out the historic photos in the bar.

Malt House, near the Museum of the Gorge, rents out six new, sparsely furnished rooms (Sb-£49, Dd-£59, CC:VM, a five-minute walk along the river from town, attached restaurant, parking, The Wharfage, TF8 7NH, tel. 01952/433-712, fax 01952/433-298, e-mail: malthse@globalnet.co.uk).

Hostels

Coalport Youth Hostel, plush for a hostel, fills an old factory at the China Museum in Coalport (most beds are in quads, but they have plenty of bunk-bed Ds for £22, including sheets). The **Ironbridge Gorge Youth Hostel,** built in 1859 as the grand Coalbrookdale Institute, is another fine hostel (a 20-minute walk from the Iron Bridge down A4169 toward Wellington, 4- to 6-bed rooms). Each hostel charges £10.15 per bed with sheets, serves meals, has a self-serve laundry, closes from 10:00–17:00, requires that you have a hostel membership (available for £11), and uses the same telephone number: tel. 01952/588-755.

Wilderhope Manor Youth Hostel, a beautifully remote and haunted 400-year-old manor house, is one of Europe's best hostels. On Saturdays, tourists actually pay to see what we hostelers sleep in for £9.15 (open mid-Feb–Oct, dinner served at 19:00, tel. 01694/771-363). It's six miles from Much Wenlock down B4371 toward Church Stretton.

Eating in Ironbridge Gorge

The best values and most local crowds are found outside of the IBG town. For a local crowd, fine spit-and-sawdust ambience, excellent ales, and surprisingly good food, try the **Coalbrookdale Inn** (dinner 18:00–20:00 except Sun, occasional folk music, across the street from the Coalbrookdale Museum of Iron, a mile from IBG, tel. 01952/433-953; run by Corrine and Mike, who are on the quest for the perfect pint). This former "best pub in Britain" (1995) has a tradition of offering free samples from a lineup of featured beers. Each is listed on a blackboard with its price and alcohol content. Ask a local to explain . . . or ask if he's ever tried a brew called the Prior's Piddle.

For a classier and more subdued atmosphere, eat well at the **Meadow Inn,** a local favorite with prizewinning pub grub (a pleasant 15-minute walk from the center, head upstream, at Dale End Park take the path along the river, the inn is just after the railway bridge, dinners nightly 18:00–21:45, CC:VM, can get crowded, no reservations taken, tel. 01952/433-193).

For a break from pub grub, you have these options in the

town center. **Oliver's** is a smoke-free vegetarian place with prices
and meals that make you want to turn—or stay—vegetarian (£6
main course, using CC adds 4 percent extra, Tue–Sat 19:00–21:00,
also Sat–Sun 12:00–14:00, High Street, reservations wise, tel.
01952/433-086). The **Ironbridge Brasserie & Wine Bar** is an
inviting bistro with an imaginative menu and real ale (Tue–Sun
18:30–23:00, also Fri–Sun 12:00–15:00, closed Mon, plenty of
indoor/outdoor seating, High Street, tel. 01952/432-716). **Da
Vinci's** serves good, though pricey, Italian food (£12 main course,
Wed–Sun 19:00–22:00, also Sun 12:00–15:00, closed Mon–Tue,
CC:VM, 26 High Street, tel. 01952/432-250). For Indian takeout,
consider **Aftab** (nightly 17:30–24:00, 25 High Street, tel.
01952/432-055). The popular **Malt House,** located in an 18th-
century beer house, offers an English menu with a European
accent (£10 main course, daily 12:00–14:30, 18:30–21:30, CC:VM,
near Museum of the Gorge, five-minute walk from the center,
also rents rooms—see above, tel. 01952/433-712).

For a pleasant evening, drive down Wenlock Edge on B4371.
At the Wenlock Edge Inn, park and walk to the cliff for a marvelous view of Shropshire at sunset (made nearly famous by the
poet A. E. Housman). Then drive farther to Much Wenlock and
eat with a fun local crowd at the **George and Dragon Pub.**

Transportation Connections—
Ironbridge Gorge
IBG is seven miles from Telford, which has the nearest train station. To get between IBG and Telford, take a bus (£1, hrly except
Sunday, 20 min) or taxi (£7.50). Although Telford's train and bus
stations are an annoying 15-minute walk apart (or a £2 cab ride),
the bus station is part of a large modern mall, an easy place to wait
for a bus to IBG. Few buses run Sunday. If you need a taxi while
in Ironbridge Gorge, call 01952/501-050.

Telford by train to: Birmingham (hrly, 45 min), **Conwy** in
North Wales (4/day, 3 hrs, with transfer in Chester), **Blackpool**
(hrly, 4.5 hrs, with several transfers), **Lake District** (allow up to
6.5 hrs total, with several transfers, at Penrith catch a bus to
Keswick, hrly except Sun 3/day, 40 min), **Edinburgh** (8 hrs, with
several transfers). Train info: tel. 0345-484-950.

By Car: Driving in from the Cotswolds and Stratford, take
M6 through Birmingham then M54 to the Telford/Ironbridge
exit. Follow the brown Ironbridge signs through lots of round-
abouts to Ironbridge Gorge. The traffic north through Birmingham is miserable from 14:00 to 20:00, especially on Fridays. From
Warwick, consider the M40, M42, Kidderminster alternative,
coming into IBG on the A442 via Bridgnorth to avoid the B'ham
traffic. Driving from IBG to Ruthin in North Wales is an easy two
hours. IBG to Conwy is 2.5 hours.

NORTH WALES

Wales' top historical, cultural, and natural wonders are found in the north. From towering Mount Snowdon to lush forests to desolate moor country, North Wales is a poem written in landscape. For sightseeing thrills and diversity, North Wales is Britain's most interesting slice of the Celtic crescent. But be careful not to be waylaid by the many gimmicky sights and bogus "best of" lists. The region's economy is poor, and they're wringing every possible pound out of the tourist trade. Sort carefully through your options.

Welsh

Language: The Welsh language, Cymru, has been a written language since about A.D. 600 and was spoken 300 years before French or German. It remains alive and well. Although English imperialism tried to kill it, today Welsh and those who speak it are protected by law. In Northwest Wales well over half the population is fluent in Welsh. It's either the first or the required second language in the public schools. Tourists hardly notice that the locals chatter away in Welsh and, as they turn to you, switch seamlessly to English. Listen in.

Welsh is a Celtic language (like Irish) and most closely related to the Breton language in western France. The common "ll" is pronounced as if you were ready to make an "l" sound and then blew it out. The language is phonetic but comes with a few tricks: the Welsh "dd" sounds like the English "th," f = v, ff = f, w = oo, and y = i. In a pub, impress your friends (or make some) by toasting the guy who just bought your drink. Say "Yeach-hid dah" ("Good health to you") and "Dee olch" ("Thank you") or "Dee olch un vowr" ("Thanks very much"). If the beer's bad, just make something up.

North Wales

Choirs: Every town has a choir (men's or mixed) that prac-
tices weekly. Visitors are usually welcome to observe and very
often follow the choir down to the pub afterward for a good,
old-fashioned, beer-lubricated singsong. Choirs welcome visitors
and practice weekly in the towns of Ruthin (mixed choir at the
Tabernacle Church, Thu 19:30–21:30), Llangollen (men's choir
Mon and Fri at 19:30 at the Hand Hotel, 21:00 pub singsong
afterward, tel. 01978/860-303), Denbigh (men's choir Mon
at 19:00 except in Aug), Llandudno (Sun 19:30–21:00, near
Conwy), and Caernarfon (Tue 19:45–21:30 at the Conservative
Club on High Street). Confirm schedules with your B&B hostess
or a local TI.

Planning Your Time

Give North Wales two nights and a day (on a three-week British
trip), and it'll give you a medieval banquet, a mighty castle, a giant
slate mine, and some of Britain's most beautiful scenery. Many
visitors are charmed and find an extra day.

Drivers interested in the medieval banquet should set up in
Ruthin and do this loop:

9:00–Drive over Llanberis mountain pass to Caernarfon (with
possible short stops in Trefriw Mill, Betws-y-Coed, Pen-y-Gwryd
Hotel, and Llanberis), 12:00–Caernarfon Castle. Catch noon tour
and 13:00 movie in Eagle Tower. See Prince Charles (of Wales)
exhibit. Climb to top for view. Walk through Caernarfon town,

lunch, shop. 14:30–Drive the scenic road (A4085) to Blaenau
Ffestiniog, 15:30–Tour Llechwedd Slate Mine, 17:30–Drive home
to Ruthin, 19:00–Arrive at home, 19:45–Medieval banquet at
castle (if not last night).

With a car and no interest in the banquet, skip Ruthin and
shorten your drive time by spending two nights in Conwy.
Without a car, skip Ruthin. From Conwy you can tour Snowdonia
and Caernarfon by bus and train.

With a second day, add the train up Snowdon (or take a hike)
and visit Conwy. With more time and a desire to hike, consider
using the mountain village of Beddgelert as a base.

Getting around North Wales

North Wales (except Ruthin) is well covered by a combination of
buses and trains. A main train line zips along the north coast from
Chester to Holyhead via Llandudno Junction, Conwy, and Bangor
(hrly). From Llandudno Junction, the Conwy Valley line goes
scenically south to Betws-y-Coed and Blaenau Ffestiniog (5/day,
1 hr). Without a car, you'll manage fine, using these two train
lines; public buses (get the Gwynedd Public Transport Guide at
any local TI); and Arriva buses, which circle Snowdonia National
Park with the needs of hikers in mind (£5 Explorer day pass available, buy on bus, tel. 01492/592-968).

RUTHIN

Ruthin (rith-in) is a low-key, workaday market town whose charm
is in its ordinary Welshness. The people are the sights. Admission
is free if you start the conversation. The market square, castle, TI,
bus station, and in-town accommodations are all within five blocks
of each other. Ruthin is Welsh as can be, makes a handy base for
drivers doing North Wales, and serves up a great medieval banquet. In the busy crafts center, you'll find the TI (Jun–Sept daily
10:00–17:30, Oct–May Mon–Sat 10:00–17:00, Sun 12:00–17:00,
tel. 01824/703-992).

Sights—Ruthin

▲▲**Ruthin Castle Welsh Medieval Banquet**—English, Scottish,
Irish, and Welsh medieval banquets are all variations on the same
touristy theme. This one is fun, more culturally justifiable (if that's
necessary), and less expensive than most. You'll be greeted with a
chunk of bread dipped in salt, which the maiden explains will "guarantee your safety." Your medieval master of ceremonies then seats
you, and the candlelit evening of food, drink, and music rolls gaily
on. You'll enjoy harp music, angelic singing, and lots of entertainment, including insults slung at the Irish, Scots, English, and even us
brash colonists. With fanfare (and historic explanation), wenches
serve mead, spiced wine, and four hearty traditional courses. Drink

Ruthin

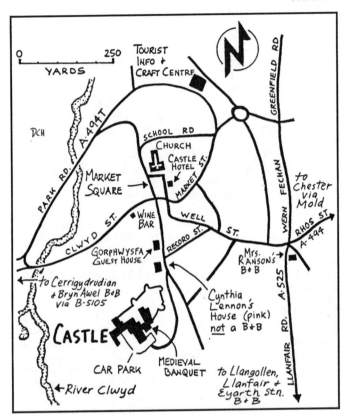

from a pewter goblet, wear a bib, and eat with your fingers and a dagger. Food and mead are unlimited—just ask for more (£28.95, CC:VMA, starts at 19:45, 2–5 nights weekly year-round, depending upon demand, vegetarian options, nonsmoking, easy doorstep parking, down Castle Street from the town square, call for reservations, tel. 01824/703-435 or, after hours, the hotel at 01824/702-664).

Walks—For a scenic and interesting one-hour walk, try the Offa's Dyke Path to Moel Famau (the "Jubilee Tower," a 200-year-old war memorial on a peak overlooking stark moorlands). The trailhead is a 10-minute drive from Ruthin.

▲▲**Welsh Choir**—The mixed choir performs at the Tabernacle Church on Thursday from 19:30–21:30 (except Aug, tel. 01824/703-757).

Sleeping in Ruthin
(£1 = about $1.70, tel. code: 01824)

Sleep Code: **S** = Single, **D** = Double/Twin, **T** = Triple, **Q** = Quad, **b** = bathroom, t = toilet only, s = shower only, **CC** = Credit Card (Visa, MasterCard, Amex).

Bryn Awel, a warm, traditional, charming farmhouse B&B with a paradise garden, is run by Beryl and John Jones in the hamlet of Bontuchel just outside of Ruthin (Db-£36–39, add £3 for one-nighters, nonsmoking, LL15 2DE Bontuchel, tel. 01824/702-481, www.accomodata.co.uk/010797.htm). Beryl, a prizewinning quilter, is helpful with touring tips, nearby walks, restaurant recommendations, booking the medieval banquet, and key Welsh words. (From Ruthin, take Bala road, #494, then B5105 Cerrigydrudion road. Turn right after the church, at the Bontuchel/Cyffylliog sign. It's on the right, 1.8 fragrant miles down a narrow road. If you get to the Bridge Hotel, backtrack 200 yards.)

Gorphwysfa Guest House, in a cozy 16th-century Tudor home between the castle and the town square, serves a royal breakfast and has a library, a grand piano, and three huge, comfortable rooms (Db-£40, Tb-£54, Qb-£64, 8a Castle Street, LL15 1DP, tel. & fax 01824/707-529, Margaret O'Riain). Gorphwysfa means "resting place" in Welsh.

Margaret Ranson's B&B is friendly, comfortable, and moderately priced (three rooms, Db-£36, strictly nonsmoking, Rhianfa, Ffordd Llanrhydd, Ruthin, Clwyd, LL15 1PP, a 10-minute walk from the castle; from Anchor Pub drive 100 yards toward the hospital; it's the first big red-brick house on right; Rhianfa sign on stone wall, tel. & fax 01824/702-971). Margaret's husband, John, a natural tour guide, will lend you an excellent North Wales road map. Or you can just play croquet in their sprawling backyard.

The Castle Hotel, not to be confused with the Ruthin Castle Hotel, is a worn, 24-room hotel on the town square (Db-£38 with this book through 2000, family suites, front rooms are larger and overlook the town square, some nonsmoking rooms, reasonable evening meals, CC:VMA, St. Peter's Square, LL15 1AA, tel. 01824/702-479, fax 01824/703-488).

Moelfa B&B, on the busy Denbigh Road, is modern and nondescript but comfortable and friendly (D-£32 with this book, leave town on Denbigh Road, first B&B sign on left, tel. 01824/702-468, Meg Jones).

Ruthin Castle, the ultimate in creaky, faded, Old World elegance for North Wales, is actually not a castle but a hotel near castle ruins (Sb-from £78, Db-from £98, show this book for 10 percent off room rates or 10 percent off their two-nights-with-a-banquet-plus-restaurant-dinner deal, CC:VMA, tel. 01824/702-664, fax 01824/705-978, www.ruthincastle.co.uk). Enjoy lavish public places, armor, antlers, ghosts, and your private snooker table (giant billiards, £1/hour). Explore the fascinating grounds, complete with a drowning pool and 40 peacocks. You'll wake up to their cry thinking it's a loony-tune damsel in distress.

For cheap beds go to the **Llangollen Youth Hostel** (15 miles from Ruthin, see below).

Eating in Ruthin

There's no reason to rush home for dinner in Ruthin if you're not going to the medieval banquet. No one place is a clear winner, but you'll eat reasonably well at the **Anchor Pub**, the **Wynnstay Arms,** the **Middleton Arms Pub** on the main square, the classier **Manor House Hotel Restaurant** (pricey), or a mile out of town in Cyffylliog at the **Red Lion** pub. **Da Vinci's,** a new wine bar, is good (The Mews, Well Street). For fish and chips, locals paddle over to **Finns** on Clwyd Street (take-away only).

LLANGOLLEN

Worth a stop if you have a car, Llangollen is famous for its musical **International Eisteddfod** (July 3–9 in 2000), a very popular and very crowded festival of folk songs and dance. Men's choir practice is held on Monday and Friday nights throughout the year (19:30 at the Hand Hotel, 21:00 pub singsong afterward, tel. 01978/860-303).

Walk or ride a horse-drawn boat down the old canal (£3.50, 45 min, 3-mile round-trip, Mar–Oct, tel. 01978/860-702) toward the lovely 13th-century **Cistercian Vale Crucis Abbey** (£2) near the even older cross called **Eliseg's Pillar.** TI: daily Apr–Oct 10:00–18:00, Nov–Mar 9:30–17:00, tel. 01978/860-828.

Llangollen has a handful of other amusements and attractions, including scenic steam train trips (daily Jun–Sept), the world's largest permanent exhibition of model railways, and the biggest "Doctor Who" exhibition anywhere.

Glasfryn B&B is good (D/Db-£35, Abbey Road, LL20 8SN, near bridge, tel. 01978/860-757, Eleanor Jones). **Gale's Hotel** is a decent value (Db-£52, £45.50 for 2 nights, good food, CC:VMA, Bridge Street 18, LL20 8PF, tel. 01978/860-089, fax 01978/861-313), and the **Llangollen Youth Hostel** is cheap (£11.30 per bed in 2- to 18-bed rooms, £2 less for members, tel. 01978/860-330).

Llangollen is a 30-minute drive from Ruthin or a bus ride (3/day except Sunday, 60 min, year-round). Hourly buses connect Llangollen with train stations at Chirk, Ruabon, and Wrexham.

CONWY

This garrison town was built at the same time in the 1280s as the castle to give Edward I an English toehold in Wales (see above). What's left today are the best medieval walls in Britain surrounding a humble workaday town and crowned by the bleak and barren hulk of a castle awesome in its day. Conwy's charming High Street

King Edward's Castles

In the 13th century the Welsh, under two great princes named Llywelyn, created a united and independent Wales. The English King Edward I fought hard to end this Welsh sovereignty. In 1282 Llywelyn was killed (and went to where everyone speaks Welsh). King Edward spent the next 20 years building or rebuilding 17 great castles to consolidate his English foothold in troublesome North Wales. The greatest of these (such as Conwy Castle) were masterpieces of medieval engineering, with round towers (tough to undermine by tunneling), a castle-within-a-castle defense (giving defenders a place to retreat and wreak havoc on the advancing enemy... or just wait for reinforcements), and sea access (safe to stock from England). These were English islands in the middle of angry Wales. Most were built with a fortified grid-plan town attached and were filled with English settlers. (With this blatant abuse of Wales, you have to wonder, where was Greenpeace 700 years ago?)

Castle lovers will want to tour each of Edward's five greatest castles. With a car and two days this makes one of Europe's best castle tours. I'd rate them in this order: **Caernarfon** is most entertaining and best presented (described below). **Conwy** is attached to the cutest medieval town and the best public transport (described below). **Harlech** is the most dramatic (£3, daily mid-May–Sept 9:30–18:00, daily Apr–mid-May and Oct 9:30–17:00, in winter Mon–Sat 10:00–16:00, Sun 11:00–16:00, tel. 01766/780-552). **Beaumaris,** surrounded by a swan-filled moat, was the last, largest, and most romantic (£2.20, same hours as Harlech, tel. 01248/810-361). **Criccieth** (KRICK-ith), built in 1230 by Llywelyn, is also dramatic and remote (£2.20, daily Apr–late Sept 10:00–18:00, closed off-season, tel. 01766/522-227).

leads from Lancester Square (with the bus stop and unmanned train station and a column honoring the town's founder, Welsh prince Llywelyn the Great) down to a fishy harbor that permitted Edward to safely restock his castle.

Since the highway was tunneled under the town, a strolling ambience has returned to Conwy. Much of the wall, with its 22 towers, is walkable and free; start at Upper Gate (the highest point) or Berry Street (the lowest) or do the small section at the castle entrance. Stroll the harbor past Britain's smallest house

Conwy

(see below), the tour boat (£2.80, 30 min), an aquarium, the town lifeboat house, and a fresh-fish trailer (Keith the Fish) selling 10p crab sticks. Beyond the castle, the mighty Telford suspension bridge is a 19th-century slice of English imperialism, built in 1826 to better connect (and control) the route to Ireland. The newly restored bridge is open to pedestrians only (£1).

Every Monday night, the gritty Malt Loaf pub hosts the Conwy Folk Music Club (across from the train station) from 20:30 on. Every Tuesday, a small market hums in the train station parking lot (year-round, but canceled if rainy). On weekends, when banks are closed, only cash machines are available for changing money. Train schedules are posted outside the station; if your train is listed with an "x," you'll need to flag down the train.

Tourist Information: The TI has to move in 2000 from the castle entrance but will stay in the town center, likely near the harbor (Apr–Oct daily 9:30–18:00, Nov–Mar daily 9:30–16:00, tel. 01492/592-248). They'll conjure up printed, personalized train schedules or driving routes for you (the first is free, the rest 10p); sell books and maps on the area (such as *Footprints' Walks around Snowdonia*, £3.50, 16 walks with maps); book rooms for a £1 fee; and do theatre bookings. Don't confuse the TI with the tacky "Conwy Visitors Centre" near the station with its goofy little 80p video show.

Car Rental: The nearest car rental agencies are in Llandudno, 1.5 miles away. Consider Aberconwy Car Hire (from £30/day, £3 fee to deliver car to your Conwy hotel or meet you at station, tel.

01492/874-669) or the pricier, "why try harder" Europcar (from
£39/day, £10 delivery to hotel, tel. 01492/878-608).
   Bike Rental: Conwy Outdoor rents bikes for £12/day,
including helmets (daily 9:00–18:00, CC:VM, packed lunches
available, 9 Castle Street, tel. 01492/593-390).

Sights—Conwy

▲**Conwy Castle**—Built dramatically on a rock overlooking the
sea with eight linebacker towers, this castle has an interesting story
to tell (£4, mid-May–Sept daily 9:30–18:00, Apr–mid-May and
Oct daily 9:30–17:00, in winter Mon–Sat 10:00–16:00, Sun 11:00–
16:00, tel. 01492/592-358). Guides wait inside to take you on a 60-
minute, £1 tour. If the booth is empty, look for the group and join
it. (These guides also do city tours; consider Neville Hortop, tel.
01492/878-209.)
St. Mary's Parish Church—Built in 1186, it's still the core of the
town and worth a look for its fine interior and wispy graveyard.
Originally a Cistercian church, it is actually older than the town.
Old Houses—On the harbor, the tiniest house in Britain is red,
72 inches wide, 122 inches high, and 50p to see. Two old houses on
High Street may tempt you. Plas Mawr, billed as the oldest house in
Wales, offers a frail look at domestic life in 16th-century Wales (£4,
includes audio tour, Tue–Sun 10:00–18:00, closed Mon). The Aberconwy House at the bottom of the street is even less exciting (£2).
▲**Bodnant Garden**—This sumptuous display of floral color—
set in the lush green of Snowdonia—is one of Britain's best. It's
famous for its magnolias, rhodies, camellias, and floral arch (£4.60,
daily 10:00–17:00 in season, best spring–June, six miles south of
Conwy, tel. 01492/650-460).

Sleeping in Conwy
(£1 = about $1.70, tel code: 01492)
Conwy has several decent budget B&Bs, each located within a
five-minute walk from the bus and train station. There's no launderette in town.
   Gwynedd Guest House, spacious, thoughtfully decorated,
and charmingly run by Margaret Young, is Conwy's best value in
the city center (S-£18, D-£32, T/Q-£50, family deals, 2 blocks
from bus and train station, 10 Upper Gate Street, LL32 8RF,
tel. & fax 01492/596-537, cell phone 0797-957-8389, e-mail:
abs.conwy@virgin.net).
   Culverlands Guest House has three slick, clean, woody
rooms worth the five-minute walk from town (Db-£32, 7 Bryn
Celyn, Cadnant Park, LL32 8PW, tel. 01492/596-744, Pauline
and Peter Hobson). From Conwy's Lancaster Square, head west
on Bangor Road, pass under city wall, turn left at Cadnant Park,
cross the bridge, and continue straight to Bryn Celyn cul-de-sac.

Town House B&B rents six tidy rooms near the entrance of the castle (S-£16.50, D-£25–27, Db-£35, CC:VM, nonsmoking, clothes washing discouraged except for "smalls," some castle views, Rosehill Street 18, LL32 3LD, tel. 01492/596-454). Avoid the dumpy, grimy Rose Hill House B&B next door.

Swan Cottage B&B is a homey place near the harbor front renting three comfortable rooms (D/Db-£30 with this book, 1 D room has panoramic harbor view, 18 Berry Street, LL32 8DG, tel. 01492/596-840, Mr. and Mrs. Roberts).

The **Pen-y-Bryn Tea Room** has two pleasant rooms above its 16th-century tearoom just off the main square (D-£35, Db-£40, nonsmoking, faint cat odor, Lancaster Square, LL32 8DE, tel. 01492/596-445).

Castle Bank Hotel has nine spacious rooms run by the gracious Karen Morton, who also serves optional dinners, with the help of her kids, for £12.50 to £15 (Db-£55, 10 percent discount with this book, CC:VM, nonsmoking, easy parking, Mount Pleasant, LL32 8NY, tel. 01492/593-888, fax 01492/596-466, e-mail: conwy@marketsite.co.uk).

Llys Llywelyn Hotel, next door, is stately but worn with nine (sometimes smoky) rooms, a big lounge, and some views (Sb-£20, Db-£39, easy parking, can pick you up from station if you request it in advance, just outside the town wall at Mount Pleasant, LL32 8NY, tel. 01492/593-257, Alan Hughes).

The big, musty old **Castle Hotel** rents 29 overpriced rooms (Db-£75 for 1 night without breakfast, Db-£80 for 2 nights includes breakfast and dinner, 10 percent discount with this book, CC:VMA, High Street, LL32 8DB, tel. 01492/592-324, fax 01492/583-351, reply@marketsite.co.uk).

Conwy's hostel is a 15-minute walk from the castle (£9 per bed in 2-, 4-, and 6-bed rooms, all with showers and lockers, family rooms, Larkhill, Sychnant Pass Road, tel. 01492/593-571, fax 01492/593-580).

Eating in Conwy

When hungry in Conwy, stroll down High Street comparing the cute teahouses and smoky pubs. At the top, on Lancaster Square, is **Alfredo's Restaurant,** a family-friendly place that serves good and reasonable Italian food (nightly 18:00–22:00, tel. 01492/592-381). At the bottom of High Street two fish-and-chips joints—**Galleon's** and **Fisherman's**—brag they're the best. Locals like **Anna's Tea Rooms,** located upstairs within the Conwy Outdoor shop (daily 10:00–17:00, near Fisherman's, 9 Castle Street, tel. 01492/580-908). The tiny **Wall Place** on Chapel Street is good for vegetarian meals (Jul-Aug daily 12:00–16:00, 19:00–22:00; otherwise weekends only, Friday lunch–Sunday lunch, slooow service, tel. 01492/596-326). **The Bridge** pub on Rosehill Street is decent. The best cheap meal in town is either a picnic from the **Spar grocery** (daily 8:00–22:00, top of High Street) or fish and chips on the harbor front with the locals.

CAERNARFON

The small and lively little town of Caernarfon (kah-NAR-von) is famous for its striking castle—the place where the Prince of Wales is "invested." The old garrison town still marches out from the castle following the original medieval grid plan laid within its well-preserved ramparts.

But Caernarfon is mostly a 19th-century town, and the most important thing in town is not the castle but the parking lot that sprawls below the castle. This was once a booming slate port shipping tidy bundles of slate from North Wales mining towns to roofs all over Europe.

The statue of local boy David Lloyd George looks over the town square. A member of parliament from 1890 to 1945, he was the most important politician Wales ever sent to London and ultimately became Britain's prime minister. Boy George began his career as a noisy nonconformist liberal advocating Welsh rights. He ended up an eloquent spokesperson for the notion of Great Britain, convincing his slate-mining constituents that only as part of the Union would their slate industry boom.

A small but lively town, Caernarfon bustles with shops, cafés, and people. Market-day activities fill its main square on Saturdays year-round; a smaller, sleepy market yawns on Monday from late May to September. The charming grid-plan medieval town is worth a wander.

The TI, across from the castle entrance, gives out a wonderful town map/guide, has train and bus schedules, sells hiking books, and books rooms here and elsewhere for a £1 fee (Apr–Oct daily 10:00–18:00, Nov–Mar daily 9:30–16:30 with a 13:00–13:30 lunch break, tel. 01286/672-232). Donna "Caernarfon is more than a castle" Goodman leads historic walks several times a week in July and August (£2, 1 hr, call 01286/677-059 for her schedule).

Within a couple of blocks of the bus stop, you'll find an Internet café (Dimensiwm 4, closed Sun, on Turf Square) and Pete's Laundromat (on Skinner Street). The only car rental agency in town is Caernarfon Rent-a-Car (on the harbor, 2 Slate Quay, tel. 01286/676-171). Two shops rent bikes: Cycle Hire (£11/day, on harbor front, tel. 01286/676-804) or Beics Castell (£13/day, High Street, closed Thu and Sun, tel. 01286/677-400).

Sights—Caernarfon

▲▲**Caernarfon Castle**—Edward I built this impressive castle 700 years ago to establish English rule over North Wales. Modeled after the striped and angular walls of ancient Constantinople, the castle—while impressive—was never finished and never really used. From the inner courtyard you can see the notched walls ready for more walls that were never built. Its fame is due to its physical grandeur and from its association with the Prince of Wales. The English king got the angry Welsh to agree that if he presented them with "a prince, born in Wales who spoke not a word of English," they would submit to the crown. In time, Edward had a son...born in Wales... who spoke not a word of English, Welsh, or any other language. In modern times, as another political maneuver, the Prince of Wales has been "invested" (given his title) here. This "tradition" actually dates only from this century and only 2 of 21 Princes of Wales have taken part.

In spite of its disappointing history, it's a great castle to tour. An essential part of any visit is the guided tour (50-minute tours for £1.50 leave on the hour from the center of the courtyard in front of the entry; if you're late, ask to join one in progress). In the huge Eagle Tower (on the seaward side) see the "Prince and Chieftains" history exhibit (ground floor), watch the 20-minute movie (a broad mix of Welsh legend and history, on the hour, upstairs, comfortable theater seats), and climb the tower for a great view. The opposite tower has an exhibit about the investiture of Prince Charles in 1969 (£4.20, Apr–Aug daily 9:30–18:30; Sept–Mar Mon–Sat 9:30–16:00, Sun 11:00–16:00; CC:VM, tel. 01286/677-617). Martin de Lewandowicz gives mind-bending tours of the castle (01286/674-369). **Men's Choir**—If spending the night, consider dropping by the local men's choir practice (Tuesday 19:45–21:30, Conservative Club on High Street).

Sleeping in Caernarfon
(£1 = about $1.70, tel code: 01286)
Isfryn B&B is just down the street from the castle and overlooks the water (6 rooms, S-£19, D-£37, Db-£42, family deals, 11 Church Street, LL5 51SW, tel. & fax 01286/675-628, Graham). **Totters Hostel** is a creative little hostel well run by Bob and Henriette (30 beds in five dorm rooms, £9.50 per bed with bedding, continental breakfast, and lockers; couples can have their own room when available; open all day, welcoming game room/lounge, use of kitchen, a block from the castle at 2 High Street, tel. 01286/672-963, www .applemaps.co.uk/totters). A fine traditional old fish-and-chips joint is on High Street, along with plenty of sandwich shops and tearooms nearby.

SNOWDONIA NATIONAL PARK
Snowdonia National Park is Britain's second-largest national park, with Mount Snowdon—the tallest mountain in England and Wales—as its centerpiece. Each year half a million people choose one of seven different paths to the top of 3,560-foot Snowdon (the

small book *The Ascent of Snowdon*, by E. G. Bowland, describes the routes, £2, sold by local TIs). Hikes take from five to seven hours. If you're reasonably fit and the weather cooperates, it's an exciting day. Trail info abounds. As you explore the area, notice the slate roofs—they're the local specialty.

Sights—Snowdonia

Betws-y-Coed—The resort center of Snowdonia National Park, Betwys-y-Coed (BET-oos-uh-coyd) bursts with tour buses and souvenir shops. Its good national park and TI are the only reason to stop here (Apr–Oct daily 10:00–18:00, Nov–Mar daily 9:30–13:00, 14:30–16:30, tel. 01690/710-426). As you drive west out of town on A5, you'll see the car park for scenic Swallow Falls, a pleasant five-minute walk from the road. A mile or so past the falls on the right you'll see "The Ugly House," built overnight to take advantage of a 15th-century law that let any quickie building avoid fees and taxes. Buses connect Conwy and Betws-y-Coed (#19, hrly in summer, 50 min). Trains run from the north coast through Betws-y-Coed to Blaenau (6/day).

Trefriw Woolen Mills—The mill in Trefriw (TREV-roo), five miles north of Betws-y-Coed, is free and surprisingly interesting if the machines are running (Apr–Oct Mon–Fri 10:00–13:00, 14:00–17:30, same hours off-season, but only weaving is demonstrated, tel. 01492/640-462). Follow the 11 stages of wool transformation: warping, weaving, carding, hanking, spanking, spinning, and so on. From June to September, the hand-spinning house (next to the WC) has a charming spinster and a petting cupboard filled with all the fibers that can be spun into cloth. Be sure to enjoy the fine woolen shop, the pleasant town (more so than Betws-y-Coed), and the coffee shop. The woolen mill at Penmachno (also near Betws-y-Coed) is smaller and less interesting.

Beddgelert—This is the quintessential Snowdon village, packing a scenic mountain punch without the tourist crowds (17 miles from Betws-y-Coed). Set on a river in the shadow of Snowdon and her sisters, with a fine variety of hikes from its doorstep and pretty good bus service, Beddgelert (BETH-geh-let) makes a good stop for those wanting to experience the peace of Snowdonia.

Locals can recommend walks. You can follow the lane along the river (three miles round-trip), walk down the river and around the hill (three hours, six miles, 900-foot gain, via Cwm Bycham), hike along (or around) Llyn Gwynant Lake and four miles back to Beddgelert (ride the bus to the lake), or try the more dramatic higher ridge walks on Moel Hebog (Hawk Hill).

Sleeping in Bleddgelert: Plas Tan Y Graig Guest House, at the village bridge, is a good value (D-£36, CC:VM, family room, fine lounge, LL55 4LT, tel. 01766/890-329, www.nwi.co.uk/plastanygraig/). Also just over the bridge,

Snowdonia Area

Brian Wheatley rents six rooms at **Plas-Gwyn** (Db-£38, non-smoking, tel. 01766/890-215). The **Royal Goat Hotel** offers well-worn, chandeliered, woody elegance in a grand hotel built for the rugged 19th-century aristocrat (Sb-£44, Db-£74, cheaper for two-night stays, some nonsmoking rooms, CC:VMA, tel. 01766/890-224, fax 01766/890-422).

Mountaineers note that this area was used by Sir Edmund Hillary and his men as they practiced for the first ascent of Mount Everest. The **Pen-y-Gwryd Hotel Pub** (at the top of the pass north of Beddgelert) is strewn with fascinating Hillary and Everest memorabilia (D-£44, Db-£54, saggy beds, smoky, old-time-elegant public rooms, those in D rooms get to use museum-piece Victorian tubs, grand five-course dinners-£16, tel. 01286/870-211). In the peaceful middle of nowhere, with a crampon ambience, this is ideal for well-bred hikers.

Llanberis—A town of 2,000 people with as many tourists on a sunny day, Llanberis is a popular base for Snowdon activities. Along with the station for the Snowdon train, there is a good information center, a few touristy museums, pony trekking, and good bus connections.

▲▲**Mount Snowdon and the Mountain Railway**—The easiest and most popular ascent of Mount Snowdon is by the Snowdon Mountain Railway, a rack-and-pinion railway from 1896 that climbs 3,500 feet over 4.5 miles from Llanberis to the summit (£15 round-trip, family discounts on early departures—until 10:00—2.5 hours, including a 30-minute stop at the summit, CC:VM, tel. 01286/870-223). The first departure is usually at 9:00. While the schedule flexes with weather and demand, they try to run several trips a day mid-March through October (two departures per hour in peak season). On sunny summer days trains fill up (waits are longer in the afternoon; arrive by lunchtime and get a departure appointment time—usually a wait of an hour or two). Off-season trains often stop short of the summit.

BLAENAU FFESTINIOG

This quintessential Welsh slate-mining town is notable for its slate-mine tour and its old steam train. The town—a dark, poor place—seems to struggle on, oblivious to the tourists who nip in and out. Take a walk. The shops are right out of the 1950s. Long rows of humble "two up and two down" houses (four rooms) feel pretty grim. There are some buses from the town to the slate mines; the road isn't pedestrian friendly. (TI, daily 10:00–13:00, 14:00–18:00, closed Oct–Easter, tel. 01766/830-360.)

Sights—Blaenau Ffestiniog

▲▲**Llechwedd Slate-Mine Tour**—Slate mining played a block-buster role in Welsh heritage, and this mine on the northern edge of the bleak town of Blaenau Ffestiniog (BLIGH-nigh FES-tin-yog) does a fine job of explaining the mining culture of Victorian Wales. The Welsh mined and split most of the slate roofs of Europe. For every ton of usable slate found, 10 tons were mined. The exhibit has three parts: a tiny Victorian mining town (free and worthwhile) and two 30-minute tours. The "deep mine" tour features a tape-recorded dramatization of social life, a serious descent, and a half mile of walking. The "tramway" tour is a level train ride with two stops, no walking, and a live guide; it focuses on working life and traditional mining techniques. Both are different and, considering the cheap combo-ticket, worthwhile. Don't miss the slate-splitting demonstration at the end of the tramway tour (£6.75 for 1 tour, £10.25 for both, Mar–Sept daily 10:00–18:00, Oct–Feb closes at 17:00, last tour starts 45 minutes before closing, tel. 01766/830-306). Dress warmly—I mean it. You'll freeze underground without a sweater.

▲**Ffestiniog Railway**—This 13-mile narrow-gauge train line was built in 1836 for small horse-drawn wagons to transport the slate from the Ffestiniog mines to the port of Porthmadog. In the 1860s horses gave way to steam trains. Today hikers and tourists enjoy these tiny titans (£13 round-trip, hrly, 2.5 hrs round-trip; diesel trains are £2 cheaper, first-class observation cars are £5 extra, tel. 01766/512-340). This is a novel steam train experience, but the full-size Llandudno–Blaenau Ffestiniog train is more scenic and works better for hikers.

Portmeirion—Ten miles southwest of Blaenau Ffestiniog, this "Italian Village" was the lifework of a rich local architect who began building it in 1925. Set idyllically on the coast just beyond the poverty of the slate-mine towns, flower-filled fantasy is extravagant. Surrounded by lush Welsh greenery and a windswept mudflat at low tide, the village is an artistic glob of palazzo arches, fountains, gardens, and promenades filled with cafés, tacky shops, a hotel, and local tourists who always wanted to go to Italy (or who are fans of the cultish British 1960s TV series *The Prisoner*). The architect explains his purpose in a videotaped slide presentation. Not worth the £4 (daily 9:30–17:30, two miles from Porthmadog, tel. 01766/770-228).

Transportation Connections—North Wales

Conwy to: Llandudno Junction (2 buses/hrly, 5 min; 4 trains/day, 5 min), **Trefriw–Betws-y-Coed–Penygwryd–Llanberis** (bus #19, hrly in summer).

Llandudno Junction by train to: Chester (2/hrly, 1 hr), **Birmingham** (2/hrly, 2.5 hrs), **London's Euston Station** (hrly, 3.5 hrs). Train info: tel. 0345-484-950.

Caernarfon by bus to: Conwy (2/hrly, hrly on Sunday, 1.25 hrs, buy ticket on bus), **Llanberis** (2/hrly, 30 min), **Beddgelert** (hrly, 30 min), **Blaenau–Ffestiniog** (hrly buses, 1.5 hrs), **Beddgelert–Penygwryd–Llanberis** (bus 95, every 2 hrs, 1.5 hrs, Jun–Sept only).

Llanberis by bus to: Beddgelert (hrly, 45 min).

Ruthin to: Llangollen (15 miles, 3 buses/day but never on Sunday, 60 min), **Betsw-y-Coed** (30 miles, allow 3–4 hrs, bus to Rhyl, train to Llandudno Junction, train to Betsw-y-Coed), **Conwy** (3 hrs by bus, with transfer at Llanrwst), **Chester** (6 buses/day, 30 min, or a £20 taxi).

Chester by train to: London (hrly, 3 hrs), **Liverpool** (2/hrly, 50 min), **Birmingham** (2/hrly, 2 hrs), points in **North Wales** (2/hrly).

Ferry Connections—North Wales and Ireland

Holyhead and Dun Laoghaire: Stena Line sails between Holyhead (North Wales) and Dun Laoghaire near Dublin (4/day, 100 min, £30–35 one-way walk-on fare, £28 round-trip in a day if you have no baggage, plus £5 tax if buying ticket in Ireland, reserve by phone as soon as you can—they book up long in advance on summer weekends, Dun Laoghaire tel. 01/204-7700, Holyhead tel. 01407/606-666, general reservations number for Stena Lines in Britain: 0990-707-070).

Holyhead and Dublin: Irish Ferries sails between Holyhead (North Wales) and Dublin (5/day, 3.25 hrs, faster ferry-1.75 hrs, slow boats are £20 one-way walk-on fare, £35 round-trip; fast boats coast £35 one way, £60 round-trip, Dublin tel. 01/638-3333, Holyhead tel. 0990-329-129, www.irishferries.ie; car fares vary-£250–350, with up to five passengers, depending on season, cheapest on Wed).

Sleeping near Holyhead dock: The fine Monravon B&B has nine smoke-free rooms (Db-£35, CC:VM, family deals, 10-minute walk from dock, Porth-Y-Felin Road, LL65 1PL, tel. & fax 01407/762-944).

Route Tips for Drivers

Ironbridge Gorge to Ruthin: Drive for an hour to Wales via A5 through Shrewsbury, crossing into Wales at the pretty castle town of Chirk. There, take A5 to Llangollen. Cross the bridge in Llangollen, turn left, and follow A542 and A525 past the romantic Valle Crucis abbey, over the scenic Horseshoe Pass, and into Ruthin. Driving to Conwy is faster via Wrexham and then the A55.

Ruthin to Caernarfon (56 miles) to Blaenau (34 miles) to Ruthin (35 miles): This route connects the top sights with the most scenic routes. From Ruthin take B5105 (steepest road off main square) and follow signs to Cerrigydrudion. Then follow A5 into Betws-y-Coed, with a possible quick detour to the Trefriw Woolen Mill (five miles north on B5106, well signposted). Climb west on A5 through Capel Curig, then take A4086 over the rugged Pass of Llanberis, under the summit of Mount Snowdon (to the south, behind those clouds), and on to Caernarfon. Park under the castle in the harborside car park (£2).

Leaving Caernarfon, take the lovely A4085 southeast through Beddgelert to Penrhyndeudraeth. (Make things even more beautiful by taking the little B4410 road from Garreg through Rhyd.) Then take A487 toward What Maentwrog and A496 to Blaenau Ffestiniog. Go through the dark, depressing mining town of Blaenau Ffestiniog on A470 into hills of slate and turn right into the Llechwedd Slate Mine.

After the mine, continue uphill on A470, snapping photos north through Dolwyddelan (passing a fine old Welsh castle ruin) and back to A5. For a high and desolate detour, return to Ruthin via the windy, curvy A543 road over the stark moors to the Sportsman's Arms Pub (the highest pub in Wales, good food), through Denbigh, and home.

BLACKPOOL

This is Britain's fun puddle. It's England's most visited attraction, the private domain of its working class, a faded and sticky mix of Coney Island, Las Vegas, and Woolworth's. Juveniles of any age love it. My kids declared it better than Disneyland.

Blackpool grew up with the Industrial Revolution. In the mid-1800s entire mill towns would close down and take a two-week break in Blackpool. They came for the fresh air—much needed after a hard year in the mills—and to drink the seawater. (Back then they figured this was healthy.) Blackpool's heydays are past now, as more and more working people can afford the cheap charter flights to sunny Spain. Still, this is an accessible and affordable fun zone for the Anne and Andy Capps of northern England. People come year after year. They stay for a week, and they love it.

Most Americans don't even consider a stop in Blackpool. Many won't like it. It's an ears-pierced-while-you-wait, tipsy-toupee kind of place. Tacky, yes. Lowbrow, O.K. But it's as English as can be, and that's what you're here for. An itinerary should feature as many facets of a culture as possible. Blackpool is as English as the queen—and considerably more fun.

Spend the day "muckin' about" the beach promenade of fortune-tellers, fish-and-chips joints, amusement piers, warped mirrors, and Englanders wearing hats with built-in ponytails. A million greedy doors try every trick to get you inside. Huge arcade halls advertise free toilets and broadcast bingo numbers into the streets; the wind machine under a wax Marilyn Monroe blows at a steady gale; and the smell of fries, tobacco, and sugar is everywhere. Milk comes in raspberry or banana in this land where people under incredibly bad wigs look normal. If you're bored in Blackpool, you're just too classy.

Planning Your Time

Ideally, get to Blackpool around lunchtime for a free afternoon and evening of making bubbles in this cultural mud puddle. For full effect, it's best to visit Blackpool during its peak season: June through early November.

Blackpool is easy by car or train. Speed demons with a car can treat it as a midday break (it's just off the M6 on M55) and continue north. If you have kids, they'll want more time here (hey, it's cheaper than Disneyland). If you're into nightlife, this town is a slam dunk. If you're before or beyond kids and not into kitsch and greasy spoons, skip it. If the weather's great and you love nature, the lakes are just a few hours north. A visit to Blackpool does sharpen the wonders of Windermere.

Orientation (tel. code: 01253)

Everything clusters along the six-mile beachfront promenade, a tacky, glittering strip mall of fun. The three amusement piers are the sedate North Pier (with theatre), the something-for-everyone Central Pier (rides plus theatre), and the noisy South Pier (rides; the theatre was replaced by a roller coaster). The piers were originally built for Victorian landlubbers who wanted to go to sea but were afraid of getting seasick. The Pleasure Beach rides are near the South Pier. Jutting up near the North Pier is Blackpool's stubby Eiffel-type tower. The most interesting shops, eateries, and theaters are inland from the North Pier. For a break from glitz, you can hike north along the waterfront path for, say, 20 miles or so.

Tourist Information: There are two TIs near the tower. The main one is on Clifton Street (Apr–early Nov Mon–Sat 9:00–17:00, Sun 10:00–16:00, off-season slightly shorter hours and closed Sun, tel. 01253/478-222, the same number gives recorded entertainment info after hours). The other TI is on the Promenade (May–early Nov). Get the city map (50p), pick up brochures on the amusement centers, and ask about special shows. The TIs do same-day room bookings for one-night stays for a £2 fee.

For a history fix, get the TI's *Heritage Trail* booklet, which takes you on an hour's walk through downtown Blackpool. Saying much about little, it is endearing (60p).

Arrival in Blackpool: The train station is just three blocks from the town center. The motorway funnels you down Yeadon Way into a giant parking zone (formerly the central station).

Car Rental: In case you decide to tour the Lake District by car, you'll find plenty of rental agencies in Blackpool, including Avis (292 Waterloo Road, tel. 01253/397-771), Budget (434 Waterloo Road, tel. 01253/691-632), and Hertz (181 Clifton Drive, tel. 01232/404-021).

Internet Access: Seek out the Warehouse Cy-bar Café, tucked into an alley behind Lloyd's Bank, off Corporation Street

(Mon–Sat 9:30–23:00, Sun 11:00–22:30, two blocks from Clifton Street TI, near North Pier).

Getting around Blackpool

Vintage trolley cars run 13 miles up and down the waterfront, connecting all the sights. This first electric tramway in Europe dates from 1885 (90p–£1.70, depending on length of trip, £4.50 for all-day pass, pay conductor, trolleys come every five minutes or so, Nov–May every 10–20 minutes, runs 6:00–24:00). Taxis are easy to snare in Blackpool.

Sights—Blackpool

▲Blackpool Tower—This mini–Eiffel Tower is a 104-year-old vertical fun center. You pay £6.50 to get in; after that, the fun is free. Work your way up from the bottom through layer after layer of noisy entertainment: circus (two acts a day Sat–Thu, usually at 14:30, big show at 19:30, nothing on Fri; you can return on a ticket), space world, dinosaur land, aquarium, and a wonderful old ballroom with barely live music and golden oldies dancing to golden oldies all day. Enjoy a break at the dance-floor-level pub or on a balcony perch. Kids love this place. With a little marijuana, adults would, too. Ride the elevator to the tip of the 500-foot-tall symbol of Blackpool for a smashing view, especially at sunset (daily 10:00–23:00, early Nov–May 10:00–18:00, tower closed when windy, tel. 01253/622-242).

▲Pleasure Beach—These 42 acres, littered with more than 80 rides (including "the best selection of white-knuckle rides in Europe"), ice-skating shows, cabarets, and amusements attract 7 million people a year. The most talked-about attraction is the Pepsi Max Big One, "the world's fastest and highest" roller coaster (235 feet, 85 mph). Another sensation is the Play Station, which rockets you straight up before letting you bungee down. Also memorable is the Passage de Terror and a frightening race called the Steeple Chase—imagine carousel horses stampeding down a roller-coaster track. Kept secret until it's unveiled in 2000, the newest ride—called Project 2000—is billed as "the most spectacular dark ride ever constructed by mankind." Admission is free, and most rides cost a couple of pounds each (Apr–early Nov daily, opens at 10:00 on weekdays, at noon on weekends, closes as early as 17:00 or as late as 22:00, depending on season, weather, and demand, tel. 01253/341-033). There are several other major amusement centers, including a popular water park called Sand Castle (across the street from Pleasure Beach, tel. 01253/343-602).

▲▲▲People Watching—Blackpool's top sight is its people. You'll see England here as nowhere else. Grab someone's hand and a big stick of "rock" (candy) and stroll. Grown men walk around with huge teddies looking for "bowlingo" places. Ponder

Blackpool

the thought of actually retiring here and spending your last years, day after day, surrounded by Blackpool and wearing a hat with a built-in ponytail. Blackpool puts people in a talkative mood. Ask someone to explain the difference between tea and supper.

▲▲**Variety Show**—Blackpool always has a few razzle-dazzle music, dancing-girl, racy-humor, magic, and tumbling shows. Box offices around town can give you a rundown on what's available (tickets £7–15). I enjoy the old-time music-hall shows. They're corny—neither hip nor polished—but it's fascinating to be surrounded by hundreds of partying British seniors swooning and waving their hankies to the predictable beat. Busloads of happy widows come from all corners of North England to giggle at jokes I'd never tell my grandma. Your B&B has the latest. If that's too lowbrow, Blackpool is second to London in theater. You can always watch a good play.

▲▲**Funny Girls**—Blackpool's current hot bar is just a block from the North Pier. Every night from 20:30 to 23:30 Funny Girls puts on a "glam bam thank you ma'am" burlesque-in-drag show that delights footballers and grannies alike. Cover is only £2 (£3 on weekends). Get your drinks at the bar unless the transvestites are dancing on it. The show, while racy, is not raunchy. The music is very loud. The crowd is young, old, straight, gay, very down-to-earth, and fun loving. Go on a weeknight; Friday and Saturday are jammed. You can pay £5 to £10 for VIP seats to avoid any weekend lines and look down on the show and crowded floor from a mezzanine level (to book, call 01253/624-901).

Blackpool's clubs and discos are cheap, with live bands and an interesting crowd (22:00–01:00). The pubs of Blackpool have a unique tradition of "and your own, luv." Say that here and your barmaid will add 20p to your bill and drop it into her tip jar. (Say it anywhere else and they won't know what you mean.)

▲**Illuminations**—Blackpool was the first town in England to "go electric" in 1879. Now, every fall (Sept 1–Nov 5 in 2000), Blackpool stretches its tourist season by illuminating its six miles of waterfront with countless lights, all blinking and twinkling. The American in me kept saying, "I've seen bigger, and I've seen better," but I filled his mouth with cotton candy and just had some simple fun like everyone else on my specially decorated tram. Look for the animated tableaux on North Shore.

Sleeping in Blackpool
(£1 = about $1.70, tel. code: 01253)
Sleep Code: **S** = Single, **D** = Double/Twin, **T** = Triple, **Q** = Quad, **b** = bathroom, **t** = toilet only, **s** = shower only, **CC** = Credit Card (Visa, MasterCard, Amex).

Blackpool's 140,000 people provide 120,000 beds in 3,500 mostly dumpy, cheap, nondescript hotels and B&Bs. Remember, the town's in the business of accommodating the people who can't afford to go to Spain. Most have the same design—minimal character, maximum number of springy beds—and charge £15 to £18 per person. Empty beds abound except September through November and summer weekends. It's only really tight on Illumination weekends. The first four listings below are on the waterfront in the quiet area they call "the posh end," a mile or two north of the tower, with easy parking and easy access to the center by trolley. The last two are near the train station. When a price range is given, the higher prices are charged during the Illuminations. Prices are soft off-season. The Albert Road Launderette, with short hours and an inconvenient location, is the only game in town (Mon–Sat 9:00–16:00, Sun 10:00–14:00, downtown—7 blocks inland—at Albert Road and Regent Road).

Robin Hood Hotel is a super place, cheery and family run, with a big, welcoming living room and 10 newly and tastefully refurbished rooms and the only sturdy beds I found (Sb-£21–26, Db-£36–42, less for two nights, family deals, CC:VM, entirely nonsmoking, trolley stop: St. Stevens Avenue and walk 1 block north; 1.5 miles north of tower across from a peaceful stretch of beach, 100 Queens Promenade, North Shore FY2 9NS, tel. 01253/351-599, Pam and Colin Webster).

Beechcliffe Private Hotel is clean, smoke free, and family run, with more charm than average (S-£15–17.50, D-£30–35, Dt-£33–38, Tt-£50–55, trolley stop: Uncle Tom's, walk a block away from the beach; can pick up from station when possible, 16 Shaftesbury Avenue, North Shore FY2 9QQ, tel. 01253/353-075, David and Brenda).

Prefect Hotel is all smiles and pink-flamingo pretty. It's run-down (with ragged towels) but clean and spacious-for-Blackpool, with fun touches—ask to see the shoe collection (Sb-£17–21, Db-£34–42, CC:VM, smoking allowed, request a view room, trolley to Bispham, 2 miles north of tower at 204 Queens Promenade, FY2 9JS, tel. 01253/352-699, Bill and Pauline Acton).

At **Burlees Hotel,** look beyond the garishly carpeted hallway to find nine bright, comfy, sedately carpeted rooms (Db-£40-52, CC:VM, 2 nights preferred, 1-nighters can book on same day only, most rooms nonsmoking, trolley stop: Uncle Tom's, from Queens Promenade walk 3 blocks inland, 40 Knowle Avenue, FY2 9TQ, tel. & fax 01253/354-535, e-mail: burleeshotel @btinternet.com, Mike and Linda Lawrence).

Valentine Private Hotel is a mix of newly renovated, attractive rooms (with bath added) and older, run-down, cheaper rooms with a bathroom down the hall. Smoking is allowed, but the breakfast room is smoke free (S-£12-15, D-£24-30, Db-£30-36, CC:VMA, family deals, plenty of showers, 3 blocks from the station at 35 Dickson Road, FY1 2AT, tel. 01253/622-775, Denise and Garry Hinchliffe).

Sandylands Guest House, a plain, "homely" little place two blocks from the station, offers optional £4 evening meals (S-£12-15, D-£24-30, smoky, 8 rooms share 2 bathrooms, 47 Banks Street, FY1 2BE, tel. 01253/294-670, www.sandylands.com, Kevin Poole).

Eating in Blackpool

Your hotel may serve a cheap, early-evening meal. The following places are all between the tower and the North Pier: For mushy peas and good fish and chips, go to the "world famous" **Harry Ramsden's** near the tower (60 The Promenade, tel. 01253/294-386); their advertising brings out the smart aleck in you. **Robert's Oyster Bar** at the corner of West Street and the Promenade, one block south of North Pier, is a fixture that actually predates the resort—as do some of its employees (daily 9:30-22:00). Around the corner on West Street is the **Mitre Bar**—drop in to survey the great photos of old Blackpool (Mon-Sat 11:00-23:00, Sun 12:00-22:30). **The Scullery,** across the street from the bar, is a humble, hardworking pantry serving healthy, hearty food for great prices (daily 10:30-20:00, till 17:00 off-season, 10 West Street). Food in the tower is terrible, but it's not much better elsewhere.

Marks & Spencer has a big supermarket in its basement (Mon-Sat 9:30-17:30, Sun 10:30-16:30, near recommended eateries, on Coronation Street and Church Street).

Transportation Connections—Blackpool

If you're heading to (or from) Blackpool by train, you'll usually need to transfer at **Preston** (3/hrly, 30 min). Train info: tel. 0345-484-950.

Preston to: Keswick, the Lake District (hrly trains, 30 min to Penrith, then catch a bus to Keswick, hrly except Sun 3/day, 40 min), **York** (hrly, 4.5 hrs), **Edinburgh** (8/day, 3 hrs).

Points south: To **Moreton-in-Marsh** in the Cotswolds (every

2 hrs, allow 5 hrs with 2 transfers), **Bath** (hrly, 4.5–5 hrs with 2 transfers), **Conwy** in North Wales (nearly hrly, allow 3 hrs with 2 transfers). Although you'll usually have transfers, you'll find fast and frequent trains. A direct train runs daily between **Blackpool** and **London** (3.5–4 hrs, more frequent, with transfer in Manchester).

Drivers entering and leaving Blackpool: As you approach Blackpool, the motorway dumps you right onto Yeadon Way, which funnels you into a huge city parking lot. Day-trippers need to park here. The quickest way out of town is to drive the Promenade to the Central Pier and turn inland. Under the bridge take an immediate left (take the exit for M55). This gets you into the huge parking lot that leads directly to the motorway.

NEAR BLACKPOOL: LIVERPOOL

Liverpool, a gritty but surprisingly enjoyable city, is a fascinating stop for Beatles fans and those who would like to look urban England straight in its problem-plagued eyes.

The TI is with everything else—on Albert Dock (daily 10:00–17:00, tel. 0151/708-8854). The bus and train stations are a 20-minute walk (or a short city bus ride) from Albert Dock.

Sights—Liverpool

▲**Albert Dock**—Opened in 1852 by Prince Albert and enclosing seven acres of water, the dock is surrounded by five-story brick warehouses. In its day, Liverpool was England's greatest seaport. It prospered as one corner of the triangular commerce of the 18th-century slave trade. As England's economy boomed, so did the port of Liverpool. From 1830 to 1930, 9 million emigrants sailed from Liverpool to find their dreams in the New World. But the port was not deep enough for the big new ships; trade declined after 1890, and by 1972 it was closed entirely. Like Liverpool itself, the docks have enjoyed a renaissance, and today they are the featured attraction of the city. The city's main attractions are lined up here out of the rain and padded by lots of shopping mall–type distractions. There's plenty of parking.

▲**Merseyside Maritime Museum**—This museum, which tells the story of this once-prosperous shipping center, gets an A for effort but feels designed for visiting school groups. The ships section is pretty dull, but the smuggling and customs, slavery, and emigration sections are interesting. The associated **Museum of Liverpool Life** offers a good look at the town's story (both daily 10:00–17:00). A £3 "NMGM8 Pass" gets you into these and a half dozen other Liverpool museums.

Tate Gallery Liverpool—This prestigious 20th-century gallery is next to the Maritime Museum. It won't entertain you as well as its London sister, but if you're into modern art, any Tate's great (free, Tue–Sun 10:00–18:00, closed Mon, tel. 0151/709-0507).

▲**The Beatles Story**—It's kind of sad to think the Beatles are stuck in a museum (and Ringo's in reruns of *Shining Time Station*). While overpriced and not very creative, the story's a great one, and even an avid fan will pick up some new information (£6.95 but discount coupons abound, try not to pay full fare, daily 10:00–18:00, tel. 0151/709-1963). The shop is an impressive pile of Beatles buyables. Die-hard Beatles fans may want to invest a couple of hours in one of several Beatles "Magical Mystery" bus tours (the lads' homes, Penny Lane, and so on, £9.50, two hours). The TI has specifics on the big bus that goes daily. You may want a more fun and intimate minibus Beatles tour from Phil Hughes (£9 per person, minimum £55 per group, three-hour Beatles tours; also offers Liverpool and regional tours; tel. & fax 0151/228-4565, mobile phone 0961-511-223).

▲**Matthew Street**—Beatles fans will want to explore Matthew Street (a 15-minute walk into the center from Albert Dock), including the site of the famous Cavern Club, the new Cavern Club nearby, and the Beatles Shop at #31.

Transportation Connections—Liverpool
By train to: Blackpool (hrly, 2 hrs, transfer at Preston), **York** (hrly, 2.5 hrs), **London** (hrly, 2.5 hrs), **Crewe** (18/day, 45 min). Train info: tel. 0345-484-950.

Route Tips for Drivers
Ruthin to Blackpool via Liverpool: From Ruthin, get to the M53, which tunnels under the Mersey River (£1). Once in Liverpool, follow signs to City Center, Pier Head, and Albert Dock, where you'll find a huge car park next to all the sights. Leaving Liverpool, drive north along the waterfront, following signs to M58 (Preston), then M6, and finally M55 into Blackpool.

    Ruthin to Blackpool (100 miles): From Ruthin, take A494 through the town of Mold and follow the blue signs to the motorway. M56 zips you to M6, where you'll turn north toward Preston and Lancaster. Don't miss your turnoff: A few minutes after Preston take the not-very-clearly signed next exit (#32, M55) into Blackpool and drive as close as you can to the stubby Eiffel-type tower in the town center. Downtown parking is terrible. If you're not spending the day, head for one of the huge £6/day garages. If you're spending the night, drive to the waterfront and head north. My top B&Bs are north on the promenade (easy parking).

LAKE DISTRICT

In the pristine Lake District, Wordsworth's poems still shiver in trees and ripple on ponds. This is a land where nature rules and man keeps a wide-eyed but low profile. Relax, recharge, take a cruise or a hike, and maybe even write a poem. Renew your poetic license at Wordsworth's famous Dove Cottage.

The Lake District, about 30 miles long and 30 miles wide, is nature's lush, green playground. Explore it by foot, bike, bus, or car. While not impressive in sheer height (Scafell Pike, the tallest peak in England, is only 3,206 feet), there's a walking-stick charm about the way nature and the local culture mix. Walking along a windblown ridge or climbing over a rock fence to look into the eyes of a ragamuffin sheep, even tenderfeet get a chance to feel very outdoorsy.

You'll probably have rain mixed with brilliant bright spells. Drizzly days can be followed by delightful evenings. Pubs offer atmospheric shelter at every turn. As the locals are fond of saying, "There's no such thing as bad weather, only unsuitable clothing."

While the south lakes (Windermere, Bowness, Beatrix Potter's cottage) get the promotion and tour crowds and are closer to London, the north lakes (Ullswater, Derwentwater, Buttermere) are less touristy and at least as scenic.

This chapter should actually be called the "North Lakes District." The town of Keswick, the lake called Derwentwater, and the vast time-passed Newlands Valley will be our focus. The area works great by car or train/bus. And Wordsworth and Potter fans can easily side-trip south to see their homes.

Planning Your Time
On a three-week trip in Britain, I'd spend two days and two nights

in the area. The quickest way in is to leave the motorway or train line at Penrith.

Those without a car will use Keswick as a springboard. Cruise the lake and take one of the many hikes in the Cat Bells area. Nonhikers can take a minibus tour.

Here's the most exciting way for drivers to pack their day of arrival: Get an early start from Blackpool or North Wales, leave the motorway at Kendal by 10:30, drive along Windermere and through Ambleside, 11:30–Tour Dove Cottage, 12:30–Backtrack to Ambleside, where a small road leads up and over the dramatic Kirkstone Pass (far more scenic northbound than southbound, get out and bite the wind) and down to Glenridding on Ullswater. You could catch the 14:40 boat. Hike six miles (15:15–18:45) from Howtown back to Glenridding. Drive to your farmhouse B&B near Keswick, with a stop as the sun sets at Castlerigg Stone Circle.

On your second day, explore Buttermere Lake, drive over Honister Pass, explore Derwentwater, and do the Cat Bells High Ridge walk. Spend the evening at the same B&B.

If great scenery is commonplace in your life, the Lake District can be more soothing (and rainy) than exciting. If you're rushed, you could make this area a one-night stand—or even a quick drive-through.

Getting around the Lake District

Those based in Keswick without a car can manage fine. Be sure to pick up the excellent *Lakeland Explorer* magazine (free from TIs and hotels), which explains all the local bus and boat schedules and outlines some great walks for the first-time visitor.

By Foot: Piles of hiking information are available everywhere you turn. Consider buying a detailed map (such as Ordnance Survey). For easy hikes, the fliers at TIs and B&Bs detailing particular routes are helpful. The best ridge walk is immediately outside of town (see "Cat Bells High Ridge Hike," below). The Lake District's TIs advise hikers to check the weather before setting out (for an up-to-date weather report, ask at TI or call 017687/75757), wear suitable clothing, and bring a map.

By Boat: A circular boat service glides you easily around Derwentwater (for a sail/hike option, see "Derwentwater," below).

By Bus: Buses take you quickly and easily (if not always frequently) to all nearby points of interest. Pick up the free 30-page *Lakeland Explorer* bus brochure for schedules and suggested bus/hike outings.

By Bus Tour: Mountain Goat Tours runs an interesting variety of half-day (£13) and all-day (£24) minibus tours from Keswick (daily Easter–Oct). They are informative, off the beaten path, led by local guides, and great for people with bucks who'd like to see the area without hiking or messing with public

Lake District

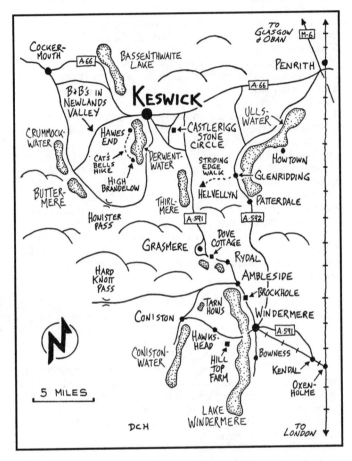

transport (office at Keswick central car park, CC:VM, tel. 017687/73962, www.lakes-pages.co.uk).

The National Trust offers more sedate, less expensive tours with an emphasis on conservation (£11/half day, £21/full day, book at TI or office at Keswick boat dock, CC:VM, tel. 017687/73780).

As a supercheap alternative to tours, take a round-trip on bus #77 from Keswick to Buttermere and back; it loops around Honister Pass (May–Oct, 2/day clockwise, 2/day "anti-clockwise," 1.5 hrs).

By Bike: Several shops rent bikes in Keswick; the most

central is Lake Pedlar (£13/day, daily 9:00–17:30, helmet included, tandems available, CC:VM, behind Bryson's Bakery on the main street, take alley to car park, tel. 017687/75752). The Keswick TI sells plasticized cycling maps and the leaflet "6 Cycle Routes from Keswick" (£1).

By Car: Nothing is very far from Keswick and Derwentwater. Get a good map, get off the big roads, and leave the car, at least occasionally, for some walking. In summer, the Keswick–Ambleside–Windermere–Bowness corridor (A591) suffers from congestion. If you want to rent a car in Keswick, Fiat is your only choice (from £32/day, Mon–Sat 8:30–17:30, closed Sun, Lake Road in town center, tel. 017687/72064).

KESWICK

As far as touristy Lake District centers go, Keswick (kezz-ick, pop. 5,000) is far more enjoyable than Windermere, Bowness, or Ambleside. An important mining center (slate, copper, lead) through the Middle Ages, Keswick became a resort in the 19th century. Its fine Victorian buildings recall those romantic days when city slickers first learned about "communing with nature." Today the compact town is lined with tea shops, pubs, gift shops, and hiking-gear shops. The lake is a pleasant five-minute walk from the town center.

Keswick is the ideal home base: plenty of good B&Bs (see "Sleeping," below), an easy bus connection to the nearest train station at Penrith, and a prime location near the best lake in the area, Derwentwater. In Keswick everything is within a five-minute walk of everything else: the market square, the TI, recommended B&Bs, a bike-rental shop, the municipal pitch-and-putt golf course, the bus stop, Mountain Goat minibus tour starting point, a lakeside boat dock, the post office (with Internet access), and a central car park. Saturday is market day, and the town square is packed and lively.

Keswick hosts an annual convention in July that books up a lot of rooms. Reserve well in advance if you plan to visit during July 15 to 29 in 2000.

Tourist Information: The helpful TI is in Moot Hall right in the middle of the main square (daily 9:30–17:30, Nov–Easter 9:30–16:30, tel. 017687/72645). They sell great 50p–£1 brochures outlining nearby hikes (including a Keswick Town Trail for history buffs), help you figure out public transportation to outlying sights, sell Lakeland Explorer bus passes (4-day £13.60 passes only, get £5.50 1-day passes on the bus), change money, book rooms, and sell Derwentwater Launch tickets at a discount of 85p per person, £1 per family.

Internet Access: Inside the P.O., just off the main square, is U-Compute (Jul–Sept Mon–Sat 8:30–20:00, Sun 10:30–16:30;

Oct–Jun until 17:30 and closed Sun; head to computers at the back to the right, don't wait in P.O. queue).

Sights—Keswick

▲▲**Daily Walks**—Walks of varying levels of difficulty led by local guides depart from the Keswick TI daily at 10:15, regardless of the weather (£4, Easter–October, bring a lunch; sometimes taxi, bus, or boat fare required; return by 17:00, tel. 017687/72645). For a list of free daily guided walks offered throughout the Lake District by "Voluntary Wardens," check the *Events 2000* booklet at any local TI. Many of the hikes start at Brockhole National Park Visitors Centre, which is an easy bus ride or a short drive from Keswick, but two hikes a week originate in Keswick (on Sun and Wed afternoons, Jul–Sept).

▲**Pencil Museum**—Graphite was first discovered centuries ago in Keswick. A hunk of the stuff proved great for marking sheep in the 15th century, and the rest is history (which you can learn all about here). While you can't tour the 150-year-old factory where the famous Derwent pencils are made, the charming museum on the edge of Keswick is a good way to pass a rainy hour (£2, daily 9:30–16:00, rentable headsets are not necessary, but the fine and free 20-minute film is; cheap brass rubbing in the shop, tel. 017687/73626).

▲**Plays**—Locals are proud of their new Theatre by the Lake, which offers events year-round and plays nearly nightly in summer. This is a fine opportunity to do something completely local (£9–16, tel. 017687/74411).

▲**Golf**—A lush nine-hole pitch 'n' putt golf course separates the town from the lake and offers a classy, cheap, and convenient chance to golf near the birthplace of the sport (daily 9:30–20:00, £3.50 for nine holes).

Swimming—The Leisure Center has a pool kids love, with a huge water slide (a short walk from the town center, tel. 017687/72760 for hours).

Sights—Derwentwater Area

▲▲**Derwentwater**—This is one of the region's most photographed and popular lakes. With four islands, good circular boat service, plenty of trails, and the pleasant town of Keswick at its north end, Derwentwater entertains.

The roadside views aren't much, so walk or cruise. You can walk around the lake (fine trail, but floods in heavy rains, nine miles, three hours), cruise it (50 minutes), or do a hike/sail mix. I suggest a hike/sail trip around the lake. From mid-March to October, boats run from Keswick about every 30 minutes—alternating clockwise and "anti-clockwise"—from 10:00 to 19:30 (during slow times until 17:30; in winter 3/day on weekends), making seven stops on each 50-minute round-trip. The best hour-long lakeside walk is the

Keswick

1.5-mile path between the docks at High Brandlehow and Hawse End. You could continue on foot along the lake back into Keswick. Lodore is an easy stop for its Lodore Falls, a 10-minute walk from the dock (falls behind Lodore Hotel, which serves lunch). The boat trip costs £5 per circle, with free stopovers, or 75p per segment. Stand on the pier or the boat may not stop. The Keswick Launch also offers a 60-minute cruise every evening mid-June through September (£5.70) and rents rowboats (£3/hr, tel. 017687/72263). ▲▲**Cat Bells High Ridge Hike**—For a great (and fairly easy) "king of the mountain" feeling, sweeping views, and a close-up look at the weather blowing over the ridge, hike about two hours from Hawes End up along the ridge to Cat Bells (1,480 feet) and down to High Brandlehow. From there you can catch the boat or take the easy path along the shore of Derwentwater to your Hawes End starting point. This is probably the most dramatic family walk in the area. From Keswick, the lake, or your farmhouse B&B, you can see silhouetted stick figures hiking along this ridge. Drivers can park free at Hawes End (not particularly safe) or at the Littletown Farm on the Newlands Valley side of Cat Bells (£1). The Keswick TI sells a "Skiddaw & Cat Bells" brochure on the hike (50p).

Cat Bells is just the first of a series of peaks all connected by a fine ridge trail. Heartier hikers continue up to nine miles along this same ridge, enjoying valley and lake views as they arc around the Newlands Valley toward (and even down to) Buttermere. After High Spy you can descend an easy path into Newlands Valley. An ultimate day plan would be to bus to Buttermere, climb Robinson, and follow the ridge around to Cat Bells and back to Keswick.

▲▲Car Hiking from Keswick—Distances are short, roads are narrow and have turnouts, and views are rewarding. Ask your B&B host for advice. Particularly scenic drives include Latrigg (from a car park just north of Keswick walk a few minutes to the top of the hill for a commanding view of the town and lake). Two miles south of Keswick on the lakeside B5289 Borrowdale Valley Road, take the small road left (signposted Watendlath) for a half mile to a packhorse bridge (a quintessential Lake District scene) and, a half mile farther, to a car park and the "surprise view" of Derwentwater. Following the road to its end, you hit the idyllic farm hamlet of Watendlath, where you can ponder the tiny lake and lazy farm animals. (On summer Sundays, free shuttle buses—offered to minimize traffic congestion—run hourly between Keswick and Watendlath. Ride to the end and hike home.) Return down to B5289 and back to Keswick or farther south to scenic Borrowdale and over the dramatic pass to Buttermere.

▲▲Buttermere—This ideal little lake with a lovely, encircling four-mile stroll offers nonstop, no-sweat, Lake District beauty. If you're not a hiker but kind of wish you were, take this walk. If you're very short on time, at least stop here and get your shoes dirty. (Parking and pubs are in Buttermere village.) Buttermere is connected with Borrowdale and Derwentwater by a great road over the rugged Honister Pass, strewn with glacial debris and curious shaggy Swaledale sheep (looking more like goats with their curly horns). In the other direction you can explore the cruel Newlands Valley or carry on through gentler scenery along Crummock Water and through the forested Whinlatter Pass (fine new Visitors Centre with a café the flying squirrels love) and back to Keswick. From May through October, bus #77 makes a round-trip loop between Keswick and Buttermere over Honister Pass (2/day in both directions, 1.5 hrs).

▲▲**Castlerigg Stone Circle**—These 38 stones, 90 feet across and 3,000 years old, are mysteriously laid out on a line between the two tallest peaks on the horizon. For maximum goose pimples (as they say here), show up at sunset (free, open all the time, 3 miles east of Keswick, follow brown signs, 3 minutes off A66, easy parking).

▲▲**More Hikes**—The area is riddled with wonderful hikes. B&Bs all have fine advice. From downtown Keswick you can walk the seven-mile Latrigg hike, which includes the Castlerigg Stone Circle (pick up 50p map/guide from TI). From the car park at Newlands Pass, at the top of Newlands Valley, an easy one-mile walk to Knottrigg probably offers more thrills per calorie burned than any walk in the region.

▲**Lakeland Sheep & Wool Centre**—If you're from farm country this is nothing special. But for a city slicker, the Sheep & Wool Centre offers an interesting and entertaining introduction to the region's most famous residents: its sheep. In the 50-minute show you'll meet 19 different breeds of sheep, watch one get sheared, and see sheepdogs do their impressive thing. Afterward you'll meet the stars of the show. It's a hands-on experience kids enjoy (£3, 4 shows daily: 10:30, 12:00, 14:00, and 15:30, only Wed–Sun in winter, unimpressive exhibition but good sheep-stuff shop, drive west from Keswick 15 minutes on A-66, at A-5086 roundabout you'll see the 300-seat auditorium on left).

Keswick Sheepdog Demonstration—Every Wednesday afternoon, five sheepdogs at various level of training (some championship) round up sheep and ducks in a field (£2, May–Sept 16:00–17:00, on Brundholme Road a mile northeast of Keswick off A66, tel. 017687/79603).

Sights—Windermere Area

▲**Brockhole National Park Visitors Centre**—Check the events board as you enter. The center offers a 20-minute introduction-to-the-lakes slide show (played upon request), an information desk, organized walks, exhibits, a bookshop, a good cafeteria, gardens, nature walks, and a large car park. It's in a stately old lakeside mansion between Ambleside and the town of Windermere on A591 (Apr–Oct daily 10:00–17:00, free entry but £3 to park, tel. 015394/46601). The bookshop has an excellent selection of maps and guidebooks. I enjoyed Hunter Davies' refreshingly opinionated (but now a bit dated) *Good Guide to the Lakes* (£6).

▲▲**Dove Cottage**—William Wordsworth, the poet whose appreciation of nature and back-to-basics lifestyle put this area on the map, spent his most productive years (1799–1808) in this well-preserved old cottage on the edge of Grasmere. Today it's the obligatory sight for any Lake District visit. Even if you're not a fan, Wordsworth's "plain living and high thinking," his appreciation of nature, his romanticism, and the ways his friends unleashed their creative talents are appealing. The 20-minute cottage tour (departures every few minutes) and adjoining museum are excellent. In dry weather the garden where the poet was much inspired is worth a wander. Even a speedy, jaded museum goer will want at least an hour here (£4.80, includes voucher for 15 percent off Rydal Mount, below, and Cockermouth, Wordsworth's birthplace, daily 9:30–17:30, tel. 015394/35544).

Rydal Mount—Wordsworth's final, higher-class home with a lovely garden and view lacks the charm of Dove Cottage. Just down the road from Dove Cottage, it's worthwhile only for Wordsworth fans (£3.50, includes voucher for 15 percent off Dove Cottage and Cockermouth, daily 9:30–17:00; Nov–Feb 10:00–16:00 and closed Tue; tel. 015394/33002).

▲**Beatrix Potter's Hill Top Farm and Other Sights**—Many come to the lakes on a Beatrix Potter pilgrimage. Sensing that, entrepreneurial locals have dreamed up a number of BP sights. This can be confusing. Most important (and least advertised) is **Hill Top Farm,** the 17th-century cottage where Potter wrote many of her Peter Rabbit books (£4, Sat–Wed 11:00–17:00, closed Thu–Fri and Nov–Mar, next to Sawrey, two miles south of Hawkshead, tel. 015394/36269). Small, dark, and crowded, it gives a good look at her life and work.

The **Beatrix Potter Gallery** (in the neighboring, likeable town of Hawkshead) shows off BP's original drawings and watercolor illustrations used in her children's books and tells more about her life and work (£3, Sun–Thu 10:30–16:30, closed Fri–Sat and Nov–Mar, Main Street, tel. 015394/36355). The gimmicky **World of Beatrix Potter** tour—a hit with children—features a five-minute video trip into the world of Mrs. Tiggy-winkle and company, a series of tableaus starring the same imaginary gang, and a 15-minute video biography of BP (not worth £3.25, daily 10:00–17:30, Sept–Easter 10:00–16:30, in Bowness near Windermere town, tel. 015394/88444).

Hard Knott Pass—Only 1,300 feet above sea level, this pass is a thriller, with a narrow, winding, steeply graded road. Just over the pass are the scant but evocative remains of the Hard Knott Roman fortress. There are great views but miserable rainstorms, and it can be very slow and frustrating when the one-lane road with turnouts is clogged by traffic (avoid in summer).

Sights—Ullswater Area

▲▲**Ullswater Hike and Boat Ride**—Long, narrow Ullswater offers eight miles of diverse and grand Lake District scenery. While you can drive it or cruise it, I'd ride the boat from the south tip halfway up and hike back. Boats leave Glenridding regularly—from four to eight a day, depending on the season (£2.85, daily

10:00–16:30, until 17:45 Jul–Aug, 35-minute ride, cheap and safe parking lot, free timetable shows walking route, tel. 017684/82229 for schedule, arrive 20 minutes before departure in summer). Ride to the first stop, Howtown, halfway up the lake. Then spend four hours hiking and dawdling along the well-marked path by the lake south to Patterdale and then along the road back to Glenridding. This is a serious seven-mile walk with good views, varied terrain, and a few bridges and farms along the way. Wear good shoes and be prepared for rain. For a shorter hike from Howtown Pier, consider a three-mile loop around Hallin Fell. Round-trip boat rides cost only 85p more than one way.

Several steamer trips chug daily up and down Ullswater. A good rainy-day plan is to ride the covered boat up and down the lake (£5.80, two hours) or to Howtown and back (£3.70, one hour). To reach Glenridding by bus from Keswick, allow two hours with a transfer at Penrith.

Helvellyn—Often considered the best high-mountain hike in the Lake District, this breathtaking, round-trip route from Glenridding includes the spectacular Striding Edge ridge walk. Be careful; do this six-hour hike only in good weather and get advice from the Glenridding TI (tel. 017684/82414). While there are shorter routes, the Glenridding ascent is best. The Keswick TI has a helpful "Helvellyn from Glenridding" leaflet on the hike (50p).

Sleeping in the Lake District
(£1 = about $1.70, tel. code: 017687)

Sleeping in Keswick
Sleep Code: **S** = Single, **D** = Double/Twin, **T** = Triple, **Q** = Quad, **b** = bathroom, **t** = toilet only, **s** = shower only, **CC** = Credit Card (Visa, MasterCard, Amex).

The Lake District abounds with attractive B&Bs, guest houses, and hostels. It needs them all when summer hordes threaten the serenity of this romantic mecca. Alert: Book well in advance if you plan to visit during Keswick's annual convention (July 15–29 in 2000).

Outside of summer, if you have a car, you should have no trouble finding a room. But to get a particular place (especially on a Saturday), call ahead. Those using public transportation should stay in Keswick. With a car, drive into a remote farmhouse experience. Lakeland hostels are cheaper and filled with an interesting crowd. The Keswick TI can give you phone numbers of places with vacancies if you call or book you a room if you drop in.

In Keswick I've featured two streets, each within three blocks of the bus station and town square. "The Heads" is a classier street lined with proud Victorian houses, close to the lake and new theatre, overlooking a golf course. Stanger Street, a bit humbler but also quiet and handy, has smaller homes. All of my Keswick listings are strictly smoke free. The launderette is around the corner from the bus station on Main Street (daily 7:30–19:30, £3 wash and dry, change machine and coin-op flake dispenser, £2 extra for full service by 10:00 or earlier; just leave clothes inside by rear door with a note and she'll do them for you).

Sleeping on The Heads

Berkeley Guest House, a big slate mansion enthusiastically run by Barbara Crompton, has a pleasant lounge, narrow hallways, and carefully appointed, comfortable rooms. The chirpy, skylight-bright £36 bathless double in the attic is a fine value if you don't mind the stairs (D-£34, Dt-£42, Db-£46, The Heads, Keswick, Cumbria, CA12 5ER, tel. 017687/74222, e-mail: berkeley@tesco.net).

Parkfield is thoughtfully run and decorated by Fay and Bob Watson. This big Victorian house is bright and pastel, with a fine, restful view lounge (8 rooms, 1 on the ground floor, Db-£44–48 with this book through 2000, CC:VM, car park, strictly nonsmoking, vegetarian options, The Heads, CA12 5ES, tel. 017687/72328, www.kencomp.net/parkfield).

Howe Keld Lakeland Hotel offers more of a guest-house feel, with 15 attractive rooms, a wide variety of breakfast selections, £12.75 evening meals, and a bar (Sb-£28, budget Db-£40, Db-£48, clarify which kind of double you have, minimum 2 nights, prices with this book through 2000, 2 ground-floor rooms, 5–7 The Heads, CA12 5ES, tel. & fax 017687/72417, www.users .globalnet.co.uk/~howekeld, David and Valerie Fisher plus their two adorable girls).

West View Guest House, next door, with seven tastefully furnished rooms, is pleasant and a decent value (D-£36, Db-£48, The Heads, CA12 5ES, tel. 017687/73638, run by friendly Carole and John Fullagar).

Sleeping on Stanger Street

Abacourt House is an old Victorian slate townhouse completely redone by Sheila and Bill Newman. Bill, who just finished climbing all the "Wainwright" peaks, is a wealth of Lake District sightseeing information and happy to point you in the most scenic direction. All five doubles have firm beds, TVs, and shiny, modern bathrooms (Db-£42, no children, 26 Stanger Street, Keswick, CA12 5JU, tel. 017687/72967, http://members.aol.com/abacourt).

Dunsford Guest House, a few doors down, has four cheery, inviting rooms run by an energetic couple who get their exercise fellrunning—running the mountain trails (Db-£39 with this book, veggie breakfast options, 16 Stanger Street, CA12 5JU, tel. 017687/75059, www.dunsford.clara.net, Pat and photographer Peter Richards).

Fell House B&B, with six charming rooms, is run by Barbara Hossack, who serves tea and homemade cakes each evening and won a "healthy heartbeat" award in 1999 for her cooking (S-£17.50, D-£35, Db-£42, 28 Stanger Street, CA12 5JU, tel. 017687/72669).

Badgers Wood B&B, at the top of the street, has six pastel, stocking-feet-comfortable rooms (S-£18, D-£36, Dt-£40, Db-£44 with this book, 30 Stanger Street, CA12 5JU, tel. 017687/72621, www.badgers-wood.co.uk, Irene and David).

Ellergill Guest House has three pleasant rooms, one with a super view (D-£36, Db-£39, 22 Stanger Street, CA12 5JU, tel. 017687/73347, e-mail: ellergill@yahoo.co.uk, Christine and Keith Taylor).

Two former hotels now operate as hostels with £10 dorm beds: **Keswick** (3- to 10-bed rooms, center of town just off Station Road, tel. 017687/72484) and **Derwentwater** (4- to 22-bed rooms, two miles south of Keswick, tel. 017687/77246).

Sleeping in Newlands Valley

With a car, I'd drive 10 minutes past Keswick down the majestic Newlands Valley. Hiking opportunities are wonderful. If the place had a lake it would be packed with tourists. But it doesn't—and it isn't. The valley is studded with 500-year-old farms that have been in the same family for centuries. Shearing day is reason to rush home from school. Sons get school out of the way ASAP and follow their dads. Neighbor girls marry sons and move in. Grandparents retire to the cottage next door. With the price of wool depressed, most of the wives supplement the family income by running B&Bs. The rooms are much plainer than in town. Traditionally, farmhouses lacked central heating, and while they are now heated, you can still request a hot-water bottle to warm up your bed.

Newlands Valley is just over the Cat Bells ridge from Derwentwater between Keswick and Buttermere. Leave Keswick heading west on the Cockermouth Road (A66). For Birkrigg, Keskadale, and Ellas Crag B&Bs, take the second Newlands Valley exit through Braithwaite and follow signs through Newlands Valley (drive toward Buttermere). You'll pass Ellas Crag first, then the curious purple house, then Birkrigg Farm B&B, and finally Keskadale Farm (about four miles before Buttermere). The road is one lane with passing turnouts. For the Low Skelgill Farm, take the first Newlands Valley exit, head through Portinscale on the Buttermere Road for three miles to Stair, then look for the sign.

Birkrigg Farm is the ideal farmhouse B&B. Mrs. Margaret Beaty offers visitors a comfy lounge, evening tea (good for socializing with her other guests), a classy breakfast, a territorial view, and perfect peace on this 220-acre working farm. Take your toast and last cup of tea out to the front yard bench (£17–18 per person in S, D, T, or Q, discounts for kids, one shower, one tub, and three WCs for six rooms, closed Dec–Feb, Newlands Pass Road, Keswick, Cumbria, CA12 5TS, tel. 017687/78278).

Keskadale Farm B&B is another great farmhouse experience, with valley views and ponderosa hospitality. This working farm has lots of curly horned sheep and three rooms to rent (D/Db-£40–44, closed Dec–Feb, nonsmoking, 1 minute farther down Newlands Pass Road to Buttermere Road on a hairpin turn, Keskadale Farm, Newlands, Keswick CA12 5TS, tel. 017687/78544, fax 017687/78150, Margaret Harryman). One of the valley's oldest, it's made from 500-year-old ship beams.

Low Skelgill Farm, with three rooms sharing two bathrooms, is immediately under Cat Bells. This is ideal for hikers, since you can leave your car there for the Cat Bells ridge walk (S-£17, D-£34, less for two nights, take the Buttermere Road to Stair, then follow the "narrow-gated" road, look for Low Skelgill, not simply Skelgill, tel. 017687/78453, Ann Grave). She also runs a rustic "camping barn" with mattresses for £3.50 a night (no bedding provided).

Ellas Crag B&B, in the same glorious setting, is a more comfortable stone house rather than a farm. This homey place, with a good mix of modern and traditional, is enthusiastically run by Tony, Jean, and Catherine Hartley, who cook up great gourmet-type breakfasts and £15 dinners with an emphasis on freshness (S-£20, Ds-£40, no twin beds, only doubles, nonsmoking, veggie options, laundry possible, Stair, Newlands Valley, CA12 5TT, tel. 017687/78217). Nearby, **Uzziar,** a sheep farm, rents three rooms (Db-£36, Newlands Valley, CA12 5TS, tel. 017687/7837).

Sleeping in Buttermere or Embleton

Buttermere: The **Bridge Hotel,** just beyond Newlands Valley at Buttermere, offers a classy, musty, Old World, countryside hotel experience (22 rooms, £65 per person with a 5-course dinner, cheaper for longer stays, £45 per person B&B only upon request, CC:VM, Buttermere, Cumbria, CA13 9UZ, tel. 017687/70252, fax 017687/70215). There are no shops within 10 miles—only peace and quiet a stone's throw from one of the region's most beautiful lakes. Buttermere also has a hostel (see below).

Embleton: Lambfoot House, run by Ruth and Howard Holden, has three cozy rooms named after sheep (S-£21, Db-£46, nonsmoking, 10 miles from Keswick, Embleton, CA13 9XL, tel. 017687/76424, fax 017687/76721, www.lambfoot .co.uk). From Keswick, take A66 (direction: Cockermouth), turn right at the second Embleton signpost and go 200 yards.

Lake District Hostels

The Lake District's inexpensive hostels, usually located in great old buildings, are handy sources of information and social fun (£6–11/bed). Local TIs have lists. The Lake District's free booking service (Easter–Oct daily 9:00–18:00, tel. 015394/31117) will tell you which of the area's 30 hostels have available beds and can even book a place on your credit card (no more than seven days in advance). Since most hostels don't answer their phones during the day and many are full, this is a helpful service. Hostelers need to be members or buy a £11 membership.

The **Buttermere King George VI Memorial Hostel,** a quarter-mile south of Buttermere village on Honister Pass Road, has good food, family rooms, and a royal setting (tel. 017687/70245). The well-run **Borrowdale Hostel** is secluded in Borrowdale Valley just south of Rosthwaite (drying rooms, tel. 017687/70245).

Eating in the Lake District

Eating in Keswick

The bus station faces a fine **supermarket** (Mon–Sat 9:00–19:00, Sun 10:00–16:00), which has a smoke-free **Coffee Shop Café** popular with locals. It features regional specialties and a menu that's healthy for your body and your pocketbook (Mon–Sat 9:30–17:00, until 18:00 Jul–Aug, Sun 10:00–16:00). **Maysons Whole Food Restaurant** is favored for its home cooking: curry, Cajun, vegetarian options, and not a chip in sight. It feels Californian (£6 meals, Jun–Oct daily 10:00–20:45, otherwise 10:30–16:30, family-friendly, on Lake Road, tel. 017687/74104). **Kitchins Cellar Bar** is the latest local favorite for its reasonable prices and good food, a cut above pub grub (daily 12:00–14:00, 18:00–21:00, same menu for restaurant or cellar bar, but "lite" meals available only in bar, CC:VM, 18 Lake Road, tel. 017687/72990).

Keswick Lodge Pub is popular for its fine pub meals and atmosphere (daily 12:00–21:00, just off the main square on Main Street, tel. 017687/74584), the **Pheasant Inn** for its pub-simple country fare (Mon–Sat 12:00–14:00, 17:30–20:00, Sun 19:00–20:00, 10-min walk, at top of Stanger Street, angle right to cross river, turn left along riverside path to Crosthwaite Road, turn right). For fish and chips, Keswickians go to **The Old Keswickian** (daily 11:15–23:30, facing TI, take out or eat upstairs).

It's easy to find ready-made sandwiches for your hike: try the supermarket or **Bryson's Bakery** on the main square or get one freshly made at the **Coffee Lounge** (down a narrow alley to the right of Bryson's as you face it).

Eating in Newlands Valley

Since most farmhouses don't serve dinner to their guests, take the lovely 10-minute drive to Buttermere for your evening meal at the **Fish Hotel** pub (£5, nightly 18:00–21:00, family-friendly, limited menu, good fish, beaucoup chips, no vegetables) or the more expensive but much cozier and tastier **Bridge Hotel** pub (£6 or £7, nightly 18:00–21:30, more interesting menu, crunchy veggies). On the Keswick side of Newlands Valley, the **Farmer's Arms** pub in Portinscale also serves good pub grub. **Swinside Inn,** the only pub actually in Newlands Valley, is a little tatty but serves decent meals.

Transportation Connections—Lake District

Keswick by bus to: Buttermere (4/day via Whinlatter Forestry Centre and Crummock Water, 40 min), **Borrowdale** (8/day to the powerfully scenic valley south of Derwentwater, Grange, and Seatoller, 30 min), **Grasmere/Ambleside/Windermere** (hrly, 1 hr), **Penrith** (£3, hrly 7:00–21:50, only three on Sunday, 40 min, offered by Stagecoach X4 and X5 buses). Buses run from the Penrith train station to **Ullswater** and **Glenridding** (6/day, 1 hr, direction: Patterdale). Bus info: tel. 01946/63222.

Penrith by train to: Oban (hrly to Glasgow, 2 hrs; then to Oban, 3/day, 3 hrs), **Edinburgh** (8/day, 2 hrs), **Blackpool** (hrly, 2 hrs, transfer in Preston), **Liverpool** (hrly, 2.5 hrs), **Birmingham** (hrly, 3 hrs), **London's** Euston Station (hrly, 4.5 hrs). Train info: tel. 0345-484-950.

Route Tips for Drivers

North Wales or Blackpool to the Lake District: The direct, easy way to Keswick is to leave the M6 at Penrith and take the A66 highway 16 miles to Keswick. For the scenic sightseeing drive through the south lakes to Keswick, exit the super M6 on A590/A591 through the towns of Kendal and Windermere to reach Brockhole National Park Visitors Centre. From Brockhole, the A road to Keswick is fastest, but the high road—the tiny road over Kirkstone Pass to Glenridding and lovely Ullswater—is much more dramatic.

For the drive north to **Oban,** see the Highlands chapter.

YORK

Historical York is loaded with world-class sights. Marvel at the York Minster, England's finest Gothic church. Ramble through the Shambles, York's wonderfully preserved medieval quarter. Enjoy a walking tour led by an old Yorker. Hop a train at Europe's greatest Railway Museum, travel to the 1800s in York Castle Museum, and head back a thousand years to Viking York at the Jorvik exhibit.

York has a rich history. In A.D. 71 it was Eboracum, a Roman provincial capital. Constantine was proclaimed emperor here in A.D. 306. In the fifth century, as Rome was toppling, a Roman emperor sent a letter telling England it was on its own, and York became Eoforwic, the capital of the Anglo-Saxon kingdom of Northumbria. A church was built here in 627, and the town was an early Christian center of learning. The Vikings later took the town, and from about 860 to 950 it was a Danish trading center called Jorvik. The invading and conquering Normans destroyed then rebuilt the city, giving it a castle and the walls you see today. Medieval York, with 9,000 inhabitants, grew rich on the wool trade and became England's second city. Henry VIII spared the city's fine minster and used York as his Anglican church's northern capital. The Archbishop of York is second only to the Archbishop of Canterbury in the Anglican Church. In the Industrial Age, York was the railway hub of North England. When it was built, York's train station was the world's largest. Today, except for its huge chocolate factory (Kit-Kats are made here), York's leading industry is tourism.

Planning Your Time

York rivals Edinburgh as the best sightseeing city in Britain after London. On even a 10-day trip through Britain, it deserves two nights and a day. For the best 36 hours, follow this plan: Catch the 19:00 city walking tour on the evening of your arrival. The next morning be at Jorvik at 9:00 when it opens (to avoid the midday crowds, or prebook at least a day ahead; see "Jorvik" below). The nearby Castle Museum is worth the rest of the morning (10:00–noon, I could spend even more time here). Three options for your early afternoon: shoppers browse the Shambles, train buffs tour the National Railway Museum, and scholars do the Yorkshire Museum. Tour the Minster at 16:00 before catching the 17:00 evensong service. Finish your day with an early evening stroll along the wall and perhaps through the abbey gardens. This schedule assumes you're there in the summer (evening orientation walk) and that there's an evensong on. Confirm your plans with the TI.

Orientation (tel. code: 01904)

The sightseer's York is small. Virtually everything is within a few minutes' walk: the sights, train station, TI, and B&Bs. The longest walk a visitor might take (from a B&B across the old town to the Castle Museum) is 15 minutes.

Bootham Bar, a gate in the medieval town wall, is the hub of your York visit. At Bootham Bar (and on Exhibition Square facing it) you'll find the TI, the starting points for most walking tours and bus tours, handy access to the medieval town wall, Gillygate (pronounced "jilly-gate," lined with good eateries), and Bootham Street, which leads to the recommended B&Bs. (In York, a "bar" is a gate and a "gate" is a street. Go ahead, blame the Vikings.)

Tourist Information: The TI at Bootham Bar sells a 75p "York Map and Guide." Ask for the free monthly *What's On* guide and the monthly *Gig Guide* for live music (Apr–Oct Mon–Sat 9:00–18:00, Sun 9:00–18:00; Jul–Aug until 19:00; Nov–Mar Mon–Sat 9:00–17:00, Sun 9:30–15:00, tel. 01904/621-756, pay WCs next door, built into gate of Bootham Bar). The TI books rooms for a £3 fee, sells theatre tickets, and can help with bus and train schedules. The train station TI is smaller but provides all the same information and services (Apr–Sept Mon–Sat 9:00–20:00, Sun 9:30–17:00, shorter hours off-season).

Arrival in York: The station is a five-minute walk from town; turn left down Station Road and follow the crowd toward the Gothic towers of the Minster. After the bridge, a block before the Minster, signs to the TI send you left on St. Leonard's Place. Recommended B&Bs are a five-minute walk from there. (For a shortcut to B&B area from station, walk along river to railway bridge, cross bridge on walkway, cross car park for B&Bs on St. Mary's Street, or duck through pedestrian walkway under tracks to B&Bs on Sycamore and Queen Anne's Road). With lots of luggage, consider a quick taxi ride (£3).

York

Helpful Hints

Festivals: *York Millennium Mystery Plays*, a series of dramas based on the Bible and involving 200 actors, covering nothing less than the story of humankind, will run from June 22 to July 22 in 2000. York's annual Early Music festival strums and hums from July 7 to 16. Book a room well in advance during festival times.

Internet Access: The Gateway, an Internet café, has eight computers (£5/hr, Mon–Wed 10:00–20:00, Thu–Sat 10:00–23:00, Sun 12:00–16:00, 26 Swinegate, tel. 01904/646-446). The Impressions Gallery has two in a hallway (£5/hr, Mon–Fri 9:30–17:30, on Castlegate, next to Fairfax House, near Jorvik).

Bike Rental: Try Trotters, just outside Monk Bar (£10/day, helmets-£2, Mon–Sat 9:30–17:00, Sun 10:30–15:30, tel. 01904/622-868).

Car Rental: If you're nearing the end of your trip, consider dropping your car upon arrival in York. The money saved by turning it in early nearly pays for the train ticket that whisks you effortlessly to Edinburgh or London. Avis (1 Layerthorpe, tel. 01904/610-460), Hertz (at train station, tel. 01904/612-586), Kenning Car & Van Rental (Micklegate, tel. 01904/659-328), and Budget (Foss Islands Road, tel. 01904/644-919) all have offices in York. Beware, car rental agencies close Saturday afternoon and all day Sunday—when dropping off is O.K. but picking up is impossible.

Tours of York

▲▲▲**Walking Tours**—Charming local volunteer guides give energetic, entertaining, and free two-hour walks through York (daily 10:15 all year, plus 14:15 Apr–Oct, plus 19:00 Jun–Aug, from Exhibition Square across from TI). There are many other commercial York walking tours. YorkWalk Tours, for example, has reliable guides and many themes to choose from (£4.50, tel. 01904/622-303, TI has schedule). The various ghost tours, all offered after nightfall, are more fun than informative.

▲**Guide Friday Hop-on Hop-off Bus Tours**—York's Guide Friday offers tour guides on speed who can talk enthusiastically to three sleeping tourists in a gale on a topless double-decker bus for an hour without stopping. Buses make the hour-long circuit, covering secondary York sights that the city walking tours skip—the workaday perimeter of town. Tickets cost £8 on the bus or from the TI (hop on and off all day, departures every 10–15 minutes from 9:20 until around 17:00; includes vouchers for discounts on York's sights, read brochure; tel. 01904/640-896). While you can hop on and off where you like, the York route is of no value from a transportation-to-the-sights point of view. I'd catch it at the Bootham Bar TI and ride it for an orientation all the way around (one hour) or get off at the Railway Museum, skipping the last five minutes. Guide Friday's competitors give you a little less for a little less.

Sights—York

▲**City Walls**—The historic walls of York provide a fine two-mile walk. Walk from Bootham Bar (gate) to Monk Bar for outstanding cathedral views. Open from dawn till dusk (barring attacks) and free.

▲▲▲**York Minster**—The pride of York, this largest Gothic church north of the Alps (540 feet long, 200 feet tall) brilliantly shows that the High Middle Ages were far from dark. The word *minster* means a place from which people go out to minister or spread the word of God.

Your first impression might be the spaciousness and brightness of the nave (built 1280–1350). The nave—from the middle period of Gothic, called "Decorated Gothic"—is one of the widest Gothic naves in Europe. Notice the Great West Window (1338) above the entry. The heart in the tracery is called "the heart of Yorkshire." The mysterious dragon's head (sticking out over the nave) was probably used as a crane to lift a font cover.

The north and south transepts are the oldest part of today's church (1220–1270). The oldest complete window in the minster, with the modern-looking grisaille pattern, is the Five Sisters' Window in the north transept (1260).

The fanciful choir and the east end (high altar) is from the last stage of Gothic, Perpendicular (1360–1470). The Great East Window (1405), the largest medieval glass window in existence, shows the beginning and the end of the world, with scenes from Genesis and the Book of Revelation. A chart (on the right, with a tiny, more helpful chart within) highlights the core Old Testament scenes in this hard-to-read masterpiece. Enjoy the art close up on the chart and then step back and find the real thing.

The "foundations" (£2) give you a chance to climb down—archaeologically and physically—through the centuries to see the roots of the much smaller, but still huge, Norman church (Romanesque, 1100) that stood on this spot and, below that, the Roman excavations. Constantine was proclaimed Roman emperor here in A.D. 306. Peek also at the modern concrete save-the-church foundations and the church treasury.

There are three more extra visits to consider. The chapter house, an elaborately decorated 13th-century Gothic dome, features playful details carved in the stonework (pointed out in the flier that comes with the 80p admission). You can step into the crypt—an actual bit of the Romanesque church excavated in modern times—which features 12th-century Romanesque art (80p) or scale the tower (£2.50, 275 steps, great view).

The cathedral opens daily at 7:00 and closes at 20:30 in summer, 18:00 in winter (tel. 01904/624-426). The chapter house, tower, and "foundations" have shorter hours, usually 9:30–18:30 (off-season 10:00–16:30 or 17:30). The crypt's hours are roughly Mon–Sat 9:30–16:30, Sun 13:30–16:30. Follow the "Welcome to the York Minster" flyer and ask about a free guided tour at the reception desk at the entry (tours go frequently, even with just one or two people; you can join one in progress). The helpful blue-armbanded Minster guides are happy to answer your questions. While a donation of £2.50 to visit the church is reasonably requested, by visiting all the small extra spots inside I give that (and more) in the form of those admissions. Just pay for and enjoy all the little extras.

Evensong is a chance to experience the cathedral in musical and spiritual action. The 45-minute evensong services are held at 17:00 on weekdays and 16:00 on weekends but are usually spoken on Monday and when the choir is off.

▲**The Shambles**—This is the most colorful old York street in the half-timbered, traffic-free core of town. Ye olde downtown York, while very touristy, is a window-shopping, busker-filled, people watcher's delight. Don't miss the more frumpy Newgate Market or the old-time candy store just opposite the bottom end of the Shambles.

▲▲▲**York Castle Museum**—Truly one of Europe's top museums, this is a Victorian home show, the closest thing to a time-tunnel experience England has to offer. It includes the 19th-century Kirkgate: a fine collection of old shops well stocked exactly as they were 150 years ago, along with costumes, armor, an eye-opening Anglo-Saxon helmet (from A.D. 750), and the entertaining "every home should have one" exhibit showing the evolution of vacuum cleaners, toilets, TVs, bicycles, stoves, and so on, from their crude beginnings to now. The one-way plan allows you to see everything: a working watermill (Apr–Oct), prison cells, man traps, World War II fashions, and old toys (£5, combined ticket with York Story-£6.30, daily 9:30–17:00, Nov–Mar daily 9:30-16:30, cafeteria midway through museum, shop, car park; the £2.50 guidebook, while not necessary, makes a nice souvenir; CC:VM, tel. 01904/653-611). Clifford's Tower (across from Castle Museum, not worth the £1.80, daily 10:00–18:00) is all that's left of York's castle (13th century, site of a 1190 massacre of local Jews—read about this at base of hill).

▲**Jorvik**—Sail the "Pirates of the Caribbean" north and back 800 years and you get Jorvik—more a ride than a museum. Innovative 10 years ago, the commercial success of Jorvik (yor-vik) inspired copycat ride/museums all over England. You'll ride a little Disney-type train car for 13 minutes through the re-created Viking street of Coppergate. It's the year 948, and you're in the village of Jorvik. Next your little train takes you through the actual excavation sight that inspired this. Finally you'll browse through a small gallery of Viking shoes, combs, locks, and other intimate glimpses of that redheaded culture (£5.35, daily 9:00–17:30, Nov–Mar closing varies from 15:30–16:30, last entry 30 minutes before closing, tel. 01904/643-211). Midday lines can be an hour long, and even past the turnstile there's a 25-minute wait. Avoid the line by going very early or very late in the day or by prebooking (call 01904/543-403 at least a day ahead, Mon–Fri 9:00–17:00, office closed on weekends CC:VM, you're given a time slot, add £1 per ticket for entry 10:00–16:00). Some love this "ride"; others call it a gimmicky rip-off. If you're looking for a serious museum, see the Viking exhibit at the Yorkshire Museum. It's better. If you're thinking Disneyland with a splash of history, Jorvik's great. I like Jorvik, but it's not worth a long line.

▲▲**National Railway Museum**—This thunderous museum shows 150 fascinating years of British railroad history. Fanning out from a grand roundhouse is an array of historic cars and engines, including Queen Victoria's lavish royal car and the very first "stagecoaches on rails." There's much more, including exhibits on dining cars, post cars, sleeping cars, train posters, and videos. This biggest and best railroad museum anywhere is interesting even to people who think *Pullman* is Japanese for "tug-o-war" (£6, kids under 17 free, daily 10:00–18:00, tel. 01904/621-261). Cute little "road trains" shuttle you between the Minster and the Railway Museum (£1, leaves Railway Museum every 30 minutes from 10:00–17:30, leaves Minster—from Duncombe Place—every 30 minutes from 10:15–17:45).

▲**Yorkshire Museum**—Located in a lush and lazy park next to the stately ruins of St. Mary's Abbey, Yorkshire Museum is the city's forgotten serious "archaeology of York" museum. While the hordes line up at Jorvik, the best Viking artifacts are here—with no crowds and in a better historical context. You have to walk through this museum, but the stroll takes you through Roman, Saxon, Viking, Norman, and Gothic York. Its prize piece is the delicately etched 15th-century pendant called the Middleham Jewel. The video about the creation of the abbey is worth a look (£4, various exhibitions can increase price, daily 10:00–17:00, tel. 01904/629-745).

Theatre Royal—Fine plays, usually British comedies, entertain the locals (20:00 almost nightly, 19:30 off-season, tickets easy to get, £6.50–14, on St. Leonard's Place next to TI and a 5-minute walk from recommended B&Bs, recorded info tel. 01904/610-041, tickets tel. 01904/623-568).

Honorable Mention—York has a number of other sights and activities (described in TI material) that, while interesting, pale in comparison to the biggies. **Fairfax House** is perfectly Georgian inside, with docents happy to talk with you (£4.25, Sat–Thu 11:00–17:30 except Sun 13:30–17:30, closed Fri except in Aug; possible guided tours offered at 11:00 and 14:00 on Friday during summer—ask in advance at TI; a tour helps bring this well-furnished building to life; on Castlegate, near Jorvik and York Story). **The York Story** offers an exhibit on the building of York and a 45-minute video on the city's past; it's good, straight history (£2, £6.30 combo ticket with Castle Museum, daily 9:30–16:45, Nov–Mar 9:30–16:00, associated with, across the car park from, and promoted by the Castle Museum). The **Hall of the Merchant Adventurers** claims to be the finest medieval guild hall in Europe (from 1361). It's basically a vast half-timbered building with marvelous exposed beams and 15 minutes worth of interesting displays about life and commerce back in the days when York was England's second city (£2, daily 8:30–17:00, Nov–Mar until 15:00, below the Shambles off Piccadilly). The **Richard III "Museum"** is interesting only for Richard III enthusiasts (£1.50, daily 9:00–17:00, Nov–Feb until 16:00, Monk Bar). The **ARC, or Archaeological Resource Center,** is a big former church full of genuine archaeological artifacts that visitors—mostly school groups—can study as pretend archaeologists (£3.60, Mon–Fri 10:00–16:00, Sat 13:00–16:00; great for kids, welcomes adults; plenty of microscopes, hands-on fun, and helpful volunteers;

just off Shambles on St. Saviourgate, tel. 01904/643-211). The **York Dungeon** is gimmicky but, if you insist on papier-mâché gore, is better than the London Dungeon (£6, daily 10:00–18:30, Oct–Mar until 17:30, 12 Clifford Street). The **Antiques Centres** are a fun browse (41 Stonegate near the Minster, and 2 Lendal near Museum Garden). At the **bowling green** on Sycamore Place near the recommended B&Bs, visitors are welcome to buy a pint of beer and watch the action.

Sleeping in York
(£1 = about $1.70, tel. code: 01904)
Sleep Code: **S** = Single, **D** = Double/Twin, **T** = Triple, **Q** = Quad, **b** = bathroom, **t** = toilet only, **s** = shower only, **CC** = Credit Card (**V**isa, **M**asterCard, **A**mex).

　　I've listed peak-season, book-direct prices. Don't use the TI. Outside of July and August some prices go soft.

Sleeping in B&Bs near Bootham Gate
These recommendations are in the handiest B&B neighborhood, a quiet residential neighborhood just outside the old-town wall's Bootham gate, along the road called Bootham. All are within a five-minute walk of the Minster and TI and a 10-minute walk or £3 taxi ride from the station. If driving, head for the cathedral and follow the medieval wall to the gate called Bootham Bar. Bootham "street" leads away from Bootham Bar. These B&Bs are all small, smoke free, and family run and come with plenty of steep stairs but no traffic noise. For a good selection, call well in advance. One-nighters will have a tougher time snagging a room, particularly on Saturday. B&Bs will generally hold a room with a phone call and work hard to help their guests sightsee and eat smartly. Most have permits for street parking. And most don't take credit cards. Regency Dry Cleaning does small loads for £8 (drop off by 9:30 for same-day service, Mon–Fri 8:30–18:00, Sat 9:00–17:00, closed Sun, 75 Bootham, tel. 01904/613-311). The cheaper Washeteria launderette is a 10–15 minute walk from the B&B neighborhood (Mon and Fri 8:00–20:00, Tue–Thu 8:00–18:00, Sat–Sun 8:00–17:30, last wash 1.5 hrs before closing, 124 Haxby Road, at north end of Gillygate, continue on Clarence, then Haxby, tel. 01904/623-379).

　　Airden House, the most central of my Bootham-area listings, has eight spacious rooms, a grandfather clock–cozy TV lounge, and brightness and warmth throughout. Susan and Keith Burrows, a great source of local travel tips, keep their place simple, clean, comfortable, and friendly (D–£40, Db–£50, 1 St. Mary's, York Y030 7DD, tel. 01904/638-915). They also rent a fully equipped apartment and a house for weeklong stays starting Saturdays (Db–£210–250, Qb–£320–350, a 5-minute walk from the Minster).

　　The Sycamore, run by Margaret and David Tyce, is a fine

York, Our Neighborhood

YARDS

- ❶ AIRDEN HOUSE
- ❷ SYCAMORE & ALCUIN
- ❸ HAZELWOOD
- ❹ ABBEYFIELDS
- ❺ CLAREMONT & WHITE DOVES
- ❻ 23 ST. MARY'S
- ❼ QUEEN ANNE'S
- ❽ CROOK LODGE
- ❾ ARNOT HOUSE
- ❿ RIVERSIDE WALK B&B
- ⓫ DEAN COURT HOTEL
- ⓬ GALTRES LODGE HOTEL

value, with seven homey rooms strewn with silk flowers and personal touches. It's at the end of a dead end opposite a fun-to-watch bowling green (D-£33, Db-£42, family deals, 19 Sycamore Place off Bootham Terrace, YO30 7DW, tel. & fax 01904/624-712).

The Hazelwood is my most hotelesque listing in this neighborhood. Ian and Carolyn McNabb, who run this spacious old house, decorate its 14 rooms with modern furnishings, pay fussy attention to details, and serve a classy breakfast (Db-£53–75 depending on room size, 2 ground-floor rooms, CC:VM, £5 laundry service; a fridge, ice, and great travel library in the plush basement lounge; CC:VM, 24 Portland Street, Gillygate, YO31 7EH, tel. 01904/626-548, fax 01904/628-032, e-mail: hazwdyork @aol.com).

Abbeyfields Guest House has nine cozy, bright rooms and a quiet lounge. This doily-free place comes without the usual clutter (S-£22, Sb-£30, Db-£50, 19 Boothham Terrace, YO30 7DH, tel. & fax 01904/636-471, www.abbeyfields.co.uk, Richard and Gwen Martin).

Claremont Guest House is a friendly house offering two delightful rooms and many thoughtful touches, including £3 laundry service (D-£32–40, Db-£36–50, 18 Claremont Terrace off Gillygate, YO31 7EJ, tel. 01904/625-158, e-mail: claremont.york @dial.pipex.com, run by Gill—pronounced Jill—and Martyn Cornell).

White Doves is a cheery little Victorian place with a comfy lounge and four tastefully decorated rooms in soothing pastels (Db-£45–48, family deals, 20 Claremont Terrace off Gillygate, YO31 7EJ, tel. 01904/625-957, Pauline and David Pearce).

23 St. Mary's is extravagantly decorated. Mrs. Hudson has done everything super-correctly and offers nine comfortable rooms, a classy lounge, and all the doily touches (Sb-£30–34, Db-£58–64 depending on season and size, 23 St. Mary's, YO30 7DD, tel. 01904/622-738, fax 01904/628-802).

Queen Anne's Guest House has six compact, clean, and cheery rooms (D-£32, Db-£36 through 2000 with this book, CC:V, family deals, 24 Queen Anne's Road, Y030 7AA, tel. 01904/629-389, fax 01904/619-529, Judy and David West).

Crook Lodge B&B is a bit more elegant than the rest, with seven tight and charming rooms (Db-£46–54, car park, 26 St. Mary's, Y030 7DD, tel. & fax 01904/655-614, Susan and John Arnott).

Alcuin Lodge is a good value, with seven pleasant rooms (Db-£42–50, 1 small top-floor D-£35, no kids, CC:VM, 15 Sycamore Place, Y030 7DW, tel. 01904/632-222, fax 01904/ 626-630, e-mail: Alcuinlodg@aol.com, Susan Taylor).

Arnot House, run by a friendly daughter and mother team, is lushly decorated with early 1900s memorabilia. Cluttered but homey, the quirky museum-quality interior merits a photo. The four well-furnished rooms have little libraries (Db-£50–55, CC:VM with £1 fee, minimum 2-night stay, nonsmoking, 17 Grosvenor Terrace, Y030 7AG, tel. 01904/641-966, Kim and Ann Robbins).

Riverside Walk B&B, on a pedestrian street along the river, has 14 small shipshape rooms, steep stairs, and a breakfast room decorated in nautical green that feels like a fisherman's cottage. Request a river view or you'll overlook a car park (two D-£37–47, Db-£52–57, nonsmoking, sun terrace on river, quiet, CC:VM for 3.5 percent extra, 8 Earlsborough Terrace, Y030 7BQ, tel. 01904/ 620-769, fax 01904/646-249, Julie Mett).

York's Youth Hotel is well run, with lots of extras, like a kitchen, a launderette, a game room, a bar, and a bike rental (S-£14, D-£26, £12 in 4- to 6-bed dorms, sheets and breakfast extra, £1 less for multinight stays, CC:VM, 10-minute walk from station at 11 Bishophill Senior Road, YO1 1EF, tel. 01904/625-904 or 01904/612-494, e-mail: youth-hotel@ymn.co.uk).

Sleeping in Hotels in the Center of York

Dean Court Hotel, facing the Minster, is a big stately place marketed by Best Western that has classy lounges and 40 comfortable rooms (small Db-£105, standard Db-£125, superior Db-£140 includes fruit, spacious deluxe Db-£155, CC:VMA, some nonsmoking rooms but even smoking rooms O.K., elevator, Duncombe Place, YO1 7EF, tel. 01904/625-082, fax 01904/620-305, www.deancourt-york.co.uk). Ask for a room in front with a Minster view; the rooms in back stare at a brick wall.

    Galtres Lodge Hotel, a block from the Minster, offers narrow hallways but comfy rooms above a restaurant in the old town center (S-£25, Sb-£35, Dt-£50, Db-£65, one refurbished Db-£75 and worth it, CC:VM, no kids under 14, nonsmoking, 54 Low Petergate, Y01 7HZ, tel. 01904/622-478, fax 01904/627-804).

Eating in York

Lunch in the Shambles

For cuteness, consider the tiny **St. Crux Parish Hall,** a medieval church now used by a medley of charities selling tea and simple snacks (Mon–Sat 10:00–16:00, at bottom end of the Shambles, at intersection with Pavement). For a smoky place with the floor still sticky from last night's spilled beer, the **Golden Fleece** pub is busy at lunch, serving famous Yorkshire pudding and hearty meals (daily 12:00–21:00, CC:VM, on Pavement and Shambles, near St. Crux). Twee, quaint eateries line the street called Pavement. **Ye Olde Starre Inn,** the oldest pub in town, has yet to learn the art of cooking.

Traditional Tea

York is famous for its elegant teahouses. Drop into one around 16:00 for tea and cakes. Ladies love **Betty's Teahouse** (£5 cream tea, daily 9:00–21:00, mostly nonsmoking, St. Helen's Square, fine people watching from a window seat on the main floor; downstairs near WC is a mirror signed by World War II bomber pilots). If there's a line for Betty's, come back at dinnertime, when the line usually disappears—because for the English, "tea time" is over, but tea time is any time at Betty's. If Betty's is just too crowded, many other tearooms can satisfy your king- or queen-for-a-day desires.

Eating near the Minster

Café Concerto has a loyal following for good reason. Their £17 three-course meal is the best I've had in York (daily 10:00–22:00, serves meals all day, traditional English or Continental cuisine, CC:VM, Petergate 21, under Bootham Bar, smart to reserve at 01904/610-478).

    The Viceroy of India—just outside Monk Bar and therefore outside the tourist zone—serves great Indian food at good prices to mostly locals; if you've yet to eat Indian on your trip, do it here (nightly 18:00–24:00, £8 plates, friendly staff, CC:VM, continue straight through Monk Bar to 26 Monkgate, notice the big old "Bile Beans keep you healthy, bright-eyed, and slim" sign on your left, tel. 01904/622-370). For Italian food, consider the popular **Little Italy** for dinner (£6–12, Tue–Sun 17:00–23:00, plus Sat 12:00–14:00, closed Mon, Goodramgate 12, just inside Monk Bar, tel. 01904/623-539). The **Royal Oak** offers pub grub throughout the day, a small nonsmoking room, and hand-pulled ale (daily 11:30–20:00, CC:VM, Goodramgate, a block from Monk Bar, a block east of the Minster, tel. 01904/653-856). **St. Williams Restaurant,** just behind the great east window of the Minster in a wonderful half-timbered 15th-century building, serves quick and tasty lunches and elegant candlelit dinners (open daily, two courses-£14, three courses-£16, traditional and Mediterranean, CC:VM, College Street, tel. 01904/634-830).

Eating near Bootham Bar and Your B&B

Walk along Gillygate and choose from an enjoyable array of eateries: For authentic Italian, consider **Mama Mia's** (£6–9, daily 11:30–14:00, 17:30–23:00, fun, *domani* service, indoor/outdoor patio, CC:VM, 20 Gillygate, tel. 01904/622-020). **Gillygate Fisheries** is a wonderfully traditional little fish-and-chips joint where tattooed people eat in and housebound mothers take out (Mel serves £3–4 meals, eat your mushy peas, 11:30–13:30, 18:00–23:30, closed Mon lunch and all day Sun, smoke-free seating, 59 Gillygate). The **Waggon and Horses** pub has local color and £5 meals (daily 11:30–14:00, 17:30–21:00 but no Sunday dinner, across from Fisheries joint, Gillygate 48). There's a pub serving grub on every block. Eat where you see lots of food. Consider the **Coach House** (nightly 18:30–21:30, 20 Marygate, tel. 01904/652-780). For the closest you'll get to Mexico in Britain, try **Fiesta Mehicana** (nightly 18:00–22:00, sit-down or take-out, CC:VM, 14 Clifford Street, tel. 01904/610-243). The **Grange Hotel's Brasserie** is easy, a couple of blocks from the B&Bs, and classier than a pub. Go downstairs— avoid the pricey ground-floor restaurant (£9 meals, Mon–Sat 12:00–14:00, 18:00–22:00, Sun dinner only, CC:VM, 1 Clifton, tel. 01904/644-744). The people who run your B&B know the latest on what's good.

Grocery stores: In the B&B neighborhood you'll find **Spar** (daily 9:00–21:00, on Queen Anne's Road and Bootham), and near Bootham Bar is **Jackson,** a little run-down but open late (daily 7:00–23:00, on Bootham). In the old town is **Marks & Spencers** (Mon–Sat 9:30–18:00, Sun 11:00–17:00, on Parliament Street); go to the top floor for a striking view of the south wall of the Minster from the menswear department.

Most atmospheric picnic spot: In the Museum Gardens (near Bootham Bar), at the evocative 12th-century ruins of St. Mary's Abbey.

Transportation Connections—York

By train to: Durham (hrly, 60 min), **Edinburgh** (2/hrly, 2 hrs), **London** (2/hrly, 2 hrs), **Bath** (via Bristol, hrly, 5 hrs), **Cambridge** (nearly hrly, 2 hrs with a change in Petersborough), **Birmingham** (8/day, 3 hrs). Luggage storage at York's train station: £2, Mon–Sat 8:30–20:30, Sun from 9:00. Train info: tel. 0345-484-950.

By bus to: Keswick (1/day, 4 hrs; X9 bus runs early May–early Sept Mon–Sat, leaves York in afternoon, Keswick in morning; off-season, when bus runs only on Saturday, train is doable though tiring: allow 4 hrs, with transfers at Newcastle, Carlisle, and Penrith, then bus to Keswick).

Route Tips for Drivers

As you near York (and your B&B), you'll hit the A1237 ring road. Follow this to the A19/Thirsk roundabout (next to river on northeast side of town). From roundabout, follow signs for York City, traveling through Clifton into Bootham. All recommended B&Bs are four or five blocks before you hit the medieval city gate (see neighborhood map). If you're approaching York from the south, take M1 till it ends, then A64 for 10 miles till you reach York.

NEAR YORK: NORTH YORK MOORS

The North York Moors are a vacant lot compared with the Cumbrian Lake District. But that's unfair competition. In the lonesome North York Moors you can wander through the stark beauty of its time-passed villages, bored sheep, and powerful landscapes.

If you're driving, get a map. Without wheels, you have several choices: take a bus/steam train combination (below); choose one of several guided bus tours from York (focusing on Herriot or Brontë country, moors, Lake District, or Holy Island, different tour every day, offered by various companies for roughly £10 half day/£16 full day); or hire a private guide. John Smith, a licensed guide and driver, can take up to three people on one of his Countrywide Tours—such as Herriot Country, a Castle Howard/steam train/Whitby combination, or a tour tailored to your interests (£15/hr, admissions extra, tel. 01904/636-653, cell phone 0850-260-511).

Sights—North York Moors

▲The Moors—Car hike across the moors on any small road. You'll come upon tidy villages, old Roman roads, and maybe even a fox hunt. The Moors Visitors Centre provides the best orientation for exploring the moors. It's a grand old lodge offering exhibits, shows, nature walks, an information desk with plenty of books and maps, brass-rubbing, a cheery cafeteria, and brochures on several good walks that start right there (free, Apr–Oct daily 10:00–17:00, Nov–Dec and March daily 11:00–16:00, Jan–Feb weekends only 11:00–16:00, a half mile from train station, tel. 01287/660-654).

▲**North Yorkshire Moors Railway**—This 18-mile, one-hour steam-engine ride between Pickering and Grosmont goes through some of the best parts of the moors almost hourly. Even with the windows small and dirty (wipe off the outside of yours before you roll) and the track mostly in a scenic gully, it's a good ride (£9.20 round-trip, CC:VM, tel. 01751/472-508).

Pickering, with its rural-life museum, castle, and Monday market, is worth a stop. You could catch an early York–Pickering bus (hrly, 75 min), see Pickering, ride the train—with a stop along the way to take a moors walk—and carry on to Grosmont, which is on a regular train line with good connections to Whitby and points north. It's not possible to leave luggage at any stop on the steam-train line—pack light if you decide to hike.

▲**Hutton-le-Hole**—This postcard-pretty town is home of the fine Ryedale Folk Museum, which illustrates "farm life in the moors" through reconstructed and furnished 18th-century local buildings (£3.25, Apr–Oct daily 10:00–17:30, tel. 01751/417-367).

Castle Howard—Especially popular since the filming of *Brideshead Revisited*, this fine, palatial 300-year-old home is about half as interesting as the Cotswolds' Blenheim Palace (£7, daily 11:00–17:00, closed Nov–early March, 2 buses/day from York, 30 min).

Rievaulx Abbey—It's a highlight of North York Moors and beautifully situated, but if you've seen other fine old abbeys, this is a rerun (£3, daily 10:00–18:00, Oct until 17:00, Nov–Mar until 16:00).

▲**James Herriot Country**—Herriot fans will be more interested in the Yorkshire Dales than the neighboring moors. Local book-lets at the TI lay out the *All Creatures Great and Small* pilgrimage route for drivers, or you could consider a tour from York (see leaflets at TI).

Staithes/Whitby—See Durham and Northeast England chapter.

DURHAM AND NORTHEAST ENGLAND

Some of England's best history is harbored in the northeast. Hadrian's Wall reminds us that Britain was an important Roman colony 2,000 years ago. After a Roman ramble, you can make a pilgrimage to Holy Island, where Christianity gained its first toe-hold in Britain. The logical next stop is Durham, to marvel at England's greatest Norman church and enjoy an evensong service. And, for a trip into the less distant past, spend a morning in the year 1913 at the Beamish Open-Air Folk Museum.

Planning Your Time

Of the sights described in this chapter, train travelers will find Durham the most convenient stop on a three-week British train trip. You can see Hadrian's Wall en route (doable with transfers, easiest late May to late Sept), a worthwhile visit for those inspired by Roman ruins. The Beamish Folk Museum is an easy day trip from Durham (hrly bus, 20 min).

By car you'll be driving right by Hadrian's Wall, Holy Island, Bamburgh, and the Beamish Folk Museum. Whitby and Staithes are seaside escapes worth a stop only for the seagulls and surf. Whitby is accessible by train, but Staithes makes sense only with a car.

By car, connect Edinburgh and York by this string of sights, spending a night near Hadrian's Wall and a night in Durham on a one-month trip, just a night in Durham on a three-week trip. For drivers (or train travelers) with 36 hours between Edinburgh and York, leave Edinburgh early, tour Hadrian's Wall and Housesteads Fort, take a walk and have lunch, and get to Durham in time to tour the cathedral and enjoy the 17:15 evensong service. Sleep in Durham. Tour Beamish (15 minutes north of Durham by car or bus) or drive through the North York Moors the next day, arriving in York by late afternoon.

DURHAM

Without its cathedral it would hardly be noticed. But this magnificently situated cathedral is hard not to notice (even if you're zooming by on the train). Durham sits, seemingly happy to go nowhere, along its river and below its castle and famous cathedral. It has a workaday, medieval, cobbled atmosphere and a scraggly peasant's indoor market just off the main square. While Durham is the home of England's third-oldest university, the town feels working-class, surrounded by newly closed coal mines and filled with tattooed and stapled people in search of job security.

Orientation (tel. code: 0191)

Tidy little Durham clusters everything safely under its castle within the tight, protective bend of its river. The longest walk you'd make would be a 15-minute walk from the train station to the cathedral.

Tourist Information: The TI, located on the town square, books rooms and local theater tickets, provides train times, and, from June through September, offers 90-minute city walks Wednesday and Saturday at 14:15 for £3 (Mon–Sat 10:00–17:30, Jul–Aug also Sun 14:00–17:00, Oct–May Mon–Sat 10:00–17:00, public WC next door in indoor market, tel. 0191/384-3720). The brochure "Guided Walks in County Durham" lists themed walks led by local experts (£1, several times weekly, some hikes start in Durham).

Arrival in Durham: From the train station, follow the road downhill and take the second pedestrian turnoff, which leads almost immediately over a bridge above busy Alexander Crescent road; then take North Road into town or to the first couple of B&Bs (take Alexander Crescent to the other B&Bs).

Helpful Hints

Internet Access: Reality-X is hard-core, with 18 computers and no food (£5/hr, daily 11:00–22:00, at the west end of Framwelgate Bridge, tel. 0191/384-5700); Saints Café has three computers as an afterthought (£4/hr, daily 10:00–18:00, behind TI, from inside covered market go downstairs in the back, or reach from river, Market Vaults, tel. 0191/386-7700).

Car Rental: The nearest brand names are in Newcastle (Avis: tel. 0191/232-5283, Budget: tel. 0191/261-8282, Hertz: tel. 0191/232-5313).

Sights—Durham

▲▲▲**Cathedral**—Built to house the much-venerated bones of St. Cuthbert from Lindisfarne, the cathedral is the best look at

Durham

CATHEDRAL DETAIL
ENTER
GALILEE CHAPEL + BEDE'S TOMB
INFO
NAVE
CENTRAL TOWER
CHOIR
ALTAR + ST CATH. TOMB
CLIMB TOWER
CHAPEL OF THE NINE ALTARS
TO CLOISTERS, TREASURY, WC + CAFETERIA
30 YDS.

300 YARDS

TO A·167 & A·691 (BEAMISH & HEXHAM)
FRAMWEL-GATE PETH
TRAIN STATION
TO YOUTH HOSTEL
PED. BRIDGE
MILBURNGATE
CLAY PATH
TO A·1 & BEAMISH
LEAZES ROAD
BOATS
BUS STN.
ALEX CRES
NORTH ROAD
ALLERGATE
MKT PL
POST
P
ELVET BR.
OLD ELVET
NEW ELVET
HAW TER.
B+B
THE AVE.
CROSSGATE
SILVER
SADDLER
CASTLE
NORTH BAILEY
FRAMWELGATE BRIDGE
MARGERY LANE
GROVE
PIMLICO SOUTH
PATH
CATHEDRAL
SOUTH
CHURCH STREET
HALLGARTH STREET
DCH
TO A·690 & A 68 (HEXHAM)
N
RIVER WEAR
QUARRY HEADS
LAST SUPPER TREES
TO A·1 MOTORWAY
B+B's:
❶ CASTLEVIEW
❷ GEORGIAN TOWN HOUSE
❸ CASTLEDENE
❹ PARK VIEW
PREBENDS BRIDGE
LANE
TO A·167 (YORK)

Norman architecture in England. You can visit the church (free
but £2.50 requested, daily 7:15–20:00; early Sept–Easter until
17:00 or 18:00; limited access Sunday morning); climb the tower
(£2, Mon–Sat 9:30–16:00; off-season 10:00–15:00, closed Sun);
ogle the treasury (£2, Mon–Sat 10:00–16:30, Sun 14:00–16:30);
and tour the Monk's Dormitory (80p, Mon–Sat 10:00–15:30,

Sun 12:30–15:00); but I'd skip the A-V show on St. Cuthbert (80p). No photos or videos are allowed.

St. Cuthbert, an inspirational leader of the early Christian church in North England, lived in the Lindisfarne monastery on Holy Island (100 miles north of Durham). He died in 687. Eleven years later his body was exhumed and found to be miraculously preserved. This stoked the popularity of his shrine, and pilgrims came in growing numbers. When Vikings raided Lindisfarne in 875, the monks fled with his body (and the famous illuminated *Lindisfarne Gospels*, now in the British Library in London). After 120 years of roaming, in 995 they settled in Durham on an easy-to-defend hairpin bend in the Wear River. The cathedral was built over Cuthbert's tomb.

The architecture of the nave is particularly harmonious because it was built in a mere 40 years (1093–1133). Few additions were made, and the bulk of what you see today is Norman (that's British for Romanesque). The round arches and zigzag carved decorations are textbook Norman. The church was also proto-Gothic, built by well-traveled French masons and architects who knew the latest innovations from Europe. Its stone and ribbed roof, first pointed arches, and first flying buttresses were revolutionary in England. It's not as cluttered as other churches for several reasons. Out of respect for St. Cuthbert, for centuries no one else was buried here. During Reformation times, sumptuous Catholic decor was high risk. And subsequent fires and wars destroyed what Protestants didn't.

A Tour Plan: From the cathedral green, notice how this fortress of God stands boldly across from the Norman keep of Durham's fortress of man. (The castle, now part of the university, is not worth touring.) At the cathedral door, the big, bronze, lion-faced knocker is a replica of the 12th-century original (in treasury), which was used by criminals seeking sanctuary (read the explanation).

Immediately inside you'll see the information desk. Church attendants happily answer questions. Ideally, follow a church tour (Mon–Sat at 10:30 and 14:00 late May–early Sept, also at 11:30 in Aug; if one's in session you're welcome to join, £3 donation). The "A Walk Round Durham Cathedral" guide pamphlet is informative but dull (50p).

The black marble strip on the floor was as close to the altar as women were allowed in the days when this was a Benedictine church (until 1540). Sit down (ignoring the black line) and let the fine proportions of England's best Norman (and arguably Europe's best Romanesque) nave stir you. Any frilly woodwork and stonework were added in later centuries.

Notice the modern window with the novel depiction of the Last Supper (above and to the left of the entry door, given to the church by a local department store in 1984) and remember that the cathedral remains a living part of the community.

Enter the Galilee Chapel in the back of the nave (late Norman, from 1175). Notice the paintings of St. Cuthbert and St. Oswald (seventh-century king of Northumbria) on the side walls of the altar niche, rare examples of Romanesque or Norman paintings. In the center is the tomb of the Venerable Bede, an early Christian scholar who wrote the first history of England; he died in 735 and was buried here in the 11th century.

Back in the main church, stroll down the nave to the center, under the highest bell tower in Europe (218 feet). Gaze up. The ropes pull hammers that ring the bells. Continuing east (all medieval churches faced east), you enter the choir. Monks worshiped many times a day, and the choir in the center of the church provided a cozier place to gather in this vast, dark, and cold building. This is the heart of the cathedral, where Mass has been said daily for 900 years. The fancy wooden chairs are from the 17th century. Behind the altar is the delicately carved stone Neville Screen (1380). From the Norman choir, step down into the Gothic east end of the church. Go up a few stairs to the tomb of St. Cuthbert. It's part of the larger 13th-century Gothic Chapel of the Nine Altars—taller, lighter, and relatively more extravagant than the Norman nave. As you leave, walking past the choir, look for the Millenium window in the south aisle. Commemorating the church's 1,000th anniversary in 1995, the scenes depict England's history, from coal mining to cows to computers.

The entry to the tower is in the south transept; the view from the tower will cost you 325 steps and £2. The following sights are within the cloisters: The treasury (well worth £2), filled with medieval bits and holy pieces, fleshes out this otherwise stark building. The actual relics from St. Cuthbert's tomb are at the far end. The "Monks' Dormitory" is now a library with an original 14th-century timber roof filled with Anglo-Saxon stones (worth 80p). The unexceptional A-V show in the unexceptional undercroft tells about St. Cuthbert (not worth 80p). The fine cafeteria (smoke free, daily 10:00–16:30, lunch 12:00–14:30), bookshop (in the old kitchen), and WCs are next to the treasury.

Evensong: For a thousand years this cradle of English Christianity has been praising God. To really experience the cathedral, go for an evensong service. Arrive early and ask to be seated in the choir. It's a spiritual Oz, as 40 boys sing psalms—a red-and-white-robed pillow of praise, raised up by the powerful pipe organ. If you're lucky and the service went well, the organist runs a spiritual musical victory lap as the congregation breaks up (begins at 17:15 Tue–Sat, Sun at 15:30, one hour, normally not sung on Mon; when choir is off during mid-July–August school break, visiting choirs often fill in; tel. 0191/386-2367).

Riverside Walk—For a 20-minute woodsy escape, walk Durham's riverside path from busy Framwelgate Bridge to sleepy Prebends Bridge. Just beyond the Prebends Bridge on the old-town side of the river, you'll find The Upper Room, a cluster of trees carved to show the Last Supper when seen from the tree-trunk throne provided. Where are the apostles? Count the tree trunks.

If the lazy river beckons, consider renting a rowboat at Brown's Boat House (£2.5/hr per person, £5 deposit, Easter–Sept daily 10:00–18:00, just east of old town, below New Elvet Bridge, tel. 0191/386-3779).

Sleeping in Durham
(£1 = about $1.70, tel code: 0191)
Sleep Code: **S** = Single, **D** = Double/Twin, **T** = Triple, **Q** = Quad, **b** = bathroom, **t** = toilet only, **s** = shower only, **CC** = Credit Card (Visa, MasterCard, Amex).
The B&Bs are a five- or 10- minute walk from the station and the town center. Durham hosts a Rowing Regatta the second weekend in June; book ahead.

The only launderette in town is at Dunelm House, the Student Union building—a 10–15 minute walk east of the B&B neighborhood (daily 8:00–21:00 during school term, otherwise 9:00–15:00, open to public, east end of Kingsgate Bridge, tel. 0191/374-3310).

Castleview Guest House, 400 yards off Framwelgate Bridge, is a good bet, with six renovated, comfortable rooms. Only the garden has a castle view (Sb-£38, Db-£50, nonsmoking, 4 Crossgate, DH1 4PS, tel. & fax 0191/386-8852, Mike and Anne Williams).

Georgian Town House, next door, has a cheery bossanova ambience with a breezy garden, plush lounge, and bright rooms decorated with care and flair. The hearty breakfast is served in the conservatory (Db-£60 with this book, nonsmoking, hand-held showers, some rooms with castle views, 10 Crossgate, DH1 4PS, tel. & fax 0191/386-8070, Jane Weil).

Castledene B&B is tidy, simple, and friendly (twin-£40, at intersection of Crossgate and Margery Lane, take stairs to pedestrian lane—running parallel to Crossgate Peth—to last house, 37 Nevilledale Terrace, DH1 4QG; drivers go south on Margery Lane a few yards past the intersection with Crossgate and turn right on Summerville, tel. & fax 0191/384-8386, Lorna and Brian Byrne).

Park View B&B, with a handy location and three pleasant rooms, overlooks a children's tiny park (Db-£45–50 with this book, family deals, big attic room, 1 Allergate Terrace, DH1 4ES, tel. 0191/386-7034, June Buxton).

The simply named **Bed & Breakfast** has two simple rooms

on a quiet dead-end street (small S-£20, D-£40, nonsmoking, no sign on door, close to train and bus station, 12 The Avenue, DH1 4ED, tel. 0191/384-1020, run by kindly Jan Metcalfe).

Farnley Tower, which bills itself as a "luxurious B&B," is indeed. Opened in mid-1999, it feels like it just came out of the box. Its eleven doubles have all the comforts, and some have views. The hotel is on a quiet dead end at the top of a hill, a five-minute uphill walk (one Sb-£40, Db-£65, CC:VM, nonsmoking, can serve drinks, easy parking, 10-minute walk from station and city center, The Avenue, DH1 4DX, tel. 0191/375-0011, fax 0191/383-9694, John and Gail Khan).

Durham Castle, a student residence actually on the castle grounds facing the cathedral, rents 100 singles and 30 doubles (Jul–Sept only, £20.50 per person, £30.50 with private facilities, CC:VM, elegant breakfast hall; parking, with luck, on the cathedral green; University College, The Castle, Palace Green, DH1 3RW, can reserve long in advance, tel. 0191/374-3863, fax 0191/374-7470, Julie Marshall). Request a room in the classy old main building or you may get one of the few bomb shelter–style modern dorm rooms.

Drivers could consider the **Bromme Farm Guest House,** which is good but two miles out of town (four rooms, S-£20, D-£35–40, across from Love's Pub, Broom Park, DH7 7QX, tel. 0191/386-4755).

Eating in Durham

Trust your host's advice, or stroll from Framwelgate Bridge through Market Place up Saddler and take what looks good. Consider **Pizzeria Venezia** for affordable Italian food (Mon–Sat 12:00–13:45, 18:00–21:45, happy hour deals 18:00–19:00, west end of Framwelgate Bridge, tel. 0191/384-6777), **Bimbi's** for fish and chips (daily 11:00–22:30, on Market Place), **Shaheen's** for healthy Indian (nightly 18:00–23:30, CC:VM, up Saddler Street just past the turnoff to the cathedral, tel. 0191/386-0960), or **The Almshouses** on the cathedral green for tasty light meals (daily 9:00–20:00, Oct–Easter till 17:00, tel. 0191/386-1054). For pub grub, consider **Hogshead Ale House** on Saddler Street in the old town, or even better, the **Court Inn,** which serves food throughout the day (daily 11:00–22:30, Court Lane, five-minute walk east of old town, take Elvet or Kingsgate Bridge, tel. 0191/384-7350). Drivers looking for a nontouristy splurge can try **Bistro 21** (Mon–Sat 12:00–14:00, 18:00–22:00, closed Sun, CC:VM, Aykley Heads, three miles north of town, tel. 0191/384-4354).

Of Durham's two supermarkets, **Safeway** has longer hours and is closer to the recommended B&Bs (Mon–Fri 8:30–20:00, Sat 8:00–18:00, in Millburngate Shopping Center, west end of Framwelgate Bridge). In the old town, try **Marks & Spencers,** just off the main square (Mon–Sat 9:00–17:30, on Silver Street, across from P.O.). You can picnic on the benches and grass just outside the cathedral entrance (but not on the Palace Green).

Transportation Connections—Durham

By train to: Edinburgh (hrly, less off-season, 2 hrs), York (hrly, 1 hr), **London** (hrly, less off-season, 3 hrs), **Newcastle** (hrly, 15 min, then train/bus to Hadrian's Wall, see Hadrian's Wall, below), **Bristol** (near Bath, 9/day, 5 hrs). Off-season, from September to May, only about half of the London–Edinburgh trains stop in little Durham; frequency drops to about six trains per day (catch train to Newscastle for more options). Luggage storage at Durham station: £2, daily 7:00–20:00. Train info: tel. 0345-484-950.

    Parking in Durham: Parking in old Durham is nearly impossible. You're best off simply following the signs into the big public parking lots at the bottom end of town (£1.60 per day).

HADRIAN'S WALL

This is one of England's most thought-provoking sights. Around A.D. 130, during the reign of Emperor Hadrian, the Romans built this great stone wall. Its actual purpose is still debated. While Rome ruled Britain for 400 years, it never quite ruled its people. The wall may have been used to define the northern edge of the empire, protect Roman Britain from invading Scottish tribes (or at least cut down on pesky border raids), monitor the movement of people, or simply give an otherwise bored army something to do. (Nothing's more dangerous than a bored army.) Stretching 74 miles coast to coast across the narrowest stretch of northern England, it was built and defended by nearly 20,000 troops. The wall was flanked by ditches, and a military road lies on the south side. At every mile of the wall a castle guards a gate, and two turrets stand between each castle. The mile castles are numbered. (Eighty of them cover the 74 miles because a Roman mile was slightly shorter than our mile.) Today, several chunks of the wall, ruined forts, and museums thrill history buffs. About a dozen Roman sites cling along the wall's route; the best are Housesteads Fort and Vindolanda. Housesteads shows you where the Romans lived; Vindolanda's museum shows how they lived.

    In 2000, at a site called Segedunum, reconstructed Roman baths will open for use by modern-day tourists (just east of Newcastle at Wallsend, call Newcastle TI for info, tel. 0191/261-0610). In 2001 (maybe earlier), it will be possible to walk the wall's route along a new path stretching from coast to coast.

Sights—Hadrian's Wall

▲▲**Housesteads Fort**—With its tiny museum, powerful scenery, and the best-preserved segment of the wall, this is your best single

Durham and Northeast England

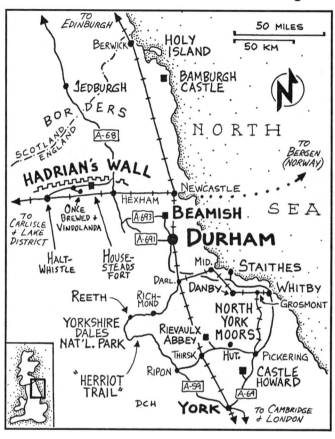

stop. All Roman forts were the same rectangular shape and design, with the commander's headquarters, barracks, and latrines (lower end); this fort even has a hospital. The fort is built right up to the wall, which is on the far side (£2.80 for site and museum, daily 10:00–18:00, Nov–May till 17:00 or dusk, £1 car park, tel. 01434/344-363). At the car park are the WCs, snack bar, and a gift shop. You can leave your baggage at the gift shop, but confirm closing hours. It's a half-mile, mostly uphill walk to the entrance of the miniscule museum and sprawling fort.

▲▲**Hiking the Wall**—From Housesteads, hike west along the wall speaking Latin. For a good, craggy, three-mile walk along the wall, hike between Housesteads and Steel Rigg. You'll pass a castle sitting in a nick in a crag (castle #39, called Castle Nick). There's a car park near Steel Rigg (take the little road up from Twice Brewed Pub). ▲Vindolanda—This larger Roman fort (which actually predates the wall by 40 years) and museum are just south of the wall. Although Housesteads has better ruins and the wall, Vinolanda has the better museum, revealing intimate details of Roman life. Eight forts were built on this spot. The Romans, by carefully sealing the foundations from each successive fort, left 20th-century archaeologists seven meters of remarkably well-preserved artifacts to excavate: keys, coins, brooches, scales, pottery, glass, tools, leather shoes, bits of cloth, and even a wig. The earliest examples of Roman writing were recently discovered here. While the actual letters, written on thin wood, are in London's British Museum, see the interesting video here and read the translations—the first known example of a woman writing to a woman is an invitation to a birthday party. These varied letters, about parties held, money owed, and sympathy shared, brings Romans to life in a way that stones alone can't.

From the car park you'll walk through 600 meters of grassy parkland decorated by the foundation stones of the Roman fort and a full-size replica chunk of the wall. At the far side of the site is the museum, gift shop, and cafeteria (£4, £5.80 combo ticket includes Roman Army Museum, May–Aug daily 10:00–18:00, Apr/Sept closes at 17:30, Mar/Oct at 17:00, Feb/Nov at 16:00, closed Dec, can leave baggage at entrance, tel. 01434/344-277). The **Roman Army Museum,** a few miles farther west at Greenhead, is redundant if you've seen Vindolanda (£3, or buy combo ticket, above, same hours).

Sleeping near Hadrian's Wall
(£1 = about $1.70, tel code: 01434)
Crindledykes Farm is a classy old farmhouse in an idyllic and peaceful setting a mile south of the wall (small D-£36, spacious twin room with view-£38, room for a child's bed, WC down the hall, nonsmoking, accessible by car only, signposted from the B6318 at Housesteads, Bardon Mill, Hexham, NE47 7AF, tel. 01434/344-316, Judy Davidson).

East Wharmley Farm rents two spacious rooms in a wonderfully rural setting; the farm's six miles from Housesteads on the A69, midway between Haydon Bridge and Hexham (D-£36, nonsmoking, tel. & fax 01434/674-259, Dorothy and Harold Foster).

Crow's Nest B&B offers three rooms in a remodeled farmhouse a quarter mile from the wall (D-£36, on B6318 road 500 meters from the Once Brewed TI and hostel at East Twice Brewed, Bardon Mill, Hexham, tel. 01434/344-348).

The nearby **Mile Castle Pub** cooks up all sorts of exotic game and offers the best dinner around, according to hungry national park rangers. Two miles west of Housesteads, the **Twice Brewed Pub**

and Hotel serves decent pub grub nightly to a local darts-and-pool crowd (S-£18, D-£36, Db-£45, dreary rooms, rarely full, tel. 01434/344-534). Next door to the Twice Brewed Pub is the comfortable **Once Brewed Youth Hostel** (£10 per bed with sheets, breakfast-£3, 4–7 beds per room, tel. 01434/344-360, fax 01434/344-045, e-mail: oncebrewed@yha.org.uk).

Transportation Connections—Hadrian's Wall

By Car: Take B6318; it parallels the wall and passes several viewpoints, minor sights, and "severe dips." (If there's a certified nerd or bozo in the car, these road signs add a lot to a photo portrait.)

By Train and Bus: A train/bus combination (or train/taxi off-season) delivers you to the wall. From England's east coast, Newcastle is the gateway to the Newcastle–Carlisle train paralleling the wall (10/day, 30 min to Hexham, 20 more min to Haltwhistle). But the train only gets you near the wall. Hadrian's Wall bus #682 gets you to the wall and all the Roman sights; get off the train at either Hexham or Haltwhistle to catch this bus (4 buses daily in each direction, late May–late Sept; Hexham–Housesteads 30 min, Housesteads–Vindolanda 10 min, Vindolanda–Haltwhistle 20 min). At Newcastle's train station, pick up a Hadrian's Wall bus schedule at the TI (Mon–Fri 10:00–20:00, Sat 9:00–17:00, Sun 10:00–16:00, tel. 0191/261-0610) or call Haltwhistle's TI, below, to get the schedule in advance. If you start from Newcastle by 11:00 (earlier is better), you can fit in both Housesteads and Vindolanda. If you visit the wall off-season (late Sept–late May), when bus service drops, you'll need to taxi to Housesteads from a nearby train station such as Haltwhistle (taxi services: Sprouls 01434/321-064, Turnbulls 01434/320-105, £8 one way); arrange for a return pickup or have the museum staff call a taxi. Haltwhistle's helpful TI gives bus information to callers (Mon–Sat 10:00–13:00, 14:00–17:00, Sun 13:00–17:00; Nov–Easter Mon–Fri 10:00–12:30, 13:00–15:30, tel. 01434/322-002, www.hadrians-wall.org).

If you're day-tripping to the wall, consider leaving your luggage at Newcastle's train station (£2–3, daily 8:00–18:00, return by 18:00 or get it the next morning). If you're staying on the wall, your B&B host can arrange a taxi for you.

Other Sights near Durham

▲▲**Beamish Open-Air Museum**—This huge museum, which re-creates the year 1913 in northeast England, takes at least three hours to explore. A vintage tram shuttles visitors around the park, stopping at each of the four stations: Coal Mine Village, Home Farm, The Town, and an 1820s Manor House. This isn't wax. If you touch the exhibits, they may smack you. Attendants at each stop explain everything.

Start with the Coal Mine Village (company village around

a coal mine), with a school, church, miners' homes, and a fascinating—if claustrophobic—20-minute tour into a real "drift" mine.

"The Town" (along with the mine tour) is the highlight. This bustling street features a 1913 candy shop, a dentist's office, a garage, a working pub (fun for a smoky beer), and a modern, smoke-free cafeteria. The old train station isn't much.

The Pockerley Manor, an 1820s manor house, is barely worth the climb, but the re-created first-ever passenger train from 1825—which takes modern-day visitors for a spin on 1825 tracks—draws railway buffs. The Home Farm is the least interesting section. (£10, daily 10:00–17:00; Jul–Aug until 18:00; from Nov–Mar only "The Town" is open, 10:00–16:00, closed Mon and Fri; check events schedule as you enter, last tickets two hours before closing, tel. 01207/231-811.)

The museum is located between the villages of Stanley and Chester-le-Street. To get to Beamish from Durham, catch a #720 bus (marked "Stanley via Beamish," hrly, 20 min, stops 700 yards from museum) or drive north on the MI to the first exit (Chester-le-Street) and follow the signs.

▲**Whitby**—Whitby is a fun coastal resort town with a busy harbor and steep and salty old streets, a carousel of Coney Island–type amusements overseen by the stately ruins of its seventh-century abbey. Whitby has been an important port since the 12th century. The **Captain Cook Memorial Museum** offers an interesting look at the famous hometown sailor and his exotic voyages (£2.60, daily 9:45–17:00, closed in winter, in the old town just over the bridge). Two of Captain Cook's boats (*Resolution* and *Endeavour*) were built in the Whitby shipyards. The TI is on the harbor next to the train and bus stations (May–Sept daily 9:30–18:00, Oct–Apr daily 10:00–12:30, 13:00–16:30, tel. 01947/602-674).

Whitby has plenty of rooms. August is the only tight month. Most rooms at **Crescent House** come with sea views (Db-£40, family deals, nonsmoking, on the bluff just south of the harbor at 6 East Crescent, YO21 3HD, tel. & fax 01947/600-091, Janet and Mike Paget). **Dolphin Hotel,** in the old-town center at the bridge overlooking the harbor, is a pub with seven rooms upstairs (Db-£50, three blocks from train station, pub closes at 23:00, CC:VM, Bridge Street, Y022 4BG, tel. 01947/602-197). The **hostel** is next to the abbey above the town (bed-£8.50, 60 beds in 8 rooms, closed 10:00–17:00, tel. 01947/602-878).

Buses connect Whitby and York (5/day, 2 hrs, tel. 01653/692-556). Trains connect Durham with Middlesbrough (8/day, 50 min); the Middlesbrough–Whitby train (4/day, 90 min) stops at Grosmont (where you can catch the Moors steam train) and Danby (a half mile from the Moors info center).

▲**Staithes**—Staithes is a short drive north of Whitby and worthwhile by car (hrly Whitby–Staithes buses; 30 min). A poor and not particularly pretty village where the boy who became Capt. James Cook got his first taste of the sea, Staithes is a salty tumble of cottages bunny-hopping down a ravine into a tiny harbor. Ten years ago the town supported 20 fishing boats—today, only three. But fishermen (who pronounce their town "steerths") still outnumber tourists in undiscovered Staithes. There's nothing to do but drop by the lifeboat house (a big deal in England; page through the history book, read the not-quite-stirring accounts of the boats being called to duty; drop a coin in the box), walk the beach, and relax to the tune of seagulls singing its praise.

I sleep in Staithes. The town is struggling. Tourists just aren't coming. It's changed little since Captain Cook's days. There are no fancy rooms. Each of these three- or four-bedroom places is cramped, with old carpets, bad wallpaper, lumpy beds, and tangled floorplans that make you feel like a stowaway. The first is on the harbor front (worth it for the view but not the rooms). **Harborside Guest House** provides basic beds, three sea-view rooms, breakfast in a café, and the sound of waves to lull you to sleep (D-£40, Seaton Garth, tel. 01947/841-296). Also consider the **Endeavour Restaurant B&B** (D-£44, Db-£55, serves great food—see below, 1 High Street, tel. 01947/840-825, Lisa Chapman) and **Salmon Cottage** (a £40 twin and a family room, High Street, tel. 01947/841-193, Isabel Elliott). Staithes' zip code is TS13 5BH.

The oddly classy-for-this-town **Endeavour Restaurant** offers excellent £20 dinners (seafood, vegetarian, reservations at 01947/840-825). **Cod and Lobster Pub** serves dinner and overlooks the harbor, with outdoor benches and a cozy living room warmed by a coal fire. **Royal George** on High Street has bar food (dinners daily 19:00–21:00, throw darts while you wait).

▲**Holy Island and Bamburgh**—This "Holy Island" was Christianity's toehold on England 1,200 years ago. It was the home of St. Cuthbert. We know it today for the *Lindisfarne Gospels*, decorated by monks in the seventh century with some of the finest art from Europe's "Dark Ages" (now in the British Museum). It's a pleasant visit, a quiet town with an evocative priory and striking castle (not worth touring), reached by a two-mile causeway that's cut off daily by high tides. Tidal charts are posted, warning you when this holy place becomes Holy Island and you become stranded (for TI and tide information, call Berwick TI at 01289/330-733, Mon–Sat 10:00–18:00, Sun 11:00–15:00, off-season Mon–Sat till 16:00, closed Sun). For a peaceful overnight, a few good B&Bs cluster in the town center (Britannia Guest House, D-£34, Db-£38, tel. 01289/389-218, Mrs. Patterson).

A few miles farther south of Holy Island is the grand **Bamburgh Castle**, overlooking Britain's loveliest beach. Its interior is worth touring (£4, daily 11:00–17:00, closed Nov–Mar, tel. 01668/214-515). This area is only worthwhile for those with a car.

EDINBURGH

Edinburgh, the colorful city of Robert Louis Stevenson, Sir Walter Scott, and Robert Burns, is Scotland's showpiece and one of Europe's most entertaining cities. Historical, monumental, fun, and well organized, it's a tourist's delight.

Promenade down the Royal Mile through the Old Town. Historic buildings pack the Royal Mile between the castle (on the top) and Holyrood Palace (on the bottom). Medieval skyscrapers stand shoulder to shoulder, hiding peaceful courtyards connected to High Street by narrow lanes or even tunnels. This colorful jumble—in its day the most crowded city in the world—is the tourist's Edinburgh.

Edinburgh (ED'n-burah) was once two towns divided by a lake. To alleviate crowding, the lake was drained, and a magnificent Georgian city, today's New Town, was laid out to the north. Georgian Edinburgh, like the city of Bath, shines with broad boulevards, straight streets, square squares, circular circuses, and elegant mansions decked out in colonnades, pediments, and sphinxes in the proud, neoclassical style of 200 years ago.

While the Georgian city celebrated the union of Scotland and England (with streets and squares named after English kings and emblems), "devolution" is the latest craze. In a 1998 election the Scots voted for more autonomy and to bring their parliament home. Though Edinburgh has been the historic capital of Scotland for centuries, parliament has not met in Scotland since 1707. In 2000—while London will still call the strategic shots—Edinburgh will resume its position as home to the Scottish Parliament. And a strikingly modern new parliament building, opening in 2002, will be one more jewel in Edinburgh's crown.

Planning Your Time

While the major sights can be seen in a day, on a three-week tour of Britain I'd give Edinburgh two days. Ideally on your arrival day, take an introductory Guide Friday bus tour in the late afternoon (when it's discounted to half price).

Day 1: Spend the morning touring the castle. The rest of the day is easily spent exploring (downhill) the Royal Mile—museum-going, lunching, shopping. Catch a walking tour of the Royal Mile at 14:00. If you tour the Holyrood Palace, do it at the end of the day and the bottom of the mile. Evening–Scottish show, folk music at pub, literary pub crawl, or haunted walk.

Day 2: Tour the National Gallery and stroll the adjacent Princes Street Gardens. After lunch, browse the New Town and visit the Georgian House; hike up King Arthur's Seat; or go swimming at the Commonwealth Pool. Evening–Show, pubs, walks, whatever you didn't do last night.

Orientation (tel. code: 0131)

The center of Edinburgh holds the Princes Street Gardens park and Waverley Bridge, where you'll find the TI; Waverley Shopping and Eating Center; the train station; the bus info office; the starting point for most city bus tours; the festival office; the National Gallery; and a covered dance-and-music pavilion. Weather blows in and out—bring your sweater.

Tourist Information: The crowded TI is as central as can be atop the Waverley Market on Princes Street (May–Jun & Sept: Mon–Sat 9:00–19:00, Sun 10:00–19:00; Jul–Aug: daily until 20:00; Nov–Mar: daily until 17:00, tel. 0131/473-3800). Buy a map (£1) but skip the misnamed *Essential Guide to Edinburgh* (£1), which shuffles a little information between lots of ads. Ask for the monthly entertainment *Gig Guide* (free) and browse the racks for brochures on the various Scottish folk shows and walking tours. *The List*, the best monthly entertainment listing, is sold for £1.95 at newsstands. Book your room direct without the TI's help. Haggis Backpackers Ltd is a good source of budget travel information (Mon–Sat 8:00–18:00, Sun 12:00–18:00, just off High Street at 11 Blackfriars Street).

Arrival in Edinburgh: Arriving by train at Waverley Station puts you in the city center and a few steps from the TI (go up the stairs) and the city bus to my recommended B&Bs. Both National Express and Scottish Citylink buses use the bus station a block from the train station in the Georgian town on St. Andrew Square.

Edinburgh's slingshot-of-an-airport is 10 miles northwest of the center and well connected by shuttle buses with Waverley Bridge (LRT "Airline" bus, £3.30 or £4.40 with all-day city bus pass, 4/hrly, 30 min, roughly 6:00–22:00; I'd skip Guide Friday's Airbus Express, which costs more, runs less often, and has shorter

Edinburgh

SCOTT MONUMENT

GEORGIAN HOUSE

CALTON HILL

REGENT ROAD

QUEEN   STREET

BUS STN.

GEORGE   STREET

C&A

ROSE   STREET

POST

G

QUEENSFERRY STREET

PRINCES   ST.

PRINCES ST. GARDENS

3

4

MILE

to A-90 & Highlands

2

ROYAL

SOUTH BRIDGE

QUEEN'S DRIVE

1

ST. GILES

HOLY-ROOD PARK

LOTHIAN ROAD

GRASSMARKET

Salisbury Crags

UNIVERSITY

MELVILLE DRIVE

Arthur's Seat

0   ¼

MILES

to Dalkeith Rd.
B&B area

❶ CASTLE ❷ NATIONAL   ❸ WAVERLEY MARKET ❹ TRAIN ❺ HOLYROOD PALACE
              GALLERY   +TOURIST INFO   STN.

hours; flight info tel. 0131/333-1000, British Midlands tel. 0870-607-0555, British Air tel. 0345-222-111). Taxi to airport: £15.

Helpful Hints

Sunday Activities: Many sights close on Sunday, but there's still a lot to do: Royal Mile walking tour, Edinburgh Castle, St. Giles Cathedral, Holyrood Palace, Royal Botanic Gardens, Arthur's Seat hike, and city bus tour. An open-air market including antiques is held every Sunday from 10:00 to 16:00 at New Street Car Park near Waverley Center. The Georgian House and National Gallery open Sunday afternoon.

   Internet Access: It's a cinch to get plugged in. Try International Telecom Centre on the Royal Mile (£1/15 min, daily 9:00–22:00, 52 High Street, half-block east of Tron Kirk and South Bridge), Café Cyberia in the New Town (Mon–Sat 10:00–22:00, Sun 12:00–19:00, 83 Hanover Street, near recommended restaurants, a few blocks northeast of TI), and Web 13 (13 Bread Street, near Grassmarket, below the castle).

   Car Rental: Avis is at 100 Dairy Road, Haymarket, tel. 0131/337-6363.

Getting around Edinburgh

Nearly all Edinburgh sights are within walking distance. City buses are handy and inexpensive (average fare 70p, LRT info office, Old Town end of Waverley Bridge, tel. 0131/555-6363). Tell the driver where you're going, drop exact change into the box or lose the excess, grab your ticket as you board, push the stop button as you near your stop (so your stop isn't skipped), and exit from the middle door. All-day "Freedom Ticket" passes are sold on buses (£2.40—four rides make it worthwhile). Buses run from about 6:00 to 23:00. Taxis are reasonable (easy to flag down, £1.20 drop charge, 80p extra after 18:00, average ride between downtown and B&B district £4.50).

Bus Tours of Edinburgh

▲Hop-on Hop-off City Bus Tours—Two companies, Guide Friday and LRT's "Edinburgh Classic Tour," offer buses that circle the town center—Waverley Bridge, around the castle, Royal Mile, Calton Hill, Georgian New Town, and Princes Street—in about an hour, with pickups about every 15 minutes and an informative narration. You can hop on and off with one ticket all day, not 24 hours. The pricier Guide Friday has a live guide, often uninspired (£8, CC:VM if bought at office at 133 Canongate, tel. 0131/556-2244). Classic Tour uses headphones and a recorded narration (£6.50; as a bonus, show ticket on bus X50, which also leaves from Waverley Bridge, to get free trip to Britannia ship and back—can be used on different day; tel. 0131/555-6363). On sunny days they go topless (the buses) but can suffer from traffic noise and congestion. First and last buses leave Waverley Bridge at 9:10 and 19:10 late May through late September (otherwise 17:10). These tours can be half-hearted—pay only half price. Prices drop 50 percent late in the afternoon (Classic Tour after 17:10 during late May–late Sept, otherwise after 15:10; Guide Friday sometime between 16:00–17:00, discounts start at Waverley Bridge, later elsewhere).

Sights—Edinburgh

▲▲▲Edinburgh Castle—The fortified birthplace of the city 1,300 years ago, this imposing symbol of Edinburgh sits proudly on a rock high above the city. While the castle has been both a fort and a royal residence since the 11th century, most of the buildings today are from its more recent use as a military garrison (£6.50, daily 9:30–18:00, Oct–Mar until 17:00, cafeteria, tel. 0131/225-9846; consider avoiding the long uphill walk from the nearest bus stop by taking a cab to the castle gate).

Entry Gate: Start with the wonderfully droll 30-minute guided introduction tour (free with admission, departs every 15 minutes from entry, see clock for the next departure; few tours run off-season). The CD-ROM audio guide is excellent, with four hours of quick digital dial descriptions (free with admission, pick up at entry gate before meeting the live guide). The clean WC at the entry annually wins "British Loo of the Year" awards (see plaques near men's room), but they use one-way mirrors above the sinks in the women's room—complain.

In the castle there are four essential stops: Crown Jewels,

Great Hall, National War Memorial, and St. Margaret's Chapel with city view. All are at the highest and most secure point—on or near the castle square—and where your guided tour ends.

The **Royal Palace** (facing castle square under the flag pole) has two unimpressive rooms (through door reading 1566). Remember, Scottish royalty only lived here when safety or protocol required. They preferred the **Holyrood Palace** at the bottom of the Royal Mile. The line of tourists leads from the square directly to the jewels. Skip this line and enter the building around to the left where you'll get to the jewels via a wonderful *Honors of Scotland* exhibition about the crown jewels.

Scotland's **Crown Jewels** are older than England's. While Cromwell destroyed England's, the Scots hid theirs successfully. Longtime symbols of Scottish nationalism, they were made in Edinburgh—of Scottish gold, diamonds, and gems—in 1540 for a 1543 coronation. They were last used to crown Charles II in 1651. Apparently there was some anxiety about the Act of Union, which dissolved Scotland's parliament into England's to create the United Kingdom in 1707—the Scots locked up and hid their jewels. In 1818 Walter Scott and a royal commission rediscovered the jewels intact.

The **Stone of Scone** sits plain and strong next to the jewels. This big gray rock is the coronation stone of Scotland's ancient kings (ninth century). Swiped by the English, it sat under the coronation chair at Westminster Abbey from 1296 until 1996. With major fanfare, Scotland's treasured Stone of Scone returned to Edinburgh on November 15, 1996. Talk to the guard for more details.

Enter the **Mary Queen of Scots room**, where in 1666 the queen gave birth to James VI of Scotland, later King James I of England. The **Presence Chamber** leads into **Laich Hall** (Lower Hall), the dining room of the royal family.

The **Great Hall** was the castle's ceremonial meeting place in the 16th and 17th centuries. In modern times it was a barracks and a hospital. While most of what you see is Victorian, two medieval elements survive: the fine hammer-beam roof and the iron-barred peephole (above fireplace on right). This allowed the king to spy on his partying subjects.

The imposing **Scottish National War Memorial** commemorates the 148,000 Scottish soldiers lost in World War I, the 57,000 lost in World War II, and the 750 lost in British battles since. Each bay is dedicated to a particular Scottish regiment. The main shrine, featuring a green Italian-marble memorial containing the original WWI rolls of honor, actually sits upon an exposed chunk of the castle rock. Above you, the archangel Michael is busy slaying the dragon. The bronze frieze accurately shows the attire of various wings of Scotland's military. The stained glass starts with Cain and Abel on the left and finishes with a celebration of peace on the right.

St. Margaret's Chapel, the oldest building in Edinburgh, is dedicated to Queen Margaret, who died here in 1093 and was sainted in 1250. Built in 1130 in the Romanesque style of the Norman invaders, it is wonderfully simple, with classic Norman zigzags decorating the round arch that separates the tiny nave from the sacristy. Used as a powder magazine for 400 years, very little survives. You'll see an 11th-century Gospel book of St. Margaret's and small windows featuring St. Margaret, St. Columba (who brought Christianity to Scotland via Iona), and William Wallace (the brave defender of Scotland). The place is popular for weddings and, since it seats only 20, particularly popular with brides' fathers.

Belly up to the bannister (across the terrace outside the chapel) to enjoy the great view. Below you are the guns—which fire the one o'clock salute—and a sweet little line of doggie tombstones, the **soldier's pet cemetery**. Beyond stretches the **Georgian New Town** (read the informative plaque).

The castle could keep you entertained all day (for instance, below, in the vaults, you can see a fine military museum and Mons Meg—a huge 15th-century siege cannon that fired 500-pound stones nearly two miles). But you've seen the essentials.

When leaving the castle, turn around and look back at the gate. There stand King Robert the Bruce (on the left, 1274–1329) and Sir William Wallace (Braveheart—on the right, 1270–1305). Wallace (newly famous, thanks to Mel Gibson) fought long and hard against English domination before being executed in London—his body cut to pieces and paraded through the far corners of jolly olde England. Bruce beat the English at Bannockburn in 1314. Bruce and Wallace still defend the spirit of Scotland.

Sights—Along the Royal Mile

(In walking order from top to bottom.)

▲▲▲**Royal Mile**—This is one of Europe's most interesting historic walks. Start at the top and amble down to the palace. I've listed the top sights of the Royal Mile working downhill.

The Royal Mile, which consists of a series of four different streets—Castlehill, Lawnmarket, High Street, and Canongate—is actually 100 yards longer than a mile. And every inch is packed with shops, cafés, and lanes leading to tiny squares. By poking down the many side alleys, you'll find a few rough edges of a town well on its way to becoming a touristic mall. See it now. In a few years tourists will be slaloming through the postcard racks on bagpipe skateboards.

Royal Mile Terminology: A "close" is a tiny alley between two buildings (originally with a door that closed it at night). A close usually leads to a "court" or courtyard. A "land" is a tenement block

Royal Mile

of apartments. A "pend" is an arched gateway. A "wynd" is a narrow winding lane. And "gate" is from an old Scandinavian word for street.

Royal Mile Walking Tours: Mercat Tours offers two-hour guided walks of the mile—more entertaining than historic (£5, daily at 11:00 and 14:00 year-round, from Mercat Cross on the Royal Mile, tel. 0131/225-6591). The guides, who enjoy making a short story long, ignore the big sights, taking you behind the scenes with piles of barely historic gossip, bully-pulpit Scottish pride, and fun but forgettable trivia. For a private guide, consider Robin Sinton (tel. 0131/661-6051) or the Voluntary Guides Association (tel. 0131/664-7180).

Castle Esplanade—At the top of the Royal Mile, the big parking lot leading up to the castle was once a military parade ground. It's often cluttered with bleachers under construction for the military tattoo—a spectacular massing of the bands that fills the square nightly for most of August (see "Edinburgh Festival," below). At the bottom, on the left, the tiny witch's fountain memorializes 300 women who were accused of witchcraft and burned here. Scotland burned more witches per capita than any other country—17,000 between 1479 and 1722. But in a humanitarian gesture, rather than burning them alive as was the custom in the rest of Europe, Scottish "witches" were strangled to death before they were burned. The plaque shows two witches: one good and one bad. (For 90 minutes of this kind of Royal Mile trivia, take the guided tour described above.)

Scotch Whiskey Heritage Centre—This touristy ambush is designed only to distill £5 out of your pocket. You get a video history, a little whiskey-keg train-car ride, and a free sample before finding yourself in the shop 45 minutes later. Small-time thrill seekers prefer the 15-minute tour—just a whiskey-keg ride and a sample—for £3.25. People do seem to enjoy it, but that might have something to do with the sample (tel. 0131/220-0441). The Camera Obscura, across the street, is just as rewarding.

▲▲**Gladstone's Land**—Take a good look at this typical 16th- to 17th-century merchant's house, complete with a lived-in furnished interior and guides in each room who love to talk (£3.40, Mon–Sat 10:00–17:00, Sun 14:00–17:00, last entry at 16:30). For a good Royal Mile photo, lean out the upper-floor window or climb the entry stairway with the golden eagle.

▲**Writers' Museum at Lady Stair's House**—This interesting house, built in 1622, is filled with manuscripts and knickknacks of Scotland's three greatest literary figures: Robert Burns, Sir Walter Scott, and Robert Louis Stevenson. It's worth a few minutes for anyone and is fascinating for fans (free, Mon–Sat 10:00–17:00, closed Sun). Wander around the courtyard here. Edinburgh was a wonder in the 17th and 18th centuries. Tourists came here to see its skyscrapers, which towered 10 stories and higher. No city in Europe was so densely populated as "Auld Reekie."

Deacon Brodie's Tavern—This is a decent place for a light meal (see "Eating," below). Read the story of its notorious namesake on the wall facing Bank Street.

▲**St. Giles Cathedral**—Wander through Scotland's most important church. Stepping inside, find John Knox's statue. Look into his eyes from 10 inches away. Knox, the great reformer and founder of austere Scottish Presbyterianism, first preached here in 1559. His insistence that every person should be able to read the word of God gave Scotland an educational system 300 years ahead of the rest of Europe. For this reason it was Scottish minds that led the way in math, science, medicine, engineering, and so on. Voltaire called Scotland "the intellectual capital of Europe."

The neo-Gothic **Chapel of the Knights of the Thistle** (from 1911, in far corner) was built in two years entirely with Scottish material and labor. Find the angel tooting the bagpipes (above the door on right). The Scottish crown steeple from 1495 is a proud part of Edinburgh's skyline (daily 9:00–19:00, until 17:00 off-season; ask about concerts—some are free, usually Thu at 13:00; fine café downstairs; see "Eating," below).

John Knox is buried out back—austerely, under the parking lot, at spot 44. The statue among the cars shows King Charles II riding to a toga party back in 1685.

Parliament House—Stop in to see the grand hall with its fine 1639 hammer-beam ceiling and stained glass. This hall housed the Scottish Parliament until the Act of Union in 1707 (explained in history exhibition adjacent). Today it's busy with wigged and robed lawyers hard at work in the old library (peek through the door) or pacing the hall deep in discussion. Greater eminence… longer wig. The friendly doorman is helpful (free, public welcome Mon–Fri 9:00–16:30, best action midmornings Tue–Fri, open-

Scottish Words

aye	yes	inch, innis	island
ben	mountain	inver	river, mouth
bonnie	beautiful	kyle	strait
carn	heap of stones	loch	lake
creag	rock, cliff	neeps	turnips
tattie	potato		

haggis rich assortment of oats and sheep organs stuffed into a chunk of sheep intestine, liberally seasoned, boiled, and eaten mostly by tourists. Usually served with "neeps and tatties." Tastier than it sounds.

to-the-public trials 10:00–16:00—doorman has day's docket, entry behind St. Giles Cathedral near parking spot 21).

Mercat Cross—This stands on the downhill side of the church. Royal proclamations were read from here in the 14th century. Today it's the meeting point of various walking tours. Pop into the police information center, a few doors downhill, for a little local law-and-order history (free, daily 10:00–22:00).

▲**Tron Kirk**—This fine old building houses an interesting (free) Old Town history display and sometimes a TI.

▲**Museum of Childhood**—This five-story playground of historical toys and games—called the noisiest museum in the world because of its delighted tiny visitors—is rich in nostalgia and history (free, Mon–Fri 10:00–16:30, closed Sun). Just downhill is a fragrant fudge shop offering free samples.

▲**John Knox House**—Fascinating for Reformation buffs, this fine 16th-century house offers a well-explained look at the life of the great reformer (£2, Mon–Sat 10:00–16:30, closed Sun, 43 High Street). While Knox never actually lived here, it was called "his house" to save it from the wrecking ball in 1850.

▲**People's Story**—This interesting exhibition traces the lot of the working class through the 18th, 19th, and 20th centuries (free, Mon–Sat 10:00–17:00, closed Sun). Curiously, while this museum is dedicated to the proletariat, immediately around the back is the tomb of Adam Smith—the author of *Wealth of Nations* and the father of modern capitalism (1723–1790).

▲**Huntly House**—Another old house full of old stuff, Huntly is worth a look for its early Edinburgh history and handy ground-floor WC. Don't miss the original copy of the National Covenant (written in 1638 on an animal skin) or the sketches of pre-Georgian

Edinburgh with its lake still wet (free, Mon–Sat 10:00–17:00, closed Sun). Just a toot farther downhill is Bagpipes Galore.

Somerville Playing Cards—This quirky little shop sells over 2,000 kinds of playing cards, from different countries and eras, in various shapes and sizes (Mon–Sat 10:30–17:30, 82 Canongate, tel. 0131/556-5225).

White Horse Close—Step into this 17th-century courtyard (bottom of Canongate, on the left, a block before Holyrood Palace). It was from here that the Edinburgh stagecoach left for London. Eight days later, the horse-drawn carriage pulled into its destination: Scotland Yard.

▲**Holyrood Palace**—The palace marks the end of the Royal Mile. The queen spends a week in Scotland each summer, during which this is her official residence and office. The abbey—part of a 12th-century Augustinian monastery—stood here first. It was named for a piece of the cross brought here as a relic by queen-then-saint Margaret. Scotland's royalty preferred living here to the blustery castle on the rock, and, gradually, the palace grew. The building is rich in history and decor. But without information or a guided tour ("there's none of either," snickered the guy who sells the boring £3.70 museum guidebooks), you're just another peasant in the dark. Docents in each room are happy to give you the answer if you know the question. After wandering through the elegantly furnished rooms and a few dark older rooms filled with glass cases of historic bits and Scottish pieces that must be fascinating, you're free to wander through the ruined abbey and the queen's gardens (£5.50, daily 9:30–18:00, Nov–Apr until 16:30—guided tour mandatory off-season, last admission 45 minutes before closing; closed last two weeks in May, 10 days in early July, when the queen's home, and whenever a prince drops in; tel. 0131/556-7371).

The building lot near the palace entrance is the site of the new Scottish Parliament, slated for completion in 2002.

More Bonnie Wee Sights

▲**Georgian New Town**—Cross Waverley Bridge and walk through Georgian Edinburgh. The grand George Street, connecting St. Andrew and Charlotte Squares, was the centerpiece of the elegantly planned New Town. The entire city plan—laid out in the late 18th century when George was king—celebrates the notion of the United Kingdom. Look at the map. You'll see George Street. Queen Street, Hanover (the royal family surname) Street, and even Thistle and Rose Streets are emblems of the two happily paired nations.

▲▲**Georgian House**—This refurbished Georgian house, set on Edinburgh's finest Georgian square, is a trip back to 1796. A volunteer guide in each room is trained in the force-feeding of stories and

trivia. Start your visit with two interesting videos (architecture/
Georgian lifestyles) totaling 30 minutes (£4.40, Mon–Sat 10:00–
17:00, Sun 14:00–17:00, 7 Charlotte Square, tel. 0131/225-2160).

Princes Street Gardens—This grassy park, a former lake bed,
separates Edinburgh's New and Old Towns and offers a wonderful
escape from the city. There are plenty of free concerts and country dances in the summer and the oldest floral clock in the world.
Join the local office workers for a picnic lunch break.

▲**National Gallery**—This elegant neoclassical building has a
small but impressive collection of European masterpieces, from
Raphael to van Gogh, and offers the best look you'll get at Scottish paintings (free, Mon–Sat 10:00–17:00, Sun 14:00–17:00, tel.
0131/624-6200).

▲**Walter Scott Monument**—Built in 1840, this elaborate, neo-
Gothic monument honors the great author, one of Edinburgh's
many illustrious sons. The 200-foot monument shelters a marble
statue of Scott. He is surrounded by busts of 16 great Scottish
poets and 64 characters from his books. Climb 287 steps for a fine
view of the city (£1, Mon–Sat 9:00–18:00, until 17:00 off-season,
closed Sun).

Royal Botanic Garden—Britain's second-oldest botanical garden,
established in 1670 for medicinal herbs, is now one of Europe's
best (free, daily 9:30–19:00 in season, £2 90-minute "rainforest
to desert" tours daily at 11:00 and 14:00, one mile north of the
center at Inverleith Row, tel. 0131/552-7171).

Museum of Scotland—Learn the story of Scotland, from 2,400
million years ago through today. Take advantage of the free
60-minute orientation tour (usually daily at 14:15 and 15:15,
plus Tuesday at 18:00) or take the included audio tour (£3, free
Tue 16:30–20:00; Mon–Sat 10:00–17:00, Tue until 20:00, Sun
12:00–17:00, Chambers Street, off George IV bridge, two long
blocks south of the Royal Mile). Admission includes entry to the
Royal Museum, next door.

Dynamic Earth—Using special effects, this new museum showcases the power of the planet, from the big bang to the whole she-
bang: volcanoes, earthquakes, glaciers, oceans, rainforests. A time
machine rewinds history from the world wars back to kings and
queens and other dinosaurs. It's family fun with an epic theme
(£6, family £16.50, Apr–Oct daily 10:00–18:00, Nov–Mar Wed–
Sat 10:00–17:00, on Holyrood Road, near palace and park, tel.
0131/550-7800).

Sights—Outer Edinburgh

Britannia—This elegant vessel, which has carted around Britain's
royal family for over 40 years and 900 voyages, is moored at Edinburgh's Port of Leith and open to the public. You can tour the
bridge, dining room, and living quarters, following in the historic

footsteps of such notables as Churchill, Ghandhi, and Reagan. Book in advance (or risk being turned away) by going in person to the Military Tattoo office (33 Market Street in Edinburgh) or calling 0131/555-5566 and booking with your credit card (£6.50, daily 10:30–16:30, until 18:00 in summer, includes audio tour, videos, café; catch X50 bus at Waverley Bridge, £2.20 round-trip, free trip if you show ticket from Classic Tour).

Edinburgh Crystal—Blowing, molding, cutting, polishing, and engraving, the Edinburgh Crystal Company glassworks tour smashes anything you'll see in Venice (£3, 35-minute tours offered year-round Mon–Fri 9:15–15:30, Apr–Sept weekends 11:00–14:30, children under 8 and large dogs not allowed in for safety reasons). There is a shop full of "bargain" second-quality pieces, a video show, and a cafeteria. A free red minibus shuttle service from Waverley Bridge departs hourly (Apr–Sept, weekdays 10:00–15:00, weekends 11:00–13:00), or you can drive 10 miles south of town on A701 to Penicuik. You can schedule a more expensive super-tour where you actually blow and cut glass (tel. 01968/675-128).

Activities in Edinburgh

▲▲**Arthur's Seat Hike**—A 45-minute hike up the 822-foot volcanic mountain (surrounded by a fine park overlooking Edinburgh), starting from the Holyrood Palace, gives you a rewarding view. You can drive up most of the way from behind (follow the one-way street from the palace, park by the little lake) or run up like they did in *Chariots of Fire*. From the parking lot (south of Holyrood Palace), you'll see two trails going up. The steep one with steps skirts the base of the cliffs; the other is longer, with an easier grade.

Brush Skiing—If you'd rather be skiing, the Midlothian Ski Centre in Hillend has a hill on the edge of town with a chairlift, T-bar, two slopes plus jump slope, and rentable skis, boots, and poles (£6/hr with gear, Mon–Sat 9:30–21:00, Sun 9:30–19:00, closed last two weeks of June, probably closed if it snows, bus LRT #4 from Princes Street—garden side, tel. 0131/445-4433).

▲**Royal Commonwealth Games Swimming Pool**—The biggest pool I've ever seen is open to the public, with a Time Out cafeteria (overlooking the pool), weight room, sauna (£6.50 extra), and plenty of water rides, including Europe's biggest waterslide flume (£2.60, Mon–Fri 9:00–21:00, Wed from 10:00, Sat–Sun 10:00–16:00, no suit rentals, tel. 0131/667-7211).

More Hikes—You can hike along the river (called Water of Leith) through Edinburgh. Locals favor the stretch between Roseburn and Dean Village, but the 1.5-mile walk from Dean Village to the Royal Botanic Garden is also good and is described in the free TI brochure "Walks in and around Edinburgh." The same brochure details the four-mile hike from nearby Cramond to

South Queensferry, which involves a ferry hop, villages, woods, and historic buildings. For either hike, a bus can get you to your starting point and carry you home when you're done (the TI can help with bus routes).

Shopping—The best shopping is along Princes Street (look for elegant old Jenner's Department Store), Victoria Street (antiques galore), and the Royal Mile (touristy but competitively priced, shops usually open 9:00–17:30, later on Thu, some closed Sun).

Edinburgh Festival

One of Europe's great cultural events, Edinburgh's annual festival turns the city into a carnival of culture. There are enough music, dance, art, drama, and multicultural events to make even the most jaded traveler drool with excitement. Every day is jammed with formal and spontaneous fun. The official and fringe festivals rage simultaneously for about three weeks each summer, with the Military Tattoo starting a week earlier. Many city sights run on extended hours, and those that normally close on Sunday (Writers' Museum, Huntly House, and Museum of Childhood) open in the afternoon. It's a glorious time to be in Edinburgh.

The official festival (August 13–September 2 in 2000) is more formal and serious, with entertainment by festival invitation only. Major events sell out well in advance (show office at 21 Market Street, £4–45, CC:VMA, booking from April on, office open Mon–Fri 10:00–16:30, tel. 0131/473-2000, www.edinburghfestivals.co.uk).

The less-formal **Fringe Festival** features "on the edge" comedy and theater (August 6–28 in 2000, ticket/info office just below St. Giles Cathedral on the Royal Mile, tel. 0131/226-5257, bookings tel. 0131/226-5138, www.edfringe.co.uk). Its many events have, it seems, more performers than viewers. Tickets are usually available at the door (or strewn on the streets).

The **Military Tattoo** is a massing of the bands, drums, and bagpipes with groups from all over what was the British Empire. Displaying military finesse with a stirring lone-piper finale, this grand spectacle fills the castle esplanade nightly except Sunday, normally from a week before the festival starts until a week before it finishes: August 4 to 26 in 2000 (£8.50–20, CC:VMA, booking starts in Jan; Fri and Sat shows sell out, Mon–Thu shows rarely do; 33 Market Street, behind Waverley train station, tel. 0131/225-1188). If nothing else, it is a really big show. The BBC airs the Tattoo in a grand TV spectacle throughout Britain on the last day of its run—August 26 in 2000. It's worth watching from anywhere in Britain.

If you do manage to hit Edinburgh during the festival, book a room far in advance and extend your stay by a day or two. While Fringe tickets and most Tattoo tickets are available the day of the show, you may want to book a couple of official events in advance.

Do it directly by telephone, leaving your credit-card number. Pick up your ticket at the office the day of the show or at the door just before curtain time. Several publications—including the festival's official schedule, the *Festival Times*, *The List*, the *Fringe Program*, and the *Daily Diary*—list and evaluate festival events.

Nightlife in Edinburgh

▲▲**Evening Walking Tours**—These walks, more than a pile of ghost stories, are an entertaining and cheap night out (offered nightly, usually 19:00 and 21:00, easy socializing for solo travelers). The theatrical and creatively staged **Witchery Tours** are the most established of the ghost tours (£7, 90 min, leave from the Royal Mile, reservations required, book your spot by calling 0131/225-6745). The fascinating-for-those-who-care **Literary Pub Tour** leaves from the Beehive Pub on Grassmarket, lasts two hours, and includes two actors and four pub stops (£7, Apr–Jun and Sept–Oct at 19:30 from Thu–Sun; Jul–Aug daily at 18:00 and 20:30; Nov–Mar Fri only at 19:30; tel. 0131/226-6665).

▲**Scottish Folk Evenings**—These £35 to £40 dinner shows, generally for tour groups, are held in huge halls of expensive hotels. (Prices are bloated to include 20 percent commissions.) Your "traditional" meal is followed by a full slate of swirling kilts, blaring bagpipes, and Scottish folk dancing with an "old-time music hall"–type emcee. You can often see the show without dinner for about half price. The TI has fliers on all the latest venues. **Carlton Highland Hotel** offers its Scottish folk evening with or without dinner, nearly nightly—ask when the next show is scheduled (£12 for show at 20:45–22:30, £36.50 includes dinner at 19:30, CC:VM, at High Street and North Bridge, tel. 0131/556-7277).

▲▲**Folk Music in Pubs**—Edinburgh is a good place for folk music. There's always a pub or two with a folk evening on. The monthly *Gig Guide* (free at TI) lists most of the live music action. **Whistle Binkies** offers nightly ad-lib traditional music from about 20:30 until late (just off the Royal Mile on South Bridge, another entrance on Niddry Street, tel. 0131/557-5114).

Grassmarket Street (below the castle) is sloppy with live music—mostly folk. This noisy nightlife center is fun to just wander through late at night. **Finnigan's Wake** has live music—often Irish folk songs—nightly (starts at 22:00, a block off Grassmarket at 9 Victoria Street, tel. 0131/226-3816). The **Fiddlers Arms, Biddy Mulligan,** and **White Hart Inn** (Tuesdays only), among others, all feature live folk music. By the noise and crowds you'll know where to go and where not to. Have a beer and follow your ear.

Theater—Even outside of festival time, Edinburgh is a fine place for lively and affordable theater. Pick up *The List* for a complete rundown of what's on.

Sleeping in Edinburgh
(£1 = about $1.70, tel. code: 0131)
Sleep Code: **S** = Single, **D** = Double/Twin, **T** = Triple, **Q** = Quad, **b** = bathroom, **t** = toilet only, **s** = shower only, **CC** = Credit Card (Visa, MasterCard, Amex).

Book ahead! The annual festival fills Edinburgh each August. Conventions, school holidays, and other surprises can make finding a room tough at almost any time. Call in advance or pay 30 percent extra for a relative dump. For the best prices, book directly rather than through the TI, which charges a £4 booking fee. "Standard" rooms, with toilets and showers a tissue-toss away, save you £10 a night.

My recommendations are south of town near the Royal Commonwealth Pool, just off Dalkeith Road. This comfortably safe neighborhood is a 20-minute walk or 10-minute bus ride from the Royal Mile. All listings are on quiet streets, a two-minute walk from a bus stop, and well served by city buses. Near the B&Bs you'll find plenty of eateries (see "Eating," below), easy free parking, and the handy Capital Laundrette (Mon–Fri 9:00–17:00, Sat 9:00–16:00, £4 for self-serve, £5.50 if they do it, drop off by 11:00 for same-day service, Jun–Sept they'll deliver your clean clothes to B&B for £1 extra, 208 Dalkeith Road, tel. 0131/667-0825).

To reach the hotel neighborhood from the train station, TI, or Scott Monument, cross Princes Street and wait at the bus stop under the small C&A sign on the department store (70p, buses #14, #21, #33, #82, or #86; red bus: exact change or pay more; green bus: makes change; ride 10 minutes to first stop 100 yards after the pool, push the button, exit middle door). These buses also stop at the corner of North Bridge and High Street on the Royal Mile. Buses generally run from about 6:00–23:00, except on Sunday morning—buses don't start running from Dalkeith into town until 9:00. Taxi fare between the station or Royal Mile and the B&Bs is about £4.50.

Room prices in this section are usually listed as a range, from low season (winter) to high season (Jul–Sept), though prices can go even higher during the August festival. Off-season prices go soft, particularly for longer stays. All recommended B&Bs have no traffic noise and are strictly nonsmoking in the bedrooms and breakfast room.

Millfield Guest House, run by Liz and Ed Broomfield, is thoughtfully furnished with antique class, a rare sit-and-chat ambience, and a comfy TV lounge. Since the showers are down the hall, you'll get spacious rooms and great prices (S-£23, D-£36–40, T-£48–52, CC:VM, CC reservation allows for late arrival, 12 Marchhall Road, EH16 5HR, tel. & fax 0131/667-4428). Decipher the breakfast prayer by Robert Burns. Then try the "Taste of Scotland" breakfast option. See how many stone (14 pounds) you weigh in the elegant throne room. This place is worth calling well in advance.

Edinburgh, Our Neighborhood

Turret Guest House is teddy-on-the-beddy cozy, with a great bay-windowed family room and a vast breakfast menu that includes haggis and vegetarian options (seven rooms, S-£20–26, D-£40–44, Db-£44–56, £2-per-person discount with this book, cheaper off-season, 8 Kilmaurs Terrace, EH16 5DR, tel. 0131/667-6704, www.turret.clara.net, Mrs. Jackie Cameron).

Kenvie Guest House, well and warmly run by Dorothy Vidler, comes with six rooms and lots of personal touches (1 small twin-£38, D-£41, Db-£49, family deals, 3 percent more with CC, 16 Kilmaurs Road, EH16 5DA, tel. 0131/668-1964, fax 0131/668-1926).

Highland Park House is simple, bright, and friendly (S-£20–25, D-£44–50 with this book, family deals, 16 Kilmaurs Terrace, EH16 5DR, tel. & fax 0131/667-9204, Margaret and Brian Love).

Ard-Na-Said B&B is an elegant 1875 Victorian house with a comfy lounge and classy rooms (1 S-£22–26, Db-£44–52, family deals, 5 Priestfield Road, EH16 5HH, tel. 0131/667-8754, fax 0131/271-0960, www.ardnasaid.freeserve.co.uk, enthusiastically run by Jim and Olive Lyons).

Amaragua Guest House, next door to Turret, is an inviting Victorian home-away-from-home decorated with a Malaysian twist—art and some furniture accumulated when the English owners lived in Kuala Lumpur (S-£18–25, Db-£36–50, £2-per-person discount with this book, 10 Kilmaurs Terrace, EH16 5DR, tel. & fax 0131/667-6775, cell 0789-987-8722, run by gracious Helen and Dave Butterworth).

Dunedin Guest House (pron. dun-EE-din) is bright, plush, Scottish, and a good value (7 rooms, S-£20–30, Db-£40–60, family rooms and deals, strong showers, good lighting, TVs with satellite channels, 8 Priestfield Road, EH16 5HH, tel. 0131/668-1949, fax 0131/668-3636, e-mail: dunedin-guesthouse@edinburgh-EH16 .freeserve.co.uk, Marcella Bowen).

Dorstan Private Hotel is personable but professional and hotelesque, with all the comforts. Several of its 14 thoughtfully decorated rooms are on the ground floor (2 Ds-£58, Db-£66, family rooms, CC:VMA, 7 Priestfield Road, EH16 5HJ, tel. 0131/ 667-6721, fax 0131/668-4644, e-mail: reservations@dorstan-hotel .demon.co.uk, Mairae Campbell).

Hotel Ceilidh-Donia (pron. kaledonia) has 13 rooms: half are state-of-the-art new and comfortable, and the other half are being refurbished. Owners Max and Annette Preston offer dinner (£5–6 entrees), run a bar, and have a high-tech security system (two D-£50–54, unrenovated Db-£50–62, deluxe Db-£55–70, CC:VM, nonsmoking except in part of bar, 14 Marchhall Crescent, EH16 5HL, tel. 0131/667-2743, fax 0131/668-2181, www.hotelceilidh-donia.freeserve.co.uk).

Salisbury Hotel fills a classy old Georgian building with 12 rooms, a large lounge, and even a dumbwaiter in the breakfast room. It's more like a hotel than its neighbors but run with B&B warmth by Brenda Wright (D-£40–56, Db-£50–60, 5 percent off with cash and this book, CC:VM, 45 Salisbury Road, EH16 5AA, tel. & fax 0131/667-1264, http://members.edinburgh.org/salisbury/).

Priestville B&B is a spacious place, with six faded rooms and charming rough edges (D-£44–50, Db-£50–56, CC:VM, family deals, small fridge per floor, 10 Priestfield Road, EH16 5HJ, tel. 0131/667-2435, e-mail: priestville@hotmail.com, Angela and Alan Aberdein).

Belford House is a tidy, homey place offering seven good rooms and a warm welcome (D-£40–44, Db-£50–54, family deals, CC:VM, 13 Blacket Avenue, tel. 0131/667-2422, Isa and Tom Borthwick).

Big, Modern, Cheap Hotels in the Center
Ibis Hotel, mid–Royal Mile behind Tron Church, is perfectly located and has 98 soulless but clean and comfy rooms and American charm (Sb-£59.50, Db-£62.50 all year, skip the £4.50 contintental

buffet breakfast, CC:VMA, nonsmoking rooms available, elevator, 6 Hunter Square, EH1 1QW, tel. 0131/240-7000, fax 0131/240-7007, e-mail: H2039@accor-hotels.com). Considering its location and the costs of other hotels in town, this is a great deal for couples.

Jurys Inn is another cookie-cutter place, with 186 dependably comfortable rooms; unlike Ibis, prices fluctuate, dropping in winter and soaring in August (Db-£39–82, CC:VM, breakfast extra, nonsmoking rooms available, some views, on quiet street just off Royal Mile, 43 Jeffrey Street, EH1 1DG, tel. 0131/200-3300, fax 0131/200-0400, www.jurys.com).

Travel Inn, the biggest hotel in Edinburgh, has even less character but a great price and a mediocre location about a mile west of the Mile. Each of its 280 rooms is modern and comfortable, with a sofa that folds out for two kids if necessary (Db-£50 for 2 adults and up to 2 kids under 15, breakfast is extra, CC:VMA, elevators, nonsmoking rooms, weekends booked long in advance, near Haymarket station west of the castle at 1 Morrison Link, EH3 8DN, tel. 0131/228-9819, fax 0131/228-9836, www.travelinn.co.uk).

Hostels
Although Edinburgh's hostels are well run and open to all and provide £12 bunk beds (an £8–12 savings over B&Bs), they don't include breakfast and are scruffy.

Castle Rock Hostel is hip and easygoing, offering cheap beds, plenty of friends, and a great central location just below the castle and above the pubs with all the folk music (15 Johnston Terrace, tel. 0131/225-9666). Their sister hostels are nearly across the street from each other: **High Street Hostel** (8 Blackfriars Street, just off High Street/Royal Mile, tel. 0131/557-3984) and **Royal Mile Backpackers** (105 High Street, tel. 0131/557-6120).

For more regulations and less color, try the IYH hostels: **Bruntsfield Hostel** (near golf course, 6 to 12 beds per room, 7 Bruntsfield Crescent, buses #11, #15, and #16 from Princes Street, tel. 0131/447-2994) and **Edinburgh Hostel** (4 to 12 beds per room, 18 Eglinton Crescent, 5-minute walk from Haymarket station, tel. 0131/337-1120).

Eating in Edinburgh
Eating along the Royal Mile
Historic pubs and doily cafés with reasonable, unremarkable meals abound. But, since chefs seem to come and go with the seasons, I have no splurge meals to recommend. These are simply handy, affordable places for a good bite to eat (listed in downhill order). **Deacon Brodie's Pub** serves soup, sandwiches, and snacks on the ground floor and good £7 meals upstairs (daily 12:00–22:00, CC:VM, tel. 0131/225-6531). Or munch prayerfully in the **Lower**

Aisle restaurant under St. Giles Cathedral (Mon–Fri 8:30–16:30;
Jul–Sept also Sun 11:00–14:00). **Bann's Vegetarian Café** serves
carnivore-pleasing veggie cuisine that goes way beyond tofu and
granola (daily 10:00–23:00, CC:VM, just off South Bridge behind
the Tron Church at 5 Hunter Square, tel. 0131/226-1112). For a
break from the touristic grind, consider the **Elephant House,**
where locals browse newspapers, listen to classic rock, and sip coffee or munch a light meal (daily, three blocks south of Royal Mile
at 21 George IV Bridge, tel. 0131/220-5355). **Food Plantation**
has good, inexpensive fresh sandwiches to eat in or take out
(Mon–Fri 7:30–17:00, 274 Canongate). **Brambles Tea Room**
serves light lunches and Starbucks coffee (Mon–Sat 10:30–16:45,
Sun 11:00–16:45, next to Huntly House at 158 Canongate).
Clarinda's Tea Room, near the bottom of the Royal Mile, is a
charming and tasty place for a break after touring the Mile or
palace (daily 9:30–16:45).
      Grassmarket Street, below the castle, is lined with sloppy
eateries and noisy pubs. This is the place for live folk music. If you
want dinner to melt into your beer, eat here.

Lunch in the New Town
Waverley Center Food Court, below the TI and above the
station, is a food circus of sticky fast-food joints—including **The
Scot's Pantry** for quick traditional edibles— littered with paper
plates and shoppers (Mon–Sat 8:30–18:00, Thu until 19:00, Sun
11:00–17:00). Local office workers pile into the friendly and family-
run **La Lanterna** for good Italian food (Mon–Sat 12:00–14:00,
17:15–22:00, closed Sun, CC:VMA, 83 Hanover Street, two blocks
off Princes Street, dinner reservations wise, tel. 0131/226-3090).
For a generation, New Town vegetarians have munched salads at
Henderson's Salad Table and Wine Bar (Mon–Sat 8:00–22:45,
closed Sun, nonsmoking section, strictly vegetarian, between Queen
and George Streets at 94 Hanover Street, tel. 0131/225-2131).
Rose Street has tubs of pubs.
      Tesco is the only supermarket in town (Mon–Sat 8:00–21:00,
Sun 9:00–19:00, on Nicolson, just south of intersection with W.
Richmond Street, 5 long blocks south of the Royal Mile, and on
the way home to B&B neighborhood).

Eating in Dalkeith Road Area, near Your B&B
All of these places except Howie's are within a five-minute walk of
the recommended B&Bs. The following simple eateries are on or
near the intersection of Newington and East Preston Streets. For
a fun local atmosphere, the smoky **Wine Glass Pub** serves filling
meals (£4, daily 12:00–14:30, 17:30–21:00 but no dinner on Fri,
closes 19:30 on Sat). **Chinatown,** next to the Wine Glass, is a
delightful—though not cheap—Chinese restaurant (£7–10 entrées,

Tue–Fri 12:00–14:00, 17:30–23:00, Sat–Sun 17:30–23:00, closed Mon, CC:VM, reservations are wise, tel. 0131/662-0555). **Chatterbox,** on the other side of the Wine Glass Pub, is fine for a light meal with tea (£3.50 meals, Mon–Fri 8:30–18:00, Sat 9:00–18:00, Sun 11:00–18:00). **Brattisanis** is your basic fish-and-chips joint serving lousy milkshakes and great haggis (daily 11:30–24:00, 87 Newington Road).

Two affordable splurges feature Scottish cooking with a French flair, are open daily, and charge about £5 to £7 for lunch and £16 to £17 for a three-course dinner. **Fenwicks** is cozy and reliable, with tasty food (daily 12:00–14:00, dinner 18:00–late, all day Sunday, CC:VM, 15 Salisbury Place, tel. 0131/667-4265). **Howies,** with a more adventurous menu, is a bit pricier and a longer walk, about 10 minutes north of the B&B neighborhood; you could get off the bus at Clerk Street on the way home (daily 12:00–14:00, 16:00–22:00, can bring own wine for £2 corkage fee, 75 St. Leonard's Street, tel. 0131/668-2917).

Hotel Ceilidh-Donia, one of the recommended hotels, serves dinner nightly (£5 to £6 meal), runs a bar with a nonsmoking section, and is open to the public (14 Marchhall Crescent, tel. 0131/667-2743).

On Dalkeith Road, the huge Commonwealth Pool's **Time Out** is a noisy cafeteria for hungry swimmers and budget travelers alike (pass the entry without paying, Mon–Fri 10:00–20:00, Sat–Sun 10:00–17:00). **Jade Palace,** several blocks south of the pool, has tasty Chinese food—takeout only (Wed–Mon 16:30–23:00, closed Tue, 212 Dalkeith Road).

Minto Hotel's bar/restaurant serves a filling high tea—hot meaty dinner with tea and scones—for £7 to £8.50 (Mon–Sat 17:00–21:00, Sun 16:00–21:00, CC:VM, on Minto Street just north of intersection with Mayfield Terrace, tel. 0131/668-1234).

Transportation Connections—Edinburgh

By train to: Inverness (7/day, 4 hrs), **Oban** (3/day, change in Glasgow, 4.5 hrs), **York** (hrly, 2.5 hrs), **London** (hrly, 5 hrs), **Durham** (hrly, 2 hrs, less frequent in winter), **Newcastle** (hrly, 1.5 hrs), **Lake District** (south past Carlisle to Penrith, catch bus to Keswick; hrly except Sun 3/day, 40 min), **Birmingham** (6/day, 4.5 hrs), Crewe (6/day, 3.5 hrs). Train info: tel. 0345-484-950.

By bus to: Oban (3/day, 4 hrs), **Fort William** (3/day, 4 hrs), **Inverness** (4/day, 4 hrs). For bus info, call National Express (tel. 0990-808-080) or Scottish Citylink (tel. 0990-505-050).

Route Tips for Drivers

Arriving in Edinburgh from the north: Rather than drive through downtown Edinburgh to the recommended B&Bs, circle the city on the new A720 City Bypass road. Approaching Edinburgh on the

M-9, take the M-8 (direction: Glasgow) and quickly get onto the A720 City Bypass (direction: Edinburgh South). After four miles you'll hit a roundabout. Ignore signs directing you into Edinburgh North and stay on A720 for 10 more miles to the next roundabout, named Sheriffhall. Exit the roundabout on the first left (A7 Edinburgh). From here it's four miles to the B&B neighborhood (see "Arriving from the south," below, and B&B neighborhood map).

Arriving from the south: Coming into town on A68 from the south, take the "A7 Edinburgh" exit off the roundabout. A7 becomes Dalkeith Road. If you see the huge swimming pool, you've gone a couple of blocks too far (avoid this by referring to B&B neighborhood map above).

Leaving Edinburgh, heading south: Edinburgh to Hadrian's Wall is 100 miles; to Durham it's another 50 miles. From Edinburgh, Dalkeith Road leads south and eventually becomes A68 (handy Cameron Toll supermarket with cheap gas is on the left as you leave Dalkeith Town, 10 minutes south of Edinburgh; gas and parking behind store). A68 takes you to Hadrian's Wall in two hours. You'll pass Jedburgh and its abbey after one hour. (For one last shot of shop-Scotland, there's a coach tour's delight just before Jedburgh, with kilt makers, woolens, and a sheepskin shop.) Across from Jedburgh's lovely abbey is a free parking lot, a good visitors centre, and public toilets (20p to pee). The England/Scotland border is a fun, quick stop (great view, ice cream, and tea caravan). Before Hexham, roller-coaster two miles down A6079 to B6318, following the Roman wall westward. (See "Hadrian's Wall" in the Durham chapter for more driving instructions.)

OBAN, ISLANDS, AND HIGHLANDS

Filled with more natural and historical mystique than people, the Highlands are where Scottish dreams are set. Legends of Bonnie Prince Charlie swirl around crumbling castles as pipers and kilts swirl around tourists. The harbor of Oban is a fruit crate of Scottish traditions, and the wind-bitten Hebrides are just an island hop, skip, and jump away.

The Highlands are cut in two by the impressive Caledonian Canal, with Oban at one end and Inverness at the other. The major sights cluster along the scenic 120-mile stretch between these two towns. Oban is a fine home base for western Scotland, and Inverness makes a good overnight stop on your way through eastern Scotland.

Planning Your Time

While Ireland has more charm and Wales has better sights, this area provides your best look at rural Scottish culture. There are a lot of miles, but they're scenic, the roads are good, and the traffic's light. In two days you can get a feel for the area with the car hike described below. To do the islands, you'll need more time. Iona is worthwhile but adds a day to your trip. Generally, the region is hungry for the tourist dollar, and everything overtly Scottish is designed to woo the tourist. You'll need more than this quick visit to get away from that.

The charm of the Highlands deserves more time and a trip farther north (ideally to the Isle of Skye). But with a car and two days to connect the Lake District and Edinburgh, this blitz tour is more interesting than two more days in England.

Day 1: 9:00–Leave Lake District (see Castlerigg Stone Circle if you haven't yet), 12:00–Rest stop on Loch Lomond, then joyride

on, 13:00–Lunch in Inveraray, 16:00–Arrive in Oban, tour whiskey distillery, and drop by the TI, 20:30–Have dinner with music at McTavish's Kitchen or dinner with class at The Studio.
Day 2: 9:00–Leave Oban, 10:00–Visit Glencoe museum and the valley's Visitors Centre, 12:00–Drive to Fort William and follow Caledonian Canal to Inverness, stopping at Fort Augustus for a wander around the locks and at Loch Ness to take care of any monster business, 16:00–Visit the evocative Culloden Battlefield near Inverness, 17:00–Drive south, 20:00–Set up in Edinburgh.

With more time, spend a second night in Oban and tour Iona, get to know Arthur Smith at Glencoe, or sleep in Inverness or Pitlochry, both fun and entertaining towns.

OBAN
Oban, called the "gateway to the isles," is a busy little ferry-and-train terminal with no important "sights" but a charming shiver-and-bustle vitality that gives you a feel for small-town Scotland. Wind, boats, gulls, layers of islands, and the promise of a wide-open Atlantic beyond give it a rugged and salty charm.

Orientation (tel. code: 01631)
Oban's business action, just a couple of streets deep, stretches along the harbor and its promenade. Everything's close together, and the town seems eager to please its many visitors. There's live, touristy music nightly in several bars and restaurants; woolen and tweed are perpetually on sale (shops open until 20:00 and on Sunday); and posters announce a variety of day tours to Scotland's wild and rabbit-strewn western islands.

Tourist Information: The TI has brochures on everything from saunas to launderettes to horseback riding to rainy-day activities as well as a fine bookshop (Mon–Sat 9:00–21:00, Sun 9:00–19:00, less Sept–Jun, on Argyll Square, just off the harbor a block from the train station, tel. 01631/563-122). Wander through their exhibit on the area and pick up a few phones to hear old-timers talk about their life on the west edge of Scotland. Check the TI's "What's On" board for the latest on Oban's small-town evening scene (free live entertainment nightly at the Great Western Hotel, with a Scottish Night every Wednesday, tug-of-war on the pier, American line dancing, and so on).

Helpful Hints
Oban Rentals rents bikes across from Tesco on Lochside Road (£6/half day, £10/day, Mon–Sat 9:00–17:30, closed Sun, tel. 01631/566-996). There's a laundrette downtown on Stevenson Street (Mon–Sat 9:00–17:00, closed Sun, self-serve or £5 for full-serve). The Oban Lawn Bowling Club has welcomed visitors since 1869. This elegant green is the scene of a wonderfully British spectacle

Oban

of old men tiptoeing wishfully after their balls. It's fun to watch, and—if there's no match and the weather's dry—for £2 each you can rent shoes and balls and actually play (two blocks above the recommended B&Bs on Dalriach Road, tel. 01631/570-808).

Sights—Oban
▲West Highland Malt Scotch Whiskey Distillery Tours—
The 200-year-old Oban Whiskey Distillery produces over 14,000 liters a week. They offer serious and fragrant 40-minute, £3 tours explaining the process from start to finish, with a free, smooth sample and a discount coupon for the shop. The exhibition preceding the tour gives a quick, whiskey-centric history of Scotland. This is the handiest whiskey tour you'll see, just a block off the harbor and better than anything in Edinburgh (Mon–Fri, in season Sat 9:30–17:00, last tour at 16:00, Jul–Sept last tour 19:30, to avoid a wait, call to reserve a place, tel. 01631/572-004).
McCaig's Tower—The unfinished "colosseum" on the hill overlooking the town was an "employ-the-workers-and-build-me-a-fine-memorial" project undertaken by an early Oban tycoon in 1900. While the structure itself is nothing to see close-up, a 10-minute hike through a Victorian residential neighborhood gets you to a peaceful garden and a mediocre view.
▲▲Day Trip to the Islands of Iona and Mull—See below.
Kerrera—This stark but very green island, nearly opposite Oban, offers a quick, easy opportunity to get that romantic island experience (ferry-£2.50 round-trip, 50p for bikes, sails upon request, at Gallanach's dock two miles south of Oban, tel. 01631/563-665).

Isle of Seil—Enjoy a drive, a walk, some solitude, and the sea. Drive 15 miles south of Oban on A816 to B844 to the Isle of Seil, connected to the mainland by a bridge. Just over the bridge on the Isle of Seil is a pub called Tigh-an-Truish ("House of Trousers"). After a 1745 English law forbade the wearing of kilts on the mainland, Highlanders used this pub to change from kilts to trousers before crossing the bridge. The pub serves great meals to those in kilts or pants (daily 12:00–14:15, 18:00–20:30, darts anytime, good seafood dish, crispy vegetables, tel. 01852/300-242). Five miles across the island, on a tiny second island, is Easdale, a historic, touristy, windy, little slate-mining town facing the open Atlantic (shuttle ferry goes the 300 yards; slate-town museum, incredibly tacky egomaniac's "Highland Arts" shop).

Sleeping in Oban
(£1 = about $1.70, tel. code: 01631)

Sleep Code: **S** = Single, **D** = Double/Twin, **T** = Triple, **Q** = Quad, **b** = bathroom, **t** = toilet only, **s** = shower only, **CC** = Credit Card (**V**isa, **M**asterCard, **A**mex).

The first five places are well located on a quiet street two blocks off the harbor, three blocks from the center, and a 10-minute walk from the train station. By car, as you enter town, turn left after King's Knoll Hotel and take first right onto Breadalbane. Each has parking from an alley behind the buildings.

Strathlachlan Guest House is a winner. Mrs. Rena Anderson's place is stocking-feet cozy, crackerjack friendly, and chocolate-box tidy. Each of its four rooms has a private bathroom next door, and they share a rest-awhile TV lounge (S-£15, D-£30, family deals, entirely smoke-free, 2 Breadalbane Street, Oban, Argyll, tel. 01631/563-861).

Tanglin B&B, next door, is another fine value. Liz and Jim Montgomery offer a bright, nonsmoking, and homey place with an easygoing atmosphere (S-£15, D-£29, Db-£36, off-season rates and family deals, 3 Strathaven Terrace, Breadalbane Street, tel. 01631/563-247, e-mail: jimtanglin@aol.com).

Gramarvin Guest House is also comfy, friendly, quiet and a great value (small D-£25, D-£30, Db-£37, Breadalbane Street, tel. 01631/564-622, Mrs. Hill).

Sand Villa Guest House rents four cheery rooms (D-£26–30, Db-£35, Tb-£45, Breadalbane Street, tel. 01631/562-803, Joyce).

Raniven Guest House is also good but a lesser value (Db-£35–40, Strathlachlan Terrace, tel. 01631/562-713, Jessie Turnbull).

Barriemore Hotel is the last place (and best value) on Oban's grand waterfront esplanade. It has a plush, dark, woody, equestrian feel and 13 spacious and comfortable non-smoking rooms furnished like living rooms (Db-£44–56, grand views, CC:VM, The Esplanade, PA34 5AQ, tel. & fax

01631/566-356, e-mail: barriemore.hotel@dnet.co.uk, Evelyn and Jim McLean).

Sleeping in Hotels

I found only tired and smoky hotels in Oban. Most have unrealistically high "rack rates" with cheaper drop-in prices most of the year. The weary old **Caledonian Hotel** dominates the center of town (Db-£91 with specials as low as £60, tel. 01631/563-133). **The Balmoral Hotel** is smaller but also very central, with street noise (Db-£50–66, CC:VMA, 4 Craigard Road, tel. 01631/562-731, fax 01631/566-810, e-mail: balmoral@oban.org.uk). **Rowan Tree Hotel** is a group-friendly place with 24 basic rooms and a central but quiet locale (Sb-£38–50, Db-£62–70, group prices, CC:VMA, easy parking, George Street, tel. 01631/562-954, fax 01631/565-071).

Sleeping in Hostels and Dorms

Oban offers plenty of £10 dorm beds. Your choice: orderly, fun, or spacey. The orderly **IYHF hostel,** on the waterfront esplanade, is in a grand building with smashing views of the harbor and islands (4- to 12-bed rooms, great facilities and public rooms, tel. 01631/562-025). **Oban Backpackers** is central, laid-back, and fun, with 6 to 12 bunks per room and a wonderful sprawling public living room (Internet access, 5-minute walk from the station on Breadalbane Street, tel. 01631/562-107). **Jeremy Inglis'** spacey B&B, a block from the TI and train station, is least expensive and feels more like a commune than a youth hostel (21 Airds Crescent, tel. 01631/565-065).

Eating in Oban

Oban has plenty of fun options. Downtown is full of cheap eateries and pubs serving decent grub: consider the harbor front **Oban Inn** (the oldest building in town) or **Coasters.**

To mix a sappy folk show inexpensively with dinner, gum haggis at **McTavish's Kitchen.** This huge eating hall is an Oban institution featuring live but tired folk music and dancing. Like anything so cliché Scottish, this is your basic tourist trap filled with English vacationers. The food is inexpensive and edible (£6 basic plate; £7 for haggis, neeps, and tatties; £13 for a super Scottish multicourse menu). The piping, dancing, and singing happen nightly May through September (20:30–22:30, mostly a fiddle and two accordions, with precious little dancing and bagpiping, the last hour is most interesting, tel. 01631/563-064). The show costs £3.50 without a meal, £1.50 with dinner, or free with dinner with a coupon from your B&B. No reservations required. Nonsmokers get the best harbor views. Smokers sit closest to the stage.

Everyone's favorite "nice dinner out" is at **The Studio,** a small, candlelit restaurant featuring serious, first-class Scottish cooking (£12 for a full Scottish meal, nightly 17:00–22:00, meals £1 off until 18:30, always make a reservation, tel. 01631/562-030). It has great trout, salmon, and a prawn-and-clam chowder that hits the spot on a stormy day.

For a genteel dining experience—pricey but worthwhile for a waterfront splurge—eat at the **Manor House Hotel** (£25 set meal, nouveau cuisine, a short drive or taxi ride south of town on the waterfront, Gallanach Road, tel. 01631/562-087).

For creative continental and vegetarian cuisine, consider the **Boxtree Restaurant** (£10 meals, nightly until 22:00, 108 George Street, tel. 01631/563-542). You'll eat good but pricey seafood at **The Waterfront Restaurant** (#1 The Pier, tel. 01631/563-110).

For a seafood appetizer drop by the **Local Shellfish** shack at the ferry dock (often free salmon samples, inexpensive coffee, meal-sized salmon sandwiches, open until the 18:00 boat unloads from Mull—a pleasant way to cap off your day trip to the islands).

Transportation Connections—Oban
Oban to: Inverness (6 buses/day, 4 hrs), **Glasgow** (3 trains/day, 3 hrs). Ferries fan out from Oban to the **southern Hebrides** (See "The Islands," below). Train info: tel. 0345-484-950. Bus info: tel. 01631/562-856. Caledonian MacBrayne Ferry info: tel. 01631/566-688.

Transportation Connections—Glasgow
Glasgow is one of the region's major transportation hubs.

Glasgow to: Edinburgh (2 trains/hrly, 1 hr), **Inverness** (hrly buses, 4.5 hrs), **Penrith** (9 trains/day, 2 hrs; 6 buses/day from Penrith to Keswick, Lake District), **London** (8 trains/day, 6 hrs). Train info: tel. 0345/484-950.

THE ISLANDS OF IONA AND MULL
For the best one-day look at the dramatic and historic Hebrides island scenery around Oban, take the Iona/Mull tour from Oban (£18, daily 10:00–17:40—but always confirm schedule). Bowman & MacDougall is the dominant and most established outfit. They offer a 10 percent discount on tours for anyone with this book (buy your ticket at the "Iona & Mull Tours" office, 3 Stafford Street facing the harbor next to the Oban Inn, tel. 01631/563-221).

Each morning travelers gather on the Oban pier and pile onto the huge Oban–Mull ferry (40 min). On board, if it's a clear day, ask a local to point out Ben Nevis, the tallest mountain in Great Britain. The ferry has a fine cafeteria and a bookshop (though guidebooks are cheaper in Oban). Five minutes before landing on Mull, you'll see the striking Duart castle on the left.

Upon arrival in Mull, you'll find your tour company's bus for the entertaining and informative 35-mile bus ride across the Isle of

Mull (75 min, single-lane road). All drivers spend the entire ride chattering away about life on Mull. They are hardworking local boys who know how to spin a yarn, making historical trivia fascinating— or at least fun.

The Isle of Mull, the third-largest in Scotland, has 300 scenic miles of coastline and castles and a 3,169-foot-high mountain. Called Ben More ("big hill" in Gaelic), it was once much bigger. The last active volcano in northern Europe, it was 10,000 feet tall—the entire island of Mull—before it blew. Calmer now, Mull has a notably laid-back population. My bus driver reported there are no deaths from stress and only a few from boredom.

On the far side of Mull the caravan of tour buses unloads at a tiny ferry town. The ferry takes about 200 walk-ons. (Confirm clearly with bus driver when to catch the boat off Iona for your return. Hustle quickly off the bus and to the dock to avoid the 30-minute delay if you don't make the first trip over.) After the 10-minute ride, you wash ashore on sleepy Iona.

Tiny Iona, just three miles by 1.5 miles, with a population of about a hundred, is famous as the birthplace of Christianity in Scotland. You'll have about two hours here on your own before you retrace your steps, docking back in Oban by about 17:40. While the day is spectacular when it's sunny, it's worthwhile in any weather.

Iona's history: St. Columba, an Irish scholar, soldier, priest, and founder of monasteries, got into a small war over the possession of an illegally copied psalm book. Victorious but sickened by the bloodshed, Columba left Ireland, vowing never to return. According to legend, the first bit of land out of sight of his homeland was Iona. He stopped here in 563 and established the abbey.

Columba's monastic community flourished, and Iona became the center of Celtic Christianity. Iona missionaries spread the gospel through Scotland and North England, while scholarly monks established Iona as a center of art and learning. The *Book of Kells*—perhaps the finest piece of art from "Dark Age" Europe— was probably made on Iona in the eighth century. The island was so important that it was the legendary burial place for ancient Scottish and even Scandinavian kings (including Shakespeare's Macbeth).

Slowly the importance of Iona ebbed. Vikings massacred 68 monks in 806. Fearing more raids, the monks evacuated most of Iona's treasures (including the *Book of Kells*, which is now in Dublin) to Ireland. Much later, with the Reformation, the abbey was abandoned, and most of its finely carved crosses were destroyed. In the 17th century locals used the abbey only as a handy quarry for other building projects.

Iona's population peaked at about 500 in the 1830s. In the

1840s a potato famine hit. In the 1850s a third of the islanders immigrated to Canada or Australia. By 1900 the population was down to 210, and today it's only around 100.

But in our generation a new religious community has given the abbey new life. The Iona community is an ecumenical gathering of men and women seeking new ways of living the Gospel in today's world, with a focus on worship, peace and justice issues, and reconciliation. A center on the island welcomes guests (tel. 01681/700-404, www.iona.org.uk, e-mail: ionacomm@iona.org.uk).

A pristine light and a thoughtful peace pervade the stark, car-free island and its tiny community. While the present abbey, nunnery, and graveyard go back to the 13th century, much of what you'll see was rebuilt in the last century. But with buoyant clouds bouncing playfully off of distant bluffs, sparkling white sand crescents, and lone tourists camped thoughtfully atop huge rocks just looking out to sea, it's a place perfect for meditation. Climb a peak—nothing's higher than 300 feet above the sea.

The village, Baile Mor, has a shop, tiny eateries, enough beds, and a meager heritage center. The Finlay Ross Shop rents bikes (near ferry dock, £4.50/half day, £8/day).

Sleeping in Iona: Enjoy the serenity of Iona by spending the night. When the day-trippers leave, you'll find that special peace. **Argyll Hotel,** built in 1868, sits proud and classy overlooking the waterfront, with basic rooms above a fine grassy yard and public spaces (15 rooms, Db-£82–90, dinner deals, CC:VM, tel. 01681/700-334, fax 01681/700-510). **Finlay B&B** rents 11 no-charm rooms in front of the ferry dock (D-£42, Db-£46, reception at Finlay Ross Shop, tel. 01681/700-357, fax 01681/700-562).

Other Island Tours—The Oban tour companies offer an array of tours. You can spend an entire day on Mull. Those more interested in nature than church history will enjoy trips to the wildly scenic Isle of Staffa with Fingal's Cave. Trips to Treshnish Island brim with puffins, seals, and other critters.

THE HIGHLANDS: OBAN TO INVERNESS

Discover Glencoe's dark secrets in the Weeping Glen, where Britain's highest peak, Ben Nevis, keeps its head in the clouds. Explore the locks and lochs of the Caledonian Canal while the Loch Ness monster plays hide-and-seek. Hear the music of the Highlands in Inverness and the echo of muskets in Culloden, where the English put down Bonnie Prince Charlie and conquered the clans of the Highlands.

Getting around the Highlands

The trains are scenic, but if schedules frustrate, take the bus. Six buses a day connect the towns from Oban to Inverness (4 hrs). Ask

Oban, Islands, and Highlands

at the station to see how schedules work for sight hopping. One great option is to ride with the postman. While locals do this to get somewhere, tourists do it to chat with the postman—great gossip on the entire neighborhood! This costs only a few pounds and works well in remote spots like Glencoe.

GLENCOE
This valley is the essence of the wild, powerful, and stark beauty of the Highlands (and, I think, excuses the hurried tourist from needing to go north of Inverness). Along with its scenery, Glencoe offers a good dose of bloody clan history.

Glencoe town is just a line of houses. One is a tiny thatched building jammed with local history. The huggable Glencoe and North Lorn Folk Museum, purely a homegrown effort, is filled with humble exhibits gleaned from the town's old closets and attics (which come to life when explained by a local). When one house was being rethatched, its owner found a cache of old rifles hidden there from the British Redcoats after the disastrous battle of Culloden (£1, Mon–Sat 10:00–17:30, closed Sun).

A couple of miles into the dramatic valley you'll find the Visitors Centre. While little more than a café, WC, and bookshop, it does show a 14-minute video about the 1692 massacre when the Redcoats killed the sleeping MacDonalds and the valley got its nickname, "The Weeping Glen" (50p, daily 9:30–17:30, shorter hours or closed off-season, just east of town on A82, tel. 01855/811-307). The nearest TI is in Ballachulish (tel. 01855/811-296).

Walks: For a steep one-mile hike, climb the Devil's Staircase (trail leaves from A82, 8 miles east of Glencoe). For a three-hour hike, ask at the Visitors Centre about the Lost Valley of the MacDonalds (trail leaves from A82, 3 miles east of Glencoe). For an easy walk from Glencoe, head to the mansion on the hill (over the bridge, turn left, fine loch views). Above Glencoe is a 365-room mansion built by a local big shot for his love—a Canadian Indian. She was homesick, so he actually replicated a Canadian garden/forest. It didn't work, and they eventually returned to British Columbia.

Glencoe's Burial Island and Island of Discussion: In the loch just outside Glencoe notice the burial island—where the souls of those who "take the low road" are piped home. (Ask a local about "You take the high road, and I'll take the low road.") The next island was the Island of Discussion—where those with disputes were put until they came to an agreement.

Sleeping in Glencoe
(£1 = about $1.70, tel. code: 01855)
Many find Glencoe more interesting than Oban for an overnight stop. In Glencoe village, Arthur Smith runs the **Cala Sona B&B,** aptly named "haven of happiness" in Gaelic. He entertains his guests with a peat fire, ghost stories, and tales of the Glencoe massacre (S-£15, D-£30, on the main street, tel. 01855/811-314). If Arthur's place is full, try the **Mack-Leven House B&B** (D-£30, Db-£32 with this book, family deals, smoke-free rooms, homey lounge, Lorn Drive, Glencoe, tel. 01855/811-215, Mackintosh family) or **Tulachgorm B&B** (D-£29, flexible on price when slow, nonsmoking, just before Cala Sona B&B, tel. 01855/811-391, Ann Blake).

While nearby hotels and pubs serve food, **Mrs. Matheson's Tea Room Restaurant** (right in the village) is your best bet for good home-cooked meals (£8 meals, nightly 17:30–20:30, tel. 01855/811-590). For evening fun, chat with your B&B host, take a walk, or drop by the "Wee Ceilidh" for music and dancing at the **Glencoe Hotel** (Mon and Fri at 20:00).

More Sights—Scottish Highlands
Ben Nevis—From Fort William, take a peek at Britain's highest peak, Ben Nevis (over 4,400 feet). Thousands walk to its summit each year. On a clear day you can admire it from a distance. Scotland's only mountain cable cars can take you to a

not-very-lofty 2,150-foot perch for a closer look (£6.50, daily 10:00–17:00, later in summer, 15-min, signposted on A82, tel. 01397/705-825).

▲**Caledonian Canal**—Three lochs and a series of canals cut Scotland in two. Oich, Lochy, and Ness were connected in the early 1800s by the great British engineer Thomas Telford. Traveling between Fort William and Inverness (60 miles), you'll follow Telford's work—20 miles of canals and locks between 40 miles of lakes, raising ships from sea level to 51 feet (Ness) to 93 feet (Lochy) to 106 feet (Oich).

While "Neptune's Staircase," a series of locks near Fort William, is cleverly named, the best lock stop is Fort Augustus, where the canal hits Loch Ness. In Fort Augustus, the Caledonian Canal Heritage Centre, three locks above the main road, gives a good rundown on Telford's work (free). Stroll to the top of the locks past several shops and eateries for a fine view.

Loch Ness—I'll admit it. I had my zoom lens out and my eyes on the water. The local tourist industry thrives on the legend of the Loch Ness Monster. It's a thrilling thought, and there have been several seemingly reliable "sightings" (monks, policemen, and sonar images). The loch, 24 miles long, less than a mile wide, and the third-deepest in Europe, is deepest near the Urquhart Castle. Most monster sightings are in this area.

The Nessie commercialization is so tacky that there are two "official" Loch Ness Exhibition Centres within 100 yards of each other. Each has a tour-bus parking lot and more square footage devoted to their kitschy shop than to the exhibit. The exhibits, while fascinating, are overpriced. The exhibition in the big stone mansion (closest to Inverness) is the better one, with a 40-minute series of video bits on the geological and historical environment that bred the monster story and the various searches (£6.50, daily 9:00–20:30, tel. 01456/450-573). The other (closest to Oban), is a high school–quality photo report followed by the 30-minute *We Believe in the Loch Ness Monster* movie, featuring credible-sounding locals explaining what they saw and a review of modern Nessie searches (£4, daily 9:00–19:30, tel. 01456/450-342).

The nearby Urquhart Castle ruins are gloriously situated with a view of virtually the entire lake (£4, daily 9:30–18:30, Jul–Aug till 20:30, tel. 01456/450-551). It's an empty shell of a castle with crowds and parking problems.

▲**Culloden Battlefield**—Scottish troops under Bonnie Prince Charlie were defeated here by the English in 1746. This last land battle fought on British soil spelled the end of Jacobite resistance and the fall of the clans. Wandering the battlefield, you feel that something terrible happened here. Locals still bring flowers and speak of "46" as if it were this century.

The excellent Visitors Centre shows a stirring 16-minute

audiovisual (3/hrly). Wander through a furnished old cottage and the battlegrounds (£3.20, Apr–Oct daily 9:00–18:00, otherwise daily 10:00–16:00, closed Jan, good tearoom, tel. 01463/790-607).

INVERNESS

The only sizable town in the north of Scotland, with 42,000 people, Inverness is pleasantly located on a river at the base of a castle (not worth a look) and has a free little museum (worth a look, cheap café). Its **Highland Music Museum** traces local music from heroic warrior songs to Gaelic rock (£2 to scan 6 hours of music, Tue–Sun 10:00–17:00, Jul–Aug till 20:00, closed Mon, live bagpiping at 17:00 during summer, Balnain House, tel. 01463/715-757). Check out the bustling pedestrian downtown and central TI (tel. 01463/234-353). Ask about the very informative "Gordon's" minibus tours to Loch Ness (£11, most days 10:30–16:30). Guide Friday buses connect Inverness and Culloden.

The Scottish Showtime evening is a fun-loving, hardworking, Lawrence Welk-ish show giving you all the clichés in a clap-along two-hour package. I prefer it to the big hotel spectacles in Edinburgh (usually Mon–Fri in season at 20:30, no meals, £12 but £2 off with this book, Cummings Hotel, Church Street tel. 0800-028-0538).

Sleeping and Eating in Inverness
(£1 = about $1.70, tel. code: 01463)

These rooms are all a short walk from the train station and town center (just up the steps from the pedestrian High Street).

Craigside Lodge B&B is a winner. Its six spacious, cheery rooms share a stay-awhile lounge with a great city view (Db-£40, CC:VM, just above Castle Street at 4 Gordon Terrace, IV2 3HD, tel. 01463/321-576, fax 01463/713-409, Wilf and Janette Skinner).

Ardconnel House is tasteful, bright, spacious, and classy (Sb-£25, D-£40, Db-£44, CC:VM, family deals, nonsmoking, TVs in rooms, 21 Ardconnel Street, IV2 3EU, tel. & fax 01463/ 240-455, new owner in 2000).

Kinloch Lodge B&B is a minimal place renting four small but cheery double rooms (no twins, S-£17, D-£32, Db-£34, 13 Ardconnel Street, tel. 01463/716-005).

Hollies is also simple but a fine value (S-£16, D-£32, T-£48, family deals, 24 Ardconnel Street, tel. 01463/231-291, well run by Mrs. Proudfoot, who doesn't appreciate soft, whiny Americans).

Melness Guest House has fine rooms and a cozy lounge but is a bit overpriced (D-£38–40, Db-£46–50, less off-season, completely smoke-free, at 8 Old Edinburgh Road, tel. 01463/220-963, e-mail: melness@joyce86.freeserve.co.uk).

For £10 beds in six-bed rooms downtown and a 10-minute walk from the train station, consider the friendly and laid-back **Inverness Student Hotel** (8 Culduthel Road, tel. 01463/236-556).

Rajah Indian Restaurant provides a tasty break from pub grub (£7–10 meals, nightly until midnight, just off Church Street at 2 Post Office Avenue, tel. 01463/237-190). Near the recommended B&B, **Redcliff Hotel** lounge is popular for its pub-style dinners. Several inviting eateries (including **Number 27**) line Castle Street.

Transportation Connections—Inverness

Trains link Inverness, **Pitlochry**, and **Edinburgh** (9/day, 3.5 hrs, tel. 01463/238-924 or tel. 0345-484-950), and buses run between Inverness and **Oban** (6/day, 4 hrs, tel. 01463/233-371). Scottish Rail does a great 20:30–7:30 sleeper service to **London** (£95 for a private compartment with breakfast). Consider dropping your car in Inverness and riding to London by train.

PITLOCHRY

This likable tourist town, famous for its whiskey, makes an enjoyable overnight stop. Its cute **Edradour Scotch Distillery**—the smallest in Scotland—offers a free one-hour guided tour, a 10-minute audio-visual show, and, of course, a tasting (3/hrly, Mon–Sat 9:30–16:45, summer Sun 12:00–16:45, a lovely 40-minute walk through the forest from downtown, tel. 01796/472-095). The big **Blair Athol Distillery** gives £3 hour-long tours with a sample at the end (2/hrly, Mon–Sat 9:30–16:00, Sun 12:00–16:00, half mile from town, tel. 01796/472-234). Pitlochry also has plenty of forest walks and a salmon ladder (free viewing area—best in May, three-minute walk from town). The town theater offers a different play every night (£16). For a unique look at jewelry made of pressed heather stems, tour **Heather-gems** (behind the TI). The TI is helpful (May–Sept daily 9:00–20:00, less off-season, tel. 01796/472-215).

Sleeping in Pitlochry
(£1 = about $1.70, tel. code: 01796)
Try **Craigroyston House,** a big Victorian country house with eight smoke-free, Laura Ashley–style rooms run by charming Gretta Maxwell (Db-£40–52, flexing with demand, next to church and TI at 2 Lower Oakfield, PH16 5HQ, tel. & fax 01796/472-053, e-mail: craigroyston@ukoline.co.uk). She can find you another B&B if her place is full. For a simpler, more rural option, drive two miles south of town on the old A9 to **Donavourd Farmhouse B&B** (D-£30–36, dinner, near distillery, tel. 01796/472-254, Mrs. Shepley). Pitlochry's fine **hostel** is on Knockard Road (£9 bunks, above the main street, tel. 01796/472-308).

Route Tips for Drivers
Lake District to Oban (220 miles): From Keswick, take A66 for 18 miles to M6 and speed nonstop north (via Penrith and Carlisle), crossing Hadrian's Wall into Scotland. The road

becomes the M74 south of Glasgow. To slip quickly through Glasgow, leave M74 at Junction 4 onto M73, following signs to M8/Glasgow. Leave M73 at Junction 2, exiting onto M8. Stay on M8 west through Glasgow, exit on Junction 30, cross Erskine Bridge (60p), and turn left on A82, following signs to Crianlarich and Loch Lomond. (For a scenic drive through Glasgow, take exit 17 off M8 and stay on A82 toward Dumbarton.) You'll soon be driving along scenic Loch Lomond. The first picnic turnout has the best lake views, benches, a park, and a playground. Halfway up the loch, at Tarbet, take the "tourist route" left onto A83, drive along Loch Long toward Inveraray via Rest-and-Be-Thankful Pass. (This colorful name comes from the 1880s, when second- and third-class coach passengers got out and pushed the coach and first-class passengers up the hill.) Stop in Inveraray, a lovely castle town on Loch Fyne. Park near the pier. (TI tel. 01499/302-063.) The town jail, now a museum, is a "19th-century living prison" (£4.50, daily 9:30–18:00, tel. 01499/302-381). Leaving Inveraray, drive through a gate (at the Woolen Mill) to A819, through Glen Aray, and along Loch Awe. A85 takes you into Oban.

Oban to Glencoe (45 miles) to Loch Ness (75 miles) to Inverness (20 miles) to Edinburgh (150 miles): Barring traffic, you'll make great time on good, mostly two-lane roads. Be careful, but if you're timid about passing, diesel fumes and large trucks might be your memory of this drive. From Oban follow the coastal A828 toward Fort William. After about 20 miles you'll see the photogenic Castle Staulker marooned on a lonely island. At Loch Leven and Ballachulish Village, leave A828, taking A82 into Glencoe. Drive through the village up the valley (Glencoe) for 10 minutes for a grand view and a chance to hear a bagpiper in the wind—Highland buskers. If you play the recorder (and no other tourists are there), ask to finger a tune while the piper does the hard work.

At the top of the valley you hit the vast Rannoch Moor— 500 square and desolate miles with barely enough decent land to graze a sheep. Then make a U-turn and return through Glencoe. Continue north on A82, over the bridge, past Fort William toward Loch Ness. Follow the Caledonian Canal on A82 for 60 miles, stop at Loch Ness, and then continuing on A82 to Inverness.

Leaving Inverness, follow signs to A9 (south toward Perth). Just as you leave Inverness, detour four miles east off A9 on B9006 to the Culloden Battlefield Visitors Centre. Back on A9 it's a won- derfully speedy, scenic highway (A9, M90, A90) all the way to Edinburgh (Inverness–Edinburgh, minimum 3 hrs).

For a scenic shortcut, head north only as far as Glencoe and then cut to Edinburgh via Rannoch Moor and Tyndrum. For directions to B&Bs, see "Edinburgh" chapter.

DUBLIN

With reminders of its stirring history and rich culture on every corner, Ireland's capital and largest city is a sightseer's delight. Dublin's fair city will have you humming "Alive, alive-O."

Founded as a Viking trading settlement in the ninth century, Dublin grew to be a center of wealth and commerce second only to London in the British Empire. Dublin, the seat of English rule in Ireland for 700 years, was the heart of a "civilized" Anglo-Irish area (eastern Ireland) known as "the Pale." Anything "beyond the Pale" was considered uncultured and almost barbaric... purely Irish.

The Golden Age of English Dublin was the 18th century. Britain was on a roll, and Dublin was Britain's second city. Largely rebuilt during this Georgian era, Dublin—even with its "tale of two cities" miserable underbelly—became an elegant and cultured capital.

Then nationalism and human rights got in the way. The ideas of the French Revolution inspired Irish intellectuals to buck British rule, and after the revolt of 1798, life in Dublin was never quite the same. But the 18th century left a lasting imprint on the city. Georgian (that's British for neoclassical) squares and boulevards gave the city a grandness. The National Museum, National Gallery, and many government buildings are in the Georgian section of town. Few buildings (notably St. Patrick's Cathedral and Christchurch Cathedral) predate this Georgian period.

In the 19th century, with the closing of the Irish Parliament, the famine, and the beginnings of the struggle for independence, Dublin was treated—and felt—more like a colony than a partner. The tension culminated in the Rising of 1916, independence, and the tragic civil war. With many of Dublin's grand streets left in ruins, the city emerged as the capital of the only former colony in Europe.

While bullet-pocked buildings and dramatic statues keep memories of Ireland's recent struggle for independence alive, it's boom time now, and the city is looking to a bright future. Locals are enjoying the "Celtic Tiger" economy—the best in Europe—while visitors enjoy a big-town cultural scene wrapped in a small-town smile.

Planning Your Time

On a two-week trip through Ireland, Dublin deserves three nights and two days. Consider this sightseeing plan:

Day 1: 10:00–Trinity College walk, 11:00–*Book of Kells* and Old Library, 12:00–Browse Grafton Street, lunch there or picnic on St. Stephen's Green, 13:30–National Museum, 15:00–Historical town walk, 17:00–Return to hotel, rest, dinner—eat well for less during "early bird specials," 19:30–Evening walk (musical or literary), 22:00–Irish music in Temple Bar area.

Day 2: 10:00–Kilmainham Jail, 12:00–Guinness Brewery tour, 13:30–Lunch (with a faint buzz), 15:00–Tour Dublin Castle, Evening–Catch a play or concert.

Orientation (tel. code: 01)

Greater Dublin sprawls with over a million people—nearly a third of the country's population. But the center of touristic interest is a tight triangle between O'Connell Bridge, St. Stephen's Green, and Christchurch Cathedral. Within this triangle you'll find Trinity College (*Book of Kells*), Grafton Street (top pedestrian shopping zone), Temple Bar (trendy nightlife center), Dublin Castle, and the hub of most city tours and buses.

The River Liffey cuts the town in two. Focus on the southern half (where nearly all your sightseeing will take place). Dublin's main drag, O'Connell Street (near Abbey Theater and the outdoor produce market) runs north of the river to the central O'Connell Bridge then continues as the main city axis—mostly as Grafton Street—to St. Stephen's Green. The only major sights outside your easy-to-walk triangle are the Kilmainham Jail and the Guinness Brewery (both west of the center).

Tourist Information

The TI fills an old church on Suffolk Street (a block off Grafton Street, Mon–Sat 9:00–17:30, Sun 9:00–14:30, closed off-season Sun, no telephone help). While packed with tourists, promotional brochures, an American Express office, a café, and traditional knickknacks, it's short on hard info. Less crowded but equally helpful TI branches are on Baggot Street and at the airport (daily 8:00–22:00). The TI gives a free newspaper with a lousy map, lots of advertisements, and the same fliers that fill racks all over town. The handy *Dublin's Top Visitor Attractions* booklet has a map and the latest on all the town's sights—many more than I list here (£2.50, sold at TI bookshop without any wait). For a schedule of happenings in town, buy the excellent *In Dublin* at any newsstand (fortnightly, £2).

Arrival in Dublin

By Train: Trains arrive at Heuston Station (serving the west and southwest) on the west end of town. Dublin's second train station, Connolly Station (serving the north, northwest, and Rosslare), is closer to the center—a 10-minute walk from O'Connell Bridge. Each station has a luggage-check facility.

Bus 90 connects both train stations, the bus station, and the city center (60p flat fee, 6/hrly, runs along river).

By Bus: Bus Eireann, Ireland's national bus company, uses the Busaras Central Bus Station next to Connolly Station (catch bus 90 to the city center).

By Ferry: Irish Ferries dock at the mouth of the River Liffey (near the town center), while the Stena Line docks at Dun Laoghaire (easy DART train connections into Dublin, at least 3/hrly, 15 min).

Dublin

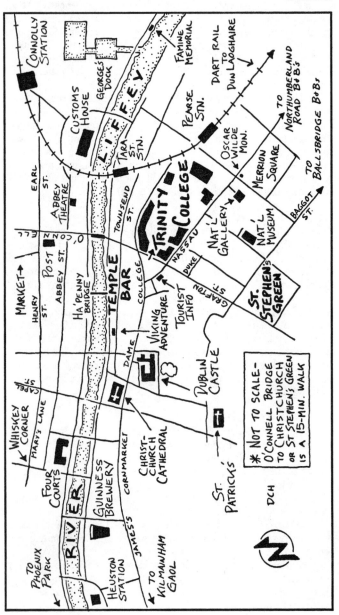

By Plane: From the airport, milk-run buses 41 and 41C go to Talbot Street, a five-minute walk to O'Connell Bridge (£1.10, 3/hrly). The faster Airlink direct bus connects the airport with the Heuston Station and Busaras Central Bus Station near Connolly Station (£3, 4/hrly, 30 min). Taxis from the airport into Dublin cost about £13.

Helpful Hints

Internet Access: On the north side of O'Connell Bridge, try Global Internet Café (£5/hr, 8 Lower O'Connell St., tel. 01/878-0295). On the south side, try Planet Cybercafé (£5/hr, off Dame Street below the castle at 23 South Great George's Street, tel. 01/679-0583).

   Laundry: Capricorn Dry Cleaners is behind Jury's Christchurch on Patrick Street (Mon–Fri 7:30–20:00, Sat 9:00–18:00, Sun 10:00–16:00, tel. 01/473-1779).

Getting around Dublin

You'll do most of Dublin on foot. Big green buses are cheap and cover the city thoroughly. Most lines start at the four quays nearest O'Connell Bridge. If you're away from the center, nearly any bus takes you back downtown. Tell the driver where you're going, and he'll ask for 60p (1 to 3 stops) or 80p (4 to 7 stops). The bus office at 59 Upper O'Connell Street has free "route network" maps and sells bus passes (1-day pass £3.30 adults, £5.50 family, 4-day adult Explorer pass £10.00, bus info tel. 01/873-4222). DART trains connect Dublin with Dun Laoghaire (ferry terminal and recommended B&Bs, at least 3/hrly, 15 min, £1.10). Taxis are honest, plentiful, friendly, and good sources of information (under £4 for most downtown rides, £20 per hour for a guided joyride, City Cabs tel. 01/872-2688).

Tours of Dublin

While the physical treasures of Dublin are mediocre by European standards, the city has a fine story to tell and people with a natural knack for telling it. It's a good town for walking tours—and the competition is fierce. Pamphlets touting creative walks are posted all over town. There are medieval walks, literary walks, Georgian Dublin walks, and more. The two evening walks are great ways to meet other travelers.

▲▲**Historical Walking Tour**—This is your best introductory walk. A group of hardworking history graduates—many of whom claim to have done more than just kiss the Blarney Stone—fill Dublin's basic historic strip (Trinity College, Old Parliament House, Dublin Castle, and Christchurch Cathedral) with the story of their city, from its Viking origin to the present. As you listen to your guide's story, you stand in front of buildings that aren't much to see but are lots to talk about. Guides speak at length about the roots of Ireland's struggle with Britain (£6, 2 hours, depart from front gate of Trinity College, May–Sept daily 11:00 and 15:00 plus Sat–Sun at 12:00; Oct–Apr only Fri, Sat, and Sun at 12:00; tel. 01/878-0227). For a private walk, contact Historical Insights (tel. 01/878-0227, www.historicalinsights.ie).

▲**Jameson Literary Pub Crawl**—Two actors take 30 or so tourists on a walk, stopping at four pubs. Half the time is spent enjoying their entertaining banter, which introduces the novice to the high craic (conversation) of Joyce, O'Casey, and Yeats. The 2.5-hour tour is punctuated with 20-minute pub breaks (free time). While the beer lubricates the social fun, it dilutes the content of the evening. Meet any night at 19:30 (plus Sunday at noon) in the Duke Pub off Grafton on Duke Street (£6.50, runs Thu–Sun in winter, tel. 01/670-5602).

▲▲**Traditional Irish-Music Pub Crawl**—This is like the Literary Pub Crawl but features music. You meet upstairs at 19:30 at Gogarty's Pub (in the Temple Bar area) and spend 40 minutes in the upstairs rooms of four pubs listening to two musicians talk about, play, and sing traditional Irish music. While having only two musicians makes the music a bit thin and Irish music aficionados will tell you you're better off just finding a good session, the evening—while touristy—is not gimmicky. The musicians demonstrate four instruments and really enjoy introducing rookies to their art (£6, boss Vinnie offers a £1 discount with this book, beer extra, nightly May–Oct, weekends only in winter, allow 2.5 hours, expect up to 50 tourists, tel. 01/478-0193).

▲**Bus Tours**—Several companies offer the basic center-of-Dublin orientation (3 hrs, £10, departing 10:15 and 14:15, from 59 Upper O'Connell Street, tel. 01/783-4222). For a hop-on hop-off bus tour, consider either **Dublin City Tour** (£7, tel. 01/873-4222) or **Guide Friday** (£7, tel. 01/676-5377). Both do identical 90-minute circuits of the town, allowing you to hop on and hop off at your choice of 12 stops (mostly topless—with running commentaries; they go to Guinness Brewery but not to Kilmainham Jail). Pay the driver when you hop on. Your ticket's good for the entire day. Buses, which leave about every 10 minutes from about 9:30 to 18:00, are especially enjoyable for photographers on sunny days. One ticket gets you on either company's buses.

Sights—Dublin's Trinity College

▲**Trinity College**—Started in 1592 by Queen Elizabeth I to establish a Protestant way of thinking about God, Trinity has long been Ireland's most prestigious college. Originally the student body was limited to rich, Protestant males. Women were admitted in 1903, and Catholics, while allowed entrance by the school much earlier, were given formal permission to study at Trinity in the

Dublin Center

1 CITY WALKS START	**10** FITZWILLIAM, BAGGOT COURT & MESPIL HOTEL	**18** POWERSCOURT TOWNHOUSE CENTRE
2 TRINITY WALKS START	**11** ALBANY HOUSE	**19** WAGAMAMA NOODLE
3 LIT. PUB CRAWL STARTS	**12** NORTHUMBERLAND ROAD	**20** YAMAMORI
4 MUSIC PUB CRAWL STARTS	**13** TOWNHOUSE OF DUBLIN & GLOBETROTTERS	**21** QV2 & TROCADERO
5 VIKING ADVENTURE	**14** CORNUCOPIA	**22** BOULEVARD CAFE
6 HERALDIC MUSEUM	**15** TOURIST OFFICE	**23** JUICE
7 HARDING / KINLAY HOTELS	**16** BEWLEYS	**24** GALLAGHER'S BOXTY
8 JURY'S INN	**17** LEO BURDOCK'S	**25** BAD ASS CAFE
9 AVALON HOUSE		

1970s. Today half of Trinity's 11,000 students are women, and 70 percent are culturally Catholic (although only about 20 percent of Irish youth are churchgoing).

▲**Trinity College Tour**—Inside the gate of Trinity, students organize and lead 30-minute tours of their campus. You'll get a rundown on the mostly Georgian architecture; a peek at student life, both in the early days and today; and enjoy a chance to hang out with a witty Irish college kid as he talks about his school (daily 10:00–15:30, the £5.50 tour fee includes the £4.50 fee to see the *Book of Kells*, where the tour leaves you).

▲▲▲*Book of Kells*/**Trinity Old Library**—The only Trinity campus interior welcoming tourists—just follow the signs—is the Old Library with its precious *Book of Kells*. The first-class *Turning Darkness into Light* exhibit puts the 680-page illuminated manuscript in its historical and cultural context and prepares you for the original book and other precious manuscripts in the treasury. The exhibit is a one-way affair leading to the actual treasury, which shows only three books under glass. Take your time in the exhibit.

Written on vellum (baby calfskin) in the eighth (or early ninth) century—probably by Irish monks in Iona (Scotland)—this enthusiastically decorated copy of the four Gospels was taken to the Irish monastery at Kells in 806 after a series of Viking raids. Arguably the finest piece of art from what is generally called the Dark Ages, the *Book of Kells* shows that monastic life in this far fringe of Europe was far from dark. It has been bound into four separate volumes. At any given time, two of the gospels are on display. You'll see four richly decorated 1,200-year-old pages—two text and two decorated cover pages—under glass. The library treasury also displays the *Book of Armagh* (A.D. 807) and the *Book of Durrow* (A.D. 680), neither of which can be checked out.

Next, a stairway leads to the 65-meter-long main chamber of the Old Library (from 1732), stacked to its towering ceiling with 200,000 of the library's oldest books. Here you'll find one of a dozen surviving original copies of the 1916 Proclamation of the Irish Republic. Patrick Pearse read these words outside the General Post Office on April 24 to start the Easter Rising which led to Irish Independence. Read the entire thing...imagining it was yours. Notice the inclusive opening phrase. (The seven signatories were each executed.) Another national icon is nearby—the oldest surviving Irish harp. From the 15th century, it's the one featured on Irish coins. Crowds are gone by the end of the day (£4.50, at Trinity College Library, Mon–Sat 9:30–17:00 all year, Sun 9:30–16:30, off-season Sun 12:00–16:30, tel. 01/608-2308).

▲▲**The Dublin Experience**—This 40-minute video giving a historic introduction to Dublin is one more tourist movie with the sound turned up. It's good—offering a fine sweeping introduction to the story of Ireland—but pricey and riding on the coattails of the *Book of Kells* (£3, discounted with combo Kells/video ticket, daily Jun–Sept 10:00–17:00 on the hour, in modern arts building next to Trinity Old Library).

Sights—Dublin, South of the River Liffey

▲▲**Dublin Castle**—Built on the spot of the first Viking fortress, this castle was the seat of British rule in Ireland for 700 years (until 1922). Located where the Poddle and Liffey Rivers came together making a black pool ("dubh linn" in Irish), Dublin Castle was the official residence of the viceroy, who implemented the will of the British royalty. Today it's used for fancy state and charity functions. The 45-minute tours offer a room-by-room walk through the lavish state apartments of this most English of Irish palaces (£3, about 4/hrly, Mon–Fri 10:00–17:00, Sat–Sun 14:00–17:00, tel. 01/677-7129). The tour finishes with a look at the foundations of the Norman tower and the best remaining chunk of the 13th-century town wall.

▲**Dublin's Viking Adventure**—This really is an adventure. You start in a box of seats that transforms into a Viking ship. Your chieftain—who hasn't washed since Norway—joins you, and suddenly you're in a storm, waves splash, smoke rolls, and you land in a kind of Viking summer camp, where you spend 30 minutes being shuttled from one friendly original Dubliner to the next (a trader, a sassy maiden, a monk building a church, and so on). A short film about the Vikings follows, with a look at artifacts recently uncovered in the adjacent excavation sight. It feels hokey, but the cast is certainly hardworking, and you leave feeling as though you'd visited if not a Viking town, at least the set for a B-grade Viking movie. It's on Essex Street a block off the riverside Essex Quay in Temple Bar—where the Vikings established their first Dublin settlement in 841 (£4.75, Tue–Sat 10:00–16:30, closed Sun and Mon, tel. 01/679-6040).

Dublinia—This tries and fails to be a "bridge to Dublin's medieval past." The amateurish look at the medieval town starts with a goofy 12-minute Walkman tour followed by a few rooms of medieval exhibits and finishes with a hard-to-follow movie dramatizing medieval political wrangling. Possibly entertaining for a school field trip, it just isn't worth the £4 or the time (daily 10:00–17:00, 11:00–16:00 in winter, tel. 01/679-4611). The ticket does get you a tower-top city view and into Christchurch Cathedral (£1 otherwise).

Christchurch Cathedral—The oldest building in Dublin, the cathedral marks the spot where the Vikings established their town on the river. The first church here was built of wood in 1038 by King Sitric. The present structure dates from a mix of periods: Norman and Gothic but mostly Victorian neo-Gothic (1870s restoration work). Because of its British past, neither of Dublin's top two churches is Catholic. Christchurch Cathedral and the nearby St. Patrick's Cathedral are both from the Church of Ireland. In Catholic Ireland they feel hollow and are more famous than visit-worthy. A choral evensong is sung at 18:00 on Wednesday and Thursday and 17:00 on Saturday.

▲▲▲**National Museum**—Showing off the treasures of Ireland from the Stone Age to the 20th century, this museum is wonderfully digestible under one dome. Ireland's Bronze Age gold fills the center. The prehistoric Ireland exhibit rings the gold, and in a corner you'll find the treasury with the most famous pieces (brooches, chalices, and other examples of Celtic metalwork) and an 18-minute video giving an overview of Irish art through the 13th century. The collection's superstar: the gold, enamel, and amber eighth-century Tara Brooch. Jumping way ahead, a special corridor features "The Road to Independence," with guns, letters, and death masks recalling the fitful birth of the "Terrible Beauty" (1900–1921, with a focus on the Easter Rising of 1916). The best Viking artifacts in town are upstairs (museum is free, Tue–Sat 10:00–17:00, Sun 14:00–17:00, closed Mon, between Trinity College and St. Stephen's Green on Kildare Street, tel. 01/677-7444). Greatest-hits tours are given several times a day (£1, 45 minutes, call for schedule).

Heraldic Museum and Genealogical Office—This small gallery, near the National Museum, displays family coats of arms. It's popular for its resource center among those tracing their Irish roots. For a worthwhile visit, come with some family details (free, behind Trinity College at 2 Kildare St., Mon–Fri 10:00–14:30, tel. 01/603-0200).

National Gallery—Along with a hall featuring the work of top Irish painters, this has Ireland's best collection of paintings by the European masters. It's impressive—unless you've been to London or Paris (free, Mon–Sat 10:00–17:30, Thu until 20:30, Sun 14:00–17:00, tel. 01/661-5133).

▲▲**Grafton Street**—Once filled with noisy traffic, today Grafton Street is Dublin's liveliest pedestrian shopping mall. A five-minute people- and busker-filled stroll takes you from Trinity College up to St. Stephen's Green (and makes you wonder why American merchants are so terrified of a car-free street). Walking by a buxom statue of "sweet" Molly Malone, you'll soon pass two venerable department stores: the Irish Brown Thomas and the English Marks & Spencer. An alley leads to the Powerscourt Townhouse Shopping Centre tastefully filling a converted Georgian mansion. The huge, glass-covered St. Stephen's Green Shopping Center and the peaceful and green green itself mark the top of Grafton Street.

▲**St. Stephen's Green**—This city park, originally a medieval commons, was enclosed in 1664 and gradually surrounded with fine Georgian buildings. Today it provides 22 acres of grassy refuge for Dubliners. On a sunny afternoon, it's a wonderful world apart from the big city.

Number 29—Tour the carefully restored house at Number 29 Lower Fitzwilliam Street for a walk through a Dublin home in 1790 (£2.50, Tue–Sat 10:00–17:00, Sun 14:00–17:00, closed Mon, includes introductory video and eager-to-teach guides scattered throughout). Nearby Merrion Square is decorated with fine doors—a Dublin trademark—and elegant Georgian knobs and knockers.

▲**Temple Bar**—This was a Georgian center of craftsmen and merchants. When it grew poor in the 19th century, lower rents attracted students and artists, giving the neighborhood a bohemian flair. With recent government tax incentives and lots of development money, the Temple Bar district has become a thriving cultural (and beer-drinking) hot spot. Today, this much-promoted center of trendy shops, cafés, theaters, galleries, pubs with live music, and restaurants feels like the heart of Dublin. Dublin's "Left Bank" (actually on the right bank) fills the cobbled streets between Dame Street and the river. The central **Meeting House Square** (just off Essex Street) hosts free street theater, a lively organic produce market (Sat 9:30–15:00), and a book market (Sat 11:00–18:00). The square is surrounded by interesting cultural centers. For a listing of events and galleries, visit the **Temple Bar Information Centre** (Eustace Street, tel. 01/671-5717, www .temple-bar.ie). Rather than follow particular pub or restaurant recommendations (mine are below under "Eating"), venture down a few side lanes off the main drag to see what looks good. The pedestrian-only **Ha' Penny Bridge,** named for the half-pence toll people used to pay to cross it, leads over the Liffey to Temple Bar. ("Bar" means a walkway along the river.)

Sights—Dublin, North of the River Liffey
▲▲**O'Connell Bridge**—The bridge crosses the River Liffey, which has historically divided the town into the wealthy and cultivated south side and the poorer, cruder north side. While there's plenty of culture on the north, even today "the north" is considered rougher and less safe.

From the bridge look upriver. The high point, near Christchurch (marked by the eyesore of the city planning commission building), is where the Vikings established Dublin in the ninth century. Across the river, the green dome marks the Four Courts, today's Supreme Court building—tragically bombed and burned in 1922 during the civil war that followed Irish independence. Between you and the dome is the elegant iron Ha' Penny Bridge, leading into the Temple Bar district. Looking downstream you'll see the tall ugly union headquarters—for now the tallest building in the Republic—and lots of cranes. Booming Dublin is developing downstream. The Irish—forever clever tax fiddlers—have subsidized and revitalized this formerly dreary quarter with great success. A short walk downstream along the north bank leads to a powerful series of modern statues memorializing the great famine of 1845.
▲**O'Connell Street**—Dublin's grandest street leads from O'Connell Bridge through the heart of north Dublin. Since the 1740s it's been a 45-meter-wide promenade. Ever since the first O'Connell Bridge connected it to the Trinity side of town in 1794, it's been Dublin's main drag. The street, while lined with fast-food and souvenir shops, echoes with history. Much of the fighting during the 1916 Easter Rising and the civil war a few years later took place here. The imposing **General Post Office** is where Patrick Pearse

read the Proclamation of Irish Independence. The GPO building itself—a kind of Irish Alamo—was the rebel headquarters and scene of a five-day bloody siege during the Rising. While there's little to see, its facade remains pockmarked with bullet holes (open for business and sightseers Mon–Sat 8:00–20:00, Sun 10:00–18:30).

Statues lining O'Connell Street celebrate great figures in Ireland's fight for independence. Daniel O'Connell (1775–1847), known as "the Liberator," founded the Irish Labor Party and was a strong voice for Irish Catholic rights in the British parliament. James Larkin founded the Irish Workers' Union. One monument that didn't wave an Irish flag—a tall column crowned by a statue of the British hero of Trafalgar, Admiral Nelson—was blown up in 1966 as locals celebrated the 50th anniversary of the Rising.

Make a point to get away from tourists' Dublin. Stroll the smaller streets north of the Liffey. Just a block west of O'Connell Street, the **Moore Street Market** is a colorful commotion of produce and hawkers. For workaday Dublin, the long pedestrian mall of Mary Street, Henry Street, and Talbot Street is a people-watchers' delight.

The prestigious **Abbey Theatre,** now a modern, ugly building, is still the much-loved home of the Irish National Theater (a block off the river on Abbey Street). **St. Mary's Pro-Cathedral** is the leading Catholic church in town but curiously is not a cathedral since Christchurch was made one in the 12th century (the Vatican has chosen to ignore the fact that it hasn't been Catholic for centuries). The **Georgian Parnell Square** has a Garden of Remembrance honoring the victims of the 1916 Rising.

The **Dublin Writers' Museum** fills a splendidly restored Georgian mansion. No country so small produced such a wealth of literature. As interesting to those interested in Irish literature as it is boring to those who aren't, this museum features the lives and works of Dublin's great writers (£3, includes slow-moving audio tour, daily 10:00–18:00, Sun and off-season till 17:00, 18 Parnell Square North, tel. 01/872-2077). With hometown wits such as Swift, Yeats, Joyce, and Shaw, literary fans will have a checklist of residences and memorials to see.

Sights—Dublin's Smithfield Village

Until recently a rundown industrial area, huge investments promise to make Smithfield Village the next Temple Bar. It's worth a look for "Cobblestores" (a redeveloped Duck Lane lined with fancy crafts and gift shops), the Ceol music museum, and the Old Jameson whiskey tour, with its chimney observatory and great Dublin views. Smithfield is two blocks north of the river behind the Four Courts (www.smithfieldvillage.com).

▲▲**Ceol Interactive Irish Music Encounter**—Throughout Ireland, musicians—lost in the traditional beat—are closing their eyes to commune with their heritage. A visit here before heading into the countryside will make your small-town pub-going more fun. Anyone interested in "trad" music will enjoy a stop at this clever introduction to Irish music. In this place filled with headphones, touch-computer screens, and music-filled TV screens, you'll go as deep as you like into the history, instruments, and regional differences of Irish music. The finale: a great 17-minute scenic and musical video tour of Ireland (£4, Mon–Sat 9:30–18:00, Sun 10:30–18:00, Smithfield Village, tel. 01/817-3820, www.ceol.ie). **The Old Jameson Distillery**—Whiskey fans enjoy visiting the old distillery. You get a 10-minute video, 20-minute tour, and a free shot in the pub. Unfortunately, the "distillery" feels fake and put together for tourism. The Old Bushmills tour in Northern Ireland, in a working factory, is a better experience. If you do take this tour, volunteer energetically when offered the chance to take the whiskey taste test at the end (£4, daily 9:30–17:30, Sow Street, Smithfield, tel. 01/807-2355).

The Jameson Chimney, built in 1895 for the distillery, is now an observatory. Ride the elevator 175 feet up for an unrivaled Dublin panorama.

Sights—Outer Dublin

The Jail and the Guinness Brewery are the main sights outside of the old center. Combine these in one visit.

▲▲▲**Kilmainham Gaol (Jail)**—Opened in 1796 as the Dublin County Jail and a debtors' prison and considered a model in its day, it was used frequently as a political prison by the British. Many of those who fought for Irish independence were held or executed here, including leaders of the rebellions of 1798, 1803, 1848, 1867, and 1916. National heroes Robert Emmett and Charles Stewart Parnell each did time here. The last prisoner to be held here was Eamon de Valera (later president of Ireland). He was released on July 16, 1924, the day Kilmainham was finally shut down. The buildings, virtually in ruins, were restored in the 1960s. Today it's a shrine to the Nathan Hales of Ireland.

Start your visit with a guided tour (60 min, including 30 min in the prison chapel for a rebellion-packed video). It's touching to tour the cells and places of execution while hearing tales of terrible colonialism and heroic patriotism—alongside Irish schoolkids who know these names well. Then browse through the excellent exhibit on Victorian prison life and Ireland's fight for independence. Don't miss the dimly lit hall off the second floor displaying the stirring last letters patriots sent to loved ones hours before facing the firing squad (£3, daily 9:30–18:00, 2 tours/hrly, last tour at 16:45; off-season Sun–Fri 10:00–17:00, closed Sat; £4 taxi, bus #51, 78a, or #79 from Aston Quay, tel. 01/453-5984).

▲**Guinness Brewery**—A visit to the Guinness Hop Store is, for

Charles Stewart Parnell (1846–1891)

Parnell, who led the Irish movement for home rule, did time in Kilmainham Jail. A Cambridge-educated Protestant and member of Parliament, he had a vision of a modern and free Irish Republic filled mostly with Catholics but not set up as a religious state. Momentum seemed to be on his side. With the British Prime Minister of the time, Gladstone, in favor of a similar form of home rule, it looked like all Ireland was ripe for independence. Then a sex scandal broke around Parnell and his mistress. The press, egged on by the powerful Catholic bishops (who didn't want a free but secular Irish state), battered and battered away at the scandal until finally Parnell was driven from office. Sadly, after that, Ireland became mired in the troubles of the 20th century: an awkward independence featuring a divided island, a bloody civil war, and sectarian violence ever since. It's said Parnell died of a broken heart. Before he did, perhaps the greatest Irish statesman requested to be buried outside of Ireland.

many, a pilgrimage. The home of Ireland's national beer welcomes visitors (for £5) with a museum, video, and drink. Arthur Guinness began brewing the famous stout here in 1759. By 1868 it was the biggest brewery in the world. Today the sprawling brewery fills several city blocks. Around the world Guinness brews more than 10 million glasses a day. You can learn as much or as little about the brewing process as you like. Highlights are the cooperage (with old film clips showing the master wood-keg makers plying their now-extinct trade) and a display of the brewery's clever ads. The video is a well-done ad for the brew that makes you feel almost patriotic as you run down to the sample bar to turn in your coupons for a pint of the real thing (£5, Mon–Sat 9:30–17:00, Sun 10:30–16:30, enter on Crane Street off Thomas Street, bus #78A from Aston Quay near O'Connell Bridge, or bus 123 from Dame Street and O'Connell Street, tel. 01/408-4800). Hop-on hop-off bus tours stop here. (Why is there no museum of Irish alcoholism, which is a serious but rarely discussed problem in this land where the social world seems to float in a sea of beer?)

▲**Gaelic Athletic Association Museum**—The GAA was founded in 1884 as an expression of an Irish cultural awakening. While created to foster the development of Gaelic sports—specifically Irish football and hurling (and ban English sports such as cricket and rugby)—it played an important part in the fight for independence.

This new museum, at the newly expanded 97,000-seat Croke Park Stadium, offers a high-tech, interactive introduction to Ireland's favorite games. Relive the greatest moments in hurling and Irish football history. Then get involved. Pick up a stick and try hurling, kick a football, and test your speed and balance. A 15-minute film clarifies the connection between sports and Irish politics (£3, May–Sept daily 9:30–17:00; Oct–Apr Tue–Sat 10:00–17:00, Sun 10:00–17:00, closed Mon; game Sundays open 12:00–17:00 to new stand ticket holders only; under the new stand at Croke Park, bus 3, 11, 11a, 16, 16a, or 123; tel. 01/855-8176).

Hurling or Irish Football at Croke Park—Actually seeing a match here, surrounded by incredibly spirited Irish fans, is a fun experience. Hurling is like airborne hockey with no injury time-outs, and Irish football is a rugged form of soccer (matches most Sunday afternoons outside of winter, tickets—£10–20—are available at the stadium except during championships).

Greyhound Racing—For an interesting lowbrow look at local life, consider going to the dog races and doing a little gambling (£3, children free, Herold's Cross, races generally Mon, Tue and Fri at 20:00, tel. 01/497-1081).

Day trips from Dublin—See "Near Dublin," at the end of the chapter, for information on Newgrange, the Wicklow Mountains, and more.

Entertainment and Theater in Dublin

Ireland produced some of the finest writers in both English and Gaelic, and Dublin houses some of Europe's finest theaters. While Handel's *Messiah* was first performed in Dublin (1742), these days Dublin is famous for its rock bands (U2, Thin Lizzie, and Sinead O'Connor all got started here).

You have much to choose from: **Abbey Theatre** is Ireland's national theater. **Gate Theatre** does foreign plays as well as Irish classics. **Point Theatre,** once a railway terminus, is now the country's top live music venue. At the **National Concert Hall,** the National Symphony Orchestra performs most Friday evenings. Street theater takes the stage in Temple Bar on summer evenings. Folk music rings in the pubs, and street entertainers are everywhere. For the latest on live theater, music, cultural happenings, restaurant reviews, pubs, and current museum hours, pick up the free *Dublin Event Guide* or a copy of the twice-monthly *In Dublin* (£2, any newsstand).

Irish Music in nearby Dun Laoghaire

For an evening of pure Irish music, song, and dance, check out the **Comhaltas Ceoltoiri Eireann,** an association working to preserve this traditional slice of Irish culture. It got started when Elvis and company threatened to steal the musical heart of the new generation. Judging by the pop status of traditional Irish music these days, Comhaltas accomplished its mission. Their "Fonntrai" evening is a costumed stage show mixing traditional music, song, and dance (£5, mid-Jun–Aug Mon–Thu at 21:00, followed by informal music session at 22:30). Fridays all year long they have a ceilidh where everyone dances (£5, 21:30–00:30). Saturday nights feature an informal session by the fireside. Performances are held in the Cuturlann na Eireann, near the Seapoint DART stop or a 20-minute walk from Dun Laoghaire, at 32 Belgrave Square, Monkstown (tel. 01/280-0295). Their bar is free and often filled with music.

Sleeping in Dublin
(£1 = about $1.50, tel. code: 01)
Sleep Code: **S** = Single, **D** = Double/Twin, **T** = Triple, **Q** = Quad, **b** = bathroom, **t** = toilet only, **s** = shower only, **CC** = Credit Card (Visa, MasterCard, Amex). Breakfast is included unless otherwise noted.

Dublin is popular and rooms can be tight. Get a reservation for weekends—especially in summer. Big and practical places (both cheap and moderate) are most central at Christchurch on the edge of Temple Bar. For classy, older Dublin accommodations you'll pay more and stay a bit farther out (east of St. Stephen's Green). For a small-town escape with the best budget values, side-trip by the convenient DART train (at least 3/hrly, 15 min) from nearby Dun Laoghaire (see below).

Sleeping in Christchurch
These places face Christchurch Cathedral, a great locale a five-minute walk from the best evening scene at Temple Bar and 10 minutes from the sightseeing center (Trinity College).

Harding Hotel is a hardwood, 20th-century, Viking-style place with 53 hotelesque rooms. The rooms are simpler than Jurys', but it's more intimate, without the tour-group mob scenes (Sb-£45, Db/Tb-£65, breakfast extra, CC:VM, elevator with an obnoxious gift of gab, Copper Alley across the street from Christchurch, tel. 01/679-6500, fax 01/679-6504, www.iol.ie /usitaccm/, e-mail: harding@usit.ie).

Jurys Christchurch Inn (like its sisters across town, in Galway and in Belfast) is well located and offers business-class comfort in all of its identical rooms. This no-nonsense, modern, American-style hotel chain has a winning keep-it-simple-and-affordable formula. If old is getting old (and you don't mind big bus-tour groups), you won't find a better value in town. All 180 rooms cost the same: £65 for one, two, or three adults or two adults and two kids, breakfast not included. Each room has a modern bathroom, direct-dial telephone, and TV. Two floors are strictly nonsmoking. Request a room far from the noisy elevator

(CC:VMA, Christchurch Place, Dublin 8, tel. 01/454-0000, fax 01/454-0012, U.S. tel. 800/843-3311, e-mail: inquiry@jurys.com). A 234-room **Jurys Custom House Inn**, on Custom House Quay, offers the same value. Bigger and not quite as well located (in a boring neighborhood, a 10-minute riverside hike from O'Connell Bridge), this Jurys is more likely to have rooms available (£62, tel. 01/607-5000, fax 01/829-0400).

Kinlay House, across the square from Jurys Christchurch Inn, is its backpackers' equivalent—definitely the place to go for cheap beds with a good location, privacy, and an all-ages-welcome atmosphere. This huge, red-brick, 19th-century Victorian building has 120 metal, prison-style beds in spartan, smoke-free rooms: singles, doubles, four- to six-bed dorms (generally coed), and a few giant dorms. It fills up most days. Call well in advance, especially for summer weekends (S-£20, D-£30, Db-£34, dorm beds-£11–13, includes continental breakfast, self-catering kitchen, launderette, internet access, left luggage, and so on, Christchurch, 2–12 Lord Edward Street, Dublin 2, tel. 01/679-6644, fax 01/679-7437, e-mail: kindub@usit.ie). **Avalon House** is 300 beds of backpacker heaven. Well located, cheap, and institutional, it's much like Kinlay House (D-£30, Db-£32, dorm beds-£8.50–13.50, CC:VMA, including continental breakfast, a few minutes off Grafton Street at 55 Aungier Street, tel. 01/475-0001, fax 01/475-0303, www.avalon-house.ie).

Sleeping East of St. Stephen's Green

Two small luxurious hotels are a five-minute walk east of St. Stephen's Green on fashionable Baggot Street. Both are newly renovated, include a fine cooked breakfast, are run with class, and offer the best value for Georgian elegance with modern comforts near the center. **The Fitzwilliam** rents 13 delightful rooms (Sb-£45, Db-£80, CC:VMA, 10 percent discount with cash, children are cheap or free, 41 Upper Fitzwilliam Street, Dublin 2, tel. 01/662-5155, fax 01/676-7488). **Baggot Court Accommodations** rents 11 similarly elegant rooms a block farther away (Sb-£35–40, Db-£80, Tb-£120, CC:VMA, nonsmoking, free car park, 92 Lower Baggot St, Dublin 2, tel. 01/661-2819, fax 01/661-0253).

Mespil Hotel is a huge, modern, business-class hotel renting 153 identical three-star rooms at a good price with all the comforts. Half the rooms overlook a canal greenbelt (Sb, Db, or Tb-£85, continental breakfast £6, Irish breakfast £9, elevator, 1 nonsmoking floor, CC:VMA, Mespil Road, Dublin 4, tel. 01/667-1222, fax 01/667-1244, e-mail: mespil@leehotels.ie).

Albany House's 33 rooms come with Georgian elegance, modern comfort, and street noise. Request the huge "superior" rooms, which are the same price (Sb-£70, Db-£100, £80 in slow times, back rooms are quieter, smoke free, CC:VMA, 1 block south of St. Stephen's Green at 84 Harcourt Street, Dublin 2, tel. 01/475-1092, fax 01/475-1093, e-mail: albany@indigo.ie).

The next two listings are on Northumberland Road. While Trinity College is only a 15-minute walk away, buses 5, 6, 7, 8, and 45 (to O'Connell Street) lumber down Northumberland Road to the city center every 10 minutes.

Northumberland Lodge is a quiet, elegant mansion (Sb-£45–55, Db-£70–90, highest on weekends and in summer, CC:VM, 68 Northumberland Road, Ballsbridge, Dublin 4, tel. 01/660-5270, fax 01/668-8679). **Glenveagh Town House** has 13 classy rooms—Victorian upstairs, modern downstairs (a new management expects to charge about Sb-£42, Db-£75, less in slow times, CC:VMA, 31 Northumberland Road, tel. 01/668-4612, fax 01/668-4559, e-mail: glenveagh@tinet.ie).

Sleeping near the Station

The **Townhouse of Dublin** is a smartly run hotel with 80 comfortable rooms filling the richly decorated, carpeted, and furnished home of a famous 19th-century playwright. It's located in a handy but grotty area midway between the train station and O'Connell Bridge (Sb-£38–47, D-£50–60, Db-£60–80, T-£65–70, depending on season and day of the week, weekends are most expensive, CC:VMA, nonsmoking rooms, 47 Lower Gardiner Street, Dublin 1, tel. 01/878-8808, fax 01/878-8787, e-mail: grotter@indigo.ie).

Globetrotters, adjacent to and run by the Townhouse (described above), is a fine slumber mill with 94 beds in 6- to 12-bed dorms (£12–15 per bed, all with private bathrooms and lockers, often special deals for three-night stays in either place).

Sleeping and Eating in nearby Dun Laoghaire
(tel. code: 01, mail: County Dublin)

Dun Laoghaire (pron: dun leary) is eight miles south of Dublin. This beach resort, with the ferry terminal for Wales and easy connections to downtown Dublin by DART commuter train, is a great small-town base for the big city.

Dun Laoghaire harbor was strategic enough to merit a line of Martello Towers (built to defend against an expected Napoleonic invasion). By the mid-19th century the huge breakwaters—reaching like two muscular arms into the Irish Sea—were completed, protecting a huge harbor. Ships sailed regularly to Wales (60 miles away), and the first train line in Ireland connected the terminal with Dublin. While still a busy transportation hub, today the nearly mile-long breakwaters are also popular with strollers, bikers, birders, and fishermen. Hike out to the lighthouse at the end of the more interesting East Pier.

While buses go into Dublin, the DART is much faster (6/hrly in peak times, at least 3/hrly otherwise, 15 min, Eurail valid, £1.10;

Dun Laoghaire

for a longer stay consider the 4-day Explorer ticket covering DART and Dublin buses). The **Dun Laoghaire TI** is in the ferry terminal (daily 10:00–21:00, off-season 9:00–17:00). The Society of the Preservation of Irish Folk Music has a lively branch in Dun Laoghaire (see above). Taxi fare from Dun Laoghaire to central Dublin is £8, to the airport £17. With easy free parking and DART access into Dublin, this area is ideal for those with cars. There's a cinema and a Laundromat (full- or self-serve) in the Sandycove "Village."

The first four listings are within several blocks of the Sandycove DART station and a seven-minute walk to the Dun Laoghaire DART station/ferry landing. The rest are closer to the Dun Laoghaire DART station. Except for the first place, all are a bit tattered around the edges.

Mrs. Kane's B&B is a modern house with three big, cheery rooms and a welcoming guests' lounge. While a few blocks farther out than the others, it's worth the walk for its great, bright, and friendly feeling (Db-£45, strictly smoke free, just above Rosmeen Gardens at 2 Granite Hall, tel. & fax 01/280-9105).

Windsor Lodge rents four fresh and cheery rooms on a quiet street a block off the harbor and a block from the DART station

(Db-£44, family deals, CC:VM, nonsmoking, 3 Islington Avenue, Sandycove, Dun Laoghaire, tel & fax 01/284-6952, e-mail: winlodge @tinet.ie, Mary O'Farrell).

Mrs. Callahan's B&B is a grandmotherly old house with decent rooms and a prizewinning garden half a block from the DART station (D-£40, Db-£45, 1 Rosemeen Gardens, tel. 01/280-6083).

Sandycove House, a creaky sprawling old place overlooking the harbor and run in a no-nonsense kind of way, rents 12 large rooms (Sb-£30, Db-£45–47, Db overlooking the sea-£50, CC:VM, 7-minute walk from the ferry landing and 2 blocks from the Sandycove DART station, Newtownsmith, Sandycove, tel. & fax 01/284-1600).

Innisfree B&B has a fine lounge and six big, bright, and comfy rooms (D-£32, Db-£37, CC:VM, from George Street follow the "Yellow Fever Vaccination Centre" sign up the ugly but quiet Northumberland Avenue to #31, tel. 01/280-5598, Brendan and Mary Smith).

Lynden B&B, with a classy 150-year-old interior hiding behind a somber front, rents four big rooms (one S-£17, D-£34, Db-£40, past Mulgrave Street to 2 Mulgrave Terrace, tel. 01/280-6404). Next door, the similar **Belmont B&B** rents three rooms (D-£34, Db-£39, tel. 01/280-1422).

Ferry House B&B, a once-upon-a-time-stately old place facing a quiet square with a tennis court rents nine borderline musty rooms. Pauline, Eamond, and family give the place a homey feel (Db-£46 with this book, CC:VM, 15 Clarinda Park North, tel. 01/280-8301, fax 01/284-6530).

The **Old School House Hostel** is a shoestring traveler's dream come true. It's two blocks from the Dun Laoghaire DART station and ferry landing with incredibly cheap beds in two- to eight-bed rooms and a hardworking, creative staff. It's a well-worn hostel: old carpets, bare walls, and a general scruffiness. Having said that, it's clean, with good beds and plenty of privacy, and feels secure and safe (£9 bunks in 6-bed dorms, £10 in a quad, £24 twins, less off-season, showers down the hall or in your room for 50p extra, breakfast not included, nonsmoking rooms, self-catering kitchen, restaurant, £3 laundry facilities, Internet access, 24-hour staff, CC:VMA; from ferry, go up Marine Road, take first right onto Eblana Avenue, tel. 01/280-8777, fax 01/284-2266, e-mail: info@hostel.ie).

Eating in Dun Laoghaire: Local diners enjoy the local "Gourmet Mile"—several fine little restaurants within an easy walk of these B&Bs.

Down the street from the Sandycove DART station is Glasthule (called simply "The Village" locally). **Bistro Vino** is the rage lately, with cozy candlelit Mediterranean ambiance and great food (£10 meals, seafood, pasta, arrive early or have a reservation, nightly early-bird special 17:00–19:00, tel. 01/280-6097). Across the street the big red **Eagle House** pub serves hearty inexpensive pub grub. The nearby **Daniel's Restaurant and Wine Bar** is also good (£15 meals, 34 Glasthule Road, tel. 01/284-1027).

The **Brasserie Na Mara** serves good contemporary Irish cuisine in a fancy former train station setting (tel. 01/280-6767). A good bet for families is the kid-friendly **De Selby's Restaurant**, serving traditional Irish food, stew, and seafood (£10 meals, nightly 17:00–23:00, a block off George Street at 17 Patrick Street, tel. 01/284-1761). **George Street,** Dun Laoghaire's main drag and three blocks inland, has plenty of eateries and pubs, many with live music.

Eating in Dublin

As Dublin does its boom-time jig, fine and creative eateries are popping up all over town. While you can get decent pub grub for £6 on just about any corner, consider holding off on pub grub for the more spit-and-potatoes countryside. And there's no pressing reason to eat Irish in cosmopolitan Dublin. Dublin's good restaurants are packed from 20:00 on, especially on weekends. Eating early (18:00–19:00) saves time and usually money (as many better places offer an early-bird special).

Eating Quick and Easy around Grafton Street

Cornucopia is a small, earth-momma, vegetarian self-serve place a block off Grafton. It's friendly, smoke free, and youthful, with great breakfasts, hearty £5 lunches, and dinner specials (Mon–Sat 9:00–20:00, closed Sun, 19 Wicklow St, tel. 01/677-7583).

Graham O'Sullivan Restaurant and Coffee Shop is a cheap and cheery cafeteria serving soup, sandwiches, and a salad bar in unpretentious ambience (Mon–Fri 8:00–19:00, Sat 9:00–17:00, closed Sun, 12 Duke St.). Two pubs on the same street (**The Duke and Davy Burns**) serve pub lunches. The **Cathach Rare Books** shop (10 Duke St.) displays a rare first edition of *Ulysses* signed by James Joyce, among other treasures in its window.

Bewleys Restaurant is an old-time local favorite serving traditional Irish and contemporary food in a fresh and bright space decorated by local art students. Light meals start at £3.50, full meals from £6.50 (daily 7:30–23:00, table service on ground floor, cafeteria upstairs, 78 Grafton Street, tel. 01/635-5470).

Blazing Salads, a crowd-pleasing vegetarian place, is just off Grafton Street, upstairs in the trendy Powerscourt Townhouse Centre (£5 meals, Mon–Sat 9:00–18:00, closed Sun, tel. 01/671-9552).

Wagamama Noodle Bar, like its popular sisters in London, is a pan-Asian slurp-athon with great, healthy noodle and rice dishes served by walkie-talkie-toting waiters on long communal tables (daily 12:00–23:00, nonsmoking, South King Street, tel. 01/478-2152).

Yamamori is a plain, bright, and mod Japanese place serving seas of sushi and noodles (£5 lunch deal served daily 12:30–17:30, £5–10 dinner 17:30–23:00, 71 South Great Georges Street, tel. 01/475-5001).

Marks & Spencer department store (on Grafton Street) has a fancy grocery store in the basement with fine take-away sandwiches and salads.

Eating Fast and Cheap near Christchurch
Many of Dublin's **late-night grocery stores** (along Dame Street at top of Temple Bar near Christchurch hotels and elsewhere) sell fine cheap salads, microwaved meat pies, and made-to-order sandwiches. A £3 picnic dinner back at the hotel might be a good option after a grueling day of sightseeing.

Leo Burdocks Fish & Chips is popular with locals (takeout only, Mon–Fri 11:00–23:00, Sat 14:00–23:00, 2 Werburgh Street, off Christchurch).

Dining at Classy Restaurants and Cafés
QV2 Restaurant serves "international with an Irish twist"—great cooking at reasonable prices with an elegant yet comfy atmosphere (£20 meals, Mon–Sat 12:00–15:00, 18:00–24:00, closed Sun, nonsmoking section, 14 St. Andrew Street, tel. 01/677-3363, run by John Count McCormack). They offer a quick £7.50 lunch special and an 18:00–19:30 early-bird special for people on the way to a theater.

Trocadero serves beefy European cuisine to locals interested in a slow romantic meal. The dressy red-velvet interior is draped with photos of local actors. Come early or make a reservation (£20 meals, nightly 18:00–24:00, nonsmoking section, 3 St. Andrew's St., tel. 01/677-5545). The three-course early-bird special at £11.50 is a fine value (18:00–19:30, leave by 20:45).

Boulevard Cafe is a mod, local, and likeably trendy place serving Mediterranean cuisine heavy on the Italian. They serve salads, pasta, and sandwiches for around £4, two-course business lunch specials (12:00–15:00, Mon–Sat), and dinner plates for £7 to £10 (nightly 18:00–24:00, 27 Exchequer Street, tel. 01/679-2131).

Eating at Temple Bar
Gallagher's Boxty House is touristy and traditional, with good, basic value in a fun old Dublin ambience (£7 meals, stews, corned beef, and boxties—the traditional Irish potato pancake filled and rolled with various meats, veggies, and sauces; daily 12:00–23:30, nonsmoking section, 20 Temple Bar, tel. 01/677-2762). Gallagher's is extremely popular. After 17:00 you'll likely get an appointment and time to wander Temple Bar.

Bad Ass Cafe is a grunge diner serving cowboy/Mex/veggie/ pizzas to old and new hippies. No need to dress up (£5 lunch and £11 dinner deals, open nearly all the time, kids specials, Crown Alley, tel. 01/671-2596).

The **Brazen Head,** famous as Dublin's oldest pub, is a hit for dinner early and live music late. A sprawling complex of smoky atmospheric rooms with a courtyard made to order for balmy evenings, it overlooks the River Liffey (on Bridge Street, a 10-minute walk upstream from Temple Bar).

Transportation Connections—Dublin

By bus to: Belfast (7/day, 3 hrs), **Ennis** (7/day, 4.5 hrs), **Galway** (10/day, 3.5 hrs), **Limerick** (10/day, 3 hrs), **Tralee** (5/day, 6 hrs), **Dingle** (4/day, 8 hrs, £16). Bus info: tel. 01/836-6111.

By train to: Rosslare (3/day, 3 hrs), **Tralee** (6/day, 4 hrs), **Galway** (4/day, 3 hrs, talking timetable tel. 01/805-4222), **Ennis** (4/day, 4 hrs), **Portrush** (5/day, 5 hrs, £20 one way, £28 round-trip; stops in Belfast on the way south), **Belfast** (8/day, 2.25 hrs, talking timetable tel. 01/855-4477). The new **Dublin–Belfast train** connects the two Irish capitals in just over two hours at 90 mph on one continuous welded rail (£17 one way, £26 round-trip; round-trip the same day only £17 except Fri and Sun; from the border to Belfast one way £9, £12 round-trip). Train info: tel. 01/836-6222.

The **Dublin Airport** is well connected to the city center, seven miles away (see "Arrival in Dublin"). British Air flies to London's Gatwick Airport (4/day, from £69 return, tel. 01/814-5201 or toll-free tel. 800/626-747 in Ireland, U.S. tel. 800/247-9297), as do Aer Lingus (tel. 01/886-8888) and British Midland (tel. 01/283-8833 in Ireland, U.S. tel. 800/788-0555). Dublin Airport info: tel. 01/814-4222. Ryanair is a new Irish cut-rate airline with unbelievable fares to European destinations (£70 flights to Frankfurt, tel. 01/609-7800, www.ryanair.ie).

Transportation Connections— Ireland and Britain

Dublin and London: The boat/rail journey takes eight hours (4/day, £40–75). Dublin train info: tel. 01/836-6222. If going directly to London, flying is your best bet.

Dublin and Holyhead: Irish Ferries sails between Dublin and Holyhead in North Wales (dock a mile from O'Connell Bridge, 2/day, 3 hrs, £25 one-way walk-on fare, Dublin tel. 01/661-0511, Holyhead tel. 0990-329-129).

Dun Laoghaire and Holyhead: Stena Line sails between Dun Laoghaire (near Dublin) and Holyhead in North Wales (4/day, 2 hrs on new HSS *Catamaran,* £36 one-way walk-on fare, reserve by phone—they book up long in advance on summer weekends, Dublin tel. 01/204-7777, recorded info tel. 01/204-7799).

Ferry Connections—Ireland and France

Irish Ferries connect Ireland (Rosslare) with France (Cherbourg and Roscoff) every other day (less Jan–Mar). While Cherbourg has the quickest connection to Paris, your overall time between Ireland and Paris is about the same regardless of which port is used on the day you sail. One-way fares vary from £40 to £80 (round-trips are much cheaper). Except for a £5 port tax, Eurailers go half price. In both directions departures are generally between 16:00 and 18:00 and arrive late the next morning. While passengers can nearly always get on, reservations are wise in summer and easy by phone. If you anticipate a crowded departure you can reserve a seat for £5. Beds in a quad start at £15. Doubles (or singles) start at £34. The easiest way to get a bed (except during summer) is from the information desk upon boarding. The cafeteria serves bad food at reasonable prices. Upon arrival in France, buses and taxis connect you to your Paris-bound train (Irish Ferries: Dublin tel. 01/661-0511, recorded info tel. 01/661-0715, Paris tel. 01 44 94 20 40, www .irishferries.ie, e-mail: info@irishferries.ie, European Ferry Guide www.youra.com/ferry/intlferries.html).

NEAR DUBLIN: NEWGRANGE, WICKLOW MOUNTAINS, KILKENNY, AND CASHEL

Newgrange, an hour's drive north of Dublin, is one of the world's most important, and one of Ireland's most talked-about, new tourist attractions. The Wicklow Mountains, while only 10 miles south of Dublin, feel remote—remote enough to have provided a handy refuge for opponents to English rule. Rebels who took part in the 1798 Irish uprising hid out here for years. When the frustrated British built a military road in 1800 to help flush out the rebels, the area became more accessible. Now known as the R115, this same road takes you through the Wicklow area to Glendalough at its south end. While the darling of the Dublin day-trip tour organizers, the valley itself doesn't live up to its hype. But two blockbuster sights make a visit worth considering.

If you're driving west to the west coast (Dingle), the best two stops to break the long journey are Kilkenny, often called Ireland's finest medieval town, and the Rock of Cashel, a thought-provoking early Christian site crowning the Tipperary Plain.

NEWGRANGE

The famous archaeological site commonly referred to as Newgrange (one of the tombs) is more properly known as Bru na Boinne—"dwelling place of the Boyne." The well-organized site is centered around a state-of-the-art museum. Visitors are given appointments for shuttle buses that ferry small groups five minutes away to one of two 5,000-year-old passage tombs, where a guide gives them a 30-minute tour. Newgrange is more famous and allows you inside. Knowth was opened more recently and is more extensive, but you can't go inside the tomb. Each is different enough, but for many, seeing one site is adequate.

Newgrange is one single mound, the most restored of the Bru na Boinne sites and the only one you actually enter. Dating from 3200 B.C., it's 500 years older than the pyramids of Giza. While we know nothing of these people, this most certainly was a sacred spot dealing with some kind of sun god ritual. During your tour you'll squeeze down a narrow passageway to a cross-shaped central chamber under a 20-foot-high igloo-type stone dome. Bones and ashes were placed here under 200,000 tons of stone and dirt to wait for a special moment. As the sun rose on the shortest day of the year (winter solstice, December 21), a ray of sunlight would creep slowly down the 60-foot-long passageway. For 17 minutes it would light the center of the sacred chamber. Perhaps this was the moment when the souls of the dead would be transported to the afterlife via that mysterious ray of life-giving and life-taking light.

Knowth is a necropolis of several grassy mounds around one 85-yard-wide grand tomb. The big mound, covering 1.5 acres, has two passages (neither open to public). They are aligned so that on the spring and fall equinox, rays from the rising and setting sun shine down the passageways to the center chamber. The Knowth site thrived from 3000 to 2000 B.C., was the domain of fairies and myths for the next 2000 years, and became an Iron Age fortress in the early centuries after Christ. Around 1000 it was an all-Ireland political center, and later a Norman fortress was built atop the mound. You'll see plenty of mysteriously carved stones, new-feeling grassy mounds, and a huge crane as the excavations continue.

Allow an hour for the excellent museum and an hour for each of the tombs you visit (£3, or £5 if you see both sights, May–Sept 9:00–18:30 or 19:00, hours a little shorter off-season, Newgrange is open year-round, Knowth only May–Oct, tel. 041/24488). The last shuttle bus leaves 1.75 hours before closing. Visits are limited, and on busy summer days, those arriving in the afternoon may not get a spot (no reservations possible). In peak season, try to arrive by 9:30 for no wait. Generally, upon arrival you'll get a bus departure time for one or both of the passage tomb sites. Spend your wait in the museum, watching the video, and munching lunch in the cheery cafeteria. Don't try to drive to the actual passage tombs. From Dublin drive north on N1 to Drogheda, where signs direct you to the Bru na Boinne Visitors Centre.

WICKLOW MOUNTAINS

By car or tour, it's easy. If you lack wheels, take a tour. It's not worth the trouble on public transport.

By Car: It's a joy. Consider a scenic detour through the Wicklow area as you drive between Dublin and the west coast.

Speed demons take the freeway south to Enniskerry, your gateway to the Wicklow Mountains. Signs direct you to the gardens and on to Glendalough. From Glendalough you can leave the valley (and pick up the highway to the west) over the famous but dull mountain pass called the Wicklow Gap.

By Tour: Wild Wicklow Tours covers the region with an entertaining guide packing every minute with information and fun craic. With a gang of 26 packed into tight but comfortable mountain-gripping buses, the guide kicks into gear from the first pickup in Dublin. Tours cover Dublin's embassy row, Dun Laoghaire, the Bay of Dublin with the mansions of Ireland's rich and famous, the windy Military Road over scenic Sally Gap, and the Glendalough monasteries (£22, Mar–Nov Wed–Sun; Sat and Sun all year, 9:10 pickup at Dublin TI, 10:00 pickup at Dun Laoghaire TI, stop for lunch at a pub—not included, home by 17:30, Dun Laoghaire-ites can use the bus to get into Dublin for the evening, tel. 01/280-1899, www.arantours.ie-wildwicklow).

Several other tour companies run day trips through the Wicklow Mountains from Dublin (Dublin Bus is cheapest). Mary Gibbon's Tours visit both the monastery and the gardens in a four-hour trip (£17, be careful—they spend an hour picking up tourists at Dublin hotels before leaving, tel. 01/283-9973).

Sights—Wicklow Mountains
▲▲**Gardens of Powerscourt**—While the mansion's interior—restored after a 1974 fire—isn't much, its meticulously kept aristocratic gardens are Ireland's best. Commissioned in the 1730s by Richard Wingfield, first viscount of Powerscourt, the gardens are called "the grand finale of Europe's formal gardening tradition... probably the last garden of its size and quality ever to be created." I'll buy that.

Upon entry you'll get a flyer laying out 40-minute and 60-minute walks. The "hour walk" takes 30 minutes at a slow amble. With the impressive summit of the Great Sugar Loaf Mountain as a backdrop and a fine Japanese garden, Italian garden, and a goofy pet cemetery along the way, this garden provides the scenic greenery I hoped to find in the rest of the Wicklow area. The lush movie *Barry Lyndon* was filmed in this well-watered aristocratic fantasy.

Powerscourt Gardens, a mile above the village of Enniskerry, cover several thousand acres within the 16,000-acre estate. The dreamy driveway alone is a mile long (£3.50, daily 9:30–17:30, great cafeteria, tel. 01/204-6000). Skip the associated waterfall (£2, three miles away).

▲▲**Military Road over Sally Gap**—This is only for those with a car. From Powerscourt Gardens and Enniskerry go to Glencree, where you ride the tiny military road over Sally Gap and through the best scenery of the Wicklow Mountains. Look for the German

military cemetery—built for U-boat sailors who washed ashore in
World War II. Near Sally Gap notice the peat bogs and the
freshly cut peat bricks drying in the wind. Many locals are nostal-
gic for the "good old days," when homes were peat-fire heated. At
the Sally Gap junction turn left, where a road winds through the
vast Guinness estate. Look down on the glacial lake "Lough Tay"
and the Guinness mansion (famous for jet-set parties). Nicknamed
the Guinness Lake, the water looks like Ireland's favorite dark
brown stout, and the sand of the beach actually looks like the head
of a Guinness beer. From here the road winds scenically down
into the village of Roundwood and on to Glendalough.

▲▲**Glendalough**—The steep wooded slopes of Glendalough (glen-
da-lock, which means "valley of the two lakes"), at the south end of
Wicklow's military road, hides Ireland's most impressive monastic
settlement. Founded by St. Kevin in the sixth century, the monastery flourished (despite repeated Viking raids) throughout the "Age
of Saints and Scholars" until the English destroyed it in 1398. While
it was finally abandoned during the Dissolution of the Monasteries
in 1539, pilgrims kept coming, especially on St. Kevin's Day, June 3.
(This might have something to do with the fact that a pope said
seven visits to Glendalough had the same indulgence value as one
visit to Rome.) While much restoration was done in the 1870s, most
of the buildings date from the 8th through the 12th centuries.

The valley sights are split between the two lakes. The lower
lake has the Visitors Centre and the best buildings. The upper
lake, with scant ruins, feels like a state park with a grassy lakeside
picnic area, school groups, and fine walks.

General Glendalough plan: Park free at the Visitors Centre.
For a complete visit, begin with the video and history exhibit in
the center (£2, daily 9:00–18:30 in summer, closes earlier off-
season, tel. 0404/45325), wander the ruins (free) around the
Round Tower, walk the traffic-free Green Road one mile to the
upper lake, and then walk back to your car. (You can drive to the
upper lake—parking £1.50.) If you're rushed, skip the upper lake.
Summer tour-bus crowds are terrible all day on weekends and
from 11:00 to 14:00 on weekdays.

Glendalough Visitors Centre: Start your visit here. The
20-minute video provides a good thumbnail background on the
monastic society in medieval Ireland. While the video is more
general than specific to Glendalough, the adjacent museum room
features this particular monastic settlement. The model in the
center of the room re-creates the fortified village in the year 1050
(although there were no black-and-white Frisian cows in Ireland
back then—they would have been red cows). A browse here shows
the contribution these monks made to intellectual life in Dark Age
Europe (such as Irish minuscule, a more compact alphabet developed in the seventh century, and illuminated manuscripts, like the

Book of Kells from the ninth century). From the center, a short and scenic walk along the Green Road takes you to the Round Tower.

The Monastic Village: Easily the best ruins of Glendalough gather around its famous 110-foot-tall Round Tower. Towers like this (60–110 feet tall, standard features in such settlements) functioned as beacons for pilgrims, bell towers, storage lofts, and places of final refuge during Viking raids. They had a high door with a pull-up ladder. Several ruined churches (8th–12th centuries) and a sea of grave markers complete this evocative scene. Markers give short descriptions of the ruined buildings.

In an Ireland without cities, these monastic communities were mainstays of civilization. They were remote outposts where ascetics (with a taste for scenic settings) gathered to commune with God. In the 12th century, with the arrival of grander monastic orders such as the Franciscans and the Dominicans and with the growth of cities, these monastic communities were eclipsed. Today Ireland is dotted with the reminders of this age—illuminated manuscripts, simple churches, carved crosses, and about 100 round towers.

Upper Lake: The Green Road continues one mile farther up the valley to the upper lake (where the marriage scene from *Braveheart* was filmed). The oldest ruins—scant and hard to find—lie near this lake. If you want a scenic Wicklow walk, start here.

KILKENNY

Famous as "Ireland's loveliest inland city," Kilkenny is a good overnight for drivers wanting to break the journey from Dublin to Dingle (necessary if you want to spend more time in the Wicklow area and at the Rock of Cashel). A night in Kilkenny comes with plenty of traditional folk music in the pubs (hike over the river and up John Street). While a small town today (under 20,000), Kilkenny has a big history. Way back, it was an important center—occasionally even capital of Ireland in the Middle Ages.

Kilkenny gives you a feel for salt-of-the-earth Ireland. A workaday town, its castle and cathedral stand like historic bookends between a higgledy-piggledy High Street of colorful shops and medieval facades.

Kilkenny Castle, dominating the town, is a stony reminder of how the Anglo-Norman Butler family dominated the town for 500 years. A local crafts center weaves and warbles across the street from the castle.

The early English Gothic St. Canice's Cathedral (13th century) is rich with stained glass, medieval carvings, and floors paved in history (daily 10:00–18:00, tel. 056/64971). The 100-foot-tall round tower, built as part of a long-gone pre-Norman church here, recalls the need for a watchtower and refuge. The fun ladder climb to the top for £1 affords a grand view of the countryside (Mon–Sat 9:00–13:00, 14:00–18:00, Sun 14:00–18:00).

The train/bus station is four blocks from John's Bridge which marks the center of town. The TI, a block off the bridge, offers hour-long guided town walks (£3, 5/day, first one at 9:15, tel. 056/51500, private guide at tel. 056/65929).

Sleeping in Kilkenny: Kilkenny Tourist Hostel, filling a fine Georgian townhouse in the town center, offers a friendly family room, well-equipped members' kitchen, wealth of local information, and cheap beds (£8 dorm beds, D-£22, 2 blocks from the cathedral at 35 Parliament Street, tel. 056/63541, fax 056/23397, e-mail: kilkennyhostel@tinet.ie).

The **Club House Hotel** is perfectly central. Originally a gentleman's sporting club, it comes with old-time Georgian elegance; a palatial, well-antlered breakfast room; and 35 large, comfy bedrooms (Sb-£38, Db-£75, CC:VMA, Patrick Street, tel. 056/21994, fax 056/71920, e-mail: clubhse@iol.ie).

Berkeley House, across the street from Club House Hotel, is smaller, less expensive, and comfortable (10 rooms, Db-£60, CC:VM, 5 Lower Patrick Street, tel. 056/64848, fax 056/64829).

Rock of Cashel

Rising high above the fertile plain of Tipperary, the Rock of Cashel is one of Ireland's most historic and evocative sites. Seat of the ancient kings of Munster (about 400–1100), this is the site where St. Patrick baptised King Aengus in about A.D. 450. In about 1100 Cashel became Church-run—an ecclesiastical center of the region. On this 200-foot-high outcrop of limestone you'll find a round tower, an early Christian cross, a delightful Romanesque chapel, and a ruined Gothic cathedral, all surrounded by my favorite Celtic cross graveyard. Begin your visit with the 15-minute video (hourly) and the tiny museum (£3, mid-Jun–mid-Sept daily 9:00–19:30, closing earlier off-season, site tel. 062/61437).

Picture the Rock with just its 12th-century round tower (nearly 100 feet tall) and the small Romanesque chapel. Cormac's Chapel was built in about 1130 by the king and bishop of Cashel, Cormac MacCarthy. Study its misty old carvings.

Outside the chapel, notice the replica of St. Patrick's high cross (the 12th-century original is in the museum where you entered). Wander through the ruined 13th-century Gothic cathedral. Then tiptoe through the tombstones. Look out over the Plain of Tipperary. Called the Golden Veil, its rich soil makes it Ireland's most prosperous farm land. A path leads to the ruined 13th-century Cistercian Hore Abbey in the fields below (free, always open and peaceful).

The huggable town of Cashel at the base of the Rock affords a good break on the long drive from Dublin to Dingle (great cafés, plenty of B&Bs, and 2 fine hostels, TI tel. 062/62511).

DINGLE PENINSULA

Dingle Peninsula, the westernmost tip of Ireland, offers just the right mix of far-and-away beauty, ancient archaeological wonders, and desolate walks or bike rides all within convenient reach of its main town. Dingle Town is just big enough to have all the necessary tourist services and a steady nocturnal beat of Irish folk music.

While the big tour buses clog the neighboring Ring of Kerry before heading east to slobber all over the Blarney Stone, Dingle—while crowded in the summer—still feels like the fish and the farm really matter. Forty fishing boats sail from Dingle, and a faint whiff of peat fills its nighttime streets.

For 20 years my Irish dreams have been set here on this sparse but lush peninsula where locals are fond of saying "The next parish is Boston." There's a closeness to the land on Dingle. When I asked a local if he was born here, he thought for a second and said, "No, it was about six miles down the road." When I told him where I was from, a faraway smile filled his eyes, he looked out to sea and sighed, "Ah, the shores of Americay."

Dingle feels so traditionally Irish because it's a Gaeltacht, a region where the government subsidizes the survival of the Irish language and culture. While English is always there, the signs, menus, and songs come in Gaelic. Children carry hurling sticks to class, and even the local preschool brags "ALL Gaelic."

Of the peninsula's 10,000 residents, 1,300 live in Dingle Town. Its few streets, lined with ramshackle but gaily painted shops and pubs, run up from a rain-stung harbor always busy with fishing boats and yachts. Traditionally, the buildings were drab grey or whitewashed. Thirty years ago Ireland's "tidy town" competition started everyone painting their buildings in playful pastels.

It's a peaceful town. The court house (1832) is open one hour a month. The judge does his best to wrap up business within a half hour. During the day you'll see teenagers—already working on ruddy beer-glow cheeks—roll kegs up the streets and into the pubs in preparation for another night of music and craic (fun conversation).

Dingle History

The wet sod of Dingle is soaked with medieval history. In the darkest depths of the Dark Ages, peace-loving, bookwormish monks fled the chaos of the Continent and its barbarian raids. They sailed to the drizzly fringe of the known world—places like Dingle. These monks kept literacy alive in Europe. Charlemagne, who ruled much of Europe in the year 800, imported Irish monks to be his scribes.

It was from this peninsula that the semimythical explorer monk, St. Brandon, is said to have set sail in the sixth century in search of a legendary western paradise. Some think he beat Columbus to North America by nearly a thousand years.

Dingle (An Daingean in Gaelic) was a busy seaport in the late Middle Ages. Along with Tralee, it was the only walled town in Kerry—castles stood at the low and high ends of Main Street, protecting the Normans from the angry and dispossessed Irish outside. Dingle was a gateway to northern Spain—a three-day sail due south. Many 14th- and 15th-century pilgrimages left from Dingle for Santiago di Compostela.

In Dingle's medieval heydays, locals traded cowhides for wine. When Dingle's position as a trading center ended, the town faded in importance. In the last century it was a linen-weaving center. Until 1970 fishing dominated. The only visitors were scholars and students of old Irish ways. In 1970 the movie *Ryan's Daughter* introduced the world to Dingle. The trickle of Dingle fans has grown to a flood as word of its musical, historical, gastronomical, and scenic charms—not to mention its friendly dolphin—has spread.

Planning Your Time

For the shortest visit, give Dingle two nights and a day. It takes six to eight hours to get there from Dublin, Galway, or the boat dock in Rosslare. I like two nights because you feel more like a local on your second evening in the pubs. You'll need the better part of a day to explore the 30-mile loop around the peninsula by bike, car, or tour bus (see "Circular Tour," below). To do any serious walking or relaxing you'll need two or three days. It's not uncommon to find Americans slowing way, way down in Dingle.

Orientation (tel. code: 066)

Dingle—extremely comfortable on foot—hangs on a medieval grid of streets between the harbor front (where the Tralee bus

Southwest Ireland

stops) and Main Street (three blocks inland). Nothing in town is more than a five-minute walk away. Street numbers are used only when more than one place is run by a family of the same name. Most locals know most locals, and people on the street are fine sources of information. Remember, locals love their soda bread, and tourism provides the butter. You'll find a warm and sincere welcome.

Tourist Information: The Bord Failte (TI) is on Strand Street by the water (Mar–Oct Mon–Sat 9:00–19:00, Sun 10:00–13:00, 14:15–18:00, off-season shorter hours and closed Sun, tel. 066/915-1188). In the summer the TI organizes town walks. For more creative help, drop by the Mountain Man shop (on Strand Street, see below).

Helpful Hints

Before You Go: Look up old issues of *National Geographic* (Apr '76, Sept '94, and for the Aran Islands, Apr '81). The local Web site (www.dingle-peninsula.ie) lists festivals and events.

Crowds: Crowds trample Dingle's charm for the first three weeks in August. The absolute craziest are the Dingle Races (second weekend in August) and Dingle Regatta (third weekend in August). July is also packed. Dingle's metabolism (prices, schedules, activities) rises and falls with the tourist crowds—October through April is pretty sleepy.

Banking: Two banks in town, both uphill from the TI on Main Street, offer the same rates (Mon 10:00–17:00, Tue–Fri 10:00–16:00). Both have cash machines.

Supermarket: The Super Valu supermarket/department store, at the base of town, has everything and is ideal for assembling a peninsula picnic (Mon–Sat 8:00–21:00, Sun 8:00–19:00, until 22:00 in summer).

Launderette: Full-service only—drop off a load and pick it up dry and folded three hours later (tiny-£3.50, regular load-£5.50, Mon–Sat 9:00–17:30, on Green Street down alley across from the church, tel. 066/915-1837).

Internet Access: Dingleweb is on Main Street (£5/hour, £1.50 per quarter hour, Mon–Sat 10:00–22:00, less on Sun and off-season, tel. 066/915-2477, e-mail: postmaster@dingleweb.com).

Bike Rental: Bike rental shops abound. Consider Paddy's Bike Hire (£6/day, £7/24 hrs, daily 9:00–19:00, helmets included, on Dykegate next to Grapevine Hostel, tel. 066/915-2311), Sciuird Tours, the Mountain Man, or the Ballintaggert Hostel. If you're biking the peninsula, get a bike with skinny street tires, not slow and fat mountain-bike tires. Plan on leaving a credit card, driver's license, or passport as security.

Dingle Activities: The Mountain Man, a hiking shop run by a local guide, Mike Shea, is a clearinghouse for information, local tours, and excursions (daily 9:00–21:00 in summer, less off-season, just off harbor at Strand Street, tel. 066/915-2400, fax 066/915-2396). Stop by for bike rentals and ideas on biking, hiking, horse riding, climbing, peninsula tours (which they offer), and trips to the Blaskets. They are the Dingle Town contact for the Dunquin–Blasket Islands boats and shuttle bus rides to the harbor (see "Blasket Islands," below).

Travel Agency: Maurice O'Connor at Galvin's Travel Agency can book you bus, train, and plane tickets and boat rides to France (John Street, tel. 066/915-1409).

Sights—Dingle Town

▲**Oceanworld**—The only place charging admission in Dingle is worth considering. This new aquarium offers a little peninsula history, 160 different species of local fish and other sea creatures in thoughtfully described tanks (including a chance to walk under the fish in the "ocean tank"), and the easiest way to see Fungi the dolphin—on video. Their mission is to teach, and you're welcome to request a quick guided tour. The petting pool is fun. Splashing attracts the rays—they're unplugged (£4.50, £12 for

Dingle Town

* NOT TO SCALE:
CHURCH TO HARBOR
IS ABOUT 200 YARDS

1 HEATON'S GUEST HOUSE
2 OCEANWORLD
3 DINGLE SAILING CLUB
4 CRUISEBOAT OFFICES
5 MAIRE DE BARRA RESTAURANT
6 MOUNTAIN MAN
7 BUS STATION
8 GREANY'S RESTAURANT
9 SUPER VALUE
10 GRAPEVINE HOSTEL
11 O'FLAHERTY'S
13 BAMBURY'S B&B
14 TRAIL TO LIGHTHOUSE
15 BALLINTAGGERT HOSTEL
16 ALPINE HOUSE
17 SCIUIRD TOURS & KIRRARY B&B
18 CORNER HOUSE B&B
19 CONNORS B&B
20 CITY PARK

21 DICK MACK
22 CRAFT GALLERIES
23 LAUNDRY
24 EL TORO
25 BENNERS HOTEL & POST
26 BANK
27 BIKE RENTAL
28 AN CAFE LITEARTA
29 MACCARTHY'S PUB
30 CAPTAIN'S HOUSE B&B
31 CINEMA
32 ADAM'S BAR & RESTAURANT
33 SMALL BRIDGE BAR
34 DOYLE'S & HALF DOOR RESTAURANTS
35 SRAID EOIN B&B
36 KELLIHER'S BALLYEGAN HOUSE
37 GREENMOUNT HOUSE
38 HILLGROVE HOTEL
39 ARD NA GREINE HOUSE B&B

families, daily 10:00–20:30 in summer, until 18:00 or earlier in off-season, cafeteria; just past the harbor on the west edge of town; tel. 066/915-2111).

▲**Fungi**—In 1983 a dolphin moved into Dingle Harbor and became a local celebrity. Fungi is now the darling of the town's tourist trade and one reason you'll find so many tour buses parked along the harbor. With a close look at Fungi as bait, tour boats are thriving (£6, kids £3; while virtually every boat sees him, you don't pay until you've seen him; 1- to 2-hour trips depart between 10:00 and 19:00 depending upon demand; book behind TI at Dolphin Trips office, tel. 066/915-2626). A hardy little fishing boat motors 4 to 30 passengers out to the mouth of the harbor, where you troll around looking for Fungi. To actually swim with Fungi, rent wetsuits and catch the morning trip.

▲**Short Harbor Walk from Dingle**—For an easy stroll along the harbor out of town (and a chance to see Fungi, 90 min round-trip), head east from the roundabout past the Esso station. Just after Bambury's B&B, take a right following signs to Skelligs Hotel. At the beach, climb the steps over the wall and follow the seashore path to the mouth of Dingle harbor (marked by a tower—some 19th-century fat cat's folly). Ten minutes beyond that is a lighthouse. This is Fungi's neighborhood. If you see tourist boats out, you're likely to see him. The trail continues to a dramatic cliff.

The Harbor—The harbor was built on land reclaimed (with imported Dutch expertise) in 1992. The new roundabout allows traffic to skirt the town center. The string of old stone shops facing the harbor was the loading station for the narrow-gauge railway that hauled the fish from Dingle to Tralee (1891–1953). The Esk Tower on the distant hill is a marker built in 1847 during the famine as a make-work project. In pre-radar days, it helped ships locate Dingle's hidden harbor. The fancy mansion across the harbor is Lord Ventry's 17th-century manor house.

Cruises—The Dingle Marina Center offers diving, sailing, and traditional currach rowing. One-man sailboats can be lent to those wanting to blow around the bay with a day membership in the Sailing Club (£15, tel. 066/915-2422). Currachs—stacked behind the building—are Ireland's traditional lightweight fishing boats, easy to haul and easy to make—cover a wooden frame with canvas and paint with tar. The currachs are owned by the Dingle Rowing Club and go out many summer evenings.

Dingle Pitch & Putt—For 18 scenic holes and a driving range, hike 10 minutes past Ocean World (£3 with gear, driving range £3 for 100 balls, daily 10:00–20:00, over bridge take first left and follow signs, Milltown, tel. 066/915-1819).

Nightlife in Dingle Town

▲▲▲**Folk Music in Dingle Pubs**—Even if you're not into pubs, take a nap and then give these a whirl. Dingle is renowned among traditional musicians as a place to get work ("£30 a day, tax-free, plus drink"). The town has 50 pubs. There's music every night and never a cover charge. The scene is a decent mix of locals, Americans, and Germans. Music normally starts around 21:30, and the last call for drinks is "half eleven" (23:30). For a seat near the music, arrive early. If the place is chockablock, power in and find breathing room in the back. By midnight the door is closed and the chairs are stacked. While two pubs, the Small Bridge Bar (An Droicheed) and O'Flahertys are the most famous for their good beer and folk music, make a point to wander the town and follow your ear. Smaller pubs may feel a bit foreboding to a tourist, but people—locals as well as travelers—are out for the craic. Irish culture is so accessible in the pubs—highly interactive museums waiting to be explored. Have a glass in an empty no-name pub and chat up the publican. Pubs are smoky and hot (leave your coat home). The more offbeat pubs are more likely to erupt into leprechaun karaoke.

The best pub crawl is along the Strand to O'Flaherty's. Rough-and-tumble Murphy's is liveliest, offering rock as well as traditional music. O'Flaherty's, with a high ceiling and less smoke, dripping in old-time photos and town memorabilia, is touristy but lots of fun, with nightly music. Then head up Green Street. Dick Mack (across from the church and therefore nicknamed "the last pew") is a tiny leather shop by day and a pub by night, with a fine snug (private booth, originally designed to allow women to drink discreetly), reliably good beer, and a smoky and strangely fascinating ambience. Notice the Hollywood-type stars on the sidewalk recalling famous visitors. Established in 1899, the original Dick Mack's grandson now runs the place. A painting in the window shows Dick Mack II with the local gang. Wander Main Street from top to bottom. MacCarthy's Pub, a smoke-stained relic at the top, is less touristy and has some fine traditional music sessions (tel. 066/915-1205). The Small Bridge Bar at the bottom—with live music nightly—is popular for good reason. Finally, head up Spa Road a few doors to An Conair—a.k.a. John Benny's, a pub attracting a more alternative Celtic folk talent (often less crowded but with good music). Further up Spa Road, the big hotel has late night dancing (see below).

Dancing—Somewhere almost every night, a pub hosts "Set Dancing," with live music (An Conair Bar Mondays after 21:30, Small Bridge Bar on Wednesdays). Hillgrove Hotel (up Spa Road a few hundred meters) is a modern hotel with traditional dances every Thursday at 23:00 and pop dancing other nights in summer. Locals say the Hillgrove "is a good time if you're pissed."

During the day, music lovers will enjoy dropping by Danlann Gallery, a music shop on Dykegate Street (Mon–Sat 10:00–22:00, Sun 11:00–18:00, less off-season). The music office, also on Dykegate—next to the Grapevine Hostel—has the latest on musical happenings.

Theater—Dingle's great little theater is The Phoenix on Dykegate. Its film club (50 or 60 locals) meets here Tuesdays

(Oct–June at 20:30). The leader runs it almost like a religion, with a homily on the film before he rolls it. Afterward, locals and tourists chat over coffee and cookies.

Sleeping in Dingle Town
(£1 = about $1.50, tel. code: 066, mail: Dingle, County Kerry)

Sleep Code: **S** = Single, **D** = Double/Twin, **T** = Triple, **Q** = Quad, **b** = bathroom, **t** = toilet only, **s** = shower only, **CC** = Credit Card (Visa, MasterCard, Amex). Prices vary with the season, with August tops.

Sraid Eoin B&B, on the quiet end of town, has four spacious and modern pastel rooms and giant bathrooms and is warmly run by Kathleen and Maurice O'Connor (Db-£34–40, family deals, 10 percent discount with this book and cash, CC:VM, smoke free, John Street, tel. 066/915-1409, fax 066/915-2156). Maurice runs Galvin's Travel Agency on the ground floor (same phone number).

Kellihers Ballyegan House is a big, plain building with six fresh, comfortable rooms on the edge of town and great harbor views. It's run by friendly Mrs. Hannah Kelliher, who provides rare strictly smoke-free rooms (Sb-£18–20, Db-£36–40, 10 percent off with this book, no CC or smokers, Upper John Street, tel. 066/915-1702).

Greenmount House sits among palm trees at the top of town, in the countryside, with a commanding view of the bay and mountains, a five-minute hike up from the town center. John and Mary Curran run one of Ireland's classiest B&Bs, with six fine rooms (Db-£40–50) and six sprawling suites (Db-£50–70) in a modern building with lavish public areas and breakfast in a solarium (CC:VM, no singles during high season or children under eight, most rooms at ground level, top of John Street, reserve in advance, tel. 066/915-1414, fax 066/915-1974, e-mail: greenmount@tinet.ie).

O'Neill's B&B is a plain but homey and friendly place with six decent rooms (Sb-£19, Db-£36–38, family deals, strictly non-smoking, John Street, tel. 066/915-1639, Mary O'Neill).

Corner House B&B is my longtime Dingle home. It's a simple, traditional place with five rooms run with a twinkle and a grandmotherly smile by Kathleen Farrell (S-£19, D-£34, T-£48, plenty of plumbing, but it's down the hall, no CC, reserve with a phone call and reconfirm a day or two ahead or risk losing your bed, central as can be on Dykegate Street, tel. 066/915-1516).

Captain's House B&B is a shipshape place fit for an admiral in the town center, with eight classy rooms and a stay-awhile garden (Sb-£35, Db-£50, great suite-£60, CC:VMA, the Mall, tel. 066/915-1531, fax 066/915-1079, e-mail: captigh@tinet.ie, Jim and Mary Milhench).

Kirrary B&B and **O Coileain B&B** stand side by side on a quiet corner in the town center, offering small, simple rooms and a homey friendliness (Db-£34–40, 10 percent discount with this book outside of August, £6 bike rental, tel. & fax 066/915-1606 or 066/915-1937, e-mail: arch@iol.ie). These are run by the same Collins—Coileain in Gaelic—family that runs the Sciuird tours recommended below. **Connor's B&B,** with 15 basic rooms, is a lesser value (Db-£40–50, CC:VMA, quiet but central on Dykegate Street, tel. 066/915-1598, fax 066/915-2376, Mrs. Connor).

Ard Na Greine House B&B is a charming, windblown, modern house on the edge of town. Mrs. Mary Houlihan rents four well-equipped, comfortable rooms to nonsmokers (Sb-£25, Db-£36, Tb-£50, CC:VM, on the edge of town an 8-minute walk up Spa Road, three doors beyond the Hillgrove Hotel, tel. 066/915-1113, fax 066/915-1898).

Alpine House Guest House looks like a monopoly hotel, but that means comfortable and efficient. Its 13 spacious, bright, and fresh rooms come with wonderful sheep and harbor views, a cozy lounge, great breakfast, and friendly management (Db-£40 except £50 in August, Tb-£60, less off-season, 10 percent discount with this book, CC:VM, Mail Road, tel. 066/915-1250, fax 066/915-1966). Driving into town from Tralee, you'll see this a block uphill from the Dingle roundabout and Esso station.

Bambury's Guesthouse, another big, modern place with views of sheep and the harbor, rents 12 big, airy, comfy rooms with a family-friendly feeling (Db-£40–55, depending on size and season, family deals, 10 percent discount with this book, CC:VM, on your left coming in from Tralee on Mail Road two blocks before Esso station, tel. 066/915-1244, fax 066/915-1786, e-mail: berniebb@tinet.ie).

Ocean View B&B rents three tidy rooms in a little water-front row house overlooking the bay (S-£16, D-£28, 5-minute walk from the center, 100 meters past Ocean World at 133 The Wood, tel. 066/915-1659, Mrs. Brosnan).

Heatons Guesthouse is a big, peaceful place on the water just west of town at the end of Dingle Bay. Their 12 rooms are thoughtfully appointed with all the comforts (Db-£50–66, CC:VM, 5-minute walk past Ocean World on The Wood, tel. 066/915-2288, fax 066/915-2324, e-mail: heatons@iol.ie, run by Cameron and Nuala Heaton).

Benners Hotel was the only place in town a hundred years ago. It stands bewildered by the modern world on Main Street, with plush and abundant public spaces and sprawling hallways leading to 52 musty but comfortable rooms (Db-£120 Jul–Aug, £90 Jun & Sept, £70 Oct–May, kids-£15 extra, CC:VMA, tel. 066/915-1638, fax 066/915-1412, e-mail: benners@tinet.ie).

Hostels in Dingle Town

Ballintaggart Hostel, a backpacker's complex, is housed in a
stylish old manor house used by Protestants during the famine as
a soup kitchen (for those hungry enough to renounce their Catholicism). It comes complete with bike rental, laundry service, kitchen,
café, classy study, family room with a fireplace, and a resident ghost
(148 beds, £8 in 10-bed dorms, £10 in quads, £14 in singles and
doubles, breakfast extra, a mile east of town on Tralee Road, tel.
066/915-1454, fax 066/915-2207, e-mail: btaggart@iol.ie, run by
Johnny V). Their shuttle bus meets each arriving inter-city bus and
does a nightly pub run—into town at 21:30, back at 23:30.

    Grapevine Hostel is a clean and friendly establishment with a
cozy fireplace lounge and a fine members' kitchen. Each four- to
eight-bed dorm has its own bathroom. Dorms are coed, but there's
usually a girls' room established (32 beds, £8–9.50 each, Dykegate
Lane, tel. 066/915-1434, e-mail: grapevine@dingleweb.com, run
by Siobhan).

    The new and modern **Marina Hostel** plans to open by
mid-2000 (next to Ocean World, tel. 066/915-1065).

Eating in Dingle Town

For a rustic little village, Dingle is swimming in good food. Budget tips: The **supermarket** stays open late nightly, fancy restaurants serve early bird specials from 18:00–19:00, many "cheap &
cheery" places close at 18:00, and pubs do amazing £5 dinners all
over town. Most pubs stop serving food around 21:00 (to make
room for maximum beer).

    Adam's Bar and Restaurant is a tight, smoky place popular
with locals for traditional food at great prices. Try their corned
beef and cabbage (£5 meals, last meal at 20:30 in summer, 17:30
off-season, closed Sun, Upper Main Street).

    An Cafe Litearta, a popular and friendly eatery hiding
behind an inviting bookstore, has good snacks and sandwiches
(10:00–17:30, Dykegate Street).

    Greany's Restaurant, just off the roundabout, is a local hit
serving fine food at decent prices in a cheery, modern atmosphere
(£10–15 dinners, fine salmon, Mon–Fri 12:30–22:00, Sat–Sun
11:00–17:30, Holyground, tel. 066/915-2244).

    Vittle's Restaurant offers good food and prices with an
early-bird special and good vegetarian selections (near the roundabout at Holyground).

    The **Global Village Restaurant** is where Martin Bealin
serves his favorite dishes, gleaned from travels around the world.
It's a smoky and eclectic healthy meat-eaters place popular with
locals for its interesting cuisine (£5 lunches, £10 dinners, daily
9:30–21:30, the Thai Curry is great, top of Main Street, tel.
066/915-2325).

El Toro offers a candlelit splash of the Mediterranean, with good seafood, salads, and pizzas (£10–15 meals, 18:00–22:30, Green Street, tel. 066/915-1820).

Maire De Barra's pub serves perhaps the best £5 dinners in town—traditional and seafood (daily 12:30–21:30, music after 21:30, the Pier). **Paudie Brosnan's** pub, a few doors down, is also good.

Dingle's long-established top-notch restaurants are **Doyle's Seafood Bar** (more famous, John Street, tel. 066/915-1174) and the **Half Door** (heartier portions, John Street, tel. 066/915-1600). Both offer £17 three-course early-dinner specials between 18:00 and 19:00 and £25 meals after that. Reservations are necessary in both places.

Transportation Connections—Dingle Town

The nearest train station is in Tralee. **Dingle bus connections: Galway** (3/day, 6.5 hrs), **Dublin** (3/day, 8 hrs), **Rosslare** (2/day, 9 hrs), **Tralee** (4/day, 75 min, £6), fewer departures on Sundays. Dingle has no bus station and only one stop, on the waterfront behind the Super Valu supermarket (bus info tel. 01/830-2222 or 066/972-3566). See "Tralee Transportation Connections," below, for more information.

Drivers choose two roads into town, the easy southern route or the much more dramatic and treacherous Conor Pass (see "Tralee Transportation Connections," below). It's 30 miles from Tralee either way.

Dingle Peninsula: Circular Tour by Bike or Car

A ▲▲▲ sight, the Dingle Peninsula loop trip is about 30 miles long (7 hrs by bike, 3 hrs by car, including stops; do only in clockwise direction). While you can take a guided tour of the peninsula (below), it's not necessary with the route described in this section. A fancy map is also unnecessary with my instructions. I've keyed in mileage to help locate points of interest. If you're driving, as you leave Dingle, reset your odometer at Oceanworld. Even if you get off track or are biking, derive distances between points from these numbers. To get the most out of your circle, read through this entire section before departing. Then go step by step (staying on R559 and following the "The Slea Head Drive" signs). Note: Roads are very congested in August.

The Dingle Peninsula is 10 miles wide and runs 40 miles from Tralee to Slea Head. The top of its mountainous spine is Mount Brandon—at 3,130 feet, the second-tallest mountain in Ireland. While only tiny villages lie west of Dingle Town, the peninsula is home to 500,000 sheep.

Leave Dingle Town west along the waterfront (0.0 miles at

Dingle Peninsula Tour

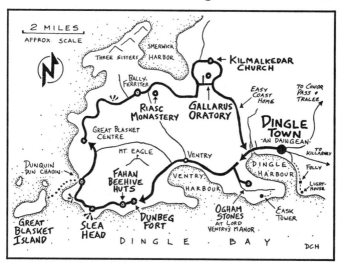

Oceanworld). There's an eight-foot tide here. The seaweed was used to nourish reclaimed land. Across the water the fancy Milltown House B&B (with flags) was Robert Mitchum's home for a year during the filming of *Ryan's Daughter*. Look back out the harbor to see the narrow mouth of this blind harbor. (That's where Fungi frolics.) Dingle Bay is so hidden, ships needed the tower (1847) on the hill to find its mouth.

0.4 miles: Turn left over the bridge. The building on the right was a corn-grinding mill in the 18th century.

0.8 miles: The Milestone B&B is named for the pillar stone (Gallaun in Gaelic) in its front yard. This may have been a prehistoric grave marker or a boundary marker between two tribes. The stone goes down as far as it sticks up. Another pillar stone stands in the field across the street in the direction of the yellow manor house of Lord Ventry. The peninsula, literally an open-air museum, is dotted with more than 2,000 monuments dating from the Bronze Age through early Christian times.

2.1 miles: Pass through a rare grove of trees and turn left ("Leather Workshop" sign). After 100 yards enter the Lord Ventry's Manor, take the first left (unmarked, through white gate—it's private but they don't seem to mind sightseers). The long one-lane drive leads past small 18th-century estate houses through a lush garden (turn right at the fork) to the Ventry Manorhouse. Lord Ventry, whose family came to Dingle as post–Cromwell War landlords in 1666, built this mansion in about 1750. Today it houses an all-Gaelic boarding school for 140 high school–age girls.

Fifty yards before the mansion, stop at the six stones. The Ogham Stones (dating from the third to seventh century, named for the Celtic goddess of writing) decorating the drive are rare examples of early Celtic writing. With variations on five straight lines, they could make 20 letters—the original bar code. Of the 380 known Ogham Stones, 80 are in Dingle. Return to the main road and turn left (3.1 miles).

In the Ventry estate and beyond you'll pass palms, magnolias, fuschias, and exotic flora introduced to Dingle by Ventry. Because of the mild climate (cradled by the gulf stream), fuschias—imported from Chile and spreading like weeds—line the roads all over the peninsula and fill the countryside with red from June to September. The mild climate—it never snows—is okay for subtropical plants.

4.1 miles: Stay off the "soft margin" as you enjoy views of Ventry Bay and its four-mile-long beach. Mt. Eagle (1,660 feet), rising across the bay, marks the end of Ireland. In the village of Ventry, Gaelic is the first language.

6.0 miles: The rushes on either side of the road are the kind used to make the local thatched roofs. Thatching, which nearly died out because of the fire danger, is more popular now that anti-flame treatments are available. Magpies fly.

6.6 miles: The Irish football star Paidi O Se (Paddy O'Shea) is a household name in Ireland. He now trains the Kerry team and runs the pub on the left.

6.9 miles: The blue house hiding in the trees 100 meters off the road on the left (view through the white gate) was kept cozy by Tom Cruise and Nicole Kidman during the filming of *Far and Away*.

7.9 miles: "Taisteaal go Mall" means "go slowly"; there's a peach-colored schoolhouse on the right. On the left is the Celtic and Prehistoric Museum, a strange private collection of dinosaur eggs, Celtic and Viking tools, coins, weapons, and an odd mechanical sheep (£3.50, closed Mon).

8.2 miles: The circular mound on the right is a late–Stone Age ring fort. In 500 B.C. it was a petty Celtic chieftain's headquarters, a stone-and-earth stockade filled with little stone houses. These survived untouched through the centuries because of superstitious beliefs that they were "fairy forts." While this is unexcavated, recent digging has shown that people have lived on this peninsula since 4000 B.C.

8.6 miles: Look ahead up Mount Eagle at the patchwork fields created by the stone fences.

9.0 miles: Dunbeg Fort, a series of defensive ramparts and ditches around a central clochan, while ready to fall into the sea, is open to tourists. While there are no carvings to be seen, the small (beg) fort (dun) is dramatic (£1, daily 9:00–20:00, descriptive handout). Forts like this are the most important relics left from Ireland's Iron Age (500 B.C. to A.D. 500). Since erosion will some-day take this fort, it has been excavated.

9.6 miles: A group of beehive huts, or *clochans*, is a short walk uphill. These mysterious stone igloos cluster together within a circular wall (£1, daily 9:00–19:00, WC). These are a better sight than the similar group of beehive huts a mile down the road. Farther on, you'll ford a stream. There has never been a bridge here; the road was designed as a ford.

10.6 miles: Pull off to the left at this second group of beehive huts. Look downhill at the scant remains of the scant home that was burned as the movie equivalent of Lord Ventry tried to evict the tenants in *Far and Away*. Even without Hollywood, this is a bleak and godforsaken land. Look above at the patches of land slowly reclaimed by the inhabitants of this westernmost piece of Europe. Rocks were cleared and piled into fences. Sand and sea-weed were laid on the clay, and in time it was good for grass. The created land was generally not tillable. Much has fallen out of use now. Look behind at the Ring of Kerry in the distance and ahead at the Blasket Islands.

11.4 miles: At Slea Head, marked by a crucifix, a pullout, and great views of the Blasket Islands (described below), you turn the corner on this tour.

11.9 miles: Pull out here to view the Blaskets and Dunmore Head (the westernmost point in Europe) and to review the road-side map (which traces your route) posted in the parking lot. The scattered village of Dunquin has many ruined rock homes—abandoned during the famine. They were built with small win-dows to minimize taxation. Some are fixed up, as this is a popular place these days for summer homes. You can see more good exam-ples of land reclamation, patch by patch, climbing up the hillside. Mount Eagle was the first bit of land Charles Lindberg saw after crossing the Atlantic on his way to Paris. Villagers here were as excited as he. Ahead, down a road on the left, a plaque celebrates the 30th anniversary of the filming of *Ryan's Daughter*.

13.4 miles: The Blasket Islanders had no church or cemetery on the island. This was their cemetery. The famous Blasket story-teller Peig Sayers (1873–1958) is buried in the center. Just past a washed-out bit of road, a lane leads left (100 yards) to a marker remembering the 1588 shipwreck of the *Santa Maria de la Rosa* of the Spanish Armada. Below that is the often tempestuous Dunquin Harbor, from where the Blasket ferry departs. Island farmers—who on a calm day could row across in 20 minutes—would dock here and hike 12 miles into Dingle to sell their produce.

13.5 miles: Back on the main road, follow signs to the Great Blasket Centre.

15 miles: Leave the Slea Head Road left for the Great Blasket Centre (described below).

15.7 miles: Back at the turnoff, head left (sign to Louis Mulcahy Pottery).

16.4 miles: Passing land that was never reclaimed, think of the work it took to pick out the stones, pile them into fences, and bring up sand and seaweed to nourish the clay and make soil for growing potatoes. On the left is a shadow of the main street of the fake poor village built to film *Far and Away*. Beyond that is the aptly named "Sleeping Giant" island—hand resting happily on his beer belly.

16.8 miles: The view is spectacular, especially when the waves are "racing in like white horses." Ahead on the right, study the top fields, untouched since the planting of 1845, when the potatoes rotted in the ground. The vertical ridges of the potato beds can still be seen—a reminder of the famine. Before the famine, 60,000 people lived on this peninsula. Today it's home to only 10,000.

20.2 miles: Ballyferriter (Baile an Fheirtearaigh), established by a Norman family in the 12th century, is the largest town on this side of Dingle. The pubs serve grub, and the old schoolhouse is a museum (£1.50, daily Easter–Sept 10:00–16:30, closed off-season). The early Christian cross looks real. Tap it . . . it's fiberglass—a prop from *Ryan's Daughter*.

21.0 miles: At the T-junction, signs direct you to Dingle (An Daingean, 11 km) either way. Go left, via Gallarus. Take a right over the bridge, still following signs to Gallarus.

21.4 miles: Just beyond the bridge and a few yards before the sign to Mainistir Riaise (Reask Monastic enclosure), detour right up the lane. After 0.2 miles (the unsigned turnout on your right) you find the scant remains of the walled Riasc Monastery (dating from the 5th to 12th centuries). The inner wall divided the community into work and religious sections. The layer of black felt marks where the original rocks stop and the excavators' reconstruction begins. The pillar stone is Celtic (from 1000 B.C.). When the Christians arrived in the fifth century, they didn't throw out the Celtic society. Instead, they carved a Maltese-type cross over the Celtic scrollwork. The square building was an oratory (church—you'll see an intact oratory at the next stop). The round buildings would have been stone igloo-type dwellings. The monasteries had cottage industries. Just outside the wall (opposite the oratory), find a stone hole with a passage facing the southwest wind. This was a kiln. Locals would bring their grain to be dried and ground, and the monks would keep a "tithe." With the arrival of the Normans in the 12th century, these small religious communities were replaced by relatively big-time state and church governments.

21.9 miles: Back on the main road, continue to the right.

23.0 miles: At the big restaurant, turn left (signs to Gallarus Oratory).

23.7 miles: At another restaurant, go right up an unmarked one-lane road.

24.0 miles: The Gallarus Oratory, built about 1,300 years ago, is one of Ireland's best-preserved early-Christian churches. Shaped like an upturned boat, its finely fitted dry-stone walls are still waterproof. Notice the holes for some covering at the door and the fine alternating stonework on the corners. A small tourist center (shop, WC, video theater, parking) charges £1.50 (you get a 17-minute video overview of Dingle Peninsula's historic sights). To park free, drive past the "Visitor Centre" sign and grab one of four spots farther up the one-lane road at the access path marked "public right-of-way" to the oratory. Continue up the rugged one-lane road.

Optional detour: The ruined Kilmalkedar church is two miles from Gallarus. This was the Norman center of worship for this end of the peninsula when England replaced the old monastic settlements in an attempt to centralize their rule.

24.6 miles: Turn left on the two-lane road, then right (to An Daingean, 7 km), where you'll crest and enjoy a three-mile coast back into Dingle Town in the direction of the Esk Tower.

27.6 miles: At the intersection, find the happy dolphin on the left. He leads the way over the bridge and back into Dingle Town (28.4 miles). Well done.

Dingle Peninsula Tours

▲▲Sciuird Archaeology Tours—These tours are offered by a father-son team with Dingle history—and a knack for sharing it—in its blood. Tim Coileain (a retired Dingle policeman) and his son Michael give serious 2.5-hour minibus tours (£8, departing at 10:30 and 14:00, depending upon demand). Drop by the Kirrary B&B (Dykegate and Grey's Lane) or call 066/915-1937 or 066/915-1606 to put your name on the list. Call early. Tours fill quickly in summer. Off-season you may have to call back to see if the necessary four people signed up to make a bus go. While skipping the folk legends and the famous sights (such as Slea Head), your guide will drive down tiny farm roads (the Gaelic word for road is "cow path"), over hedges, and up ridges to hidden Celtic forts, mysterious stone tombs, and forgotten castles with sweeping seaside views. The running commentary gives an intimate peek into the history of Dingle. Sit as close to the driver as possible to get all the information. They do two completely different tours: west (Gallarus Oratory) and east (Minard Castle and a wedge tomb). I enjoyed both. Dress for the weather. In a literal gale with horizontal winds Tim kept saying, "You'll survive it."

Moran's Tour does three-hour guided minibus trips around the peninsula with a more touristic slant (£8, normally at 10:00 and 14:00 from the Dingle TI, tel. 087/241-2488 or 066/915-1155). There are always enough seats. If no one shows up, consider a private Moran taxi trip around the peninsula (3 people, £24, cabby narrates the ride). The **Mountain Man** also offers three-hour minibus tours of the peninsula (tel. 066/915-2400).

Blasket Islands

This rugged group of six islands off the tip of Dingle Peninsula seems particularly close to the soul of Ireland. The population of Great Blasket Island, home to as many as 160 people, dwindled until the government moved the last handful of residents to the mainland in 1953. Life here was hard. Each family had a cow, a few sheep, and a plot of potatoes. They cut their peat from the high ridge and harvested fish from the sea. There was no priest, pub, or doctor. These people were the most traditional Irish community of the 20th century—the symbol of antique Gaelic culture.

Their special closeness to their island—combined with their knack for vivid storytelling—is inspirational. From this primitive but proud fishing/farming community came three writers of international repute whose Gaelic work—basically tales of life on Great Blasket—is translated into many languages. You'll find *Peig* (by Peig Sayers*), Twenty Years a-Growing* (Maurice O'Sullivan), and *The Islander* (Thomas O'Crohan) in shops everywhere.

In the summer there may be a café, shop, and hostel on the island, but it's little more than a ghost town overrun with rabbits on a peaceful, grassy, three-mile-long poem. The Blasket ferry runs on the hour (weather permitting) and on the half hour (demand and weather permitting). In 2000 there should be two or three buses a day from Dingle Town to Dunquin (usually around 9:00, 14:00, and 16:00, returning about 10:00, 14:30, and 18:00, tel. 066/915-6533). Buses are coordinated with ferry departures; check at the Mountain Man shop in Dingle Town (£3 each way by bus, £10 round-trip with boat trip to Blasket, Dunquin ferry tel. 066/915-6455). There is a fine hostel in Dunquin.

▲▲**Great Blasket Centre**—This state-of-the-art Blasket and Gaelic heritage center gives visitors the best look possible at the language, literature, and way of life of the Blasket Islanders. See the fine 20-minute video (shows on the half hour), hear the sounds, read the poems, browse through old photos, and then gaze out the big windows at those rugged islands and imagine. Even if you never got past limericks, the poetry of these people—so pure and close to each other and nature—will have you dipping your pen into the cry of the birds (£2.50, Easter–Oct daily 10:00–18:00, until 19:00 July and August, cafeteria, on the mainland facing the islands, well signposted, tel. 066/915-6444). Visit this center before visiting the islands.

▲▲**Blasket Islands Adventure Cruise**—Three-hour cruises take visitors around nine islands and provide a wild Atlantic dose of bird, fish, and natural scenery (around £15 "depending upon the success of the sightseeing," shuttlebus to and from Dingle about £6; pack for rain and cold, bring a barf bag; departs daily at noon, weather permitting; coffee and snacks included, booking required, tel. 066/915-6533).

Sights—East of Dingle Town
▲**Minard Castle**—Three miles southwest of Annascaul is Minard Castle, the largest fortress on the peninsula. Built by the Norman Knights of Kerry in 1551, it was destroyed by Cromwell in about 1650.

Wander around the castle. With its corners undermined by Cromwellian explosives, it looks ready to split. Look up the garbage/toilet chute. As you enter the ruins, find the faint scallop in the doorway—the symbol of St. James. The castle had a connection to Santiago de Compostela in Spain. Medieval pilgrims would leave from here on a seafaring pilgrimage to northern Spain. Inside, after admiring the wall flowers, re-create the floor-plan: ground floor for animals and storage; main floor with fireplace; thin living quarters floor; and, on top, the defensive level.

The setting is dramatic, with the Ring of Kerry across the way and Storm Beach below. Storm Beach is notable for its sandstone boulders that fell from the nearby cliffs. Grinding against each other because of the wave and tidal action, the boulders eroded into cigar-shaped rocks. Some of these rocks, inscribed by prehistoric people, became the Ogham Stones (see "Circular Tour," above).

▲**Puicin Wedge Tomb**—While pretty obscure, this is worth the trouble for its evocative setting. Above the hamlet of Lispole in Doonties, park your car and hike 10 minutes up a ridge. At the summit is a pile of rocks made into a little room with one of the finest views on the peninsula. Beyond the Ring of Kerry you may just make out the jagged Skellig Rock, noted for its sixth-century monastery.

Inch Strand—This four-mile sandy beach, shaped like a half-moon, was made famous by *Ryan's Daughter*.

TRALEE
While Killarney is the tour-bus capital of county Kerry, Tralee is its true leading city. Except for the tourist complex around the TI and during a few festivals, Tralee feels like a bustling Irish town.

Tralee's famous Rose of Tralee International Festival (five days in late August), while a celebration of arts and music, climaxes with the election of the "Rose of Tralee"—the most beautiful woman at the festival. While the rose garden in the

Castle Gardens surrounding the TI is in bloom from summer through October, Tralee's finest roses are going about their lives in the busy streets of this workaday town.

Orientation (tel. code: 066)

For the tourist, the heart of Tralee is Ashe Memorial Hall, housing the TI and Kerry the Kingdom, located near the rose garden and surrounded by the city park. Beyond the park is the Aqua Dome and steam railway that, if you were here 50 years ago, would chug-chug you to Dingle. Today it goes only to the touristy windmill.

Tourist Information: The TI is in Ashe Memorial Hall but may relocate in 2000 (Jul–Aug daily 9:00–19:00, shorter hours off-season, tel. 066/21288).

Arrival in Tralee: From the train and bus station (located in the same building, with bike rental available), the Ashe Memorial Hall is a 10-minute walk through the center of town. From the station head down Edward Street, then turn right on Castle Street and left on Denny. It's at the end of Denny. Drivers should knock around the town center until they find a sign to the TI. Parking on the street requires a disk (40p per hour, sold at TI and news-stands, have them date it for you).

Sights—Tralee

▲▲**Kerry the Kingdom**—This is the place to learn about life in Kerry. The museum has three parts: Kerry slide show, museum, and medieval town train ride. Get in the mood by relaxing for 20 minutes through the Enya-style, continuous slide show of Kerry's spectacular scenery, then wander through 7,000 years of Kerry history in the museum (well described, no need for rentable head-phones). The Irish say that when a particularly stupid guy moved from Cork to Kerry, he raised the IQ in both counties—but this is pretty well done. The museum starts with good background on the archaeological sights of Dingle and goes right up to a video showing highlights of the Kerry football team (a fun look at Irish football). The attempted finale is a 12-minute four-person train ride down Tralee's Main Street in 1450 (£5.50, daily 10:00–18:00, until 19:00 in August, less in winter, tel. 066/712-7777, 40p disk at TI for one-hour parking). Before leaving, garden enthusiasts will want to ramble through the rose garden in the adjacent park.

Blennerville Windmill—On the edge of Tralee, just off the Dingle road, spins a restored mill originally built in 1800. Its eight-minute video tells of the famine (£3, Apr–Oct daily 10:00–18:00, closed off-season, tel. 066/712-1064). A restored narrow-gauge steam railway runs hourly from Tralee's Ballyard Station to the windmill (£3 round-trip, tel. 066/712-1064 for services). In the 19th century Blennerville was a major port for America-bound emigrants.

Blennerville's Jeanie Johnston Shipyard—This features a life-size replica of the tall ship that made 16 successful voyages to North America (1847–1858) during and after the famine (£3, Visitors Centre daily 9:00–18:00 year-round, tel. 066/712-9999).

Siamsa Tire Theatre—The National Folk Theater of Ireland, Siamsa Tire (pron: shee-em-sah tee-rah), stages two-hour dance and theater performances based on Gaelic folk traditions. The songs are in Irish, but there's no dialogue (£11, 20:30 most evenings May–mid-Oct, next to Kingdom of Kerry building in park, tel. 066/712-3055).

Swimming—The Aqua Dome is a modern-yet-fortified swim center—the largest indoor waterworld in Ireland—at the Dingle end of town. Families enjoy the huge slide, wave pool, and other wet amusements (£6, £4 for kids, Jun–Aug daily 10:00–22:00, less off-season, tel. 066/712-9150).

Music and Other Distractions—Tralee has a fine pub scene, with several pubs within a few blocks of each other offering live traditional music most evenings. There's greyhound racing (ten 30-second races every 15 minutes 20:00–22:15, Tue & Fri year-round plus Sat in summer, 10-min walk from station or town center, tel. 066/718-0008). It costs £4 plus what you lose gambling (kids free). At just about any time of day you can drop into a betting office to see the local gambling scene.

Sleeping in Tralee
(£1 = about $1.50, tel. code: 066, mail: Tralee, County Kerry)

O'Shea's B&B, a simple, tidy, modern house, rents four comfy rooms (Sb-£22, Db-£34, Tb-£45, leaving the station, walk five minutes up Oakpark Road to #2 Oakpark Drive, tel. & fax 066/718-0123, Mairead O'Shea).

Two good and central hostels with £8 dorm beds and £20 doubles without breakfast are **Finnegan's Hostel** (in a stately Georgian house from 1826, a block in front of the TI in the town center at 17 Denny Street, rustic cellar restaurant serving fine meals, CC:VM, tel. 066/712-7610) and the homey **Lisnagree Hostel** (£8 beds in shared quads, D-£18, Db-£22, a mile from the center just off N21, follow Boherboy to Ballinorig Road, tel. 066/712-7133). **Atlas House Budget Accommodation** also offers cheap dorms and tidy doubles (D-£30, Db-£35, £9 beds in 4- to 8-bed rooms, with continental breakfast, CC:VM, two blocks from train station, just off Castle Street, tel. 066/712-0722, fax 066/712-0747, e-mail: atlashousetralee@tinet.ie).

Collis-Sandes House, a mile north of the station and town center, is a run-down neo-Gothic mansion in a peaceful forest with 100 cheap beds (£7 beds in 4- to 8-bed rooms, D-£20, Db-from £24, sheets included, breakfast-£1, CC:VMA, from the station head up Oakpark Drive, after about eight blocks you'll see the sign on the left, tel. & fax 066/712-8658, e-mail: colsands @indigo.ie). They have a free shuttle service from the station (ring upon arrival) and a Tralee pub run on summer evenings.

Transportation Connections—Tralee

By train to: Dublin (4/day, 3/day on Sunday, 4 hrs), **Rosslare** (1/day, 5 hrs). Train info: tel. 066/712-3522.

By bus to: Dingle (7/day, less off-season and on Sunday, 75 min, £6), **Galway** (5/day), **Limerick** (5/day, 2 hrs), **Doolin/Cliffs of Moher** (daily at 9:30 and 15:30), **Ennis** (5/day, 3 hrs), **Rosslare** (3/day, 7 hrs, £16), **Shannon** (5/day). Tralee's bus station is at the train station. Bus info: tel. 066/712-3566.

Car Rental: Duggan's Garage Practical Car Hire rents Fiat Unos (£35/24 hours, £70/48 hours, includes everything but gas, CC:VM, two blocks from train station on Ashe Street, tel. 066/712-1124, fax 066/712-7527).

Kerry Airport, a 45-minute drive from Dingle Town, now offers direct flights to **Dublin, London** (daily, £86), and even points on the **Continent** (tel. 066/976-4644 or 066/976-4350).

Route Tips for Drivers

Between Tralee and Dingle: Drivers choose between the narrow, but very exciting, Conor Pass road or the faster, easier, but still narrow N86 through Lougher and Anascaul. On a clear day Conor Pass comes with incredible views over Tralee Bay and Brandon Bay, the Blasket Islands, and the open Atlantic. Pull over at the summit viewpoint to look down on Dingle Town and the harbor. While in Kerry listen to Radio Kerry FM 97. To practice your Gaelic, tune into FM 94.4.

Between Tralee and Galway/Burren/Doolin: The Killimer–Tarbert ferry connection allows those heading for the Cliffs of Moher to avoid the 80-mile detour around the Shannon River. If you're going to Galway, the Limerick route is faster, but the ferry route is more scenic (hrly trips, 20 min, £9/carload, leaves on the half hour going north and top of the hour going south in peak times, tel. 065/53124).

GALWAY, ARAN ISLANDS, AND COUNTY CLARE

GALWAY

Galway feels like a boomtown—rare in western Ireland. With 60,000 people, it's the area's main city—a lively university town and the county's industrial and administrative center. Amid the traditional regions of Connemara, James Joyce country, and the Aran Islands, it's also a Gaelic cultural center.

Galway offers tourists plenty of traditional music, easy bus connections to Dublin (hrly, 3.5 hrs, £5), and a convenient jumping-off point for a visit to the Aran Islands.

While Galway has a long and interesting history, its British overlords (who ruled here until 1922) had little use for anything important to the Irish heritage. Consequently, precious little from old Galway survives. What does survive has the interesting disadvantage of being built in the local limestone, which, even if medieval, looks like modern stone construction. A spirit of preservation came with the city's quincentennial celebration in 1984.

What Galway lacks in sights it makes up for in ambience. Spend an afternoon just wandering its medieval streets, with their delightfully mix of colorful facades, labyrinthine pubs, weather-resistant buskers, and steamy eateries.

Blustery Galway heats up after dark, with fine theaters and a pub scene Dubliners travel for. Visitors mix with old-timers and students as the traditional music goes round and round.

If you hear a strange language on the streets and wonder where those people are from ... it's Irish, and so are they.

Galway History

The medieval fishing village of Galway went big time when the Normans captured the territory from the O'Flaherty family in

Galway, Aran Islands, and County Clare

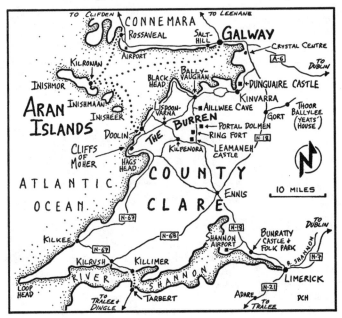

1234. Making the town a base, they invited in their Anglo friends, built a wall (1270), and kicked out the Irish. Galway's Celtic name (Gaillimh) comes from an old Irish word, *gall*, which means "foreigner." Except for a small section in the Eyre Square Shopping Center and a chunk at the Spanish Arch, that Norman wall is gone.

In the 14th century, 14 merchant families, or "tribes," controlled Galway's commercial traffic, including the lucrative wine trade with Spain and France. These English families constantly clashed with the local Irish. While the wall was built to "keep out the O's and the Macs," it didn't always work. A favorite prayer at the time was "From the fury of the O'Flaherty's good Lord deliver us."

Galway's support of the English king helped it prosper. But with the rise of Oliver Cromwell, Galway paid a price. After sieges in 1651 by Cromwell and in 1691 by the Protestant King William, Galway declined. It wasn't until the last half of this century that it regained some of its importance and wealth.

Galway Legends
Because of the dearth of physical old stuff, the town milks its legends. Here are a few you'll encounter repeatedly:

In the 15th century, the mayor, one of the Lynch tribe, condemned his son to death for the murder of a Spaniard. When no one in town could be found to hang the popular boy, the dad—who loved justice more than his son—did it himself.

Columbus is said to have stopped in Galway in 1477. He may have been inspired by tales of the voyage of St. Brandon, the Irish monk who is thought by some (mostly Irish) to have beaten Columbus to the New World by nearly a thousand years.

On the main drag you'll find a pub called the King's Head. It was originally given to the man who chopped the head off of King Charles I in 1649. For his safety he settled in Galway, about as far from London as an Englishman could go back then.

Every sight in town finds a way to tell you the story about the Claddagh ring—so I won't.

Planning Your Time

Galway's sights are little more than pins on which to hang the old town. The joy of Galway is its street scene. You could see its "sights" in three hours, but without an evening in town, you missed the best. Many spend three nights here and two days: one for the town and another for a side trip to Connemara, the Burren, or the Aran Islands. Tour companies make day trips to all three regions cheap and easy.

Orientation (tel. code: 091)

The center of Galway is Eyre Square. Within two blocks of the square you'll find the TI, Aran boat offices, a bike rental shop, a tour pick-up point, the best cheap beds, and the train station. The train and bus station butt up against the Great Southern Hotel, a huge gray railroad hotel that overlooks and dominates Eyre Square. The lively old town lies between Eyre Square and the river. From Eyre Square, Williamsgate Street leads right through the old town (changing names several times) to Wolfe Tone Bridge. Nearly everything you'll see and do is within a few minutes' walk of this spine.

Tourist Information: The TI, just off the lower side of Eyre Square at the corner of Victoria Place and Merchants Road, is a busy center with a bookshop and many booking services (Jul–Aug daily 9:00–20:00, off-season Mon–Sat 9:00–17:45, Sun 9:00–12:45, tel. 091/563-081). Pick up the TI's *Galway Magazine* (£1, includes three walking tours). The free "List," a bimonthly entertainment newsletter, lists all the happenings in town.

Helpful Hints

Crowd Control: Expect huge crowds—and higher prices—during the Galway Arts festival (15 days in mid-July) and the Galway Races (late July/early August, three days in mid-September, and three days in late October).

Bike Rental: Irish Cycle Hire is next to the Great Western Hotel opposite the station (£6 for 24 hours, daily 9:30–18:00, tel. 091/561-498).

Laundry: Prospect Hill Launderette (Mon–Sat 8:30–18:00, closed Sun, £4 self-serve, £7 drop off, 44 Prospect Hill, 100 meters from town square, tel. 091/568-343).

Internet Access: Internet Arcade in Fun World on Eyre Square rents Internet access for £3 per hour (tel. 091/561-415).

Sights—Medieval Galway's "Latin Quarter"

From the top of Eyre Square, **Williamsgate Street** (named for the old main gate of the Norman town wall that once stood here) is the spine of medieval Galway, leading downhill straight to the Corrib River. While the road changes names several times (William, Shop, High, and Quay Streets), it leads generally downhill and straight past these sights:

Lynch's Castle (now a bank), Galway's best surviving 16th-century fortified townhouse, was the home of the Lynch family— the most powerful of the town's 14 tribes. More than 60 Lynch mayors ruled Galway in the 16th and 17th centuries.

St. Nicholas' Church (half a block off the main street on the right) is the finest surviving medieval building in town (1320) and is dedicated to St. Nicholas of Myra, the patron saint of sailors. Columbus is said to have worshiped here in 1477 while undoubtedly contemplating a scary voyage. Its interior is littered with obscure town history (£1 donation for admission). On Saturday morning a wonderful market surrounds the church.

Quais Pub and Restaurant, once owned by "Humanity Dick," an 18th-century member of Parliament who was the original animal-rights activist, is worth a peek inside for its lively interior. The lane just before it leads to the 100-seat Druid Theatre. Drop by to see if anything's playing tonight (£8 tickets for top-notch contemporary Irish theater).

Spanish Arch/City Museum, overlooking the Corrib River, is the best surviving chunk of the old city wall. The Spanish Arch (1584), the place where Spanish ships would unload their cargo, is a reminder of the trading importance Galway once enjoyed. The tiny museum is humble—but if it's fragments of old Galway you're looking for, this is where they're kept (£1, May–Oct daily 10:00–13:00, 14:15–17:15, closed off-season, tel. 091/567-641). The Fisheries Tower (nearby on Wolfe Tone Bridge) expects to open in 2000 with more of the same.

At the **Corrib River** you'll find a riverside park perfect for a picnic (although the town's best chippie, McDonagh's, is across the street). Over the river (southeast of the bridge) is the modern housing project that, in the 1930s, replaced the original Claddagh. The Claddagh was a picturesque Gaelic-speaking fishing village with

Galway

a strong tradition of independence—and open sewers. This gaggle of thatched cottages actually functioned as an independent community with its own "king" until early in this century. Nothing survives today except for the tradition of the popular Claddagh ring—two hands holding a heart—which comes with a fascinating story.

Notice the monument (just before the bridge), given to Galway by the people of Genoa, celebrating Columbus' visit here in 1477. (That acknowledgment, from a town known in Italy for its stinginess, helps to substantiate the murky visit.) From the bridge look up the river. The green copper dome marks the new city cathedral. Down the river is a tiny harbor with a few of Galway's famous square-rigged "hooker" fishing ships tied up and on display. Beyond that a huge park of reclaimed land is popular with the local kids for Irish football and hurling. From there the promenade leads to the resort town of Salthill.

Siamsa, Galway's folk theatre, features Irish music, singing, dancing, and folk drama mid-June through August at 20:45 (Claddagh Hall, Nimmos Pier, tel. 091/755479).

Sights—Galway

▲**Walking Tour**—Kay Davis enjoys taking small groups on grandmotherly two-hour walks through old Galway. Starting at the TI, she covers Eyre Square, the cathedral, and the old town and then finishes up at the Spanish Arch (£3.50 tickets at TI, Jun–Sept Mon–Fri at 11:30, Kay also does private walks, tel. 091/792-431). Western Heritage does a similar walk at 14:30 (same price and starting point, specifics at TI).

▲**Quick City Bus Tours**—Lally Tours' open-top double-deck bus tour of greater Galway gives a good 60-minute overview of the downtown sights and an interesting look at Galway beyond where you'll be walking (£5, 2/hrly, departing from top of Eyre Square, tel. 091/562-905).

▲**Eyre Square**—In the Middle Ages this was a green just outside the town wall. The square is named for the mayor who, in 1710, gave the land to the city. While still called Eyre Square, it now contains John F. Kennedy Park—established in memory of the Irish-descended president's visit in 1963 a few months before he was assassinated. (While Kennedy is celebrated as the first Irish Catholic president, there have been a dozen Irish presidents of Protestant Ulster stock.) On a sunny day Eyre Square is a popular grassy hangout. Walk to the rust-colored Quincentennial Fountain (built in 1984 to celebrate the 500th anniversary of the incorporation of the city). The sails represent Galway's "hooker" fishing ships and the trading vessels that made Galway a trading center so long ago. The Browne Doorway, from a 1627 fortified townhouse, is a reminder of the 14 family "tribes" that once ruled the town. Each had a town castle—much like the towers that characterize the towns of Tuscany with their feuding noble families. So little survives of medieval Galway that the town makes a huge deal of any surviving window or crest. The cannons are from the Crimean War (1854). The statue is of Patrick O'Connor, Galway's favorite Gaelic poet, who'd sit on a limestone wall, as sculpted, recording the local life.

The Eyre Square Shopping Center (arcaded entry from the square) leads to a surviving piece of the old town wall that includes two reconstructed towers. Today it's a busy, modern shopping mall.

▲▲**Cathedral (of our Lady Assumed into Heaven and Saint Nicholas)**—Opened by American Cardinal Cushing in 1965, this is one of the last great stone churches built in Europe. The interior is a treat: mahogany pews set on green Connemara marble floors under a Canadian cedar ceiling. The acoustically correct cedar accompanies the church's fine pipe organ. Two thousand worshipers sit in the round facing the central altar. A Dublin woman carved 14 larger-than-life stations of the cross. The carving above the chapel (left of entry) is from the old St. Nicholas church. Explore the modern stained glass. Find the Irish holy family—with Mary knitting and Jesus offering Joseph a cup of tea. The window depicting the Last Supper is particularly creative— find the 12 apostles. Church bulletins at the doorway tell of upcoming masses and concerts (tel. 091/563-577).

Salmon Weir Bridge—This bridge was the local bridge of sighs. It led from the courthouse (opposite the church) to the prison (torn down to build the church—unlikely in the United States). Today the bridge provides a fun view of the fishing action. Salmon run up this river most of the summer (look for them). Fishermen, who wear waders and carry walking sticks to withstand the strong current, book long in advance to get half-day appointments for a casting spot.

Canals multiplied in this city (sometimes called the Venice of Ireland) to power more water mills.

Sights—Outer Galway

▲**Galway Irish Crystal Heritage Center**—This is a grand-sounding name in a grand new building for a sight made to order for big bus groups. Still, this cheap and handy (for drivers) tour is the place to see the making of Irish crystal. Tours go every half hour. After a guided tour through the museum and a quick look at craftsmen cutting crystal (Mon–Fri only), you sit for 10 minutes while a video subliminally sells you crystal while wowing you with Galway sights. The museum, more interesting than Galway's City Museum, gives you a good rundown on the Claddagh Village and a chance to see a large "hooker" named Fiona (£2, Mon–Fri 9:00– 20:00, Sat 9:00–18:00, Sun 10:00–18:00, less off-season, good cafeteria, five minutes out of Galway on the Dublin road N6, or take the Merlin Park bus—every 20 minutes—from Eyre Square, tel. 091/757-311).

▲**Salthill**—This small resort packs pubs, discos, a splashy water park, amusement centers, and a fairground up against a fine mile-long beach promenade. For sunny time on the beach, a relaxing sunset stroll, late-night traditional music, or later-night disco action, Salthill hops (bus #1 or #2 from Eyre Square).

Dog Racing—Join the locals and cheer on the greyhounds on Tuesday and Friday evenings from 20:15 to 22:00 (£3, barking distance from my recommended B&Bs, a 10-min walk from Eyre Square).

Tours to the Burren and Connemara—Several companies do all-day £10 tours of the regions of interest near Galway. Connemara tours include the Quiet Man Cottage, Kylemore Abbey, Clifden, and the Famine Village. Burren tours cover Kinvara, Aillwee Cave, the Poulnabrone Dolmen, and the Cliffs of Moher (tours go most days about 10:00–17:00, Lally tours tel. 091/562-905, O'Neachtain tours tel. 091/553-188).

Nightlife in Galway

▲**Traditional Irish Music in Pubs**—Galway (like Dingle and Doolin) is a mecca for good Irish music (nightly 21:30–23:30). Unlike Dingle and Doolin, this is a university town (enrollment: 12,000), and many pubs are often overrun with noisy students. Still, the chances of landing a seat close to a churning band surrounded by new Irish friends are good any evening of the year. Touristy and student pubs are found and filled along the main drag down from Eyre Square to the Spanish Arch and across Wolfe Tone Bridge along William Street West and Dominick Street Upper. Across the bridge start at **Monroe's** with its vast and music-filled interior. Several other pubs feature almost-nightly traditional music within earshot.

Pubs along the main drag known for Irish music include **Taaffe's** (nightly music, plus Thu, Fri, and Sat at 17:00, Shop Street, across from St. Nicholas Church) and **The Quays** (very young scene, Quay Street).

For a place with an older crowd, I like **The Lisheen**—with live traditional music nightly at 22:00. Enjoy the painting of the firelit "crossroads dance," an event that still takes place (5 Bridge Street, tel. 091/563-804). And **Pucan Pub**, a smoky cauldron of music and beer drinking with an older crowd, is also worth a look (just off Eyre Square on Forster Street).

Sleeping in Galway
(£1 = about $1.50, tel. code: 091)
Sleep Code: **S** = Single, **D** = Double/Twin, **T** = Triple, **Q** = Quad, **b** = bathroom, **t** = toilet only, **s** = shower only, **CC** = Credit Card (Visa, MasterCard, Amex).

There are three price tiers for most beds in Galway: high season (Easter–October), off-season, and charge-what-you-like festival times (e.g., race weekends and the last three weeks in July). I've listed high-season rates. B&Bs simply play the market. If you're on a tight budget, call a few and see what the prices do. All B&Bs include a full fried breakfast.

Sleeping in Hotels

Park House Hotel, a plush business-class hotel, is ideally located a block from the train station and Eyre Square. Its 57 spacious rooms come with all the comforts you'd expect (Db-£90 is the "corporate rate" you should get most of the year, ask for a discount, Sunday night is slow and rooms can rent for Db-£75, CC:VMA, elevator, free garage, Forster Street, tel. 091/564-924, fax 091/569-219, e-mail: parkhouse@tinet.ie).

Great Southern Hotel, filled with palatial Old World elegance, marks the end of the Dublin–Galway train line and the beginning of Galway. Since 1845, it's been Galway's landmark hotel (Db-£125–140, some discounts during slow times, CC:VMA, at the head of Eyre Square, tel. 091/564-041, fax 091/566-704, e-mail: res@galway.gsh.ie).

Jurys Galway Inn offers all the American comforts in a 128-room modern hotel centrally located where the old town hits the river. Big bright rooms have two double beds and huge modern bathrooms (£66 for all rooms, whether filled by a single, a couple, 3 adults, or a family of 4; £52 off-season, breakfast is extra, elevator, lots of tour groups, parking-£5, CC:VMA, nonsmoking floor, Quay Street, tel. 091/566-444, fax 091/568-415, U.S. tel. 800/843-3311, e-mail: inquiry@jurys.com).

Sleeping in Hostels

Kinlay House is the no-nonsense place for budget train travelers to sleep. Just 100 yards from the train station, it's a smoky slumber mill with 150 beds (1–8 beds per room) in bare, clean, and simple rooms. Prices range from £8 for a bed in an eight-bed room to £30 for a Db (CC:VM, includes continental breakfast, elevator, self-service kitchen, Internet access, launderette, luggage storage, and budget USIT travel agency downstairs, across from TI on Merchants Road, tel. 091/565-244, fax 091/565-245, e-mail: kingal@usit.ie).

Great Western House, even closer to the station, is similarly big, plain, scruffy, and cheap (270 beds, S-£18, D-£28, Db-£32, Q-£12.50 per bed, dorm beds-£10, includes continental breakfast, lockers free with deposit, elevator, kitchen, Frenchville Lane, tel. 091/561-150, e-mail: shaungwh@iol.ie). Easygoing people of any age feel comfortable in either of these hostels.

Sleeping in B&Bs on College Road

Drivers, following city center signs into Galway, drive right by a string of B&Bs just after the greyhound racing stadium. These are a five-minute walk from Eyre Square. The first two listed are the best values. Most are clever and scheming in the battle for the tourist punt. The last one is cheapest and is equally central, but it's in a different area.

College Crest Guest House, a proud establishment with 10 big, fresh rooms and a cushy lounge, feels like a small hotel (Sb-£26–28, Db-£40–50, Tb-£60, CC:VM, nonsmoking, closest to town at 5 College Road, tel. & fax 091/564-744). Marion Fitzgerald enjoys her work and runs this place with flair, offering the best value on the street.

Petra House, a peaceful-feeling brick building, rents six fine rooms, including one family room (Sb-£30, Db-£45, CC:VM, second door from stadium on right at 29 College Road, tel. & fax 091/566-580, run by Joan and Frank Maher).

Balcony House B&B rents nine decent rooms (Db-£36, family deals in quads, 27 College Road, tel. 091/563-438, Michael and Teresa Coyne).

The Graduate B&B rents 10 rooms; some are wonderful, but the ones on the garden out back are cramped and overpriced (Db-£40–50, CC:VM, 26A College Road, tel. 091/569-534, e-mail: libran@indigo.ie).

Copper Beech House B&B rents five rooms a bit cheaper than its neighbors but with no lounge, tight quarters, and an absentee owner (Db-£32–45, CC:VM, 26 College Road, tel. 091/569-544).

Aaron House B&B rents 14 sleepable rooms (Sb-£25, Db-£35 through most of the year, CC:VM, 25 College Road, tel. & fax 091/563-315, e-mail: aaron@indigo.ie).

Lynfield House B&B rents five plain, practical rooms (small Db-£25, Db-£40, CC:VM, 9 College Road, tel. 091/567-845, fax 092/463-346, e-mail: lynfield@tinet.ie).

Prospect Hill Road (leaving Eyre Square from Richardson's Bar) is lined with small row houses, many of which do B&B. Mrs. **Bridie Flanagan's B&B** is a humble, friendly old home with a welcoming living room and four rooms—two big and two cramped (tiny D-£30, fine Db-£32, T-£42, 85 Prospect Hill, tel. 091/561-515).

Sleeping out of Town in Salthill

Carraig Beag B&B, the classiest, friendliest, and most peaceful of all, is a big brick home on a residential street a block off the beach just beyond the resort town of Salthill. Catherine Lydon, with the help of her husband Paddy, rents six big, bright, fresh, and comfy rooms with a welcoming living room and a social breakfast table (Sb-£30–35, Db-£36–40, family room-£50–60; 8-minute drive from Galway, follow the beach past Salthill, take 2nd right after golf course on Knocknacarra Road, and go 2 blocks to 1 Burren View Heights; tel. 091/521-696). The #2 bus (90p, 3/hrly) goes from Eyre Square to the Knocknacarra stop at the B&B's doorstep. Catherine can arrange for tour pickups at her place.

Eating in Galway

Being a tourist and college town, the city is filled with colorful, inexpensive eateries. People everywhere seem to be enjoying their food. Each of these places is at the bottom of the old town within a block or two of Jurys Inn.

River God is a bistro/restaurant passionately run by Patric Juillet, who cooks fine "world French" cuisine. He slices, dices, and prices as if his bottom line is filling people with very good food (£5 lunch deals, £12 three-course dinners, Mon–Sat 12:00–22:00, Sun 16:00–22:00, no reservations—but a great corner pub downstairs to enjoy an ancient snug and a fresh beer until your table's ready, you can bring your beer to dinner, 2 Quay Street, tel. 091/565-811).

Brasserie KC is a mod, candlelit place serving good Continental food (£10–15, nightly 17:00–22:30, next to Jurys at Quay Street, tel. 091/561-826).

Kirwan's Lane Creative Cuisine, considered Galway's best restaurant, is a dressy place where reservations are required (£25 dinners, open from 18:00, Kirwan's Lane a block from Jurys, tel. 091/568-266).

Busker Brownes is a confusing complex of three eateries in a smoky, sprawling, pubby place popular for its good cheap food (£6 meals, 11:00–20:30, walk far to the back for better seating, Cross Street and Kirwan's Lane, tel. 091/563-101).

McDonagh's Fish and Chips is a favorite chippie. They have a fast, cheap section and a classier restaurant. If you're determined to try Galway oysters, remember that they're in season September through April only. Other times you'll eat Pacific oysters—which doesn't make much sense to me (£3 cheap lunch, £10 in restaurant, Mon–Sat 12:00–24:00, Sun 17:00–24:00, non-smoking, 22 Quay Street, tel. 091/565-01).

The **Galway Bakery Company (GBC)** is a popular and basic place for a quick Irish meal (£3–6 meals in the ground-floor cafeteria, more pricey restaurant upstairs, 9 Williamsgate Street, near Eyre Square).

If you have a car, consider a **Dunguaire Medieval Castle Banquet,** in Kinvarra, a 30-minute drive south of Galway (for more information, see "Kinvarra," near end of chapter). The 17:30 banquet can be done very efficiently as you're driving into or out of Galway (B&Bs are accustomed to late arrivals if you call).

Transportation Connections—Galway

By train to: Dublin (4/day, 3 hrs). For **Limerick, Tralee,** and **Rosslare,** you'll change in or near Dublin. Train info: tel. 091/564-222.

By bus to: Ennis (5/day, 1 hr), **Doolin/Cliffs** (3/day, 2.5 hrs), **Rosslare** (3/day, 6.5 hrs), and **Dublin** (8/day, 3.5 hrs, L6). Bus info: tel. 091/562-000 or 091/563-555. Nestor Travel, among other companies, runs a cheap and fast bus service from Galway (Forster Street Bus Park) to Dublin (Tara Street Dart Station at George's Quay) and the Dublin airport (£5, 4/day, 3 hrs, tel. 091/797-144 for specifics).

ARAN ISLANDS

The Arans—an extension of the Burren—are made up of three limestone islands: Inishmor, Inishmaan, and Inisheer. The largest, Inishmor (eight miles by two miles), is by far the most populated, interesting, and visited. The landscape of all three islands is harsh—windswept, rocky fields divided by stone walls and steep, rugged cliffs. During the winter severe gales sweep the islands; because of this, most of the settlements on Inishmor are found on its more peaceful eastern side.

There's a stark beauty about these islands and the simple lives its inhabitants eke out of six inches of topsoil and a mean sea. Precious little of the land is productive; in the past its people made a precarious living from fishing and farming. The layers of limestone rock meant that there was little natural soil. Farming soil has been built up by the islanders—the result of centuries of layering seaweed and sand together. The fields are small, divided by several thousand miles of dry-stone wall. Most of these are built in the Aran "gap" style, where angled upright stones are filled with smaller stones. This allows a farmer who wants to move stock to dismantle and rebuild the walls easily. Nowadays tourism boosts the local economy.

The islands are a Gaeltacht area. While the islanders speak Irish among themselves, they happily speak English for their visitors. Many of them have direct or personal connections with America and will ask you if you know their cousin Paddy in Boston.

Today the 900 people of Inishmor (literally, "the big island") greet as many as 2,000 visitors a day. The vast majority of these are day-trippers. They'll hop on a minibus at the dock for a 2.5-hour tour to the Dun Aengus fort and spend an hour or two browsing through the few shops or sitting at a picnic table outside a pub with their Guinness.

The other islands, Inishmaan and Inisheer, are smaller, much less populated, and less touristed. While extremely quiet, they have B&Bs, daily flights, and ferry service. For most, the big island is quiet enough.

Kilronan, on Inishmor

By far the Aran Islands' largest town, Kilronan is still just a village. Groups of backpackers wash ashore with the landing of each ferry. Minibuses, bike shops, and a few old men in pony carts sop up the tourists. There are five or six shops and about as many pubs, restaurants, and B&Bs. Most of Kilronan huddles around the pier.

The Heritage Center, post office, bank (open only on Wednesday), and best folk-music pub are a few blocks inland. The huge SPAR supermarket, two blocks inland from the harbor, seems too big for the tiny community. Several huts rent bikes (about £3/4 hrs, £6/24 hrs).

Tourist Information: The TI is helpful, but don't rely on them for accommodations. The only people who work with them are out of town and desperate (daily 10:00–18:45 in summer, shorter hours Mar–Oct, faces the harbor, tel. 099/61263).

Getting around Inishmor

Just about anything rolling functions as a taxi. A trip from Kilronan to Dun Aengus costs about £2 in a shared minibus. Flag them down and don't hesitate to bargain. Pony carts cost about £20 per load for a trip to the west end of the island. Biking is great. Bikers take the high road over and the low road back—fewer hills, scenic shoreline, and at low tide, 50 seals sunbathing.

Sights—Inishmor

▲**Aran's Heritage Center**—This little museum, while nothing impressive, offers a worthwhile introduction to the island that covers the island's geology, its archeological wonders, and the traditional lifestyle (£2.50, or £4 combo ticket with movie, daily 10:00–19:00, tel. 099/61355).

Man of Aran—The 1934 movie *Man of Aran*, giving a good look at traditional island life with an all-local cast, is shown at the Heritage Center (£2.50, 6 shows/day in summer, one hour). The movie features *currachs* (canoelike boats) in a storm, fishing for sharks with hand-held harpoons, how the fields were made from bare rock, and turn-of-the-century life when you couldn't rent bikes.

▲**Island Minibus Tours**—There couldn't be more than 100 vehicles on the island, and the majority of them seem to be minibuses. A line of buses, awaiting the arrival of each ferry, offer 2.5-hour, £5 island tours. Talk with several to find a driver who likes to talk. I learned that 900 islanders live in 14 villages, with three elementary schools and three churches. Most own a small detached field where they keep a couple of cows (sheep are too much trouble). When pressured for more information, my guide explained that there are 400 different flowers and 19 different types of bees on the island. The tour, a convenient time-saver, zips you to the end of the island for a quick stroll in the desolate fields, gives you 10 minutes to wander through the historic but visually unimpressive "seven churches," and then drops you for 90 minutes at Dun Aengus (20 minutes to hike up, 30 minutes at the fort, 20 minutes back, 20 minutes in café or shops at drop-off point) before running you back to Kilronan. Ask your driver to take you back

Inishmor Island

along the smaller coastal road (scenic beaches and sunbathing seals at low tide).

▲▲▲**Dun Aengus**—This is the island's blockbuster sight. The stone fortress hangs spectacularly and precariously on the edge of a cliff 300 feet above the Atlantic. The crashing waves seem to say, "You've come to the end of the world." Little is known about this 2,000-year-old Celtic fort. Its concentric walls are 13 feet thick and 10 feet high. As an added defense, the fort is ringed with a commotion of spiky stones sticking up like lances called a *chevaux-de-frise* (literally, "Frisian horses"; named for the Frisian soldiers who used pikes like these to stop a charging cavalry). Slowly, as the cliff erodes, hunks of the fort fall into the sea. Dun Aengus doesn't get crowded until after 11:00. I enjoyed half an hour completely alone at 10:00 in the tourist season. Be there early or late if you can (free, always open, 5.5 miles from Kilronan). A small museum displays findings from recent digs and tells the story of the fort.

Seven Churches (Na Seacht Teampaill)—Close to the western tip of the island, this gathering of ruined chapels, monastic houses, and fragments of a high cross dates from the 8th to 11th centuries. The island is dotted with early Christian reminders of how, in the fifth century, Christianity was brought to the islands by St. Enda, who established a monastery on the island. Many great monks studied under Enda. Among these "Irish apostles," who started

Ireland's "Age of Saints and Scholars" (A.D. 500–900), was Columba, the founder of the monastery of Iona in Scotland. **Kilmurvey**—The island's second village sits below Dun Aengus. With a gaggle of homes, a laid-back hostel (listed below), a B&B, a great sheltered beach, and a pub, this (except for the folk music in the pub) is the place for solitude.

Pub Music—Several pubs in Kilronan offer live music nearly nightly in summer. Off-season you're likely to find music on Wednesday, Friday, and Saturday evenings. Joe Watty's Pub, just past the post office, has reliably good Irish folk music and tons of tourists. Tigh Fitz, on the airport road, has a more locals and folk music and dancing on Friday, Saturday, and Sunday.

Other pubs offer Irish tunes but with musical detours beyond the tin whistle. The town hall (Halla Ronain) becomes a dance hall on most Saturday and Sunday nights, when from midnight to 02:00 locals have a *ceilidh* (kay-lee), the Irish equivalent of a hoedown.

Sleeping in Kilronan, Inishmor
(£1 = about $1.50, tel. code: 099, mail: Kilronan, Aran Islands)

Remember, this is a poor island. Most rooms are plain with sparse plumbing. No one takes credit cards.

The Pier House stands solidly a hundred yards beyond the pier offering 12 decent rooms, a cozy sitting room with a fireplace, a dramatic setting, and sea views from each of its rooms (Db-£40, tel. 099/61417, fax 099/61122).

Clai Ban, about the only really cheery place in town, is worth the 10-minute walk from the pier (Db-£30–34, walk past the bank out of town and down a lane on the left, tel. 099/61111, fax 099/61423, Marion Hernon).

St. Brendan's B&B, hiding a cozy living room behind ivy-covered walls and a wind-blown garden, rents eight rooms (D-£26, Db-£30, about £5 less outside of summer, save £2 if you take a continental breakfast, tel. 099/61149).

Bayview House, the biggest place in town overlooking the harbor, rents eight smoky ghost-town rooms (D-£36, Db-£40 in July and August, less otherwise, tel. & fax 099/61260).

Costello's B&B has four plain rooms in a plain home in a fine garden setting (D-£28, Db-£32, tel. 099/61241, Sally Costello).

Kilronan Hostel, overlooking the harbor above the Joe Mac Pub, is cheap but noisy (£9 beds, 4- to 6-bed rooms, self-service kitchen, laundry service, tel. 099/61255).

Dun Aengus Hostel is for those who really want to get away from things. It's located near Dun Aengus, five miles from Kilronan, and is surrounded by birds, stone walls, and vast views It's also near a pub (with good music), a restaurant, and a fine beach (£7 per bed in 2- and 8-bed rooms, communal kitchen, small shop, free pick-up upon arrival if you call, tel. 099/61318, run by friendly manager, Janette).

While Kilronan is getting pretty touristy, you can get out into the Aran countryside and find true peace. The **Man of Aran B&B** is as classy as a thatched cottage can be. Rooms are quiet and rustic and have fireplaces. The restaurant uses all organic, home-grown vegetables and herbs (£15 meals), and the setting is pristine (this is where the movie was filmed, D-£36, Db-£42, reserve well in advance, 100 meters past the Dun Aengus turnoff, four miles out of Kilronan, tel. 099/61301).

Eating in Kilronan

Kilronan's cafés dish up soup, soda bread, sandwiches, and tea. Joe Watty's Bar does hot pub lunches. The Sein Ceibh is popular for its take-away fish and chips. The Aran Fisherman does a good dinner. The SPAR supermarket has all the groceries you'll need (Mon–Sat 9:00–20:00, Sun 10:00–17:00).

Transportation Connections—Aran Islands

By ferry from Rossaveal: Island Ferries sails to Inishmor from Rossaveal, a port 20 miles west of Galway (3/day in summer, 2/day off-season, 40-minute crossing but allow two hours including bus connection from Galway, £15 round-trip boat crossing, £5 round-trip Galway–Rossaveal shuttle bus, walk-in customers usually buy the boat ticket and get the bus connection for £1). Shuttle buses depart from Galway 75 minutes before the boat sails and return to Galway immediately after each boat arrives. Summer schedule: from Rossaveal at 10:30, 13:30, and 18:30; from Inishmor at 9:00, 12:00, and 16:30. Island Ferries has two offices, each within a block of the Galway TI (tel. 091/561-767). Boats go in anything less than a gale (only a couple departures a year are canceled). Don't worry about seat availability; buses and boats are added as needed.

By ferry from Doolin: This ferry is handy if you're in Doolin, but it's notorious for being canceled because of wind or tides (for specifics, see "Doolin," below).

By plane: Aer Arann, a friendly and flexible little airline, flies four planes a day and stops at all three islands (£35 round-trip, groups of 4 or more: £29 each). They fly their nine-seat planes from the Connemara Regional Airport, 20 miles west of Galway (not the Galway airport). A shuttle bus—£5 round-trip—runs from Galway for each flight. The Kilronan airport is small (baggage is transported from the plane to the "gate" in a shopping cart). A minibus shuttle to and from Kilronan costs £2 round-trip (two miles from the airport). For reservations and late seat availability, tel. 091/593-034, fax 091/593-238. Ask for a 10 percent discount—they have lots of coupons out.

COUNTY CLARE AND THE BURREN

Those connecting Dingle in the south with Galway, the urban center of the west, can entertain themselves along the way by skipping through the fascinating landscape and tidy villages of County Clare. Ennis, the major city of the county, with a medieval history and a market bustle, is a workaday Irish town ideal for anyone tired of the tourist crowds. The Cliffs of Moher, a series of dramatic cliffs overlooking the Atlantic, offer tenderfeet a thrilling hike. The Burren is a unique, windblown, limestone wasteland that hides an abundance of flora, fauna, caves, and history. For your evening entertainment you can join a tour bus in a castle for a medieval banquet at Kinvarra or join traditional Irish music enthusiasts from around Europe at tin-whistling Doolin.

Planning Your Time

By train and bus, your gateway to this region is Ennis on the south and Galway from the north. By car the region can be an enjoyable daylong drive-through or a destination in itself. None of the sights has to take much time. But do get out and hike a bit.

If driving between Dingle/Tralee in the south and Galway/Aran Islands in the north, here's a day I'd prefer to the fast road via Limerick: north from Tralee to catch the Tarbert–Killimer car ferry (avoiding the 80-mile drive around the Shannon estuary, see "Route Tips" at the end of Dingle chapter), then drive the scenic coastal route to the Cliffs of Moher for an hour break. The scenic drive through the Burren, with a couple of stops and a tour of the caves, takes about two hours. There's a 17:30 medieval banquet at the Dunguaire Castle near Kinvarra (just 30 minutes south of Galway).

Sights—County Clare and the Burren

▲▲▲**Cliffs of Moher**—A visit to the Cliffs of Moher is one of Ireland's great natural thrills. For five miles the dramatic cliffs soar as high as 700 feet above the Atlantic. Drivers park at the Visitors Centre (£1, TI office—daily at least 9:30–17:30, shop, and cafeteria; three public buses stop here daily in the summer). From the center, walk 200 yards past harpists and accordion players along a low wall of the local Liscannor slate (notice the squiggles made by worms, eels, and snails a few years ago when the slate was still mud on the sea floor) to the cliff edge. O'Brien's Tower (1853) marks the highest point.

For the best thrill, read the warning, consider the risk, then step over the slate barrier and down onto the stone platform. Here there are no crowds. If you're a risk-taking fool, gingerly belly out to peek over the ledge. You'll find yourself in a dramatic world where the only sounds are the waves, the wind, the gulls, and your stomach signaling frantically for help. There's a particularly

peaceful corner of the platform over on the far right. On the far left, watch the birds play in the updrafts. In the distance, on windy days, the Aran Islands can be seen wearing their white necklace.
Doolin—This town is a strange phenomenon. Tourists go directly from Paris or Munich to Doolin. It's on the touristic map for its three pubs that feature Irish folk music nightly. A few years ago, this was a mecca. Irish musicians came together here to jam before a few lucky aficionados. But now the crowds and the foreigners are overwhelming the musicians, and the quality of music is not as reliable. Still, Irish as well as European music lovers crowd the pubs, and the bodhran beat goes on. In 2000 Doolin plans to entertain visitors with a new heritage music center—a museum of traditional Irish music.

Doolin has plenty of accommodations (see "Sleeping," below), several good restaurants, and a Greek island-without-the-sun ambience. Each pub serves decent dinners before the music starts. The "town" is just a few homes and shops strung out along a valley road from the tiny harbor. Nearest the harbor, the Lower Village (Fisherstreet) has **O'Connor's Pub** (tel. 065/707-4168) and is the closest thing to a commercial center. A mile farther up the road, the Upper Village (Roadford) straddles a bridge with the other two destination pubs, **McGann's** (tel. 065/707-4133) and **McDermott's** (tel. 065/707-4328). Music starts around 21:30 and finishes around midnight. On my last trip I hit Doolin on a medi-ocre music night. The craic is fine regardless.

From Doolin you can hike or bike (rentals in town) up the Burren Way for three miles to the Cliffs of Moher. (Get advice locally on the trail condition and safety.)

The boats from Doolin to the Aran Islands can be handy but are often canceled. Even a balmy day can be too windy (or the tide can be too low) to allow for a sailing from Doolin's crude little port. If you are traveling by car and have time limits, don't risk sailing from Doolin. Without a car you can travel on from the Aran Islands by the bigger boats, so Doolin might work for you (one-hour cruise, one departure/day, leaving at 10:00, returning at 16:00, £20 return, tel. 065/707-4455 to see what's sailing).
Lisdoonvarna—This town of 1,000 was known for centuries for its spa and its matchmakers. Today, except for a couple of Septem-ber weeks during its Matchmaking Festival, it's pretty sleepy. (The bank is open one day a week.) Still, it's more of a town than Doolin and, apart from festival time, less touristy. Lisdoonvarna has reliably good traditional music in its pubs. I'd stay here rather than in Doolin (a couple miles away, see "Sleeping," below) and commute.
▲▲**The Burren**—Literally, the "rocky place," the Burren is just that. The 50-square-mile limestone plateau is so barren a disap-pointed Cromwell surveyor described it as "a savage land, yielding

The Burren

neither water enough to drown a man, nor a tree to hang him, nor soil enough to bury him." But he wasn't much of a botanist, because the Burren is a unique ecosystem, with flora that has changed little since the last Ice Age 10,000 years ago. It's also rich in prehistoric and early Christian sights. The first human inhabitants of the Burren came about 6,000 years ago. Today this "Limestone Land" is littered with more than 2,000 historic sites, including about 500 Iron Age stone forts.

Botany of the Burren in Brief: The Burren is a story of water, rock, geological force, and time. It supports the greatest diversity of plants in Ireland. Like nowhere else, Mediterranean and Arctic wildflowers bloom side by side in the Burren. It's an orgy of cross-pollination that attracts more insects than Doolin does music lovers—even beetles help out. Limestone, created from layers of sea mud, is the basis of the Burren. (This same basic slab resurfaces 10 miles or so out to sea to form the Aran Islands.) The earth's crust heaved it up. The glaciers swept it bare—dropping boulders as they receded. Rain slowly drilled potholes into the surface. Rainwater cut through weak parts in the limestone, leaving crevices on the surface and Europe's most extensive system of caves below. These puddles grew algae, which dried into a powder. That, combined with bug parts and rabbit turds (Irish hares abound in the Burren), creates a very special soil. Plants and flowers fill the cracks in the limestone. Grasses and shrubs don't do well here, and wild goats eat down any trees that try to grow, giving tender little flowers a chance to enjoy the sun. Different flowers appear at different months, sharing space rather than competing. The flowers are best in June and July.

Sightseeing the Burren: The drive from Kilfenora to Ballyvaughan offers the best quick swing through the historic Burren.

Kilfenora (five miles southeast of Lisdoonvarna) is a good starting point. Its humble but hardworking community-run Burren Centre gives a quick tour of its one-room museum followed by an intense 12-minute video explaining the geology and botany of the region (£2.50, daily 9:30–18:00 in summer, closed in winter, tel. 065/88030). You'll see copies of a fine eighth-century golden collar and ninth-century silver brooch (now in Dublin's National Museum). A bigger and better center is planned for 2000. The ruined church next door has a couple of 12th-century crosses but isn't much to see. Mass is still held in the church, which claims the Pope as its bishop. (In the 16th century, when the Anglican English were taking over Ireland, the Pope defended the town as best he could—by personally declaring himself its bishop.) For lunch in Kilfenora consider the cheap and cheery Burren Centre lunchroom or the more atmospheric Vaughan's Pub (tel. 065/88004).

At **Leamaneh Castle**, a ruined shell of a fortified 17th-century house not open to anyone these days, turn north on R480 (direction: Ballyvaughan). After about five miles you'll hit the start of the real barren Burren and see a stone table a few hundred yards off the road (to the east, toward an ugly gray metal barn building).

This is the **Portal Dolmen** (also called the Poulnabrone Dolmen—a stone table). Two hundred years ago, locals called this a "druid's altar." Four thousand years ago it was a grave. Wander over for a look. (It's crowded in midday with tour buses, but it's all yours early or late.)

Be a geologist. Wander for some quiet time with the wildflowers. You're walking across a former seabed. Look for fossils: white smudges were coral. Scratches on rocks were ground by other rocks in a retreating glacier. The boulder debris was left by the glaciers. V-shaped valleys were carved by glacial runoff.

The **Cahercommann ring fort** (one of 500 or so in the area) can be seen on the crest of a hill just off the road about a half mile south of the Portal Dolmen. (You can park at the intersection and walk up the gray farm's driveway and through the gate marked "stone fort" for a look, but there's little to see.) The stretch from Portal Dolmen north to Ballyvaughan offers the starkest scenery.

The Aillwee Caves are touted as "Ireland's premier showcave." I couldn't resist a look. While fairly touristy and not worth the time or money if you've seen a lot of caves, they offer your easiest look at the massive system of caves that underlie the Burren. Your guide walks you 300 yards into the plain but impressive cave, giving a serious 30-minute geology lesson. During the Ice Age underground rivers carved countless caves like these. Brown bears, which became extinct a thousand years ago in Ireland, found this cave great for hibernating. But at a constant 50 degrees, I needed my sweater (£4, £14 family deal, daily 10:00 to about 18:00, clearly signposted just south of Ballyvaughan, tel. 065/77036).

In Ballyvaughan, **Burren Exposure** is your best first stop if you're entering the Burren from Galway. In a modern little building overlooking Galway Bay at the edge of the bleakness, its excellent three-part video presentation tells the geological, human, and floral story of this unique chunk of Ireland (£3.50, four 35-minute shows per hour, Apr–Oct 10:00–17:00, closed in winter, plush seaview cafeteria, tel. 065/77277).

Kinvarra—This two-pub town, between Ballyvaughan and Galway (half an hour from each), is waiting for something to happen in its minuscule harbor. It faces the Dunguaire Castle, a four-story tower house from 1520 standing a few yards out in the bay. (For B&Bs, see "Sleeping," below.)

The **Dunguaire Medieval Castle Banquet** is Kinvarra's most tourist-worthy sight. The 500-year-old Dunguaire Castle hosts a touristy but fun medieval banquet (17:30 and 20:30 almost nightly, tel. 091/637-108). The evening is as intimate as 55 tourists gathered under one time-stained barrel vault can be. For £30 you get a decent three-course meal with wine (or mead if you ask sweetly) served amid an entertaining evening of Irish tales and folk songs. Remember that in medieval times it was considered polite to flirt with wenches. It's a small and multitalented cast: one harpist and three singer/actors who serve the "lords and ladies" between tunes. The 40-minute medieval stage show that comes with dessert is the highlight (but the Ruthin banquet in North Wales is better).

Ennis—This simple little market town, the main town of County Clare (pop: 15,000), provides those relying on public transit with a handy transportation hub (good connections to Limerick, Dublin, and Galway; see "Transportation Connections," below) and a chance to wander around a workaday Irish town that is not reliant upon the tourist dollar.

The Franciscan monks arrived here in the 13th century. The town grew up around their friary. The Ennis Friary, from 1300, with some fine limestone carvings in its ruined walls, is worth a look (£1 includes a personalized tour, daily in summer 9:30–18:30). Ask the guide to fully explain the crucifixion symbolism in the 15th-century *Ecce Homo* carving. (Ennis regional TI tel. 065/682-8366.)

The town has its history, but apart from the friary, it's best simply wandered through. If you spend the night (see "Sleeping," below) you'll find plenty of live music in the pubs. In fact, Ennis is emerging as the next Doolin on the traditional music scene. **May Kearney's Pub** hosts paid musicians on Thursday, Friday, and Sunday nights and ad-lib music on other nights (across bridge from Friary, 100 meters up Newbridge Road, tel. 065/682-4888). **Quinn's** on Lower Merket Street and **Ciaran's Pub** and **Cruise's Pub,** both on Abbey Street, are also likely to have live music. **Bunratty Castle and Folk Museum**—I'd leave this most commercial and least lively of all European open-air folk museums to the jet-laggy big bus American tour groups (located just a potty stop from the Shannon Airport past Limerick on the road to Ennis).

Sleeping in County Clare and the Burren
(£1 = about $1.50)

Sleeping in Doolin (tel. code: 065)
Harbour View B&B is a fine modern house a mile from the Doolin fiddles overlooking the valley. Mrs. Cullinan keeps the fire on in the guests' living room (which is stocked with touring books and games) and serves a classy breakfast (Sb-£22, Db-£36, larger family room deals, on the main road halfway between Lisdoonvarna and the Cliffs of Moher next to the Statoil gas station, tel. 065/707-4154, fax 065/707-4935, e-mail: kathlen@tinet.ie). **Doolin Hostel,** right in Doolin's Lower Village, caters creatively to all the needs of backpackers there for the music (£8 dorm beds, D-£19, Lower Village, tel. 065/707-4006).

Sleeping in Lisdoonvarna (tel. code: 065)
Each of these three places is on the main "Galway" road near the center square and church. **Marchmont B&B** rents two large twin/family rooms and two small doubles in a fine old house (Db-£34, just past the post office, tel. 065/707-4050, Eileen Barrett). **Banner County Lodge** (D/Db-£30, tel. 065/707-4340) and **St. Genevieve's B&B** (D-£24–28, Db-£28–32, open May– Oct only, tel. 065/707-4074) are closer to the square but bigger, scruffier, and less personal.

Sleeping in Kinvarra (tel. code: 091)
Cois Cuain B&B is a small but stately house with a garden overlooking the square and harbor of the most charming village setting you'll find. Mary Walsh rents three super-homey rooms for nonsmokers (Db-£36, The Harbour, tel. 091/637-119).

Sleeping in Ennis (tel. code: 065)
These three places are clustered a block toward the town center from the train/bus station. **Greenlea B&B** is a charming little

place with three spacious and comfy rooms run in a simple way by Mary Conway (S-£13.50, D-£27, £1.50 less per person with a continental breakfast instead of a full fry, Station Road, tel. 065/682-9049). **Grey Gables B&B**, just across the street, is a bit more upscale and has four rooms (2 small D-£32, 3 large Db-£36, small breakfast, Station Road, tel. 065/682-4487, e-mail: marykeane .ennis@tinet.ie, Mary Keane). **St. Jude's B&B** rents three sleepable rooms in a bunkerlike annex (Db-£32, twin room is much better than the cramped doubles, around the corner from Grey Gables, tel. 065/684-2383, Catherine Quinn).

The **Clare Hostel** is well run and has good dorm beds (£10, two blocks from the market up Summerhill at the N18, tel. 065/682-9370, e-mail: stay@clarehostel.ie).

Transportation Connections—Ennis
By train to: Limerick (6/day, 40 min), **Dublin** (7/day, 3 hrs). Train info: tel. 065/684-0444.

By bus to: Galway (6/day, 1 hr), **Dublin** (5/day, 4 hrs), **Rosslare** (2/day, 5 hrs), **Limerick** (4/day, 70 min), **Doolin/Lisdoonvarna** (2/day), **Tralee** (5/day, 3 hrs). Bus info: tel. 065/682-4177.

By car: For ideas on driving from Galway to Portrush in Northern Ireland, see the Antrim Coast chapter.

NORTHERN IRELAND

Ireland was once part of Great Britain—a colony made more distant from London than its Celtic cousins not so much by the Irish
Sea as by its Catholicism. Protestant settlers from England and
Scotland were "planted" in Ireland to help assimilate the island
into the British economy. These "Scotch-Irish" established their
own cultural toehold on the island, but the Catholic Irish held
strong to their culture.

Over the centuries, British rule was never easy. But in the
beginning of this century the sparse Protestant population could
no longer control the entire island. Ireland won its independence,
but the northern six counties (the only ones with a Protestant
majority) voted to stay with Britain.

With 94 percent of the Republic of Ireland Catholic and only
6 percent Protestant, there was no question who was dominant.
But in the North, the Catholic minority was a sizable 35 percent
that demanded attention. Discrimination was considered necessary
to maintain the Protestant status quo in the North, and this led to
"The Troubles" that have filled headlines since the late 1960s.

It is not a fight over Catholic and Protestant religious differences. It's whether Ireland will be free or part of Britain. And the
indigenous Irish, who generally want a united and independent
Ireland, happen to be Catholic.

When Ireland won its independence (a 1921 treaty gave it
dominion status within the British Commonwealth—like Canada),
the issue of unity with the North had to be dealt with. It was
uncertain what the final arrangement would be. In the North the
long-established Orange Order and the newly mobilized Ulster
Volunteer Force (UVF) worked to defend the union with Britain.
The UVF became the military muscle of the Unionists. This

would be countered on the Catholic side by the Irish Republican Army (IRA). With the Republic's neutrality and the North's enthusiastic support of the Allied cause in WWII, Ulster won a spot close to London's heart. After WWII the split seemed permanent, and Britain invested heavily in Northern Ireland to bring it solidly into the United Kingdom fold.

With the Civil Rights movement of the 1960s, Irish rights needed to be addressed. Extremists polarized issues, and demonstrations became violent. As Protestants and Catholics clashed in 1969, the British Army entered the fray. They've been there ever since. In 1972, a watershed year, combatants moved from petrol bombs to guns. A new, more violent IRA emerged. In the most recent 25-year chapter in the struggle for an independent and united Ireland, more than 3,000 people have been killed.

A 1985 agreement granted Dublin a consulting role in the Northern Ireland government. Unionists bucked this, and violence escalated. In that same year, the Belfast City Hall draped a huge and defiant banner under its dome proclaiming "Belfast Says No."

In 1994 the banner came down. In the 1990s, with Ireland's membership in the European Union, the growth of its economy, and the weakening of the Catholic Church's influence, the consequences of a united Ireland are less threatening to the people of the north. A strong movement toward peace seems to be underway.

In 1994 the IRA declared a cease-fire. The Protestants followed suit, and talks are underway. The Republicans want British troops out of Ireland and political prisoners released. The Unionists want the IRA to turn in its arms and figure their prisoners are terrorists and jail is where they belong. Optimists hail the signing of the Good Friday Accord in 1998. Major hurdles to a solid peace persist, but the downtown checkpoints are history, "bomb damage clearance sales" are over, and more tourists than ever are venturing to Belfast.

Terminology

Ulster consists of nine counties in the northern part of the island of Ireland. Six of those make up Northern Ireland (three counties remain part of the Republic). *Unionists* want the North to remain with Britain. *Republicans* (and *Nationalists*) want a united and independent Ireland ruled by Dublin. *Sinn Fein* is the political wing of the *Irish Republican Army* (IRA). In 1996 Sinn Fein (whose leader is Gerry Adams) got its best election ever, with 15 percent of the vote in Northern Ireland. Orange, and the red, white, and blue of the Union Jack, are the favored colors of the Unionists. Green is the color of the Republicans.

Northern Ireland Is a Different Country

When you leave the Republic of Ireland and enter Northern Ireland, you are crossing an international border. You change money, stamps, phone cards—and your Eurailpass is no longer valid. The Irish punt (while worth nearly one British pound sterling) must be changed. Northern Ireland issues its own Ulster pound and also uses English pounds. Like the Scottish pound, Ulster pounds are interchangeable with English pounds. But it's best to change your Ulster pounds into English ones before returning to England (free at any bank in either region).

Safety
Tourists in Northern Ireland are no longer considered courageous (or reckless). Traveling there is as safe as traveling in England. You really have to look for trouble to find it here. Just don't seek out spit-and-sawdust pubs in working-class Protestant neighborhoods and sing Catholic songs. July 12 is Orange Day, the day Protestants parade and flex in favor of remaining separate from the Republic of Ireland. Catholics have their similar days in mid-August. Lie low if you stumble onto any big green or orange parades.

BELFAST

Seventeenth-century Belfast was only a village. With the influx, or "plantation," of Scottish and English settlers, Belfast boomed, spurred by the success of the local linen, rope-making, and ship-building industries. The Industrial Revolution took root with a vengeance. While the rest of Ireland remained rural and agricul-tural, Belfast earned its nickname, "Old Smoke," when many of the brick buildings you'll see today were built. The year 1888 marked the birth of modern Belfast. After Queen Victoria granted city status to this boomtown of 300,000, its citizens built the city's centerpiece, City Hall.

Belfast is the birthplace of the *Titanic* (and many ships that didn't sink). The two huge, mustard-colored cranes (the biggest in the world, nicknamed Samson and Goliath) rise like skyscrapers above the harbor as a reminder of this town's shipbuilding might.

It feels like a new morning in Belfast. Security checks, once a tiresome daily routine, are now rare. What was the traffic-free security zone has shed its gray skin and is now a bright and bustling pedestrian zone. On my last visit, the children dancing in the street were both Catholics and Protestants. They were part of a community summer-camp program giving kids from both com-munities reason to live together rather than apart.

Still, it's a fragile peace and a tenuous hope. Mean-spirited wall murals, hateful bonfires built a month before they're actually burnt, and pubs with security gates are reminders that the island is split and about a million Protestants prefer it that way.

Planning Your Time

Big Belfast is thin on sights. For most, a day of sightseeing is plenty.

Day trip from Dublin: With the handy 130-minute Dublin–Belfast train (and its cheap £17 day-return tickets, £26 on Friday or Sunday) you could make Belfast a day trip: 7:00–Catch the train from Dublin; 10:30–City Hall tour, browse the pedestrian zone, lunch, ride a shared cab up Falls Road; 15:00–Take city walking tour, visit Ulster Museum or side-trip out to the Ulster Folk and Transport Museum; Evening–Return to Dublin (last train 20:10).

Two days in Northern Ireland from Dublin: Take the train to Portrush for two nights and a day to tour the Causeway Coast (castle, whiskey, Giant's Causeway, resort fun), then follow the Belfast-in-a-day plan above.

Two days in Belfast: This allows time to splice in the Living History tour, Ulster Museum, Botanic Gardens, and some low or high after-dark culture.

Orientation (tel. code: 028)

For the first-time visitor in Belfast for a quick look, the town is pretty simple. There are three zones of interest: central (Donegall Square/City Hall/pedestrian shopping/TI), southern (Ulster Museum/Botanic Gardens/university), and western (working-class sectarian neighborhoods beyond the freeway). Belfast's "Golden Mile"—stretching from Hotel Europa to the university district—connects the central and southern zones with many of the best dinner and entertainment spots. To call Northern Ireland from the Republic of Ireland, dial 08, then 28, then the eight-digit local number.

Tourist Information: This modern TI has an enjoyable book-shop (Mon–Sat 9:00–19:00, Sun 12:00–16:00; closes in winter at 17:15 and Sunday; north edge of city center at 59 North Street—may relocate in 2000 near City Hall, tel. 028/9024-6609). Get the fine free city map and *The List*, a biweekly entertainment guide covering pub music, concerts, theater, movies, restaurants, and cultural news. Refer to this for your evening fun.

Arrival in Belfast: Arriving by fast train, you'll go direct to Central Station. Slower trains arc through Belfast, stopping at several downtown stations, including Central Station, Great Victoria Station (most central, near Hotel Europa and Donegall Square), Botanic (close to the university and Botanic Gardens), and Adelaide (near several recommended B&Bs).

Helpful Hints

Laundry: The Laundry Room is at 37 Botanic Avenue (£4.40-self-serve, £6-drop off, Mon–Fri 8:00–21:00, Sat 8:00–18:00, Sun 12:00–18:00).

Internet Access: Revelations Internet Café is at 27 Shaftsbury Square, near Belfast Hostel (£5/hour, tel. 028/9032-0337).

Bike Rental: McConvey Cycles is at 10 Pottingers

Entry, off High Street near Lagan Lookout (£7/24 hrs, tel. 028/9049-1163).

Getting around Belfast

If you line up your sightseeing logically, you can do most of the town on foot.

By Bus: Handy buses with friendly drivers go from Donegall Square East to Malone Road and all recommended accommodations (#70 and #71, 90p/ride, all-day £2.40 pass). A free Centerlink bus loops from Central Station to Donegall Square and to Shaftesbury Square, stopping near the TI on North Street (free with any new or old local train or bus ticket, 4/hrly, not Sunday).

By Taxi: Taxis are reasonable and should be considered. Rather than use their meters, many cabs charge a flat £3 rate for any ride up to two miles. It's £1 per mile after that. Ride a shared cab if you're going up Falls Road (explained below).

Tours of Belfast

▲**Walking Tour**—A 90-minute Town Walk introducing you to the historic core of town leaves from the TI (£4, Saturday at 14:00, call TI for additional times, tel. 028/9024-6609).

▲**Bus Tours**—The "Belfast: A Living History" bus tour offers the best introduction to the city's recent and complicated political and social history. You'll cruise the Catholic and Protestant working-class neighborhoods with a commentary explaining the political murals and places of interest—mostly dealing with "The Troubles" of the last 25 years. You see things from the bus and get out only for a tea break (£8, Wednesday and Saturday for City Tour, Sunday for Living History Tour, 2.5 hours, from Castle Place, tel. 028/9045-8484).

Rodney's Tours: Minibus tours leave from Belfast International City Hostel daily at 10:30. They cover the troubled areas in more depth, with time for photo stops (£7.50, two hours, book in advance, tel. 028/9032-4733). The same guide, Rodney McComb, also offers minibus tours of the Antrim Coast (£20, rope bridge, Giant's Causeway, Bushmills Distillery, and Dunluce Castle, Apr–Oct daily 9:30–17:45 depending on demand, book through and depart from hostel, tel. 028/9032-4733) and works as private guide (tel. 028/9086-3976, cell tel. 0836/676-258).

Sights—Belfast

▲▲**City Hall**—This grand structure, with its 173-foot-tall copper dome, dominates the town center. Built between 1898 and 1906, with its statue of Queen Victoria scowling down Belfast's main drag and the Union Jack flapping behind her, it's a stirring sight. In the garden you'll find memorials to the *Titanic* and the landing of the U.S. Expeditionary Force in 1942—their first stop en route

Belfast

to Berlin. Take the free 45-minute tour (summer Mon–Fri usually at 10:30, 11:30, and 14:30, Sat at 14:30; off-season only at 14:30, call to check schedule and book, tel. 028/9032-0202 ext. 2346). If you can't manage a tour, at least step into the interior, with its marble swirl staircase, and drop into the "What's on in Belfast" room just inside the front door. (Politely ask the receptionist for the free City Hall booklet and postcard that tour takers get.)

    The tour gives you a rundown on city government and an

explanation of the decor that makes this an Ulster political hall of fame. Queen Victoria and King Edward VII look down on city council meetings. The 1613 original charter of Belfast granted by James I is on display. Its Great Hall—bombed by the Germans in 1941—looks as great as it did the day it was made.

Linen Hall Library—Across the street from City Hall, the 200-year-old Linen Hall Library welcomes guests (Mon–Sat 9:30–17:30, Sat 9:30–16:00, 17 Donegall Square North, tel. 028/9032-1707). It has a fine, hard-bound ambience, a coffee shop, a royal newspaper reading room, and a top floor of papers and posters documenting "The Troubles" (top floor by tour only—call for schedule).

Golden Mile—This is the overstated nickname of Belfast's liveliest dining and entertainment district, which stretches from the Opera House to the university district.

The **Grand Opera House**, originally built in 1891, bombed and rebuilt in 1991 and bombed and rebuilt again in 1993, is extravagantly Victorian and the place to take in a concert, play, or opera (closed to sightseers, ticket office across the street, tel. 028/9024-1919). **Hotel Europa**, next door, while considered the most bombed hotel in the world, feels pretty casual.

Across the street is the museum-like **Crown Liquor Saloon**. Built in 1850, it's now a part of the National Trust. A wander through its mahogany, glass, and marble interior is a trip back into the day of Queen Victoria (although the privacy provided by the snugs—private booths—allows for un-Victorian behavior; open 11:30–24:00). Upstairs, **Flannigan's Bar** serves pub grub, is decorated with historic photos, and is the starting point for the **Bailey's Historical Belfast Pub Walk** (2 or 3 evenings a week, tel. 028/9024-9476).

Lagan Lookout Visitors Centre—This center shows off the fruits of the city's £750 million investment in its harbor. The tides of the River Lagan left the town with daily unsightly mud flats. The weir, built in 1994, controls the tides, stabilizing the depth of the harbor. It also doubles as a free pedestrian bridge over the river, affording walkers a fine view of the harbor area, including the big cranes and the new convention center. The Visitors Centre, while mildly entertaining and enthusiastically "interactive," is not really worth the £1.50 entry fee (Mon–Fri 11:00–17:00, Sat 12:00–17:00, Sun 14:00–17:00, closed Mon in winter, a short walk from TI, just past the tipsy—four feet off center—Albert clock tower, tel. 028/9031-5444).

▲▲**Falls Road**—It will be a happy day when the sectarian neighborhoods of Belfast have nothing to be sectarian about. For a look at one of the original home bases of the "The Troubles," explore the working-class Catholic Falls Road neighborhood.

At the end of Castle Street you'll find a square filled with old black cabs—and the only Gaelic-language signs in downtown Belfast. These shared black cabs efficiently shuttle residents from outlying neighborhoods up and down Falls Road and to the city center. This service originated when the troubles began and locals would hijack city buses and use them as barricades in the street fighting. When bus service was discontinued, local paramilitary groups established the shared taxi service. Any cab (except those in the "Whiterock" line) goes up Falls Road and past Sinn Fein headquarters and lots of murals to the Milltown Cemetery (70p, sit in front and talk to the cabbie). Hop on and off. Easy-to-flag-down cabs run every minute or so in each direction on Falls Road. Twenty trained-guide cabbies do one-hour tours for £15 (cheap for a small group).

The Sinn Fein office and bookstore are near the bottom of Falls Road. The bookstore is worth a look. Page through books featuring color photos of the political murals that decorate the buildings. Money raised here supports families of imprisoned members of the IRA.

A sad corrugated wall called the Peace Line runs a block or so north of Falls Road, separating the Catholics from the Protestants in the Shankill Road area.

At the Milltown Cemetery walk past all the Gaelic crosses down to the far right-hand corner (closest to the highway), where the IRA "Roll of Honor" is set apart from the thousands of other graves by little green railings. They are treated like fallen soldiers. Notice the memorial to Bobby Sands and the 11 other hunger strikers who starved in protest for a united Ireland in 1981.

Sandy Row—While you can ride a shared black cab through the Protestant Shankill Road area (departing from the end of North Street, 30 minute loop, £1.20), the easiest way to get a dose of the Unionist side is to walk Sandy Row. From the Hotel Europa, walk a block down Glengall Street, then turn left and enjoy a 10-minute walk along a working-class Protestant street. A stop in the Unionist memorabilia shop, a pub, or one of the many cheap eateries here may give you an opportunity to talk to a local. You'll see murals filled with Unionist symbolism. The mural of William of Orange's victory over the Catholic King James II (Battle of the Boyne, 1690) stirs Unionist hearts. (From the south end of Sandy Row, it's a 10-minute walk to the Ulster Museum.)

▲**Ulster Museum**—While mediocre by European standards, this is Belfast's one major museum. It's free and pretty painless: Ride the elevator to the top floor and follow the spiraling exhibits downhill—there's a cheery café halfway down. You'll find an interesting *Made in Belfast* exhibit just before an arch that proclaims "Trade is the golden girdle of the globe." The delicately worded history section is given an interesting British slant (such as the implication that the famine was caused by the Irish population doubling in 40 years—without a mention of various English contributions to the suffering). After a wander through the *Early Medieval Ireland* exhibit and a peek at a pretty darn good mummy, top things off with the Girona Treasure. Soggy bits of gold, silver, leather, and wood were salvaged from the Spanish Armada's shipwrecked *Girona*—lost off the Antrim Coast north of Belfast in 1588 (free, Mon–Fri 10:00–17:00, Sat 13:00–17:00, Sun 14:00–17:00, tel. 028/9038-3000).

▲**Botanic Gardens**—This is the backyard of Queen's University. On a sunny day, you couldn't imagine a more relaxing park setting. On a cold day, step into the Tropical Ravine for a jungle of heat and humidity. Take a quick walk through the Palm House, reminiscent of the Palm House in London's Kew Gardens, but smaller (free, Mon–Fri 10:00–12:00, 13:00–17:00, Sat–Sun 13:00–17:00, less in winter, tel. 028/9032-4902).

Sights—Near Belfast

▲▲**Ulster Folk and Transport Museum**—This 180-acre, two-museum complex straddles the road and rail at Cultra, midway between Bangor and Belfast (eight miles out of town).

The Folk Museum, an open-air collection of 34 reconstructed buildings from all over the nine counties of Ulster, showcases the region's traditional lifestyles. After wandering through the old town site (church, print shop, schoolhouse, humble Belfast row house, and so on), you'll head off into the country to nip into cottages, farmhouses, and mills. Most houses are warmed by a wonderful peat fire and a friendly attendant. It can be dull or vibrant, depending upon when you visit and your ability to chat with the attendants. Drop a peat brick on the fire.

The Transport Museum (downhill, over the road from the folk section) consists of three buildings. Start at the bottom and trace the evolution of transportion from 7,500 years ago—when people first decided to load an ox—to modern times. The lowest building holds intriguing sections on the local Gypsy culture and the sinking of the Belfast-made *Titanic*. In the next two buildings you roll through the history of bikes, cars, and trains. The car section rumbles from the first car in Ireland (an 1898 Benz) through the "Cortina Culture" of the 1960s to the local adventures of John De Lorean and a 1981 model of his car. (£4, £11 for families, Jul–Aug Mon–Sat 10:30–18:00, Sun 12:00–18:00; Apr, May, Jun, and Sept Mon–Fri 9:30–17:00, Sat 10:30–18:00, Sun 12:00–18:00; Oct–Mar closes daily at 16:00; check schedule for special events on the day of your visit, allow three hours, a handy and free shuttle bus runs on busy summer days but expect lots of walking, tel. 028/9042-8428.)

From Belfast reach **Cultra** by taxi (£8), bus #1 or #2 (2/hrly, 30 min from Oxford Street), or train (2/hrly, 15 min, from any Belfast train station or Bangor). Trains and buses stop right in the park. Public transport schedules get skimpy on Saturday and Sunday. There's a complete schedule on the wall at the bottom building in the transport area. Drivers can drive from one section to the next.

Sleeping in Belfast
(£1 = about $1.70, tel. code: 028; to call Belfast from the Republic of Ireland, dial 08-28 before the local number)
Sleep Code: **S** = Single, **D** = Double/Twin, **T** = Triple, **Q** = Quad, **b** = bathroom, **t** = toilet only, **s** = shower only, **CC** = Credit Card (Visa, MasterCard, Amex).

Many of Belfast's best budget beds cluster in a comfortable area just south of the Ulster Museum and the university. Two train stations (Botanic and Adelaide) are nearby, and buses zip down Malone Road every few minutes. Any bus on Malone Road goes to Donegall Square East. Taxis, cheap in Belfast, zip you downtown for £3 (your host can call one). Belfast is more of a business town than a tourist town, so business-class room rates are lower or soft on weekends.

Ulster People's College Residential Centre rents 30 beds in 10 rooms year-round on a quiet street near the stop for the bus into town (S-£16, D-£32, £2 per bed cheaper with a continental rather than Irish breakfast, free laundry, 30 Adelaide Park, tel. 028/9066-5161, fax 028/9066-8111).

Malone Guest House is a classy stand-alone Victorian house fronting the busy Malone Road. It's homey and well run by Mrs. Millar who rents two spacious singles and six large, pastel twins (Sb-£35, Db-£50 with this book, 79 Malone Road, Belfast BT9 6SH, tel. 028/9066-9565, fax 9022-3020).

Camera House Guest House rents large smoke-free rooms and comes with an airy, hardwood feeling throughout (Sb-£35, Db-£45–52, CC:VM, 44 Wellington Park, Belfast BT9 6DP, tel. 028/9066-0026, fax 028/9066-7856, Paul Drumm).

Windermere House rents 11 rooms, including several small but pleasant singles, in a large Victorian house (S-£22, very small D-£30, D-£44, Db-£46, T-£47, 60 Wellington Park, tel. 028/9066-2693, Brian).

Malone Lodge Hotel provides slick, modern, business-class comfort and professionalism in a charming environment on a quiet, leafy street (newly remodeled, Db-probably around £100, weekend deals, CC:VMA, elevator, 60 Eglantine Avenue, Belfast BT9 6DY, tel. 028/9038-2409, fax 028/9038-2706).

On the same quiet street you'll find **George B&B** (D-£36, Db-£42, 9 Eglantine Avenue, tel. 028/9068-3212, Hugh McGuinness), **Eglantine Guest House** (S-£20, D-£38, T-£54, 21 Eglantine Avenue, tel. 028/9066-7585, Lou Cargill will mother you—even do your laundry), and the grand old **Marine House B&B** (11 rooms, S-£22, Sb-£27, D-£38, Db-£44, 30 Eglantine Ave, tel. & fax 028/9066-2828).

Botanic Lodge rents 20 decent rooms on a lively but stylish "University Ave"-type street with lots of fun eateries nearby (D-£40, Db-£45, CC:VM, 10-minute walk to City Hall at 87 Botanic Avenue, Belfast BT7 1JN, tel. & fax 028/9032-7682).

Sleeping in Big, Modern, Inexpensive Chain Hotels

Jurys Inn, a huge American-style place that rents its several hundred identical modern rooms for one simple price, is perfectly located two blocks from the City Hall (up to three adults or two adults and two kids for about £65, breakfast extra, CC:VMA, nonsmoking floor, Fisherwick Place, tel. 028/9053-3500, fax 028/9053-3511, e-mail: info@jurys.com).

Granada Travelodge is a basic Jurys-style business hotel with 83 cookie-cutter rooms high on value, low on character (Db-£50, often huge weekend discounts for Friday or Saturday nights, no breakfast, CC:VMA, quiet but extremely central, a block from Hotel Europa and City Hall at 15 Brunswick Street, Belfast BT2 7GE, tel. 028/9033-3555, fax 028/9023-2999).

Belfast Holiday Inn Express is cheaper but not as central as Jurys Inn, with the same basic formula (Db-£60, often weekend deals, kids free, includes continental breakfast, CC:VMA, nonsmoking floors, elevator, 106 University Street, tel. 028/9031-1909, fax 028/9031-1910, e-mail: express@holidayinn-irelandl.com).

Sleeping in Hostels and Dorms

Belfast International City Hostel is big, basic, and creatively run with 40 twins and quads. It's located near the Botanic train station in the heart of the lively university district and close to the center. Features include free lockers, left luggage, self-serve £3 laundry, a cheap cafeteria, an elevator, and no curfew (S-£17, D-£24, beds in a quad-£11, includes breakfast, CC:VM, 22 Donegall Road, tel. 028/9032-4733, fax 028/9043-9699, e-mail: info@hini.org.uk). This is the starting point for Rodney's Tours (see "Tours of Belfast," above).

The Ark, a smaller, more hip, youthful, and easygoing hostel, is in the university district near the Botanic train station (£7.50 per bed in 4-bed dorms or D-£28, 18 University Street, tel. 028/9032-9626).

Linen House Youth Hostel fills an old linen factory with a 120-bed industrial-strength hostel. It's on a dark, scary-at-night street in a very central location (£8 dorm beds, S-£12, D-£20, no breakfast, plenty of facilities, 18 Kent Street, tel. 028/9058-6400, fax 028/9058-6444, e-mail: info@belfasthostel.com).

Queen's Elms Halls of Residence is a big brick Queen's University dorm renting 300 bleak institutional rooms to travelers during summer break (mid-Jun–mid-Sept only, S-£14, D-£28, cheaper for students, free laundry service and self-serve kitchen, 78 Malone Road, tel. 028/9038-1608, fax 028/9066-6680).

Sleeping and Eating in Bangor
(£1 = about $1.70, tel. code: 028)

To stay in a laid-back seaside hometown—with more comfort per pound—sleep 30 minutes south of Belfast in Bangor. Formerly a slick Belfast seaside escape, Bangor is now sleepy and almost residential feeling. But with easy train connections to downtown Belfast (2/hrly, 30 min), elegant old homes facing its newly spruced-up harbor, and a lack of even a hint of big-city Belfast, Bangor appeals. The harbor is a five-minute walk from the train station.

Pierview House B&B is a chandeliered winner, with three of its five spacious rooms overlooking the sea (D-£32, grand Db-£34, family room, CC:VM, 28 Seacliff Road, tel. 028/9146-3381, Mr. and Mrs. Watts). **Battersea Guest House,** one of a row of tall, stately homes overlooking the yacht basin, rents four rooms (small D-£34, grand sea-view double-£40, 47 Queen's Parade, tel. 028/9146-1643, Rene and John Brann). **Royal Hotel** is a fine old place right on the harbor with good weekend rates on its 50 rooms (Db-£75 weekdays, £65 on weekends, view rooms are pricier, CC:VMA, 26 Quay Street, BT20 5ED, tel. 028/9127-1866, fax 028/9146-7810).

Your hosts can direct you to their favorite eatery. The welcoming bar at **Royal Hotel** (facing the harbor) serves good £6 dinners. **Steamer Bar** (next door, upstairs from the pub) is also popular. **Dragon House** provides a tasty Chinese break from pub grub (76 High Street, tel. 028/9145-9031). **Los Amigos Restaurant** serves good Mexican food (9 Crosby Street, tel. 028/9124-7060).

Transportation Connections—Bangor

By train to Belfast: Trains go from Bangor station (the end of the line, don't use Bangor West) into Belfast via Cultra (Ulster Folk and Transport Museum). The journey (2/hrly, 30 min) gives you a good close-up look at the giant Belfast harbor cranes. Belfast Central has a free Rail-Link shuttle bus to the town center (4/hrly, not Sunday). Stay on until the Botanic train station for the Ulster Museum, the Golden Mile, and Sandy Row.

Transportation Connections—Belfast

By train to: Dublin (8/day, 2 hrs), **Larne** (hrly, 1 hr), **Portrush** (7/day, 2 hrs). Train info: tel. 028/9089-9411.

By bus to: Portrush (6/day, 2 hrs), **Glasgow** (2/day, 6 hrs, £26), **Edinburgh** (2/day, 8 hrs), **London** (2/day, 12 hrs, £32). Ulsterbus tel. 028/9033-7003. The bus station is behind Hotel Europa.

By plane: British Air flies to **Glasgow** (3/day, 45 min, £62 one day in advance) and **London** (5/day, 1 hr, £77 one way, but you can buy a £55 round-trip ticket and forget to return—it's allowed).

By ferry: Consider sailing overnight from Belfast to **Liverpool**—with a bed, dinner, and breakfast—for £40 via North Irish Ferries (8 hrs, nightly, tel. 028/9077-9090) and **Stranraer, Scotland** (via Sea Cat catamaran or Stena Line ferry—£25, tel. 028/9074-7747). P&O Ferry goes from **Larne** (20 miles north of Belfast) to **Cairnryan, Scotland** (Brit tel. 0990-980-777).

ANTRIM COAST
AND PORTRUSH

The Antrim Coast—the north of Northern Ireland—is one of the most interesting and scenic coastlines in Britain and Ireland. Within a few miles of the train terminal of Portrush, you can visit some evocative castle ruins, tour the oldest whiskey distillery, risk your life on a bouncy rope bridge, and hike along the famous Giant's Causeway—a World Heritage Site.

The homely seaside resort of Portrush used to be known as "the Brighton of the North." While it's seen its best days, it retains the atmosphere and buildings of a genteel, middle-class seaside resort. Portrush fills its peninsula with family-oriented amusements, fun eateries, and B&Bs. Summertime fun seekers promenade along the toy harbor and tumble down to the sandy beaches, which extend in sweeping white crescents on either side.

Superficially, it has the appearance of any small British seaside resort, but its history and high population of young people (students from the University of Coleraine) give Portrush a little more personality. Along with the usual arcade amusements, there are nightclubs, restaurants, summer theater in the town hall, and convivial pubs that people from Belfast travel for. At the end of the train line and just a few miles from several important sights, it's an ideal base for exploring the highlights of the Antrim Coast.

Planning Your Time
You need a full day to explore the Antrim Coast, so allow two nights in Portrush. An ideal day might be a bike tour lacing together Dunluce Castle, Old Bushmills Distillery, and the Giant's Causeway, followed by nine holes on the Portrush pitch-and-putt course. Consider this side trip north from Dublin.

Day 1: 11:00–16:00–Train from Dublin to Portrush.

Day 2: All day for Antrim Coast sights and Portrush.
Day 3: 8:00–10:00–Train to Belfast, all day in Belfast; 19:00–21:00–Train back to Dublin.

Orientation (tel. code: 028)

Portrush's pleasant and easily walkable town center features sea views in every direction. On one side is the harbor and restaurants, and on the other are Victorian townhouses and vast salty views. The tip of the peninsula is marked by a lighthouse and a park filled with tennis courts, lawn-bowling greens, and putting greens.

The city is busy with students during the school year. July and August are beach resort boom time. June and September it's laid-back and lazy. Families pack Portrush on Saturdays, and revelers from Belfast pack its hotels on Saturday nights.

Tourist Information: The TI, more generous and helpful than those in the Republic, is in the big, modern Dunluce Centre (mid-Jun–Aug daily 9:00–19:00, otherwise Mon–Fri 9:00–17:00, Sat–Sun 12:00–17:00, closed in winter, tel. 028/7082-3333). Get their free North Ireland driving map, the "Places to Visit" brochure, and a free Belfast map if you're Belfast-bound.

Arrival in Portrush: The train tracks stop at the base of the tiny peninsula that Portrush fills. (The small station has no bag check.) The TI is three long blocks from the train station (follow signs down Eglinton Street and turn left at fire station). All listed B&Bs are within a five-minute walk of the train station (see "Sleeping," below). The bus stop is two blocks from the train station.

Getting around the Antrim Coast

By Bus: In July and August, open-top "Bushmills" buses connect Portrush, Dunluce Castle, Old Bushmills Distillery, and the Giant's Causeway every two hours (maybe hourly in summer, weather permitting). You could spend two hours at Bushmills and the causeway, but you'd be bored at the castle (£3.20 round-trip, buy ticket from driver, pick up a schedule at TI).

By Car: Distances are short, and parking is easy. Don't miss the treacherously scenic coastal route down to the Glens of Antrim.

By Taxi: Groups (up to four) go reasonably by taxi, which costs only £7 from Portrush to Giant's Causeway.

By Bike: Portrush's only bike-rental place has closed. Ask around if anyone's renting bikes.

Sights—Portrush

Barry's Old Time Amusement Arcade—This is a fine chance to see Northern Ireland at play (open weekends and summer only). Just below the train station on the harbor, it's filled with candy floss (cotton candy) and little kids learning the art of one-armed

Portrush

BELVEDERE TOWN HOUSE
BETHEL HOUSE
RECREATION CENTRE
HOSTEL
BATH TERR
HARBOR & RAMORE WINE BAR
MAIN
KERR ST
PENINSULA HOTEL
EGLINTON HOTEL
ARDENLEE & WEST STRAND B & B
MARING B & B
EAST STRAND
BARRY'S ARCADE
TRAIN STN.
EGLIN. ST.
CAUSEWAY STREET
PITCH-N-PUTT GOLF COURSE
T.I. DUNLUCE CENTRE
TO GIANT'S CAUSEWAY
WEST STRAND
TO COLERAINE & BELFAST
DCH
½ MILE

bandits—2p at a time. Get £1 worth of 2p coins from the machine and go wild.

Pitch-and-Putt at the Royal Portrush Golf Course—Irish courses, like those in Scotland, are highly sought after for their lush but dry greens in glorious settings. While serious golfers can get a tee time at the Royal Portrush, rookies can get a smaller dose of this wonderful golf setting at the neighboring "Skerry 9 Hole Links" pitch-and-putt range. You get two clubs and balls for £4.50, and they don't care if you go around twice (Apr–Sept daily 8:30–19:30, five-minute walk from station, tel. 028/7082-2285).

Portrush Recreation Grounds—For some easygoing exercise right in town, this well-organized park offers lawn-bowling greens (£3/hr with gear), putting greens, tennis courts, a great kids' adventure play park, and a café (tennis shoes, balls, rackets, etc., all rented for a small price, daily Easter–Sept Mon–Sat 10:30–dusk, Sun 13:00–dusk, tel. 028/7082-4441). Other major Portrush amusements include the **Dunluce Center** and **Waterworld**.

Sights—Antrim Coast

▲**Dunluce Castle**—These romantic ruins, perched dramatically on the edge of a rocky headland, are a testimony to this region's turbulent past. During the Middle Ages it resisted several sieges. But on a stormy night in 1639 dinner was interrupted as half the kitchen fell into the sea, taking the servants with it. That was the last straw for the lady of the castle. The Countess of Antrim packed up and moved inland, and the castle "began its slow submission to the forces of nature." While it's one of the largest castles in Northern Ireland and is beautifully situated, there's precious little to see among its broken walls.

Expansion of the castle was financed by the salvaging of a shipwreck. In 1588 the Spanish Armada's *Girona*—returning home after an aborted English mission and laden with sailors and valuables of three abandoned sister ships—sank. More than 1,300 drowned, and only five washed ashore. The shipwreck was excavated in 1967, and a bounty of golden odds and silver ends ended up in Belfast's Ulster Museum.

Castle admission includes a little impromptu guided tour of the ruins and a 15-minute video that's interesting for its effort to defend the notion of "Ulster, a place apart—facing Scotland, cut off from the rest of Ireland by dense forests and mountains..." (£1.50, Apr–Sept Tue–Sun 10:00–18:00, closed Mon; in winter 10:00–16:00, with shorter hours on Sunday, tel. 028/7073-1938).

▲▲**Old Bushmills Distillery**—Bushmills claims to be the world's oldest distillery. While King James I (of Bible fame) granted their license to distill "Aqua Vitae" in 1608, whiskey has been made here since the 13th century. Distillery tours waft you through the process, making it clear that Irish whiskey is triple-distilled—and therefore smoother than Scotch whiskey (distilled merely twice). The 45-minute tour starts where the mash pit is filled with a porridge that eventually becomes whiskey. (The leftovers of that porridge are fed to the county's particularly happy cows.) You'll see thousands of oak casks—the kind used for Spanish sherry— filled with aging whiskey. The finale, of course, is the tasting in the 1608 Bar—the former malt barn. When your guide asks for a tasting volunteer, raise your hand quick and strong. Two volunteers per tour get to taste test eight different whiskeys (Irish versus Scotch and bourbon). Everyone else gets a single glass of their choice. Non–whiskey enthusiasts might enjoy their cinnamon and cloves hot toddy. To see the distillery at its lively best, visit when the 100 workers are manning the machinery—Monday morning

Northern Ireland's Antrim Coast

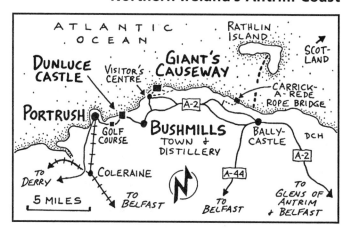

through Friday noon (weekend tours see a still still). Tours are limited to 35 and book up. In summer call in your name to get a tour time before you arrive (£3.50, daily Mar–Oct, tours depart on the half hour from 9:30, last tour at 16:00, Sunday from 12:00, in winter only Mon–Fri, with shorter hours, tel. 028/2073-1521). The distillery is a signposted quarter mile from Bushmills town center. (Valley View Farm B&B rents rooms at 6a Ballyclough Road, Bushmills, tel. 028/2074-1608).

▲▲**Giant's Causeway**—This four-mile-long stretch of coastline is famous for its bizarre basalt columns. The shore is covered with hexagonal pillars that stick up at various heights. It's as if Earth is offering God his choice of 37,000 six-sided cigarettes.

Geologists claim the Giant's Causeway was formed by volcanic eruptions 60 million years ago. As the lava surface cooled, it contracted and cracked into hexagonal shapes. As the layer of hardened but alligatored rock settled, it broke into its many stair steps.

In actuality, the Giant's Causeway was formed by an Ulster warrior giant named Finn MacCool who wanted to reach his love on the Scottish island of Staffa. At that time the causeway stretched to Scotland, way back when the two lands were connected. Today, while the foundation has settled, the formation still extends undersea to Staffa, just off the Scottish coast. Finn's causeway was ruined (into today's "remnant of chaos") by a rival giant. As the rival fled from ferocious Finn back to his Scottish homeland, he ripped up the causeway so Finn couldn't chase him.

For cute variations on the Finn story, as well as details on the ridiculous theories of modern geologists, start your visit in the

Visitors Centre. The worthwhile video gives a history of the Giant's Causeway and a regional overview (£1, 4/hrly, 12 min). The real information is on the walls of the exhibition. A gift shop and cafeteria are standing by.

A minibus (60p each way, 4/hrly) zips lazy ones a half mile directly to the Grand Causeway, the highlight of the entire coast. For a better dose of the causeway, consider this play: follow the high cliff-top trail from the Visitors Centre 10 minutes to a great viewpoint, then five minutes farther on you reach the Shepherd's Stairway. Zigzag down to the coast; at the T, go 100 yards right to the towering pipes of "the Organ." Then retrace your steps and continue left to the "Giant's Boot" for some photo fun and the dramatic point where the stairs step into the sea. Just beyond that, at the asphalt turnaround, you'll see the bus stop for the lift back to the Visitors Centre. You could walk the entire five-mile Giant's Causeway. The 75p hiking guide points out the highlights named by 18th-century guides (Camel's Back, Giant's Eye, and so on). The causeway is always free and open (Visitors Centre daily 10:00–17:00, until 19:00 Jul–Aug, £3 to park, tel. 028/2073-1855).

Causeway Coast Bike Ride—(At last check, no one was renting bikes in Portrush—ask around.) It's an eight-mile, one-hour pedal from Portrush past Dunluce Castle and Bushmills to the Giant's Causeway Visitors Centre. From Portrush to Dunluce Castle, allow 20 minutes. Bike along the Royal Portrush Golf Course and past some beautiful beach scenery (a bike-friendly sidewalk keeps timid riders away from traffic). It's another 20 minutes to Bushmills; the distillery is a quarter-mile detour inland from the town square. Bushmills is a good place for a lunch break; choose among the fancy Bushmills Inn, several pantries, and a happy Hip Chip chippie. From Bushmills the Giant's Causeway is 20 minutes farther over gentle hills.

▲▲Carrick-a-Rede Rope Bridge—For 200 years fishermen have strung a narrow 80-foot-high bridge (planks strung between wires) across a 65-foot-wide chasm between the mainland and a tiny island. The bridge (not the original) still gives access to the salmon nets that are set during the summer months to catch the fish turning the coast's corner. (The complicated system is described at the gateway.) The island affords fine views and, especially during nesting season, great seabird watching (free, Apr–Sept daily 10:00–18:00, Jul–Aug till 20:00, gone in winter, 15-min walk from the £2 car park).

▲Antrim Mountains and Glens—Not particularly high (never more than 1,500 feet), the Antrim Mountains are cut by a series of large glens running northeast to the sea. Glenariff, with its waterfalls, especially the "Mare's Tail," is the most beautiful of the nine glens.

Sleeping in Portrush
(£1 = about $1.70, tel. code: 028, zip code: BT56 8DG)

Sleep Code: **S** = Single, **D** = Double/Twin, **T** = Triple, **Q** = Quad, **b** = bathroom, **t** = toilet only, **s** = shower only, **CC** = Credit Card (Visa, MasterCard, Amex).

Portrush's many B&Bs all seem well worn. But small-town well worn is better than big-town well worn. August and Saturday nights can be tight. Otherwise it's a "you take a half a loaf when you can get it" town. Rates vary with the view and season—probe for softness. Each listing faces the sea, though sea views are worth paying for only if you get a bay window. Ask for a big room (some doubles can be very small; twins are bigger). Lounges are invariably grand and have bay-window views. All places listed have lots of stairs but are perfectly central and within a few minutes' walk of the train station. Parking is easy.

Peninsula Hotel is a big, new place right in the town center with huge, fresh rooms, modern decor, and comforts. Ask for a room far from its disco, which can be a problem on party nights (Db-£50, Tb-£75, breakfast-£5—eat better and cheaper down the street, CC:VMA, elevator, 15 Eglinton Street, BT56 8DX, tel. 028/7082-2293, fax 028/7082-4315, e-mail: reservations @peninsulahotel.freeserve.co.uk).

Eglinton Hotel, Portrush's smoky old-time hotel, is central but noisy and impersonal. It's a dark place with small doubles and bigger twins (Db-£50–70 with demand, CC:VMA, across the street from train station, 49 Eglinton Street, BT56 8DZ Portrush, tel. 028/7082-2371, fax 028/7082-3155).

Belvedere Town House, a stately place on the quiet side of town with 13 spacious, relatively well-appointed rooms, is the best value in town (S-£14, Sb-£17, D-£28–30, Db-£34–36, 5 percent extra for CC, farthest from station but ideal for drivers, at 15 Lansdowne Crescent, tel. 028/7082-2771, Sammy and Winnie Dunn).

Ardenlee B&B is enthusiastically run by Rodney Montgomery and has six bigger-than-average rooms and a fine location near the station (S-£15, Db-£35–40, £5 discount for two-night stays, 10 percent discount with this book, 19 Kerr Street, Portrush BT56 8DG, tel. 028/7082-2639).

Maring B&B rents 14 cramped, well-worn rooms (S-£15, Sb-£20–25, D-£35, Db-£35–40, 10 percent discount with this book, family loft room, CC:VMA, 17 Kerr Street, tel. & fax 028/7082-2765, Anne and Robin Rossborough).

West Strand Guest House has 15 tight, musty rooms, none with private bathrooms (S-£15–17, D-£30–34, fine view lounge, 18 Kerr Street, tel. 028/7082-2270, Muriel Robinson).

Bethel House B&B is a cozy, completely smoke- and alcohol-free Christian-run place overlooking the sea on the quiet side of town. Request the bigger or view rooms. Some top-floor doubles are tiny, but all are nicely refurbished (S-£17, Sb-£22, D-£34, Db-£44, big homey lounge used nightly in the summer for a 30-minute hymn-singing fellowship, 7 Lansdowne Crescent, tel. 028/7082-2354, Tom and Marie Graham). May be under a different management in 2000.

MacCool's Portrush Youth Hostel is a friendly and laid-back place with 20 beds in four rooms (two, four, six, and eight beds each, £7 per bed, one tiny £16 double, one all-girls' room, lockers, guests' kitchen, game-stocked lounge, nonsmoking, Internet access, bike rental to residents only, 5 Causeway View Terrace, midway between station and tip of peninsula, tel. 028/7082-4845).

Drivers may want to stay just out of town at **Glenkeen Guest House** (10 rooms, Sb-£25, Db-£38–42, some smoke-free rooms, CC:VMA, seven-minute walk from the station, 59 Coleraine Road, tel. 028/7082-2279, Mrs. Little) or **Summer Island House** (four rooms, Sb-£20, Db-£35–40, family room, five-minute walk from station, 14 Coleraine Road, tel. 028/7082-4640, Vivian Shields).

Eating in Portrush

Being a university town and a get-away-from-Belfast town, Portrush has more than chips joints. Eglinton Street is lined with cheap and cheery eateries. For pub grub consider the **Eglinton Hotel** or **Peninsula Hotel**. **Don Giovanni** serves decent Italian.

Three restaurants within 50 yards of each other, all under the same ownership and overlooking the harbor, are just about everyone's vote for the best eating values in town.

Ramore Restaurant, dressy black and white, is the spot for fine dining (£15 main courses, full dinners for £25–30, Tue–Sat 18:30–22:30, closed Sun–Mon, CC:VM, reservations wise, tel. 028/7082-4313).

While the Ramore Restaurant upstairs is exclusive and pricey, the salty, mod, and much-loved **Ramore Wine Bar** is bursting with happy eaters enjoying the same quality cooking at half the price. The most inviting menu I've seen in Ireland offers huge £7 meals ranging from steaks to vegetarian. Their good red wine (from £1.80 glass) is a welcome break after all the Guinness. Come early for a table or sit at the bar (£5.50 lunch specials, dinner 17:30–21:30, no CC, closed Sun, tel. 028/7082-3444).

The **Harbor Restaurant** (run by the Ramore folks with the same winning formula) offers a more subdued, darker bistro ambience and meals for a few pounds more than the wine bar (£5.50 lunches 12:15–14:15, £7–10 dinners 17:30–22:00, closed Mon, tel. 028/7082-2430).

The **Harbor Bar,** upstairs from the Harbor Restaurant, is a plush, overstuffed lounge with a toasty fire and grand views—a great place to enjoy a drink.

Transportation Connections—Portrush

By train to: Coleraine (2/hrly, 12 min, sparse on Sunday morning), **Belfast** (7/day, transfer in Coleraine, 4/Sunday, 2 hrs), **Dublin** (7/day, 1/Sunday, 5 hrs, several tight but easy connections, £21 one way, £28 round-trip with Belfast stopover, buy ticket in Coleraine).

By bus to: Belfast (along scenic coast, 2/day, 3.5 hrs, £6).

Driving from Galway to Portrush

Allow a long day for the drive from Galway to Portrush with these interesting stops along the way (leave Galway heading north on N17):

Knock—In 1879 the Virgin Mary and Joseph appeared to locals atop the church in the tiny town of Knock. Word of miraculous healings turned the trickle of pilgrims into a flood and put Knock solidly on the pilgrimage map. Today you can visit the shrine. At the edge of the site a small but interesting folk museum shows "evidence" of the healings, photos of a papal visit, and interesting slices of traditional life.

Belleek Pottery Visitors Centre—After a stretch of scenic coastline and just over the Northern Ireland border you reach the cute town of Belleek, famous for its pottery. The Belleek Parian China factory welcomes visitors with a small gallery and museum (daily 9:00–18:00, less on weekends and off-season), a video, a cheery cafeteria, and fascinating 30-minute tours of its working factory (£2 tours, Mon–Fri 9:30–16:15, call to confirm schedule and reserve a spot, tel. 028/6865-8501).

Ulster American Folk Museum—North of Omagh, this museum shows life before emigration, on the boat, and in America for the many Irish who left their homeland during hard times in the 19th century.

Derry—The town of Derry (or Londonderry to Unionists) is the mecca of Ulster unionism. The Foyle River was the logical border between the North and the Republic. Unfortuately, Derry (occupying a bit of land over the river) was kept by the north for sentimental reasons. Consequently, it's been much contested throughout "the Troubles." You can walk the ramparts of the finest walled town in Ireland, study the political murals, and chat with locals in pubs that rarely see a tourist. Get specifics from the helpful TI as you enter the town. Stephen McPhilemy does great city tours (tel. 028/7128-9051, e-mail: nirelandtours@wiredup.net). Park House Hotel has the only real restaurant in the town center.

From Derry it's less than an hour's drive to Portrush, a town much more clearly British.

APPENDIX

BRITAIN

Britain was created by force and held together by force. It's really a nation of the 19th century. Its traditional industry, buildings, and the popularity of the notion of "Great" Britain are a product of the wealth derived from the empire that was at its peak through the Victorian age … the 19th century. Generally, the nice and bad stories are not true and the boring ones are. To best understand the many fascinating guides you'll encounter in your travels, have a basic handle on the sweeping story of this land.

What's So Great about Britain?

Regardless of the revolution we had 200 years ago, many American travelers feel that they "go home" to Britain. This most popular tourist destination has a strange influence and power over us.

Britain is small (about the size of Uganda or Idaho)—600 miles long and 300 miles at its widest point. Its highest mountain is 4,400 feet, a foothill by our standards. The population is a quarter that of the United States. Politically and economically, Great Britain is closing out the 20th century only a weak shadow of the days when it boasted that "the sun never sets on the British Empire."

At one time Britain owned one-fifth of the world and accounted for more than half the planet's industrial output. Today the Empire is down to token and troublesome scraps, such as the Falklands and Northern Ireland. Great Britain's industrial production is about 5 percent of the world's total, and Italy has a higher per-capita income.

Still, Britain is a world leader. Her heritage, her culture, and her people cannot be measured in traditional units of power. The United Kingdom is a union of four countries—England, Wales, Scotland, and Northern Ireland. Cynics call it an English Empire ruled by London, and there is some tension between the dominant Anglo-Saxon English (46 million) and their Celtic brothers and sisters (10 million).

In the Dark Ages the Angles moved into this region from Europe, pushing the Celtic inhabitants to the undesirable fringe of the islands. The Angles settled in Angle-land (England), while the Celts made do in Wales, Scotland, and Ireland.

Today Wales, with 2 million inhabitants, struggles with a terrible economy, dragged down by the depressed mining industry. A great deal of Welsh pride is apparent in the local music and the bilingual signs—some with the English spray-painted out. The Welsh language is alive and well.

Scotland is big, accounting for one-third of Great Britain's land area, but sparsely inhabited, with only 5 million people. Only about 80,000 speak Gaelic, but the Scots enjoy a large measure of autonomy with their separate Church of Scotland, their own legal system, and Scottish currency (interchangeable with the British). In a 1998 vote, Scotland has decided to "devolve" further. In 2000 it will pull its members of Parliament from Westminster and, for the first time in nearly 300 years, reestablish its own parliament. International affairs will still be decided in London, but Edinburgh will call most of the local shots.

Ireland is divided. Most of it is the completely independent Catholic Republic of Ireland. The top quarter is Northern Ireland, ruled from London. Long ago the Protestant English and Scots moved into the north—the Catholic, industrial heartland of Ireland—and told the Catholic Irish to "go to hell or go to Connemara." The Irish moved to the bleak and less productive parts of the island, like Connemara, and the seeds of today's "Troubles" were planted. There's no easy answer or easy blame, but the island has struggled—its population (3 million) is only one-third of what it used to be—and the battle continues. Recently the moderate center (which, in spite of what the headlines imply, is the vast majority) has voted major concessions to each side. Protestants acknowledged Catholics have equal rights in the North, and Catholics removed the lines from the Republic's constitution refusing to recognize British rule in Ulster.

Just as the United States Congress is dominated by Democrats and Republicans, two parties dominate Britain's Parliament: Labor and Conservatives. (Ronald Reagan would fit the Conservative Party and Bill Clinton the Labor Party like political gloves.) Today Britain's Labor Party, currently in charge, is shoring up a social service system undercut by years of Conservative rule (Thatcher, Major). While in charge, the Conservatives (who consider themselves proponents of Victorian values—community, family, hard work, thrift, and trickle-down economics) took a Reaganesque approach to Britain's serious problems.

This eventually led to a huge Labor victory and the prime ministership of Tony Blair. He's the most popular PM in memory, and his party rules Parliament with a vast majority. Blair's Labor Party is "New Labor"—akin to Clinton's "New" Democrats. It's fiscally conservative but with a keen sense for the needs of the people. Conservative Party fears of old-fashioned, big-spending, bleeding-heart, Union-style liberalism have proven unfounded. The Liberal Parliament is more open to integration with Europe. The economy is booming, and inflation, unemployment, and interest rates are all very low. Social programs such as health, education, and the minimum wage are being bolstered but in ways more measured than Conservatives predicted. It looks like Britain is in for a long period of Labor rule.

Basic British History for the Traveler

When Julius Caesar landed on the misty and mysterious isle of
Britain in 55 B.C., England entered the history books. The primitive
Celtic tribes he conquered were themselves invaders who had earlier
conquered the even more mysterious people who built Stonehenge.
The Romans built towns and roads and established their capital at
"Londinium." The Celtic natives in Scotland and Wales, consisting
of Gaels, Picts, and Scots, were not subdued so easily. The Romans
built Hadrian's Wall near the Scottish border to consolidate their
rule in the troublesome north. Even today, the Celtic language and
influence are strongest in these far reaches of Britain.

As Rome fell, so fell Roman Britain, a victim of invaders and
internal troubles. Barbarian tribes from Germany and Denmark,
called Angles and Saxons, swept through the southern part of the
island, establishing Angle-land. These were the days of the real
King Arthur, possibly a Christianized Roman general fighting
valiantly, but in vain, against invading barbarians. The island was
plunged into 500 years of Dark Ages—wars, plagues, and
poverty—lit only by the dim candle of a few learned Christian
monks and missionaries trying to convert the barbarians. The
sightseer sees little from this Saxon period.

Modern England began with yet another invasion. William
the Conqueror and his Norman troops crossed the English Channel from France in 1066. William crowned himself king in Westminster Abbey (where all subsequent coronations would take
place) and began building the Tower of London. French-speaking
Norman kings ruled the country for two centuries. Then followed
two centuries of civil wars, with various noble families vying for
the crown. In one of the most bitter feuds, the York and Lancaster
families fought the War of the Roses, so-called because of the
white and red flowers the combatants chose as their symbols. Battles, intrigues, kings, nobles, and ladies imprisoned and executed in
the Tower—it's a wonder the country survived its rulers.

England was finally united by the "third-party" Tudor family.
Henry VIII, a Tudor, was England's Renaissance king. He was
handsome, athletic, highly sexed, a poet, a scholar, and a musician.
He was also arrogant, cruel, gluttonous, and paranoid. He went
through six wives in 40 years, divorcing, imprisoning, or behead-
ing them when they no longer suited his needs.

Henry also "divorced" England from the Catholic Church,
establishing the Protestant Church of England (the Anglican
Church) and setting in motion years of religious squabbles. He
also "dissolved" the monasteries (around 1540), leaving just the
shells of many formerly glorious abbeys dotting the countryside
and pocketing their land and wealth for the crown.

Henry's daughter, Queen Elizabeth I, who reigned for 45
years, made England a great trading and naval power (defeating

the Spanish Armada) and presided over the Elizabethan era of great writers (such as Shakespeare) and scientists (Francis Bacon).

The long-standing quarrel between England's "divine right" kings and nobles in Parliament finally erupted into a civil war (1643). Parliament forces under the Protestant Puritan farmer Oliver Cromwell defeated—and beheaded—King Charles I. This civil war left its mark on much of what you'll see in England. Eventually, Parliament invited Charles' son to take the throne. This "restoration of the monarchy" was accompanied by a great colonial expansion and the rebuilding of London (including Christopher Wren's St. Paul's Cathedral), which had been devastated by the Great Fire of 1666.

Britain grew as a naval superpower, colonizing and trading with all parts of the globe. Her naval superiority ("Britannia rules the waves") was secured by Admiral Horatio Nelson's victory over Napoleon's fleet at the Battle of Trafalgar, while the Duke of Wellington stomped Napoleon on land at Waterloo. Nelson and Wellington—both buried in London's St. Paul's—are memorialized by many arches, columns, and squares throughout England.

Economically, Britain led the world into the industrial age with her mills, factories, coal mines, and trains. By the time of Queen Victoria's reign (1837–1901), Britain was at the zenith of power, with a colonial empire that covered one-fifth of the world.

The 20th century has not been kind to Britain. Two world wars devastated the population. The Nazi blitzkrieg reduced much of London to rubble. The colonial empire has dwindled to almost nothing, and Britain is no longer an economic superpower. The "Irish Troubles" are constant, as the Catholic inhabitants of British-ruled Northern Ireland fight for the independence their southern neighbors won decades ago. The war over the Falkland Islands in 1982 showed how little of the British Empire is left but also how determined the British are to hang on to what remains.

But the tradition (if not the substance) of greatness continues, presided over by Queen Elizabeth II, her husband Prince Philip, and Prince Charles. With economic problems, the turmoil of Charles and the late Princess Diana, the Fergie fiasco, and a relentless popular press, the royal family is having a tough time. But the queen has stayed above it all, and most British people still jump at an opportunity to see royalty. With the death of Princess Diana and the historic outpouring of grief, it's clear that the concept of royalty is alive and well as Britain enters the third millennium.

Britain's Royal Families

802–1066	Saxon and Danish kings
1066–1154	Norman invasion (William the Conqueror), Norman kings
1154–1399	Plantagenet
1399–1461	Lancaster

1462–1485	York
1485–1603	Tudor (Henry VIII, Elizabeth I)
1603–1649	Stuart (civil war and beheading of Charles I)
1649–1659	Commonwealth, Cromwell, no royal head of state
1660–1714	Stuart restoration of monarchy
1714–1901	Hanover (four Georges, Victoria)
1901–1910	Edward VII
1910–present	Windsor (George V, Edward VII, George VI, Elizabeth II)

Architecture in Britain

From Stonehenge to Big Ben, travelers are storming castle walls, climbing spiral staircases, and snapping the pictures of 5,000 years of architecture. Let's sort it out.

The oldest ruins—mysterious and prehistoric—date from before Roman times back to 3000 B.C. The earliest sites, such as Stonehenge and Avebury, were built during the Stone and Bronze Ages. The remains from these periods are made of huge stones or mounds of earth, even man-made hills, and were created as celestial calendars and for worship or burial. Britain is crisscrossed with lines of these mysterious sights (ley lines). Iron Age people (600 B.C. to A.D. 50) left desolate stone forts. The Romans thrived in Britain from A.D. 50 to 400, building cities, walls, and roads. Evidence of Roman greatness can be seen in lavish villas with ornate mosaic floors, temples uncovered beneath great English churches, and Roman stones in medieval city walls. Roman roads sliced across the island in straight lines. Today, unusually straight rural roads are very likely laid directly on ancient Roman roads.

As Rome crumbled in the fifth century, so did Roman Britain. Little architecture survives from Dark Ages England, the Saxon period from 500 to 1000. Architecturally, the light was switched on with the Norman Conquest in 1066. As William earned his title "the Conqueror," his French architects built churches and castles in the European Romanesque style.

English Romanesque is called Norman (1066–1200). Norman churches had round arches, thick walls, and small windows; Durham Cathedral and the Chapel of St. John in the Tower of London are typical examples. The Tower of London, with its square keep, small windows, and spiral stone stairways, is a typical Norman castle. You'll see plenty of Norman castles—all built to secure the conquest of these invaders from Normandy.

Gothic architecture (1200–1600) replaced the heavy Norman style with light, vertical buildings, pointed arches, soaring spires, and bigger windows. English Gothic is divided into three stages. Early English (1200–1300) features tall, simple spires; beautifully carved capitals; and elaborate chapter houses (such as the Wells Cathedral).

Decorated Gothic (1300–1400) gets fancier, with more elaborate tracery, bigger windows, and ornately carved pinnacles, as you'll see at Westminster Abbey. Finally, the Perpendicular style (1400–1600, also called "rectilinear") returns to square towers and emphasizes straight, uninterrupted vertical lines from ceiling to floor, with vast windows and exuberant decoration, including fan-vaulted ceilings (King's College Chapel at Cambridge). Through this evolution, the structural ribs (arches meeting at the top of the ceilings) became more and more decorative and fanciful (the most fancy being the star vaulting and fan vaulting of the Perpendicular style).

As you tour the great medieval churches of England, remember that nearly everything is symbolic. For instance, on the tombs, if the figure has crossed legs, he was a Crusader. If his feet rest on a dog, he died at home; but if the legs rest on a lion, he died in battle. Local guides and books help us modern pilgrims understand at least a little of what we see.

Wales is particularly rich in English castles, which were needed to subdue the stubborn Welsh. Edward I built a ring of powerful castles in Wales, including Caernarfon and Conwy.

Gothic houses were a simple mix of woven strips of thin wood, rubble, and plaster called wattle and daub. The famous black-and-white Tudor, or half-timbered, look came simply from filling in heavy oak frames with wattle and daub.

The Tudor period (1485–1560) was a time of relative peace (the War of the Roses was finally over), prosperity, and renaissance. Henry VIII broke with the Catholic Church and "dissolved" (destroyed) the monasteries, leaving scores of England's greatest churches gutted shells. These hauntingly beautiful abbey ruins (Glastonbury, Tintern, Whitby) surrounded by lush lawns are now pleasant city parks.

Although few churches were built during the Tudor period, this was a time of house and mansion construction. Warmth was becoming popular and affordable, and Tudor buildings featured small square windows and many chimneys. In towns where land was scarce, many Tudor houses grew up and out, getting wider with each overhanging floor.

The Elizabethan and Jacobean periods (1560–1620) were followed by the English Renaissance style (1620–1720). English architects mixed Gothic and classical styles, then Baroque and classical styles. Although the ornate Baroque never really grabbed England, the classical style of the Italian architect Andrea Palladio did. Inigo Jones (1573–1652), Christopher Wren (1632–1723), and those they inspired plastered England with enough columns, domes, and symmetry to please a caesar. The Great Fire of London (1666) cleared the way for an ambitious young Wren to put his mark on London forever with a grand rebuilding scheme, including the great St. Paul's and more than 50 other churches.

The celebrants of the Boston Tea Party remember England's Georgian period (1720–1840) for its lousy German kings. Georgian architecture was rich and showed off by being very classical. Grand ornamental doorways, fine cast-ironwork on balconies and railings, Chippendale furniture, and white-on-blue Wedgewood ceramics graced rich homes everywhere. John Wood Jr. and Sr. led the way, giving the trend-setting city of Bath its crescents and circles of aristocratic Georgian row houses. "Georgian" is English for "neoclassical."

The Industrial Revolution shaped the Victorian period (1840–1890) with glass, steel, and iron. England had a huge new erector set (so did France's Mr. Eiffel). This was also a Romantic period, reviving the "more Christian" Gothic style. London's Houses of Parliament are neo-Gothic—just 100 years old but looking 700, except for the telltale modern precision and craftsmanship. Whereas Gothic was stone or concrete, neo-Gothic was often red brick. These were England's glory days, and there was more building in this period than in all previous ages combined.

The architecture of our century obeys the formula "form follows function"—it worries more about your needs than your eyes. England treasures its heritage and takes great pains to build tastefully in historic districts and to preserve its many "listed" buildings. With a booming tourist trade, these quaint reminders of its—and our—past are becoming a valuable part of the British economy.

British TV

British television is so good—and so British—that it deserves a mention as a sight-seeing treat. After a hard day of castle-climbing, watch the telly over tea in the living room of your village B&B.

England has five channels. BBC-1 and BBC-2 are government regulated, commercial free, and traditionally highbrow. Channels 3, 4, and 5 are private, are a little more Yankee, and have commercials—but those commercials are clever and sophisticated and provide a fun look at England. Broadcasting is funded by an £80-per-year-per-household tax. Hmmm, 35 cents per day to escape commercials and public television pledge drives.

Britian is about to leap into the digital age ahead of the rest of the TV-watching world. Ultimately every house will enjoy literally hundreds of high-definition channels with no need for cable or satellites.

Whereas California "accents" fill our airwaves 24 hours a day, homogenizing the way our country speaks, England protects and promotes its regional accents by its choice of TV and radio announcers. Commercial-free British TV, while looser than it used to be, is still careful about what it airs and when.

American shows (such as *Frasier* and *ER*) are very popular. The visiting viewer should be sure to tune the TV to a few typical English shows, including a dose of English situation and political comedy fun and the top-notch BBC evening news. Quiz shows are taken very seriously here. Michael Parkinson is the Johnny Carson of Britain for late-night talk. For a tear-filled, slice-of-life taste of British soap dealing in all the controversial issues, see the popular *Brookside*, *Coronation Street*, or *Eastenders*.

Benny Hill comedy has become politically incorrect but is rumored to be coming back. And if you like Monty Python–type comedy, you've come to the right place.

IRELAND

Irish History

One surprising aspect of Ireland is the richness of its history. While the island is not particularly well endowed with historic monuments, it is soaked in history. Here's a thumbnail overview.

The story of Ireland can be broken into four sections:

500 B.C.–A.D. 500	Iron Age
500–900	"Age of Saints and Scholars"
900–1900	Age of invasions and colonization
20th century	Independence and the question of a united Ireland

The Celtic people left the countryside peppered with thousands of ancient sights from the Iron Age. While most of what you'll see will be little more than rock piles that take a vigorous imagination to reconstruct (ring forts, wedge tombs, monumental stones, and so on), just standing next to a megalith that predates the pharaohs while surrounded by lush Ireland is evocative. The finest gold, bronze, and iron work of this period is in the National Museum in Dublin.

The Romans called Ireland Hibernia, or "Land of Winter"; it was apparently too cold and bleak to merit an attempt to take over and colonize. The biggest nonevent in Irish history is that the Romans never invaded. While the mix of Celtic and Roman contributes to what makes the French French and the English English, the Irish are purely Celtic. If France is *boules* and England is cricket, then Ireland is hurling. This wild Irish national pastime (like airborne hockey with no injury time-outs) goes back to Celtic days, more than 2,000 years ago.

Celts worshipped the sun. Perhaps St. Patrick had an easy time converting the locals because they had so little sun to worship. Whatever the case, a former Roman slave boy, Patrick, helped Christianize Ireland in the fifth century. From this period on, monks established monastic centers of learning that produced great Christian teachers and community builders. They traveled, establishing monastic communities all over Ireland, Britain, and Europe. One of the monks, St. Brandon, may have even sailed to America.

While the collapse of Rome left Europe a mess, it meant nothing to Ireland. Ireland was and remained a relatively cohesive society based on monastic settlements rather than cities. While Europe was rutting in the Dark Age mud, the light of civilization shone brightly in Ireland during a Golden Age that lasted from the fifth through the ninth centuries. Irish monks—such as those imported by Charlemagne to help run his Frankish kingdom in 800—actually carried the torch of civilization back to Europe. Perhaps the greatest works of art of Dark Age Europe are the manuscripts (such as the ninth-century *Book of Kells*, which you'll see in Dublin) illuminated, or richly illustrated, by Irish monks. Impressive round towers dot the Irish landscape—silent reminders of this impressive age.

Viking invasions of the ninth century wreaked repeated havoc on the monasteries and shook Irish civilization. Vikings established trading towns (such as Dublin) where before there were only Celtic settlements and monasteries.

The Normans, who invaded and conquered England after the Battle of Hastings (1066), were Ireland's next uninvited guests. In 1169, the Anglo-Normans invaded Ireland. These invaders, big-time organizers, ushered in a new age in which society (government, cities, and religious organizations) was organized on a grander scale. Individual monastic settlements (the basis of Irish society in the Age of Saints and Scholars) were eclipsed by monastic orders just in from the Continent, such as the Franciscans, Augustinians, and Cistercians.

The English made a concentrated effort to colonize Ireland in the 17th century. Settlers were "planted," and Irish society was split between an English-speaking landed gentry and the local Irish-speaking landless or nearly landless peasantry.

During the 18th century Ireland thrived under the English. Dublin was Britain's second city. Over time, greed on the top and dissent on the bottom required colonial policies to become more repressive. The Enlightenment provided ideas of freedom, and the Revolutionary Age emboldened the Irish masses. (Even the non-Catholic Dubliner Jonathan Swift—dean of St. Patrick's cathedral in the early 18th century—declared "Burn all that's British, except its coal.")

To counter this Irish feistiness, English legislation became an out-and-out attack on the indigenous Gaelic culture. The harp, symbol of Irish culture, was outlawed. Written and unwritten laws made life for Catholics and Irish-speakers very difficult.

The potato famine of 1845–1849 was a pivotal event in Irish history. The stature of Ireland and its language never recovered. In a few years Ireland's population dropped from 8 million to 5 million (3 million either starved or emigrated). Ireland's population has not grown since. Britain's population, on the other hand, has grown from 12 million in 1845 to around 60 million today.

(During this period, Ireland's population, as a percent of England's, has dropped from 67 percent to about 8 percent.)

While the English are likely to blame the famine on over-population (Ireland's population doubled in the 40 years leading up to the famine), many Irish say there actually was no famine—just a calculated attempt to starve down the local population. In fact, there was plenty of food grown on the island for export. It was only the potato crop that failed ... and that happened to be what the Irish subsisted on.

The average farmer grew fancier export products for his landlord and was paid in potatoes, which, in good years, he grew on the side. (If this makes you mad at the English landlords, consider American ownership of land in Central America, where the landlord takes things one step further by not growing the local staple at all. He devotes all the land to more profitable cash crops for export and leaves the landless farmer no alternative but to buy his food—imported from the United States—at plantation wages, in the landlord's grocery store.)

The famine was a turning point in Irish history. Before the famine, land was subdivided—each boy got a piece of the family estate (which grew smaller with each generation). After the famine, the oldest son got the estate and the younger siblings, with no way to stay in Ireland, immigrated to Britain, Australia, Canada, and the United States. Today there are 40 million Irish Americans.

After the famine, Irish became the language of the peasant. English was for the upwardly mobile. Because of the huge immigration to the United States, Ireland began to face west, and American influence increased. (As negotiations between Northern Ireland and the Irish Republic continue, American involvement in the talks is welcomed and considered essential by nearly all parties.)

The tragedy of the famine inflamed the nationalist movement. Uprising after uprising made it clear that Ireland was ready to close this thousand-year chapter of invasions and colonialism. Finally, in 1919, Ireland declared its independence. While the northern six counties (the only ones without a Catholic majority) voted to stay with Britain, the independent Republic of Ireland was born. (For a review of the ongoing "Troubles" between the North and the Republic, see the Northern Ireland chapter.)

The Irish Pub

When you say "a beer, please" in an Irish pub, you'll get a pint of Guinness (the black beauty with a blonde head). If you want a small beer, ask for a half-pint. Never rush your bartender when he's pouring a Guinness. It takes time—almost sacred time. If you don't like Guinness, try it in Ireland. It doesn't travel well and is better in its homeland. Murphy's is a very good Guinness-like stout but a bit smoother and milder.

In an Irish pub you're a guest on your first night; after that you're a regular. Women traveling alone need not worry—you'll become part of the pub family in no time.

It's a tradition to buy your table a round and then for each person to reciprocate. If an Irishman buys you a drink, thank him by saying, "*Guh rev mah a gut.*" Offer him a toast in Irish—"*Slahn chuh!*" A good excuse for a conversation is to ask to be taught a few words of Gaelic.

Craic (crack), the art of conversation, is the sport that accompanies drinking in a pub. People are there to talk. If you feel a bit awkward, remind yourself of that.

Here's a goofy excuse for some *craic*: Ireland—small as it is—has many dialects. People from Cork are famous for talking very fast (and in a squeaky voice)—so fast that some even talk in letters alone. ABCD fish? (Anybody see the fish?) DR no fish. (There are no fish.) DR fish. (There are fish.) CDBD Is? (See the beady eyes?) OIBJ DR fish. (Oh aye, be Jeeze, there are fish.) For a possibly more appropriate spin, replace the fish with "bird" (girl). This is obscure, but your pub neighbor may understand and enjoy hearing it. If nothing else, you won't seem so intimidating to him anymore.

You might ask if the people of one county are any smarter than the next. Kerry people are considered by some of their neighbors to be a bit out of it.

Traditional Irish Music

Traditional music is alive and popular in pubs throughout Ireland. "Sessions" (musical evenings) may be planned and advertised or impromptu. Traditionally, musicians just congregate and jam. There will generally be a fiddle, a flute or tin whistle, a guitar, a bodhran (goatskin drum), and maybe an accordion. Things usually get going around 21:30 or 22:00. Last call for drinks is around 23:30.

The bodhran is played with a small two-headed club. The performer's hand stretches the skin to change the tone and pitch. The wind and string instruments embellish melody lines with lots of improvised ornamentation. Occasionally the fast-paced music will stop and one person will sing an a cappella "lament." This is the one time when the entire pub will stop to listen as sad lyrics fill the smoke-stained room. Stories—ranging from struggles against English rule to love songs—are always heartfelt. Spend a lament enjoying the faces in the crowd. A *ceilidh* (kay-lee) is an evening of music and dance... an Irish hoedown.

The music comes in sets of three songs. Whoever happens to be leading determines the next song only as the song the group is playing is about to be finished. If he wants to pass on the decision, it's done with eye contact and a nod.

A session can be magic or lifeless. If the chemistry is right, it's one of the great Irish experiences. The music churns intensely while the group casually enjoys exploring each other's musical style. The drummer dodges the fiddler's playful bow with his cigarette sticking half-ash straight from the middle of his mouth. Sipping their pints, they skillfully maintain a faint but steady buzz. The floor on the musicians' platform is stomped paint-free, and barmaids scurry artfully through the commotion, gathering towers of empty cream-crusted glasses. Make yourself right at home, drumming the table or playing the 10-pence coins. Talk to your neighbor. Locals often have an almost evangelical interest in explaining the music.

Let's Talk Telephones
Here's a primer on making direct phone calls. For more information, see "Telephones" in the Introduction.

Dialing Direct
Calling between Countries: First dial the international access code, then the country code, the area code (if it starts with zero, drop the zero), and the local number.

Calling Long Distance within a Country: First dial the area code (including its zero), then the local number.

Europe's Exceptions: France, Italy, Spain, Portugal, Norway, and Denmark have dispensed with area codes entirely. To make an international call to these countries, dial the international access code (usually 00), the country code (see chart below), and then the local number in its entirety (okay, so there's one exception: for France, drop the initial zero of the local number). To make long-distance calls within any of these countries, simply dial the local number.

International Access Codes
When dialing direct, first dial the international access code of the country you're calling from. For the U.S. and Canada, it's 011. Virtually all European countries use "00" as their international access code; the only major exception is Finland (990).

Country Codes
After you've dialed the international access code, then dial the code of the country you're calling.

Austria—43	Greece—30
Belgium—32	Ireland—353
Britain—44	Italy—39
Canada—1	Netherlands—31
Czech Republic—420	Norway—47
Denmark—45	Portugal—351
Estonia—372	Spain—34
Finland—358	Sweden—46
France—33	Switzerland—41
Germany—49	U.S.A.—1

Calling-Card Operators

You can call direct much more cheaply by using a British or Irish phone card from any phone booth, but if you'd prefer to use an AT&T, MCI, or Sprint calling card, these are the numbers you'd use.

	AT&T	MCI	Sprint
Britain	0800-89-00-11	0800-89-02-22	0800-89-08-77
Ireland	1800-55-00-00	1800-55-10-01	1800-55-20-01

Useful Numbers in Britain

Emergency (police and ambulance): 999
Operator Assistance: 100
Directory Assistance: 192 (free from phone booth, otherwise expensive)
International Info: 153 (80p)
International Assistance: 155
United States Embassy: 020/7499-9000
Eurostar (Chunnel Info): 0990-848-848
Train and Boats to Europe Info: 0990-848-848

Note: Understand the various prefixes: 0891 numbers are telephone sex–type expensive. Prefixes 0345 and 0845 are local calls nationwide. And 0800 numbers are entirely toll free. If you have questions about a prefix, call 100 for free help.

Useful Numbers in Ireland

Emergency: 999
Operator Assistance: 10
Directory Assistance: 1190 (free from phone booth, or 34p)
Directory Assistance for Britain: 1197 (free from phone booth)
International Assistance: 1198 (free from phone booth)

London's Airports and Airlines

Heathrow

General Information: 020/8759-4321 (transfers to airport, arrivals, airline phone numbers, etc.)
Air Canada: 020/8745-6584
American: 0345-789-789
British Air: 0345-222-111, 020/8759-5511
British Midlands: 0870-607-0555, 01332/854-000
Scandinavian Airlines System: 020/8750-7675
United Airlines: 0845-844-4777

Gatwick

General Information: 01293/535-353 for all airlines, except British Airways, 0990-444-000.

Stansted
Ryanair (cheap fares): 0541/569-569

Climate
The chart below gives average daytime temperatures and average number of days with more than a trickle of rain.

	J	F	M	A	M	J	J	A	S	O	N	D
London	43°	44°	50°	56°	62°	69°	71°	71°	66°	58°	51°	45°
	15	13	11	12	11	11	12	11	13	14	15	15
S. Wales	45°	45°	50°	56°	61°	68°	69°	69°	65°	58°	51°	46°
	18	14	13	13	13	13	14	15	16	16	17	18
York	43°	44°	49°	55°	60°	67°	70°	70°	65°	57°	49°	45°
	17	15	13	13	13	14	15	14	14	15	17	17
Edinburgh	42°	43°	46°	51°	56°	62°	65°	64°	60°	54°	48°	44°
	17	15	15	14	14	15	17	16	16	17	17	18
Dublin	40°	41°	44°	47°	52°	57°	60°	59°	56°	50°	45°	42°
	13	10	10	11	10	11	13	12	12	11	12	14

Numbers and Stumblers
- Europeans write a few of their numbers differently than we do. 1 = 1, 4 = 4, 7 = 7. Learn the difference or miss your train.
- In Europe, dates appear as day/month/year, so Christmas is 25-12-00.
- Commas are decimal points and decimals commas. A dollar and a half is 1,50 and there are 5.280 feet in a mile.
- When pointing, use your whole hand, palm downward.
- When counting with fingers, start with your thumb. If you hold up your first finger to request one item, you'll probably get two.
- What we Americans call the second floor of a building is the first floor in Europe.
- Europeans keep the left "lane" open for passing on escalators and moving sidewalks. Keep to the right.
- And please... don't call your waist pack a "fanny pack."

Weights and Measures
1 British pint = 1.2 U.S. pints
1 imperial gallon = 1.2 U.S. gallons or about 4.5 liters
1 stone = 14 pounds (a 168-pound person weighs 12 stone)
28 degrees Centigrade = 82 degrees Fahrenheit
Shoe sizes = about .5 to 1.5 sizes smaller than in the United States

British–Yankee Vocabulary

advert advertisement
afters dessert
anticlockwise counterclockwise
aubergine eggplant
Balloons Belgians
banger sausage
bangers and mash sausage and mashed potatoes
bank holiday legal holiday
bap hamburger-type bun
billion a thousand of our billions (a million million)
biro ballpoint pen
biscuit cookie
black pudding sausage made from dried blood
bobby policeman ("copper" is more common)
Bob's your uncle there you go (with a shrug), naturally
bomb success
bonnet car hood
boot car trunk
braces suspenders
bridle way path for walkers, bikers, and horse riders
brilliant cool
bubble and squeak cold meat fried with cabbage and potatoes
bum bottom or "backside"
candy floss cotton candy
car boot sale temporary flea market with car trunk displays (a good place to buy back your stolen goods)
caravan trailer
cat's eyes road reflectors
ceilidh (kay-lee) informal evening of song and folk fun
cheap and nasty cheap and bad quality
cheerio good-bye
chemist pharmacist
chips french fries
chock-a-block jam-packed
cider alcoholic apple cider
clearway road where you can't stop
coach long-distance bus

concession discounted admission
cotton buds Q-tips
courgette zucchini
craic (crack) good conversation (Irish and spreading to England)
crisps potato chips
cuppa cup of tea
dear expensive
dicey iffy, risky
digestives round graham crackers
dinner lunch or dinner
diversion detour
donkey's years until the cows come home
draughts checkers
dual carriageway divided highway (four lanes)
face flannel washcloth
fag cigarette
fagged exhausted
faggot meatball
fanny vagina
fell hill or high plain
first floor second floor
football soccer
force waterfall (Lake District)
fortnight two weeks
Frogs French people
Full Monty The whole shabang. Everything.
gallery balcony
gangway aisle
gaol jail (same pronunciation)
give way yield
glen Scot. narrow valley
goods wagon freight truck
grammar school high school
half eight 8:30 (not 7:30)
heath open treeless land
holiday vacation
homely likable or cozy
hoover vacuum cleaner
ice lolly Popsicle
interval intermission
ironmonger hardware store
jelly Jell-O
Joe Bloggs John Doe
jumble sale, rummage sale

jumper sweater
keep your pecker up be brave
kipper smoked herring
knackered exhausted (Cockney: cream crackered)
knickers ladies' panties
knocking shop brothel
knock up wake up or visit
ladybird ladybug
let rent
loo toilet or bathroom
lorry truck
mac mackintosh coat
mate buddy (boy or girl)
mean stingy
mews courtyard stables, often used as cottages
minced meat hamburger
nappy diaper
natter talk and talk
neep Scottish for turnip
nought zero
noughts & crosses tic-tac-toe
off license store selling take-away liquor
pasty crusted savory (usually meat) pie
pavement sidewalk
petrol gas
pissed (rude), paralytic, bevvied, wellied, popped up, ratted, pissed as a newt drunk
pillar box postbox
pitch playing field
plaster Band-Aid
poppers snaps
publican pub manager
public convenience toilets
public school private "prep" school (Eton)
put a sock in it shut up
queue line
queue up line up
quid pound (money, worth about $1.70)
randy horny
redundant, made fired
Remembrance Day Veterans' Day
return ticket round-trip
ring up call (telephone)
rubber eraser

sanitary towel sanitary pad
sausage roll sausage wrapped in a flaky pastry
Scotch egg hard-boiled egg wrapped in sausage meat
self-catering aprtment with kitchen, rented weekly
sellotape Scotch tape
serviette napkin
single ticket one-way ticket
sleeping policeman speed bumps
smalls underwear
snogging kissing cuddling
solicitor lawyer
starkers buck naked
starters appetizers
stone 14 pounds (weight)
subway underground pedestrian passageway
surgical spirit rubbing alcohol
suss out figure out
swede rutabaga
ta thank you
taxi rank taxi stand
telly TV
theater live stage
tick a check mark
tight as a fish's bum cheap-skate (water-tight)
tights panty hose
tipper lorry dump truck
tin can
to let for rent
top hole first rate
topping excellent
top up refill a drink
torch flashlight
towpath path along a river
tube subway
twee quaint, cute
underground subway
verge grassy edge of road
verger church official
Wellingtons, wellies rubber boots
wee urinate
whacked exhausted
witter on gab and gab
yob hooligan
zebra crossing crosswalk
zed the letter "z"

Road Scholar Feedback for
GREAT BRITAIN & IRELAND 2000

We're all in the same travelers' school of hard knocks. Your feedback helps us improve this guidebook for future travelers. Please fill this out (or use the on-line version at www.ricksteves.com/feedback), attach more info or any tips/favorite discoveries if you like, and send it to us. As thanks for your help, we'll send you our quarterly travel newsletter free for one year. Thanks! **Rick**

Of the recommended accommodations/restaurants used, which was:

Best _____

     Why? _____

Worst _____

     Why? _____

Of the sights/experiences/destinations recommended by this book, which was:

Most overrated _____

     Why? _____

Most underrated _____

     Why? _____

Best ways to improve this book:

_____

I'd like a free newsletter subscription:

_____ Yes   _____ No   _____ Already on list

_____
Name

_____
Address

_____
City, State, Zip

_____
E-mail Address

Please send to: ETBD, Box 2009, Edmonds, WA 98020

Jubilee 2000—Let's Celebrate the Millennium by Forgiving Third World Debt

Let's ring in the millennium by convincing our government to forgive the debt owed to us by the world's poorest countries. Imagine spending over half your income on interest payments alone. You and I are creditors, and poor countries owe us more than they can pay.

Jubilee 2000 is a worldwide movement of concerned people and groups—religious and secular—working to cancel the international debts of the poorest countries by the year 2000.

Debt ruins people: In the poorest countries, money needed for health care, education, and other vital services is diverted to interest payments.

Mozambique, with a per-capita income of $90 and life expectancy of 40, spends over half its national income on interest. This poverty brings social unrest, civil war, and often costly humanitarian intervention by the U.S.A. To chase export dollars, desperate countries ruin their environment. As deserts grow and rain forests shrink, the world suffers. Of course, the real suffering is among local people born long after some dictator borrowed (and squandered) that money. As interest is paid, entire populations go hungry.

Who owes what and why? Mozambique is one of 41 countries defined by the World Bank as "Heavily Indebted Poor Countries." In total, they owe $200 billion. Because these debts are unlikely to be paid, their market value is only a 10th of the face value (about $20 billion). The U.S.A.'s share is under $2 billion.

How can debt be canceled? This debt is owed mostly to the U.S.A., Japan, Germany, Britain, and France either directly or through the World Bank. We can forgive the debt owed directly to us and pay the market value (usually 10 percent) of the debts owed to the World Bank. We have the resources. (Norway, another wealthy creditor nation, just unilaterally forgave its Third World debt.) All the U.S.A. needs is the political will . . . people power.

While many of these poor nations are now democratic, corruption is still a concern. A key to Jubilee 2000 is making certain that debt relief reduces poverty in a way that benefits ordinary people: women, farmers, children, and so on.

Let's celebrate the new millennium by giving poor countries a break. For the sake of peace, fragile young democracies, the environment, and countless real people, forgiving this debt is the right thing for us in the rich world to do.

Tell Washington, D.C.: If our government knows this is what we want, it can happen. Learn more, write letters, lobby legislators, or even start a local Jubilee 2000 campaign. For details, contact Jubilee 2000 (tel. 202/783-3566, www.j2000usa.org). For information on lobbying Congress on J2000, contact Bread for the World (tel. 800/82-BREAD, www.bread.org).

Faxing Your Hotel Reservation

Faxing is more accurate and cheaper than telephoning. Use this handy form for your fax (or find it online at www.ricksteves.com /reservation). Photocopy and fax away.

One-Page Fax

To: _____ @ _____
           hotel   *fax*

From: _____ @ _____
            name   *fax*

Today's date: ___ /_____ /___
              day *month* *year*

Dear Hotel _____,

Please make this reservation for me:

Name: _____

Total # of people: _____   # of rooms: _____   # of nights: _____

Arriving: ___ /_____ /___ My time of arrival (24-hr clock): _____
          day *month* *year*   (I will telephone if I will be late)

Departing: ___ /_____ /___
           day *month* *year*

Room(s): Single___ Double___ Twin___ Triple___ Quad___

With: Toilet___ Shower___ Bath___ Sink only___

Special needs: View___ Quiet___ Cheapest Room___

Credit card: Visa___ MasterCard___ American Express___

Card #: _____

Expiration date:_____

Name on card: _____

You may charge me for the first night as a deposit. Please fax or mail me confirmation of my reservation, along with the type of room reserved, the price, and whether the price includes breakfast. Thank you.

_____
Signature

_____
Name

_____
Address

_____
City   *State*   *Zip Code*   *Country*

_____
E-mail Address

INDEX